ANTHOLOGIZING
CANADIAN
LITERATURE

ANTHOLOGIZING
CANADIAN
LITERATURE
Theoretical and
Cultural Perspectives

ROBERT LECKER, editor

**WILFRID LAURIER
UNIVERSITY PRESS**

This book has been published with the help of a grant from the Canadian Federation for the Humanities and Social Sciences, through the Awards to Scholarly Publications Program, using funds provided by the Social Sciences and Humanities Research Council of Canada. Wilfrid Laurier University Press acknowledges the support of the Canada Council for the Arts for our publishing program. We acknowledge the financial support of the Government of Canada through the Canada Book Fund for our publishing activities. This work was supported by the Research Support Fund.

Library and Archives Canada Cataloguing in Publication

    Anthologizing Canadian literature : theoretical and cultural perspectives / Robert Lecker, editor.

Includes bibliographical references and index.
Issued in print and electronic formats.
ISBN 978-1-77112-107-1 (pbk.).—ISBN 978-1-77112-110-1 (epub).—
ISBN 978-1-77112-109-5 (pdf)

    1. Anthologies—History. 2. Canadian literature (English) —History and criticism. 3. Canon (Literature). 4. National characteristics, Canadian, in literature. 5. Canada—in literature. I. Lecker, Robert, [date], editor

PS8071.5.A58 2015   C810.9'971   C2015-902044-1
                                                                                C2015-902045-X

Front-cover image: *Death by Landscape (for M.A.), or The Girl Disappears #4* (oil and acrylic on canvas over wood panel; 120 x 84 inches), 2013, by Kim Dorland. Photo by Eden Robbins. Cover and text design by Angela Booth Malleau.

This book is printed on FSC® certified paper and is certified Ecologo. It contains post-consumer fibre, is processed chlorine free, and is manufactured using biogas energy.

Printed in Canada

Every reasonable effort has been made to acquire permission for copyright material used in this text, and to acknowledge all such indebtedness accurately. Any errors and omissions called to the publisher's attention will be corrected in future printings.

CONTENTS

ACKNOWLEDGEMENTS

I am grateful to the Social Sciences and Humanities Research Council of Canada for a grant that enabled me to explore Canadian literary anthologies, and to the Awards to Scholarly Publications Program of the Federation for the Humanities and Social Sciences for its support of the collection. This book would never have been published without the expertise, patience, and persistence of two wonderful professionals at Wilfrid Laurier University Press: Lisa Quinn, Associate Director and Acquisitions, and Rob Kohlmeier, Managing Editor. I also want to thank my research assistant, Matthew Rettino, for his invaluable help in bringing the manuscript to publication. And of course, my thanks go to all the contributors to this volume. Together, they have taken me to places I might never have explored.

INTRODUCTION

Robert Lecker

I

Editing a collection of critical essays on anthologies is much like editing an anthology. You begin with an idea of producing something that will be original, transformative, representative of certain values, and (hopefully) somewhat coherent. Then you realize that you are not fundamentally in control. Neither are the contributors. They do not share your vision, and besides, they never knew what it was in the first place. They do not have a sense of the collective body they have joined, even though they have willingly agreed to be part of it. Some of them have promised you one thing and delivered another. Others have not played by the rules you established—rules about subject matter, format, methods of citation, deadlines, delivery time. You soon understand that the act of bringing these essays together, like the act of editing an anthology, is highly disciplinary: somehow, the material must be bent together, organized in a way that makes sense. Surely, if you look long enough, some coherence will emerge. Surely, if you order and reorder, a narrative line will take shape. This shaping happens in certain ways—you can cajole and force it a bit—but in other ways the book will resist you, even mock you and your assumptions about coherence and value. The collection of essays sits on your desk; like Robert Kroetsch's stone hammer, it becomes an existential object that takes on a life of its own. The manuscript's very presence undoes the completion it was supposed to embody. It will not be seduced through structure or the pretensions of an introduction that wants to civilize the fundamental randomness of these narratives that have been brought together. You look at the manuscript with suspicion. And you know that, finally, it will never bend to your will.

This little meditation on the relation between essay collections and anthologies was meant to introduce certain tropes that are part of the anthologizing process. I wanted to resist the usual observations about anthology-making that have been disempowered by their inevitable invocation in books of this kind, even though some of those books are excellent starting points. When I say "books of this kind," I am referring to essay collections and single-author studies that are devoted to what Jeffrey R. Di Leo calls (in the subtitle of his monograph) the "politics and pedagogy" of anthology-making. These studies include articles and books by Benedict; Churchman; Dike; Fraistat; Graff; Johnson; Jusdanis; Korte, Schneider, and Lethbridge; Kuipers; Lauter; Longenbach; Nelson; Parry; Price; Rasula; and Schrift. An important symposium on anthology formation, including commentary by Leitch, Johnson, McGowan, Finke, and Williams, appeared in 2003 (see Leitch). In the study of Canadian anthologies, there are a number of central works, including articles by Brydon, Davey, Knight, Fee, Gerson, Irvine, Kamboureli, Keith, Lecker, MacGillivray, Mandel, Miki, and Sugars. My history of English-Canadian anthologies, *Keepers of the Code*, was published in 2013.

Di Leo's excellent collection focuses on some crucial issues regarding anthology formation and the forces accounting for the canonical implications of anthological value. He discusses the ways in which the "formative power of anthologies is often magical to students and regulative to teachers" (1). Those anthologies carry with them quasi-magical and religious attributes. They are often instruments of power that replicate the authority of the institutions that make them required reading for students. In this context, the teacher becomes a secular preacher. The required anthology becomes the central text uniting the class; it embodies the codes that lead to enlightenment.

It is no coincidence that anthologies are typically seen as agents of canon formation, but the conjunction between canons and congregations is not mentioned very often. The etymology of the word "canon" is ecclesiastical. It comes from the Greek "κανών," meaning "rule" or "measuring stick." The concept of authority embedded in the term was adopted in Late Latin descriptions of Christian scripture, where it came to mean "church law" or church decrees enacted to govern moral and religious values. The clergyman who transmits this canon is referred to as a *"canonicus"* because he is "living under a rule." The congregation that receives this rule is not unlike the modern school class, which is assigned its required reading by a teacher or professor whose task it is to transmit canonical norms. Even those teachers whose work is consciously devoted to undermining the canon or questioning its assumptions reinforce the power of the canon as a dominant opponent worthy of attack. In the meeting of university, classroom, teacher, and anthological text, we find the secular equivalents of church, congregation, priest, and sacred word.

The idea that the canon comprises a set of texts that are used by anthologists to promote the idea of cultural inheritance is indebted to the theories of Pierre Bourdieu and other thinkers who have followed him, including John Guillory, who describes literary canons as forms of "cultural capital" used to transmit social values through the educational system. This collection asks how Canadian anthologies employ this cultural capital. To what extent do they transmit ideas about the nature and value of the nation whose literature they represent? What forms does this representation take? How have those forms changed over time?

Early anthologies were often described as literary feasts that offered sustenance to a wide variety of readers. However, as Barbara Benedict points out, "in its elevation of appetite to cultural capital, the metaphor of consumption is significant. Literary miscellanies and anthologies, indeed, promote the commodification of literature itself" (*Making the Modern Reader* 11). Although the etymology for "anthology" comes from the Greek word for garland, or a bouquet of flowers, the process of editing anthologies of national literatures is seldom a sweet-smelling affair. In fact, editors are routinely taken to task for upsetting the status quo, or for making choices deemed to be overly conservative or overly subversive in the way they reproduce or reject existing literary values. National literature anthologies are frequently identified as the focal points for debate about the makeup of the literary canon, mainly because arguments about the canon are displaced arguments about the makeup of the nation. The challenge to the canon that marks the study of American literature over the past four decades is implicitly a rethinking of the nation. This challenge finds its most fervent expression in the rise of feminist theory, and in revisions to the canon prompted by a reconfigured concept of the nation that is plural, multi-ethnic, and open to interrogation. Such revisions, and all the tensions they invoke, are nowhere better represented than in some of the ambitious national literature anthologies that have appeared over the last twenty years. But let's go back in time a bit first.

The first American national poetry anthology was edited by Elihu Hubbard Smith in 1793. As Alan C. Golding notes, "Smith's Federalism underlies what he saw as the use of his anthology: to build America's sense of identity by gathering an independent national literature to match and strengthen the country's newly achieved political independence." Golding observes that "the term 'American literature,' rarely used before the 1780s, became commonplace after the 1783 Treaty of Paris" (281). It was this kind of intense literary nationalism, always equated with the creation of a national literary canon, that drove literary anthology-making in the United States well into the twentieth century, until the canon itself became the object of intense scrutiny and questioning.

The most prominent late-twentieth-century example of the controversial nature of anthology-making is Paul Lauter's editorship of *The Heath Anthology of American Literature* (originally published in 1989). Lauter's anthology was the end product of a project called Reconstructing American Literature begun by The Feminist Press in the late 1970s. During this period, Lauter realized, some academics began to see that the American canon was not complete. His controversial anthology significantly revised the canon by introducing a wide variety of previously excluded or marginalized works. The debate about Lauter's anthology project consists of two questions: Should national anthologies collect great works, and if so, "great" by whose standards? And should national anthologies collect those works that have survived the test of time, or should they reflect the contemporary writing of the culture that will use them? These questions are directly related to the concept of nation. In the instructor's guide to the current edition of *The Heath Anthology of American Literature*, for example, the editor encourages students who read her collection "to see themselves as active participants in the process of cultural definition and transformation through their interpretation of and response to the texts in this anthology as well as through their participation in the institutionalized study of culture—in other words, to see the literature class itself as a kind of cultural work" (Coryell 4).

Anthologies of Canadian literature have always been preoccupied with similar questions as they navigate the intertwined concepts of canon and nation. In one of the first anthologies of Canadian poetry, entitled *Selections from Canadian Poets* (1864), the editor, Edward Hartley Dewart, argued that "[a] national literature is an essential element in the formation of national character. It is not merely the record of a country's mental progress: it is the expression of its intellectual life, the bond of national unity, and the guide of national energy" (ix). Dewart's equation of literature and nation would be reinforced again and again in dozens of national literature anthologies, especially those published in the years following Canada's centennial, in 1967. A commonly held assumption among the editors of these collections is that reading Canadian literature anthologies involves people in the activity of constructing Canada; every anthology presents them with textual versions of the country they know or are getting to know. But consider the extent to which the idea of "country" embodied in any given anthology is the product of a series of negotiations concerning the representation of nation. Editors must carefully consider the weight they give to different geographic regions, the balance between selections of writing by men and women, the need to recognize ethnic and racial diversity, and the desire to resist various forms of genre suppression encouraged by the anthology-making act. To add to the complexity of these negotiations, the editor is faced with further challenges about how the nation is represented through the organizational structure of the text. If the anthology is organized in terms of thematic groupings, to what extent does this reduce the nation to convenient categories that bear no real relation to the unstable and multiform qualities of national life? Should the anthology include aboriginal texts? That question bears on the issue of when a national narrative actually begins. How far back should a national literature anthology go in order to identify a genesis? Is there a definable beginning, or does the starting point of national literary history shift over time? And if the starting point shifts, what kind of valid commentary can the editor offer in terms of asserting a tradition? Should the editor resist asserting tradition, in the knowledge that this imposes the kind of deterministic historical pattern that has been undermined by poststructuralist thought?

The idea of Canada presented in anthologies varies widely and is constantly changing in response to shifting concepts of the country and to notions of literary value current in any given period. And different anthologists working in the same era often construct Canada in very different ways. By doing so, they show how the idea of Canada is multiple and evolving. Beyond the extrinsic constructions of nation that shift from collection to collection and over time, every anthology displays anxieties about the form it takes, the values it enshrines, the structure it imposes, and the way it frames its unstable national subject. Depending on the perspective of its editor, a national literature anthology may construct a modern nation, a postmodern nation, or a nation composed of intermingling voices that defy classification. Paradoxically, the anthological construction of the nation today is in many ways about the deconstruction of national identity, a process that has been assisted by the rise of on-demand publishing, which turns every instructor into an anthologizer capable of envisioning the nation from multiple and shifting perspectives. In this environment, the nation is dynamic and polyvalent. However, if one's understanding of community and citizenship is in some ways a function of a shared sense of national assumptions, or values, to what extent does the breakdown of conventional anthological authority make the notions of community and citizenship problematic? Do national literature anthologies—or the absence of them—say something about how nations are understood? Or do such anthologies encourage nations to be *mis*understood? That could be their most valuable function.

II

In suggesting that anthologies—and particularly national literature anthologies—prompt us to reconfigure their central subject, I am also suggesting that anthologies are metaphoric objects. But they are not usually treated in this way. Ever since the canon wars emerged in the early 1990s, anthologies have been seen as relatively pragmatic constructs that transmit or repudiate canonical norms. Di Leo describes many of the practical factors associated with anthological activity. He observes that anthologies provide map-like access to the disciplines that produce them. In this way, they are not only "reflective of the laws of their domain" but also vehicles that transmit "authority and orthodoxy through the pedagogical, political, and economic implications of using and publishing anthologies" (1). As canonical objects, they valorize "political and cultural agendas" and are "illustrative of ideological currents" while also announcing "new and emerging areas of inquiry" and helping us "to organize and understand the past" (2).

Di Leo points to three triadic areas that draw the attention of anthology reviewers. The first triad focuses on coverage (what does it include or exclude?), introductions (how is the material framed?), and comparison (how does it compare to others in terms of its selections?). The second triad includes editing (how has the material been shaped, and is it accurate?), organization (how is the material structured?), and paraphernalia (what kind of textual apparatus is included?). The third triad focuses on the material conditions of the anthology's production: how it is sold (who distributes it and what stores carry it?), how it is manufactured (what kind of paper is used, and how does the book design influence its content?), and what it costs (to what extent is the publication of the anthology a money-making or money-losing activity, and why?). Di Leo argues that it is the last of these triads—which concerns the material conditions of production—that receives the least coverage, even though "investigation into the third holds the greatest potential for increasing our critical understanding of the world of anthologies" (9).

Despite the best intentions of their editors, material conditions and limitations inevitably lead to decisions that distort the canon and literary history. This may result in the creation of bold and creative anthologies, but it will in no way result in a selection that accurately represents the larger picture. This is ironic, given the fact that anthologies are usually perceived, in terms of synecdoche, as vehicles that use parts to represent the whole. Another way of saying this is to assert that national literature anthologies paradoxically become the opposite of what they are designed to be. So when we use such anthologies to introduce students to Canadian literature, for example, we are really introducing them to a severely compromised narrative governed largely by material concerns.

I'd like to discuss a few of these concerns as I've experienced them.

National literary anthologies are pretty big beasts. Before commissioning such a project the publisher will have made detailed calculations about a number of related questions. How many pages can be printed? At what cost? What is the budget for permissions? Is the permissions budget sufficient to obtain current work? Is it sufficient to include works by the best-known writers? If not, how can the anthology be representative? How much money will be spent on copy-editing? On visual material? How much compensation will the editor demand? Are his or her name and experience worth the cost?

Permissions fees, and the actual cost of reproducing poems of a given size, can have a dramatic impact on the kind of material that is included in an anthology. One of the most prominent genres in Canadian poetry is the long poem, or serial poem. Many of Canada's most accomplished poets have done their best work in this form, and some of these poems can run to forty pages or more. In other words, they are short books. Obviously, it isn't always possible to include the entire work. The typical way of dealing with this problem is to use an excerpt. But then professors complain that their students don't really see the entire landscape, and that what started out as a long poem can in fact look like a much shorter poem in its excerpted form. Ironically, the book budget has erased the long poem form and in doing so has denied students exposure to a crucial genre of Canadian poetry.

Just as cost factors influence the ways in which long poems are handled, so do they influence the kind of fiction that is selected to represent the canon. Since every printed page costs money, editors have to be constantly aware of the length of the material they are selecting. This makes the process of anthology selection particularly hard on authors who favour the novella, including writers such as Eden Robinson, John Metcalf, Bill Gaston, or Alice Munro. The budgetary constraints that result in space limitations take a big toll on the ways in which genre is represented. Some anthologies—particularly the Norton anthologies—try to deal with this issue by including one or more chapters from canonical novels. But in the eyes of the student, these excerpts assume the status of a short story; the anthologizing process tends to reconfigure longer works as shorter works by selecting a chapter to represent the whole, or by truncating the original works in other ways, through excerpting, condensation, or elision. The net effect on new readers of the national canon is their sense that canonical works are more or less consistent in length, generally short, and generally not novels. The material conditions affecting selection introduce an unstated bias against longer forms by excluding or modifying length. If *The Great Gatsby* can be reduced to its first chapter, something has gone terribly wrong.

Material limitations affect not only the size of poems or works of fiction included in anthologies. They affect the range of poems available to editors as they make their choices. For example, Anne Carson is one of Canada's most accomplished and famous poets, yet her current publisher charges fees well above the average for her most recent work, mainly because she has become so well known. Those publishers, and perhaps Carson herself, have done us a disservice, for now, faced with these escalating permissions costs, anthologists turn to her earlier work, which can be obtained at a lower cost. The result? Students are not exposed to her most recent poetry, and cannot get an accurate sense of her evolution as a poet, mainly because the recent poetry is so seldom seen outside its original book publication, which few students can afford. To make matters worse, Carson frequently employs the long poem form, which to an editor only signals further monetary hurdles to be overcome.

Often, an editor will not know for certain whether a specific author can be included until the entire process of arriving at a final table of contents has run its conflicted course. For only after a tentative table of contents has been selected and then modified in response to various forms of review can the ideal table of contents be established. Even then, however, *that* ideal table of contents is subject to revision, for only when the ideal contents are established will the publisher actually attempt to determine the permissions costs. If those costs are too high, the contents will have to be modified again and again until the budget ceiling is met. So a convoluted series of editorial negotiations over selection and cost is finally modified by an overarching determination of total cost. In the midst of these negotiations, the abstract idea of nation that first mobilized the editor to work on the collection becomes even more distorted than it once was.

Editors can't help but be aware of these material restrictions. Or, if they are not, they will be rudely awakened. For many, this awakening produces some obvious cost-saving strategies. One temptation is to seek out authors whose work is in the public domain and therefore free for anyone to reproduce, a status obtained in North America fifty years after the author's death. Since cost is a factor in the creation of any anthology, editors are naturally drawn to material that can be obtained without charge. There is a tension between the desire to use this free material and the realization that it is frequently not the best material and is never current. For example, Duncan Campbell Scott, a respected poet, died in 1947. Therefore his work has been in the public domain for eighteen years. Recent anthologies are using more of Scott's work. Why? Has opinion about the quality of his work shifted radically? No. The increase is due to the fact that his work entered the public domain after 1997. So the inclusion of early Canadian poetry may be driven by its inherent quality, but it may equally be driven by the desire to flesh out the historical perspective through the use of works that have paradoxically lost their currency in terms of cold, hard cash.

Material conditions often lead to the exclusion of experimental writers whose work cannot be easily reproduced within the anthology's given design. For example, concrete and visual poets such as bpNichol or bill bissett often present their work in very unconventional ways: as paper fragments emerging from a box, as a series of coloured prints or paintings interlaced with printed words, as visual fragments that run across the page or are housed in books of odd dimensions that can accommodate the visual elements. Contemporary writers such as Lisa Robertson and Erin Mouré use exaggerated fonts to create visual effects, and their writing often challenges conventional book margins. In order to publish works of this kind, these poets found friendly publishers who were often as interested in the book as artifact as they were in the poetry those books contained. Design and content went hand in hand. But the large-scale anthology is never friendly to printing and design experimentation. Once the margins are established and the book gutters set, it becomes very expensive to run signatures of the book that defy these overall parameters, just as it becomes costly to introduce colour. As a result, such boundary-breaking works are often made to fit the pre-established anthology mould, or the editor is forced to make selections that will fit that mould. The process robs the work of its subversive elements, or distorts them by civilizing their presence. In many cases, the work that cannot be accommodated is simply omitted, so that students gain only a partial sense of the writer's experimental methods.

If we examine the supply side with a bit more cynicism it becomes clear that there are even crasser material factors at work in the creation of national literary canons as they are exemplified by these national literature anthologies. Take, for example, weight. I am not talking about the weightiness of ideas here. I am talking about pure physical poundage. In the peer review of my own anthology *Open Country*, I was made all too aware of how important weight is. My reviewers reminded the publisher repeatedly that the final anthology must not be too heavy. One said it should be designed in such a way as to fit comfortably into a backpack. And the paper should not be too thin. But it had to be acid-free and environmentally friendly. And lots of room should be left on the pages for notes. What else could be done with this canonical waistline? Chop an inch off the overall dimensions of the book? That's good for the backpack, but it reduces the margins inside. Bad for note-takers. Bad for the experimental poets who like to play with the distinction between margin and centre. Bad for the overall look of the book, which will seem cramped. Yes, it's true, every book encounters design limitations, but in this case, I would argue that the material appearance of one anthology—which is itself a function of mediation and compromise—transmits a different sense of the canon than another anthology that appears in a different physical form, even if the contents are identical. So national literary canons truly can be perceived in terms of physical appearance and weight; one's response to holding that canon or stuffing it into a backpack is directly related to the kind of reception that canon will receive. In short, the gross materiality of the product contributes to its reception just as much as the content itself. The same holds true for the nation embodied in that anthology. Will it be slim or chubby? Backpackable or not? To add to this perception of the book's value, we could also consider such material factors as the kind of artwork selected for the anthology's cover, the technology involved in printing and binding the book in a cost-efficient manner, the amount allocated to marketing and promoting the title, and so on.

Because most small and medium-sized publishing houses will not be able to compete with larger houses in offering the editor an advance against royalties, or in making a substantial financial commitment to the permissions budget and other costs associated with production, large-scale national literature anthologies tend to be published by a few well-known companies that have truly cornered the market. This situation differs markedly from the conditions that apply to other kinds of smaller and less costly anthologies, which are often undertaken by independent publishing companies. But the big literature anthology seems by definition to be the creation of a few big companies, and it is necessarily imprinted with the institutional values that allow those companies to succeed. So, in fact, the presentation of national literary canons is always restricted and partial, and always a function of the corporate material resources available to the companies that produce them. It is never simply a matter of editorial innovation or intelligence. There are too many material factors that stand in the way.

III

I have been discussing the canonical and material dimensions of anthology formation. But there is another aspect of anthologies that interests me, and that is their metaphorical qualities. In order to explain my understanding of these qualities, I would like to retrace the steps that made me aware of them. When I was a student, as is the case for most of my students today, anthologies represented unproblematized collections of material that had somehow been deemed worthy of study by my professors. And, of course, the material itself, and the ways in which it was discussed, usually conjured up a version of literary history designed to demonstrate that history had continuity, that concepts such as influence and tradition existed, that there was an order to the literary universe and it could be encapsulated in a single book. When I became a teacher and had to select the anthologies that would be used in my own courses, I tended to fall back on those collections that had established their authority. In Canadian literature, in my time, this meant anthologies such as Gary Geddes and Phyllis Bruce's *15 Canadian Poets* (and its various permutations), or different editions of the big anthologies edited by Bennett and Brown.

It was only after I became involved in editing and publishing Canadian literature that I was approached to edit my own anthology. So, for the first time, I had to think about what I wanted to achieve. I had no desire to create a volume that would be of interest to the general reading public, and I never even thought about that possibility, a fact that indicates the extent to which I understood implicitly, even at an early stage in my career, that anthologies of national literatures were fundamentally designed to serve curricular communities rather than a broader reading audience. I also understood, early on, that a canon of Canadian literature existed, that professors relied upon it, and that to challenge it in any kind of detail would probably result in poor uptake by the academic community I was trying to serve. I see now that my attempt to "serve" that community underlined the way in which editors of national literature anthologies are the footmen of academia. Step out of line, or refuse to toe the line, and you stand a good chance of being figuratively fired. This was not a worry for me because I fully intended to serve my masters, and in fact I worked hard to devise ways in which their needs could be met and surpassed. At the same time, my experience began to acquaint me with the material side of anthologizing, because I had to become familiar with permissions budgets and costs, with grumpy authors who did not want certain works reproduced, and with the host of limitations imposed upon the editor by the processes of editing, design, production, and marketing. Eventually, my editorial activities became cynical, mainly because I could see that it was almost impossible to create a national literature anthology that deviated from the accepted canonical norms, and that publishers were reluctant to support works that challenged the status quo; they feared that doing so would lose them academic sales. There was an unstated agreement between academics and publishers that neither side would rock the boat. Of course, there were many radical anthologies, and many anthologies of experimental or subversive work, but these never posed a challenge to the major anthologies because they did not generate the kind of pan-Canadian academic following that was necessary to sustain the costs of producing expensive national literature anthologies. This meant that students—for the better part of Canadian literary history—were being fed a homogenized view of Canadian literature that was heavily reliant upon canonical norms established in the nineteenth century.

It was partly my interest in anthologies as canonical objects that led me to wonder about the extent to which anthologies contributed to the historical formation of literary value in Canada. Before any kind of commentary could be made on this formation, it had to be defined. In an attempt to begin this process of definition, I compiled (with Peter Lipert and Colin Hill) a detailed bibliography of Canadian literary anthologies published between 1837 and 1997. In that 150-year period, close to 2,000 anthologies representing various configurations of Canadian literature were published, certainly a testimony to the enduring power of anthologies as instruments of literary value, and particularly impressive given the material limitations of publishing books in Canada, especially before the impact of the Massey Commission report in 1951. The wide variety of anthologies appearing in every part of the country also revealed the extent to which marginal, experimental, subversive, and ex-centric anthologies define the Canadian literary landscape. In fact, one could easily show, using this bibliographical information, that more antho-logical attention in Canada has been devoted to undermining conventional notions of a Canadian literary tradition than to supporting it. The majority of Canadian literary anthologies question the very existence of such a tradi-tion, and allow us to realize that we could as easily define Canadian literary history by asking how anthologies relentlessly illustrate the impossibility of defining it in any monolithic terms. As these anthologies make eminently clear, Canadian literary history is all over the map.

And yet, the myth of a Canadian literary tradition that can be described and captured in anthologies persists, right up to the present day. It is partic-ularly the big national literature anthologies that are devoted to sustaining this myth, which is shared by editors and professors. These big national liter-ature anthologies are designed to be used in courses founded on a profound determinism, on a belief in literary causality, on a code of inheritance and influence. Even the terms used to describe this code indicate the extent to which such anthologies support a national-idealist agenda that is rooted in capital, sometimes called the currency of canonical texts. John Guillory is right to argue that anthologies preserve and disseminate cultural capital. Achieving cultural literacy is a function of obtaining that capital and handing it down to the next generation of believers.

I have tried to suggest, perhaps somewhat obviously, that national liter-ature anthologies are more than the product of material conditions or one editor's set of selections. They document a ritual of succession. Their edi-tors participate in this ritual and understand their activities in quasi-myth-ical terms. Because they are involved in constructing a national narrative, editors imagine themselves as mythologizers, and, from this imagining, it does not take much more for them to see themselves as the principal actors in a creation narrative. In articulating a model of Canadian literary history and evolution through their selections, they are involved in constructing a foundational story. Quasi-gods, they give breath and voice to this genesis, and they are responsible for determining what unfolds after the moment of creation. Not surprisingly, then, editors of anthologies that set out to represent the development of Canadian literature often see themselves and their project in archetypal terms, a point I develop more fully in *Keepers of the Code*.

If we grant that anthologies are material constructions that are also deeply symbolic structures, many things begin to change. We can begin to examine the ways in which anthologies are themselves narratives with their own patterns of development and, indeed, their own plots. This allows us to read anthologies in a different way. For example, take any anthology of Canadian literature. What is its opening selection? How does that opening provide a door that frames the work? What values are embedded in this opening? And then what does this opening give onto? How does the story unfold? What kind of narrative continuity or discontinuity is mapped out as we move from one selection to the next, if we read the text in the order in which it is presented? Each selection stands alone, yes, but each is also part of an overall picture, brush strokes in a painting. How can we articulate the nature of those brush strokes and the total canvas they achieve?

In trying to describe this painting, however, we soon come to understand that we cannot do it innocently, because the canvas is troubled. We cannot just describe the total painting because that would be to ignore its parts. Yet we understand that, at some level, the editor wants us to absorb the total effect—the totalizing effect—while ignoring the frictions posed by its constituent parts. When we begin to focus on those parts—they may be poems or stories or excerpts—we see that, individually, they are themselves small paintings with their own distinctive styles. In order to meld them to the overall canvas, the editor has to recognize their individuality and difference while at the same time subduing it, so that the overall picture can emerge. In this sense, the anthological act is always violent and repressive as it seeks to illustrate a totality out of parts that might not normally cohere. This is the kind of painting I like to look at, mainly because it is so troubled by the fact of its own existence. Its presumption of coherence—of depicting *something*—is radically undercut by all of the literary energy it is at pains to collect, and civilize. If the subject of the canvas is the nation itself, and certainly that is the subject of any national literature anthology, then we can begin to talk about the way in which the narratives developed in these anthologies are deeply conflicted. And we can also try to describe the way in which the total picture of the nation presented in the anthology is paradoxically self-destructive.

The radical energy of national literature anthologies does not come from the coherence of the narrative they present. It comes from the coherence they can never obtain, from the discrepancy between what the editor wants and what the editor knows he or she will never achieve. National literature anthologies are potent and interesting precisely because they articulate the narrative of their own failure. Once we begin to focus on the metaphors aligned with anthologizing, a new world opens up. Anthologies can be seen as ritualized objects that desire archetypal status. Their editors, acting as canonizers, are involved in the secular equivalent of what is fundamentally a religious pursuit. The texts they produce—shared by a congregation of students from generation to generation—also have biblical import. The development of the anthological text may be viewed as a harmonized and conflicted narrative that expresses the editor's impossible desire for coherence. Or the poems and stories comprising an anthology might be described as individual voices on a stage, each one determined to speak its part, so that by the end of the anthology—a play—we have heard each speak but our overall impression is one of cacophony. We cannot put the final picture together, and can only describe a few of the many voices we have heard. This is much like describing the country that the anthology purports to represent through its literature: it is not coherent, not whole, and its energy comes from its cacophony. The picture does not make sense, it is perpetually conflicted, and that is exactly what gives it dynamism and depth. Or, as A. J. M. Smith might put it, this is the beauty of strength, broken by strength and still strong.

I've invoked Smith here for two reasons. First, because his numerous efforts as an anthologizer of Canadian literature are all informed by a desire to know the country through its poetry and fiction and are predicated on the notion that such knowledge is obtainable though editorial action. Second, because Smith's "The Lonely Land," like his anthologies, defines the country as a site of paradoxical conflict, as a place that is both broken and strong, or (to use Smith's anthological lexicon) as a place that is native and cosmopolitan all at once. We can read Smith's anthologies for what they say about the country, or we can read them as narratives about their editor's own anxious attempts to come to terms with the subject of his inquiry: the anthology, the country. The use value of anthologies is often determined in relation to the way they serve or don't serve particular curricular agendas. The pedagogical currency of an anthology is typically measured in terms of *what* is represented. But to interrogate anthologies at a more challenging level, we need to ask how they represent *themselves* as narrative entities, what identities they seek out through their selections, and what anxieties those selections display. From this perspective, every anthology becomes a rich, self-contained story in its own right, and every national literature anthology becomes the expression of the ways in which its editor manipulates that story in an attempt to capture a dream of nation. And precisely because it is a dream, anthological narratives are richly symbolic, fascinating and inexplicable at the same time.

In this context, we understand that there are many kinds of anthologies, and many kinds of anthological narratives. Anthologies are not just books. They might also be museums, or civic spaces, or albums of popular music, or any powerful combination of human expressions that are brought together by an editorial force that may be curatorial, or political, or creative, or pedagogical, or religious. Any collection of things that is brought together through human intervention is a form of anthology. We live in an anthological universe. There are many kinds of anthological control that affect the way we live from day to day. How far can we take this metaphor? Quite far, I think. Anthologies have always had power because they are reflective of the human condition. Anthologies are existential vessels.

IV

How does such a conception of anthologies relate to this book? To answer that question I need to return to some of my opening statements in this introduction, where I was suggesting that this collection of critical essays is much like an anthology. Perhaps it is an anthology. It has an editor who has sought out and selected a group of works that are all related to the subject of Canadian literature. The essays have generally been ordered in relation to the historical period they cover, so as to provide a rough chronological perspective on the history of anthology formation in Canada. I could have introduced another order. I am reminded of the "crazy sundials" in Irving Layton's "The Fertile Muck"; they never get built. So, in this collection, I have more or less failed to disturb my penchant for historical order and my belief that one thing still leads to another. But this does not mean that what is "anthologized" here is not suggestive and rich. In what follows, I want to introduce the essays in this book by allowing myself the freedom to let them take me in different directions, not in order to explain them, but to let them operate as symbolic narratives in their own right, much like the narratives that are brought together in any anthology.

The collection opens with Richard Cavell's meditation on the metaphor of anthology-making, and on anthologies as metaphors. Moving among a number of diverse but anthemic texts, he demonstrates that anthologies are tropes of violence, continuity, discontinuity, contagion, influence, and rejection, to name but a few of the powerful forces associated with the formation and reception of anthologies. As he says, every anthology "implies a political allegory" because "the anthology, like writing itself, is founded upon the idea of the cut, the glyph." The richness of the anthological text is also a function of the way we read it. What do our reading methods say about our political understanding of anthological texts? Do we read them in an orderly fashion, from beginning to end? Do we skip from selection to selection, looking for those pieces that provide us with certain kinds of satisfaction? Or do we read anthologies backward in an attempt to undo the chronology they propose? Cavell uses A. M. Klein's *The Second Scroll* as a metaphoric point of reference for his inquiry into "the politics and poetics of the anthology in Canada." He reads it as a kind of ur-text that illustrates the fundamental violence at the heart of anthology-making. National anthology-making embodies a particular kind of violence because the nation "can only be known in fragments." Cavell examines the nature of this violence as it emerges in three influential collections: Bertram Brooker's *Yearbook of the Arts in Canada* (1929), Malcolm Ross's *Our Sense of Identity* (1954), and Cavell and Peter Dickinson's *Sexing the Maple* (2006). In looking at the discourse of nation that emerges in these three very different texts, Cavell argues that national literature anthologies "must *always* fail to represent the nation because there is no nation to represent." This is largely because the nation itself is always in the process of being narrated. Anthologies are a testimony to any nation's fluid status.

D. M. R. Bentley's commentary on the origins and editing of W. D. Lighthall's *Songs of the Great Dominion* (1889) provides ample evidence of the extent to which anthologies may serve as testing grounds for national ideals. Bentley shows that once Lighthall was named editor of the volume by the London publisher Walter Scott, the contents of his anthology came under the scrutiny and influence of Charles G. D. Roberts, who was attempting to promote a number of poets from his own generation. They were aligned with the idea that the poems selected for inclusion in the anthology should not focus on "manifestly Canadian subjects and themes." In arguing that Lighthall could break with tradition by selecting poets whose work was international in scope and subject matter, Roberts encouraged a series of conflicts that made this anthology "the most editorially vexed and problematic anthology in the history of Canadian literature." Perhaps the only other anthology that could be described in these words would be A. J. M. Smith's *The Book of Canadian Poetry* (1943), which became the subject of a virulent attack by John Sutherland, who objected to the distinction that Smith made, in his introduction, between what he called the "native" and "cosmopolitan" traditions in Canadian poetry. However, as Bentley's essay makes clear, this distinction between the native and the cosmopolitan does not begin with Smith. It finds its first articulation in Lighthall's collection, which was a product of the interaction between his "patriotic agenda" and his eventual desire to see Canada and its literature in the context of nation, empire, and, ultimately, "the union of mankind." Bentley demonstrates how deeply Lighthall, his publisher, and Roberts and his circle saw the anthology as a testing ground for conceptions of nation, and how fully they associated the selections made by Lighthall with a depiction of the country. From this point onward, and perhaps as far back as 1864 (when Edward Hartley Dewart published his *Selections from Canadian Poets*), Canadian literature anthologies would be involved in the vexed issues of representing nation.

As Bentley shows, nation is not only represented through subject matter. Editors also construct ideas of nation by favouring certain authors, styles, genres, or periods. As well, they have to decide what people constitute the nation as it is represented through their selections. At what point did Canadian anthologists begin to admit translated works by immigrant writers into their anthologies? Or when did they begin to illustrate the origins of English-Canadian literature through a selection of native songs in translation? While it might seem odd to open an anthology of English-Canadian literature with indigenous work in translation, this became a trend after Ralph Gustafson introduced his Pelican *Anthology of Canadian Poetry (English)* in 1942 with two Haida songs in translation. In her essay, Margery Fee shows that many other editors had included poems about native peoples prior to 1942. However, Gustafson's was the first anthology to use poems by indigenous peoples in translation to introduce a book of English-Canadian poetry, as if those Haida songs were somehow foundational to the development of English-Canadian literature. But they were nothing of the kind, simply because the vast majority of Canadian writers did not know them, and even if they did, Gustafson was presenting indigenous work in translation, a gesture that replicated the colonization of the very people whose language set them apart from the tradition that was now annexing them.

Fee traces the inclusion of "Indian poems" in anthologies appearing since 1893, comparing the inclusion rates of poems by E. Pauline Johnson with those of Duncan Campbell Scott. She observes that because of his powerful position as the Deputy Superintendent of the Department of Indian Affairs from 1913 to 1932, and because of his close association with powerful literary figures of the time, Scott's Indian poems tend to be represented more frequently than Johnson's, especially after her death in 1913. It was partly modernism that "effectively took all her poems out of the canon from 1940 to 1990"; as Fee argues, "modernist critics drove Johnson—and most other women poets—out of the canon." Johnson's removal from the canon was also a result of the ways in which her poetry represented native people. While many of her poems "directly criticized colonial power," Scott's "racist" and "sexist" poetry exoticized natives and often portrayed them (and particularly women) as debased sexual beings. He foregrounded their polygamous relations and focused on their "exotic and primitive customs," while Johnson portrayed Indian women as "active and often articulate." Yet, in a contemporary canon that is so highly influenced by modernist values, Scott's Indian poems have survived in anthologies, while (until quite recently) Johnson's Indian poems have languished.

Issues concerning the representation of indigenous peoples are often linked to ideas about the origins of Canadian literature. By including Haida verses in translation, Gustafson was indicating his belief that, somehow, English-Canadian literature found its point of origin there. But he was also following the lead of the American anthologist Mark van Doren, who had included translated Haida verses in his *American and British Literature since 1890* (1939), which appeared three years prior to Gustafson's work. Both Gustafson and van Doren were wrestling with the problem of how to begin their anthological narratives; they were struggling to define a myth of origin in a modernist universe that had rejected conventional models of genesis. They were not alone in this struggle. In the first true anthology of Canadian literature—Dewart's *Selections from Canadian Poets*—the editor pictures himself as a wanderer in an unexplored land. In his preface, Dewart says that in undertaking the anthology "I entered on an untrodden path, without any way-marks to guide me" (vii). And in the introduction, he speaks of his editorial efforts in terms of the metaphor of genesis: "Whatever is discovered as new in the records of creation, in the capacities and relations of things, in the history of the mind's operations, or in the forms of thought and imagery by which in its higher moods soul speaks to soul, will always demand some suitable embodiment in literature" (ix). Both Gustafson and Dewart were asking how it all begins, and by asking that question in relation to the literature of a specific place, they were also asking *where* it all begins, or, as Northrop Frye famously wondered in his conclusion to the *Literary History of Canada*: "Where is here?"

That is precisely the question Cheryl Cundell approaches in her essay on exploration writing in Canadian anthologies. In reviewing the exploration writing collected in fourteen anthologies, she explores the conflicted ideas about origin and place that characterize the presentation of Canadian writing. She recognizes an immediate paradox in the representation of exploration writing, for by anthologizing it various editors have sought to transform one genre that was not meant to be "literary" into another genre that defines what is literary in Canadian terms. As she says, "exploration writing is frequently devalued as literature because of habits of reading that read its non-fictional status—by transposition—as a *non-literary status*. Thus, it becomes canonical non-literature." For this reason, the inclusion of exploration writing in these anthologies "involves them in a paradox of place" because the idea of "place" denotes "both literary situation and geographical delineation." Different editors choose to represent different points of origin, not only because they disagree about historical departure points in defining the beginnings of Canadian literature, but also because they have multiple conceptions about "what constitutes literature" in the first place. One feels the anxiety implicit in this problem. If editors cannot agree on where or when Canada begins, how are readers supposed to position themselves in relation to the past? Cundell quotes from Leon Surette's influential article about topocentrism in Canadian literature and concurs that "English-Canadian critics and writers reject the Canadian polity as an organizing principle for Canadian literary history because they desire 'a Canadian story or myth'" (52). Although many anthologists include exploration writing in their collections, they are often reluctant to make assertions about its originary status, mainly because the early explorers did not understand themselves as Canadians. Yet, Cundell argues, "exploration writing must be the nation's earliest literature because without its observations, maps, and directions—without its arrival—Canadian literature would be lost."

If we don't know—and never will know—where Canadian literature begins, its instability as a subject of study becomes even more apparent. Looking back at the claims made by Canadian anthologists over 150 years, one is struck by the absurdity of the idea—held in common by virtually every editor of a national literature anthology—that a nation can be apprehended through a selective representation of its literature. The viability of such a representation is further eroded by a host of exclusionary values at play in such anthologies. In surveying English-Canadian literary anthologies published between 1920 and 1950, Peggy Lynn Kelly provides ample evidence demonstrating the extent to which "systemic biases affected the choices made by publishers, editors, and curriculum developers" during the period. Specifically, the canon that emerged in these years "perpetuated the distinctly Anglo-Saxon, white, and masculine traditional canon that had been developing since the arrival of European settler-invaders." Virility and "manliness" in poetry was valued over "feminine, emotional, domestic art forms." Frequently barred from entering the masculine domain that was advanced and protected by male editors, women sought alternative publishing venues, which were often aligned with literary associations that produced anthologies, often on an annual basis. Yet, as the history of anthology formation in Canada demonstrates, works that appeared in the association anthologies were seldom reprinted in mainstream anthologies ("academic-professional anthologies") of Canadian literature, which meant that they were doubly marginalized: first, in being ignored by Canadian publishers, all of whom were men, and second, in being ignored by Canadian anthology editors, almost all of whom were men. In this pattern of exclusion, one sees hard evidence of the ways in which the English-Canadian canon is skewed, but also a strong illustration of the various factors "that relate to a gendered imbalance of financial and cultural power."

Bonnie Hughes enters this discussion of anthologies at the historical point that Kelly leaves off: the 1950s. Hughes looks specifically at the selection of works by Susanna Moodie and John Richardson in four influential anthologies published during the 1950s and 1960s: Carl F. Klinck and Reginald E. Watters's *Canadian Anthology* (1955), their revised edition of the same work (1966), the third edition of A. J. M. Smith's *The Book of Canadian Poetry* (1957), along with his *The Book of Canadian Prose* (1965). She notes that these works are located in the second stage of what she describes as four stages of anthology development in Canada: "the literary historical, from 1922 to the late 1940s; the literary nationalist, from the 1950s to the late 1960s; the thematic, occurring throughout the 1970s and into the early 1980s; and the pluralistic, from the early 1980s to the present." She asks how these prominent editors positioned Richardson and Moodie during the literary nationalist phase. Richardson was presented to demonstrate the nationalist ideals of the era. In their 1955 edition, Klinck and Watters link Richardson to the War of 1812 and praise his attention to historical detail in *The Canadian Brothers* (1840) rather than *Wacousta* (1832), because they saw the Grantham brothers in the later work as realistic figures in a war that was central to Canada's survival. In 1966, they replaced the chapters excerpted from *The Canadian Brothers* with a section from *War of 1812* (1902), Richardson's posthumously published memoir of his war experiences. In this way, they lent even more credence to Richardson as a defender of Canada, rather than as a novelist. Like Klinck and Watters, Smith focuses on *War of 1812* in his 1965 anthology because, Hughes says, it "links the war with national unity." In this way, Smith upholds "earlier assessments of the connections between war, national identity, and affiliation with Britain." Klinck and Watters also made strategic decisions concerning the promotion of national identity through their selection of Moodie's work. Rather than choosing excerpts from *Roughing It in the Bush* (1852), which was well known, they made selections from *Life in the Clearings* (1853) and *Mark Hurdlestone* (1853) in order to position her "as an important contributor to the growth and development of the nation's literature." In their later edition, Klinck and Watters placed even more emphasis on Moodie's place in the Canadian canon, positioning her as a good example of "Canada's extant literary culture." Smith, on the other hand, chose poems from *Roughing It* for his 1957 edition, in order to demonstrate the realistic qualities of Moodie's writing. For Hughes, this reveals Smith's interest "in detailing national history and unique traits." When Smith returned to Moodie in 1965, he focused more on her divided personality, and on the ways in which her experiences in the woods, as represented in *Roughing It*, approached a kind of archetypal status, perhaps anticipating Northrop Frye's comments on the role of landscape in Canadian literature that appeared in his conclusion to the *Literary History of Canada*, published in the same year as Smith's revised work.

The 1950s and '60s were crucial years in the development of Canadian literature, especially because the effects of the Massey Commission report, issued in 1951, were being felt across the country. The founding of the Canada Council in 1957 was a direct product of the Commission's recommendations. By the mid-1960s, new publishing houses and magazines started to appear across the country, and a variety of reading communities began to affiliate themselves with the different political agendas associated with these venues. Perhaps most important, Canadians from coast to coast began to see and hear Canadian writers, an activity we take for granted today but which was a startling innovation for Canadian readers in these years. It was the CBC that brought this innovation into Canadian homes.

We need to recall that Canadian writers were rarely discussed on Canadian radio before World War II. It was only with the introduction of Robert Weaver's radio program *Canadian Short Stories*, in 1948, that the reading public began to get a sense of contemporary Canadian writing. But Canadian writers could not be seen on national television until 1952, when CBC started broadcasting from coast to coast. The radio successor to *Canadian Short Stories* was Weaver's *Anthology*, which allowed people to hear Canadian writers reading their own work, starting in 1954. As Joel Deshaye notes, *Anthology* "contributed greatly to the boom in Canadian literature in the 1960s and '70s," and helped to make a number of Canadian writers media personalities. Deshaye is interested in the kind of writing that *Anthology* promoted, which tended to be realistic rather than sentimental or melodramatic. Because they were presented with realistic forms of writing that were experimental at that time, Canadians were implicitly encouraged to understand their country through a new discursive mode that tacitly bore witness to the nation's pragmatic existence. Although Weaver may have "demurred when his work was associated with nationalism," as Deshaye says, its alignment with CBC's nationalist mandate, and with the broadcasting vehicle of CBC itself, tied the essence of the show to a literary-nationalist ethos that continues to the present day.

Historically, CBC programming has operated implicitly and explicitly on the assumption that nationally broadcast programs devoted to Canadian culture are crucial to the promotion and survival of national unity. In this sense, the message behind Weaver's radio anthology shares many of the values associated with the print anthologies that preceded it. These values were also transferred to the print version of his radio show—*The Anthology Anthology*. In quoting Donna Bennett's review of the book, Deshaye draws our attention to the perception of such collections as national symbols. Bennett speaks of the way in which the book reminds us of the show, which she calls "the voice of the land," and of how it is a "talisman" because "to speak the words that define ourselves is virtually a ritualistic act in Canada." Here Bennett articulates the frequent positioning of Canadian literary anthologies as oracular artifacts that carry symbolic weight.

It hardly seems fitting to describe some of the anthologies that appeared in the 1970s as oracular objects. Many of them, inspired by countercultural politics, were doing their best to challenge the status quo, both in terms of design and content. One of these challengers was Gary Geddes and Phyllis Bruce's *15 Canadian Poets*, which first appeared in 1970 under their joint editorship, and then was revised, by Geddes alone, in several expanded editions over the next four decades. Whereas previous national literary anthologies had sought to represent numerous poets from different periods, Geddes and Bruce focused on a new generation of writers who were coming to public attention. For this reason, I speculate, their anthology appealed to a new generation of scholars who were obtaining doctorates in the fields of Canadian literature and following the writers of their day, particularly those who were attached to what Geddes calls "the Canadian literary renaissance of the 1960s, which brought Al Purdy, Gwendolyn MacEwen, Leonard Cohen, Margaret Atwood, and Michael Ondaatje into the public eye." But the success of *15 Canadian Poets* also had something to do with its design. Here was an anthology that seemed fresh and user-friendly, with its author photographs and conversational comments by those authors about their craft. One might think that the editorial values underlying such a successful volume had been deliberated in great detail, but, as Geddes reveals in the memoir included in this volume, he was "appalled by the lack of a decent and representative teaching anthology" and was mainly interested in reproducing material that he could use in the classroom as a first-time teacher of Canadian literature. Because he was resistant to poetry that was "academic, or experimental for its own sake," Geddes tended to favour poetry that would "provide ammunition for the student who, like [himself], had to struggle against the undue authority and privileging of critics, and who preferred to spend his or her time engaging with the primary texts rather than quoting and synthesizing secondary materials." Either because there were no viable contemporary alternatives, or because a new generation of Canadian literature academics agreed with his literary taste, Geddes's anthologies struck a chord that continues to resonate. And certainly the way in which he engaged in the process of selection as something that was existential, rather than academic, presented a model of the ways in which anthology-making could be grounded in a structure that was personal and self-reflective. The directness of that mode of selection is reflected in the openness of the voice we encounter in Geddes's contribution to this collection.

While successful anthologies such as Geddes's tend to dominate curricular choices, they comprise only a small part of overall anthological activity. As Janet Friskney's detailed analysis shows, anthology-making in Canada has been a diverse and prolific enterprise, marked by conflicting editorial standards that emerge in a competitive marketplace. By writing literary history through bibliographical analysis, she draws our attention to the many publishing companies that have invested most heavily in anthologizing Canadian literature (see her table 3). At the same time, her analysis allows us to see just how the profile of anthology publishing devoted to Canadian literature has shifted historically and regionally. Perhaps most revealing are the statistics she provides concerning the growth of anthology publishing. Of all the Canadian literature anthologies surveyed, only 1.42 percent were published prior to 1900, a figure that jumps to 30.26 percent between 1990 and 1999. From this perspective, we can see that Geddes's *15 Canadian Poets*, first published in 1970, was at the beginning of a wave that saw anthology production rise from 6.38 percent in the 1960s to 23.48 percent in the 1970s, a massive jump that attests to the presence of a period that is often called the "explosion" in Canadian literature.

The results of that explosion were multiple. New publishing houses were established. Small magazines entered the scene. Scholarly journals devoted to the study of Canadian literature appeared from coast to coast. Libraries began to invest much more heavily in acquiring Canadian writing. Authors benefited through the introduction of outright grants, along with travel grants to support touring. Funding was made available to university departments and cultural organizations that allowed them to bring in visiting speakers from across the country. If Canadian literature had a golden decade in the twentieth century, this was it. By the end of the 1970s, the market for Canadian literature had matured to the point that alternative anthologies could make it into university courses, a situation that would have been unthinkable just a decade earlier, when the anthology landscape was dominated by the large, commercial publishing houses such as Oxford University Press Canada and McClelland and Stewart.

The same golden decade saw the canonization of many new Canadian writers, among them Michael Ondaatje. He had been actively involved in promoting experimental writing, especially in the years following the publication of *The Collected Works of Billy the Kid* in 1970. By the time he edited *The Long Poem Anthology* for Coach House Press, in 1979, he had achieved considerable power, and he was connected with a network of poets who were challenging convention. The long poem—at least as it was understood by its practitioners at the time—was a potent form of this kind of challenge. It was perceived as embodying subversive values that undermined traditional notions of historical determinism and the nature of the literary subject. Partially inspired by American postmodernism, but also by Black Mountain poetics and (a bit later) by poststructuralist French theory, Canadian long poems proposed a radical reformulation of human consciousness, a questioning of historical certitude, and a profound doubt about mimetic theories of art.

Ondaatje's anthology embodies these various modes of subversion while at the same time validating his role as an agent of change. In her powerful deconstruction of *The Long Poem Anthology*, Karis Shearer shows us how compromised a volume that anthology really is. While it ostensibly presents a collection of long poems that challenge "the normal hierarchy whereby small-press poetry was selected and fed into the academic market via commercial presses," in fact it sought to enter into this hierarchy by framing its contents in terms that would make the anthology inviting to the academic market it wanted to exploit. While it sought to engage and promote alternative ideas of the long poem's "public," it courted the professors and professionals aligned with existing canonical values. Ondaatje understood this academic market well, mainly because his own books had been granted entry to it. Shearer traces the process through which a literary work—or in this instance a collection of works sharing certain political values—are depoliticized through their commodification via the anthology. In this case, the anthology becomes a civilizing force, domesticating the originally radical texts that, when united under a single cover, allow the editor to claim that his anthology is original and timely. But no sooner have terms such as "original" and "timely" been introduced than we begin to see the anthological paradox, for these works—which reject ideas of essence, originality, and timeliness—are subdued through their editorial regrouping, transformed into canonical expressions that are amenable to study in precisely those academic circles that replicate canonical norms. By virtue of their anthologization, these long poems are neutered, deprived of the power that warranted their inclusion in the first place. Much the same happens to the design elements of these long poems, each of which was originally published as a self-contained artifact in which the appearance of the work—from cover, to paper selection, to interior layout and font selection—are part and parcel of the overall aesthetic. However, *The Long Poem Anthology*, like any anthology, eradicates the visual distinctions that make each work unique, standardizing them in relation to a template that is far removed from the original work.

Shearer shows that the three claims made on the book cover also point to how this anthology undermines the value of what it collects. It was not true that "more than half of these poems are presently out of print," or that "the complete texts appear." In making these claims, the publisher presented the anthology as something that would reinstate these long poems' value by bringing them back to print. But many were not out of print, although the appearance of the anthology now threatened the survival of the original editions in the market. Coach House claimed that the full texts of each poem appeared (with the exception of *The Martyrology*). But it could only make this claim by ignoring the original design of each text, which was certainly part of the "complete" text. Finally, the anthology was positioned as a collection that "for the first time" (there is the originary metaphor) "makes possible the serious study of this form and these poems in university and college classrooms," as if they could not be studied "seriously" before the appearance of the anthology, and as if the very presence of the anthology somehow made the subject matter more viable for use in classrooms than it was before. What the publisher actually meant was that the material had been repackaged in such a way as to make it acceptable to the canonical gatekeepers.

The business of packaging and repackaging poetry to make it saleable is central to the anthologizing act. As Lorraine York explains in her study of a recent collection that brings together only poems by authors whose first name is Susan, there is a long tradition of quirky anthologies in Canada, and many of these works use humour to exploit what are fundamentally nationalist values. Although they may poke fun at those values by focusing exclusively on iconic tropes such as the RCMP or hockey or beavers, their popularity rests on the common assumption that national self-recognition is crucial to anthology formation. After all, *Tributes to the Scarlet Riders: An Anthology of Mountie Poems* is published by Heritage House, a company that describes its mission as "telling Canada's stories" (Heritage House website).

By laughing at ourselves and our national symbols, we also recognize ourselves, and, through that process of recognition, we reaffirm the values that unite us. Northrop Frye was right when he argued that comedy leads to social reconciliation and integration. His insight even works at very basic levels. For example, as a strategy in special teaching situations (and just to warm things up), you can ask the students in a classroom what a Canadian is supposed to say when he or she is responsible for clearing everyone out of a swimming pool. The students, being young, do not know the stale answer to this question, so you provide it: "Would everyone please get out of the pool?"

I've found that this bad joke always brings a class together, particularly in a moment of exegetical need. Perhaps they are laughing at its badness, but that doesn't matter. The mechanism is an example of the way in which humour unites us, and the editors of anthologies devoted to panties, or Mounties, or poets named Susan know this well. Such anthologies invite us to play, as do essays on them. In reading York's essay, I was reminded of the fact that I almost never encounter students named Susan, which made me realize that, at one level, the editors of *Desperately Seeking Susans* are seriously out of date, or, at best, they are appealing to a generation of readers that has nothing to do with contemporary Canada. Had they done their research, as I did, they would know that the most popular names for girls in Canada today are Emma and Olivia. Could they not have appealed to a younger market?

York also points out that one reviewer suggested there might be a follow-up volume, titled something like *What About Bob?* Now here, speaking as a Robert who has lived some years in the United States, I want to say boldly that this title suggestion is a mistake, because as any genuinely *Canadian* Robert knows, you are Robert in Canada, but Bob in the United States. If you have lived your whole life as a Robert, and then start working in the United States, your American colleagues will immediately call you Bob without a second thought. You are given a new identity, on the spot. Soon you understand: there are no Roberts in the United States. From my existential experience, I know that "Bob" in an anthology title will not sell books in Canada. Canadian readers will understand that such an anthology is fundamentally traitorous, a text inspired by American imperialism; they will reject it out of hand. Besides, even if a crafty publisher used "Robert" in an anthology title, they would be repeating the mistake of using "Susan": both names hark back to a bygone era that is deeply *passé*. To confirm this, I did a quick bit of research on babynamewizard.com. From this I learned that Susan was the tenth most popular name in the 1940s but that in 2010 it dropped to 792nd place. What a plunge to oblivion! Poor Susans. My name was number one in the 1920s and 1930s (not much consolation there), and then began to fade from view in the 1960s, giving way to James, of all things. From this kind of detailed scholarly research, we can see that names are connected to their age, but also to the social values connected with the act of naming. By giving me one of North America's most popular names when I was born (*not* in the 1920s), my parents were saying that they were part of a community, that they understood their place within the social fabric, and that by naming their son as they did they wanted to perpetuate the values aligned with their middle-class ethos.

Although York's own sense of play in her essay permits (I hope) this kind of quirky editorial digression, she remains aware, throughout, of what seems to be the perpetual link between anthologizing and nationalism in Canada. She also shows that although we typically categorize anthologies as either "popular" or "academic" in terms of their strategies and subject matter, the actual values underlying their conception and promotion do not always reinforce the binary. Although "quirkily themed anthologies ... have served at various times to uphold or challenge prevailing ideas about the relationship between the quirky or humorous and national culture," even those anthologies that challenge the status quo perform the function of recognizing its value as an object worthy of attack. In this way, subversive anthologies may actually serve to reinforce conventional ideas of nation, or region, by identifying them as prevailing norms. As York observes, "national clichés ... are more difficult to overthrow than it would seem, and one sign that at least some of these quirky anthologies are working in tandem with those clichés rather than challenging them is their record of library holdings," which demonstrate that library holdings of offbeat anthologies that have nationalist themes "are far more extensive than those of other, less nationally themed collections." Similarly, quirky anthologies that can be classed as "Canadiana" are "more likely to attract media coverage, and will tend to be bought by libraries here and abroad" because "the force of national narratives" resonates in both the commercial and academic marketplace.

As I argue in *Keepers of the Code*, mainstream English-Canadian literature anthologies have endorsed and transmitted these "national narratives" ever since John Simpson published Canada's first anthology—*The Canadian Forget-Me-Not*—in 1837. In this way, Canadian anthologies have supported literary nationalism and conveyed to generations of readers—and especially students—a particular vision of the country, one constructed by a line of editors who pursued their dream of anthological power and inheritance. These editors made the country teachable through its poetry and fiction. Their anthologies promoted the idea that the nation could be represented through strategic selections. Those who had been empowered to make such selections entered an elite club.

Even this brief description of the anthologizing process conveys the extent to which anthologies have traditionally been conceived of as privileged constructions—as signs of class, prestige, and knowledge; of literary power. This power reigned unchecked for decades, since few people were willing to stand up and say that the idea of representing any nation through a subjective selection of some of its literature was patently absurd. Those are some of the thoughts I have when reading Frank Davey's meditation on the impact of anthologies. In his early years as a writer and teacher, Davey recalls, anthologies were approached as relatively innocent objects. They were purchased to provide a glimpse into the work of specific writers or to illustrate particular formal or historical concerns. At the same time, some anthologies were obviously presented as instruments of power. Salespeople would arrive at the professor's door bearing sample copies, pushing for an annual adoption of texts that would become required reading for hundreds of students, year after year. Professors saw these big, ostensibly authoritative anthologies as symbols of power, but they also understood that, as professionals charged with choosing one anthology over another, *they* had power. In this exchange, the actual contents of the book became subordinate to the reinforcement of professorial authority through an economic transaction. In choosing one anthology over another, the professor also understood that he or she had joined a camp. There would be those who used one anthology because they held certain values in common; and then there were the others, who were following a different anthological path. Yet everyone seemed to have the same destination: something called Canadian literature. Anthological allegiances in the name of nation reinforced the idea of nation.

Until quite recently, as Davey points out, the nature of this destination called nation was relatively clear. One could teach Canadian literature by relying on an anthology that was more or less experimental, more or less interested in notions of tradition, more or less focused on the lives of its "representative" authors. Yet it was all about endorsing the idea that a national literature existed. But then came the course pack, which dramatically undercut the authority that editors of anthologies had wielded (in Canada) for more than 150 years. In the world of the course pack there was no central anthological vision to be shared by professors, and not even a few different versions to choose from. It had come down to individual choice, embodied in the course pack designed by a specific instructor for a specific course, with no allegiance to the national ideals that had mobilized anthologists historically. As Davey says, "the course pack has become the invisible anthology, the one that leaves little or no textual residue." Meanwhile, changes in copyright law and fair usage guidelines have undermined the authority of the author to control the reproduction of his or her work. The result is that course packs, so widely used in contemporary classrooms, disempower individual writers both politically and economically. At the same time, those course packs grant even more power to the professor. They transform the perception of the nation's literature into a series of texts selected by one person. Divorced from any connection to the anthological sense of community and consensus, the course pack becomes a solipsistic construction that promotes a hermetic view of the nation as a fundamentally private affair.

Because course packs negatively impact authors and their publishers, and because they promote the idea that the representation of nation is something unique to a specific professor's class, they are ultimately alienating devices that will eventually destroy what they claim to support: Canadian writing. This situation is not unique to Canada, but in Canada the destruction will happen faster, because the economics of the writing and publishing infrastructure are inherently weak, easily affected by the smallest blow. Faced with the competition from course packs, how many Canadian publishers will continue to invest in anthologies? And if we lose those publishers (many are already gone), further damage will be done to those few houses that still support Canadian writing.

It is too early to predict the death of anthologies. However, simply thinking about their demise allows us to meditate on how they have served us, and what they have become. This is precisely the kind of meditation we find in the closing essay of this volume, Anne Compton's "The Poet and Her Library: Anthologies Read, Anthologies Made." While there are many perceptive observations here about specific anthologies that have influenced Compton and her career as poet, editor, critic, and teacher, I am most interested in the way she turns her meditation toward the conception of anthologies as metaphors. In this sense, her essay reflects back on many of the essays brought together in this volume, and particularly on Richard Cavell's opening essay, which similarly seeks to position the anthology as a metaphorical force that is not so much about a particular selection of material as it is about a way of thinking and being.

As I was making my notes for this introduction and rereading the essays included here, I had in hand my highlighter, which I used to isolate ideas or connections that struck me most powerfully in each contributor's work. I started highlighting Compton's essay at the point where she reminds us how "an encounter with an anthology can be a determinant in a writer's career." Part of her essay illustrates this point through her recollection of the processes leading to the creation of *Coastlines*, an anthology of Atlantic literature. But she also demonstrates the extent to which her personal encounter with a variety of anthologies changed her as a person, as if, in encountering these very different collections, she was meeting a host of metaphors, each of which profoundly affected her inner sense of self. It is fascinating to consider some of these metaphors. For Compton, the anthology is a house, or perhaps it is the reverse: "a house is itself an anthology of rooms, each room with a story of its own." Like houses, anthologies have their own architecture, and each one "has designs on your mind, your taste, and future reading." Or perhaps, Compton proposes, the anthology is another kind of metaphor: "Perhaps it's a library," and the anthologist "a librarian of sorts, ranging widely, choosing judiciously, although, inevitably, choices will be affected by the anthologist's position in time and space, and by sensibility and experience."

Earlier in this introduction, I suggested that anthologies could be viewed as different kinds of narratives with their own landscapes, voices, characters. Compton seems to concur. She points out that "an anthology is *also* a setting of sorts," or it is "a book of beginnings," or (expanding the metaphor still further) it is "a search engine" that brings together genesis and Google, origins and apocalypse. Compton never mentions apocalypse, or genesis, for that matter. Yet there is a richness in the associations she makes with anthological consciousness that permits this kind of liberty, I think. For her, "the anthology is an occasion for exploration" that "links present to future, reader to writer." The anthology is "a little life." Or we can put it another way: anthologies are little worlds.

When I began this introduction, I did not know what I would say. And now I have come to the point of asserting that anthologies are worlds. That is a lot of distance covered. While this collection of essays is intended to stimulate discussion about anthological activity in Canada, it strikes me as having broader applications, especially if we follow the suggestion, made by virtually every contributor, that anthologies possess a symbolic power that makes them more than local or national in significance. The idea that anthologies are narratives in their own right has scarcely been explored. Similarly, anthological studies have not focused on the way in which the beginnings, endings, and contents of different anthologies serve to define specific literary periods or genres. A comparative study of different national literature anthologies, for example, would reveal a range of possible beginnings. By engaging in a comparison of this kind, we can open up the plurality of geneses assigned to national literatures, and by doing so, we can destabilize the concept of origins in a positive and productive way.

Unlike particular poems, or short stories, or novels, anthologies are the only literary vehicles that posit the concept of literary origin, and that fact alone makes them eminently worthy of investigation. Once we think of the starting point of national literature anthologies in originary terms, the metaphor of beginning becomes even richer, for now we can begin to imagine the ways in which the opening of an anthology might be prelapsarian, while the close of an anthology might represent the world after the fall that is embodied in the collection itself. To what extent do anthologies trace the story of a transition from innocence to experience? Is the anthological act of selection a kind of editorial fall? To what extent do anthologies question whether such a fall can even be conceived as the result of an editorial act? Perhaps national literature anthologies exist in order to undermine the evolutionary model they normally propose. Perhaps they offer the paradoxical proof that they have failed to establish the historical trajectory they sought to illustrate through their selections. Perhaps anthologies demonstrate, in the end, that literary history does not exist, or that it cannot be captured in the pages of a book that claims to be a container of literary history.

Beset by their own internal contradictions, anthologies always fail spectacularly. It is that failure—of conception, of execution, of imagination—that makes anthologies so troubled and exciting as literary forms. This collection seeks to open up a conversation about anthologies, to see them as historical objects that have contributed to our contemporary and historical understanding of Canadian literature. At the same time, it seeks to problematize those anthologies and to show that they are anxious objects, unstable at the best of times. I don't think this collection reaches any kind of consensus about anthology formation in Canada. But it does convince me that this formation is compelling, and worthy of more detailed study.

WORKS CITED

Benedict, Barbara. *Making the Modern Reader: Cultural Mediation in Early Modern Literary Anthologies.* Princeton: Princeton UP, 1996. Print.

———. "The Paradox of the Anthology: Collecting and *Différence* in Eighteenth-Century Britain." *New Literary History: A Journal of Theory and Interpretation* 34.2 (Spring 2003): 231–56. Print.

Bode, Katherine. "Beyond the Colonial Present: Quantitative Analysis, 'Resourceful Reading' and Australian Literary Studies." *Journal of the Association for the Study of Australian Literature.* Special Issue: The Colonial Present (2008): 184–97. Print.

Brydon, Diana. "Metamorphosis of a Discipline: Rethinking Canadian Literature within Institutional Contexts." *Trans.Can.Lit: Resituating the Study of Canadian Literature.* Ed. Smaro Kamboureli and Roy Miki. Waterloo: Wilfrid Laurier UP, 2007. Print.

Churchman, Philip H. "The Use of Anthologies in the Study of Literature." *Modern Language Journal* 7.3 (Dec. 1922): 149–54. Print.

Coryell, Patricia A. "Pedagogical Introduction." *Instructor's Guide. The Heath Anthology of American Literature.* Boston: Houghton Mifflin, 2002. Print.

Davey, Frank. "Poetry, Audience, Politics and Region." *Canadian Poetry: Studies, Documents, Reviews* 30 (1992): 6–17. Print.

Dettmar, Kevin J. H. "Writers Who Price Themselves Out of the Canon." *Chronicle of Higher Education.* Web. 4 Aug. 2006. <http://chronicle.com/temp/reprint.php?id=vl9fh16khq36622631flxckjlxr95y01>

Dewart, Edward Hartley. *Selections from Canadian Poets with Occasional Critical and Biographical Notes and an Introductory Essay on Canadian Poetry.* Montreal: John Lovell, 1864. Print.

Dike, E. B. "Improve the Anthologies." *College English* 5.8 (May 1944): 447. Print.

Di Leo, Jeffrey R. *On Anthologies: Politics and Pedagogy.* Lincoln: U of Nebraska P, 2004. Print.

Fee, Margery. "English-Canadian Literary Criticism, 1890–1950: Defining and Establishing a National Literature." Diss. University of Toronto, 1981. Print.

Finke, Laurie. "The Hidden Curriculum." Di Leo 395–404. Print.

Fraistat, Neil. "The Place of the Book and the Book as Place." *Poems in Their Place: The Intertextuality and Order of Poetic Collections.* Ed. Neil Fraistat. Chapel Hill: U of North Carolina P, 1986. Print.

Gerson, Carole. *A Purer Taste: The Writing and Reading of Fiction in English in Nine-teenth-Century Canada*. Toronto: U of Toronto P, 1989. Print.

Golding, Alan C. "A History of American Poetry Anthologies." *Canons*. Ed. Robert von Hallberg. Chicago: U of Chicago P, 1983. 279–307. Print.

Graff, Gerald. *Professing Literature: An Institutional History*. Chicago: U of Chicago P, 1987. Print.

Irvine, Dean. *Editing Modernity: Women and Little-Magazine Cultures in Canada, 1916–1956*. Toronto: U of Toronto P, 2008. Print.

Johnson, Glen M. "The Teaching Anthology and the Canon of American Literature: Some Notes on Theory in Practice." *The Hospitable Canon: Essays on Literary Play, Scholarly Choice, and Popular Pressures*. Ed. Virgil Nemoianu and Robert Royal. Philadelphia: John Benjamins, 1991. 111–35. Print.

Jusdanis, Gregory. *The Necessary Nation*. Princeton: Princeton UP, 2001. Web. 1 June 2013.

Kamboureli, Smaro. "Canadian Ethnic Anthologies: Representations of Ethnicity." *ARIEL: A Review of International English Literature* 25.4 (Oct. 1994): 11–52. Print.

Keith, W. J. "Editors and Texts: Reflections on Some Recent Anthologies of Canadian Poetry." *Canadian Poetry: Studies, Documents, Reviews* 12 (1983): 77–86. Print.

Knight, Alan. "Growing Hegemonies: Preparing the Ground for Official Anthologies of Canadian Poetry." *Prefaces and Literary Manifestoes/Préfaces et manifestes littéraires*. Ed. E. D. Blodgett, A. G. Purdy, and S. Tötösy de Zepetnek. Edmonton: Alberta UP, 1990. 146–57. Print.

Korte, Barbara, Ralf Schneider, and Stefanie Lethbridge, eds. *Anthologies of British Poetry: Critical Perspectives from Literary and Cultural Studies*. Amsterdam: Rodopi, 2000. Print.

Kuipers, Christopher M. "The Anthology/Corpus Dynamic: A Field Theory of the Canon." *College Literature* 30.2 (Spring 2003): 51–71. Print.

Lauter, Paul. "Taking Anthologies Seriously." *MELUS: The Journal of the Society for the Study of the Multi-Ethnic Literature of the United States*. 29.3–4 (Fall-Winter 2004): 19–39. Print.

——. "Teaching with Anthologies." *Pedagogy: Critical Approaches to Teaching Literature, Language, Composition, and Culture* 3.3 (Fall 2003): 329–39. Print.

Lecker, Robert. "Anthologizing English-Canadian Fiction: Some Canonical Trends." *Open Letter* 9.1 (1994): 25–80. Print.

——. *English-Canadian Literary Anthologies: An Enumerative Bibliography*. Teeswater, ON: Reference P, 1997. Print.

——. *Keepers of the Code: English-Canadian Literary Anthologies and the Representation of Nation*. Toronto: U of Toronto P, 2013. Print.

——. "Nineteenth-Century English-Canadian Anthologies and the Making of a National Literature." *Journal of Canadian Studies* 44.1 (Winter 2010): 91–117. Web. 2 July 2013. Print.

Leitch, Vincent B., Barbara Johnson, John McGowan, Laurie Finke, and Jeffrey J. Williams. "Editing a Norton Anthology." *College English* 66.2 (Nov. 2003): 173–77. Print.

Longenbach, James. "The Question of Anthologies." Rev. of Anne Ferry, *Tradition and the Individual Poem*. *Raritan: A Quarterly Review* 21.4 (Spring 2002): 122–29. Print.

MacGillivray, S. R. "Bouquets from the Bush Garden: Some Recent Canadian Anthologies." *Lakehead University Review* 7 (1974): 93–101. Print.

Mandel, Eli. "Masks of Criticism: A. J. M. Smith as Anthologist." *Canadian Poetry: Studies, Documents, Reviews* 4 (1979): 17–28. Print.

Miki, Roy. "The Future's Tense: Some Notes on Editing, Canadian Style." *Interventing the Text: Open Letter* 8.5–6 (1993): 182–96. Print.

Nelson, Cary. "Murder in the Cathedral: Editing a Comprehensive Anthology of Modern American Poetry." *American Literary History* 14.2 (Summer 2002): 311–27. Print.

Parry, John J. "A Plea for Better Anthologies." *College English* 5.6 (Mar. 1944): 318–24. Print.

Price, Leah. *The Anthology and the Rise of the Novel: From Richardson to George Eliot*. Cambridge: Cambridge UP, 2000. Print.

Rasula, Jed. "The Empire's New Clothes: Anthologizing American Poetry in the 1990s." *American Literary History* 7.2 (Summer 1995): 261–83. Print.

Said, Edward W. *The World, the Text, and the Critic*. Cambridge: Harvard UP, 1983.

Schrift, Alan D. "Confessions of an Anthology Editor." *symplokē* 8.1–2 (2000): 164–76. Print.

Sugars, Cynthia, and Laura Moss, eds. *Canadian Literature in English: Texts and Contexts*. Toronto: Pearson/Penguin, 2008. Print.

Surette, Leon. "Here Is Us: The Topocentrism of Canadian Literary Criticism." *Canadian Poetry* 10 (1982): 44–57. Web. 28 May 2013.

ANTHEMS AND ANTHOLOGIES

Richard Cavell

> *"this hard community has a beauty of its own"*
> —Leonard Cohen, *Flowers for Hitler*[1]

An anthem is a song and an anthology is a collection of songs.[2] Etymologically the words are diverse, yet they share the goal of finding unity in diversity. Anthems and anthologies are thus sites of tension, of multiple voices on which a single voice is superimposed; this emerges in the etymology of "anthem," which derives from "antiphon," part of the call and response in religious ceremonies (hence the original meaning of anthem as "hymn"). The tensions inherent in anthems and anthologies are explored in *The Second Scroll* (1951) of A. M. Klein, in which the Montreal narrator is sent by his newspaper editor to collect an anthology of poetry from the newly created state of Israel. In the following pages, Klein's novel serves as the antiphon to an inquiry into the politics and poetics of the anthology in Canada.

An anthology is literally a collection of flowers—verbal flowers: the first Canadian anthology was named a *Forget-Me-Not*[3] and was published in 1837, fifteen years after Rudolf Ackermann had published the first literary annual in Britain, *Forget-Me-Not: A Christmas and New Year's Present for 1823*.[4] Ackermann's annuals had a religious element (indicated by the engraving of the Madonna on the frontispiece of the first edition) that is also evident in the early Canadian anthology; they were meant as Christmas gifts, and were directed toward a female audience, highlighting, thus, the gendered complexities of these works, in which women were "represented" through their absence (Lecker, "Nineteenth-Century" 98). Here we approach the dynamics of inclusion and exclusion that characterize both the gendered and the raced aspects of the anthology, and that point toward the violence that subtends such collections. The paradox of a bouquet of flowers is that it is born of violence, a violence that remains a venerable trope of literature, from Eve plucking the apple to Baudelaire's *Flowers of Evil*, and is powerfully conveyed by Leonard Cohen's *Flowers for Hitler*, the romanticism of the flower balanced by the brutality of its plucking, which, in this case, implies a political allegory. The flower must be plucked, uprooted, deracinated in order to be collected. The anthology, like writing itself, is founded upon the idea of the cut, the glyph.[5] In the political context, the anthology becomes the form *par excellence* of the delayed nation—*die verspätete Nation*[6]—a nation such as Canada, where "all the things that couldn't happen when they should have happened keep happening all the time," as the late Milton Wilson memorably put it (89). What is declared in this context is the paradox of an "original secondariness,"[7] one that proclaims its originality precisely through an abrogation of linear concepts of space and time; hence postmodernism and postcolonialism and all the other "posts" that have their "origin" in the "discovery" of a "new" world that is geomorphically and culturally older than that of the colonizers, as Enrique Dussel has compellingly argued.

Anthology-making in the context of canonization is a Möbius strip: in compiling an anthology of Canadian literature, one produces a version of the literature of Canada that didn't exist before the process of making the anthology, and only exists as such within that particular anthology. As Robert Lecker remarks, "national literature anthologies serve to underline the fact that nations are plural and unstable, unmappable in any form. As edited collections, these anthologies are necessarily self-defeating" ("Nineteenth-Century" 94). Part of what defeats them is the attempt to impose a narrative on what is by definition fragmentary. The narrativizing impulse reflects, on the political level, the inheritance of imperialism, the sun that never sets on the British empire demanding a coherent story of race and colonization: W. D. Lighthall's *Songs of the Great Dominion* sought to reflect "'the common heritage of the Imperial Race'" (qtd. in Lecker, "Nineteenth-Century" 102). Canada, in this context, becomes the flower of the empire, and the empire is thus naturalized. Anthology and imperialism coincide; while the anthology is "conceptually democratic," it is "ultimately undemocratic in its final realization" (Lecker, "Watson" 15).

The Second Scroll begins under the sign of the uncle, Uncle Melech, with whom the narrator becomes obsessed, his search for his uncle mapping onto his editorial quest for the poetry of the new state of Israel. The uncle is an appropriate source of origin for an anthology because he is at one remove from the father; the paternity of the anthology is always already displaced.

To put it another way, the anthology collected in the service of the nation is a quest for the patriarch—for "true patriot love"—that must always fail; like original sin, its originality can only be secondary. Its origin is displaced, like that of Uncle Melech, whose appearance is likewise unknown—it can only be known in fragments, its totality always escaping the narrator.

The novel consists of five chapters, modelled on the five books of the Pentateuch, and five glosses on these books; it immediately imposes in this way a problematic of reading that is characteristic of the anthology: do you read it straight through, as if it were a narrative, or do you dip into it, moving back and forth between (in this case) chapter and gloss? The anthology oscillates between this idea of wholeness and totality and a practice of fragmentation and disarticulation. Klein increases the tension by including poems, an expository essay, a play, and a series of citations in his text, which reproduces a number of languages and scripts; it is "complete" neither in its totality nor in the elaboration of its quest—the search for Uncle Melech and for the new poetry of Israel both fail. If we are to read the novel as an allegory of Canadianness,[8] then this further accentuates the notion of displacement; Canada is displaced by Israel, but Israel is itself displaced into a fragmentary gloss on an unachievable national narrative, and Melech, at the end, suffers the *sparagmos* of another Holocaust. The anthology cannot make whole, and that lack of wholeness, of totality, of identity is ultimately what the narrator returns *with*—and *to*.

This sense of absence, of displacement, questions the notions of nation and narration—how it might be possible to represent a nation through the fragmented "narration" of the anthology. Bertram Brooker's *Yearbook of the Arts in Canada* (1929), Malcolm Ross's *Our Sense of Identity* (1954), and Richard Cavell and Peter Dickinson's *Sexing the Maple* (2006) testify against the notion of a national plenitude, of a wholeness and completeness that might be represented anthologically, and they bear scrutiny for that reason. While they might be understood as responding to the formal constraints of anthologizing, I argue here that they are responding as well to the implied mimeticism of the task. In this, the works are paradigmatic, rather than exceptional.

Brooker's *Yearbook*[9] is in some senses closest to the notion of the annual—an "eclectic annual" (back jacket flap)—as published in Britain by Ackermann. Like those books, it presents itself as "an appropriate gift book for the growing number of artistically-minded people whose interest and encouragement is very necessary to the stimulation of a vigorous art in this country" (front jacket flap).[10] Published in 1929, it is exactly contemporary with the London publication of *The New Forget-Me-Not*,[11] which specifically sought to revive "Mr. Ackermann's *Forget-Me-Not*" (vii), with decorations by society artist Rex Whistler, and was meant as a Christmas gift. Like Whistler's book, Brooker's is brilliantly designed.

The overriding concern of Brooker is to declare a particular modernity in and for Canada. To this end, he is less concerned with the time-bias of canon than with the space-bias of contemporaneity;[12] the back jacket flap represents Brooker as someone whose "weekly letter on 'The Seven Arts,' now being published by the six Southam newspapers, is read by thousands of art-lovers from Ottawa to Vancouver" (leaving one wondering what those east of Ottawa were doing), which suggests the role played by the "new" media in establishing this space-bias. The time-bias is no longer a credible criterion for artistic production because "with the tremendously widened and inten-sified means of communication—by newspapers, movies, radio, etc.—new ideas are given so much publicity that we become accustomed to them and accept in a twelvemonth what in medieval times would have taken at least a century to become absorbed" (Brooker 10). Brooker quotes appositely in an epigraph cited from the preface to Whitman's *Leaves of Grass* that the "direct trial of him who would be the greatest poet is to-day. If he does not flood himself with the immediate age ... let him merge in the general run, and wait his development" (n. pag.). Likewise, Brooker's preface disavows any "representative" status for the volume, which "is not intended to be looked upon as an official guidebook to the art activities of Canada" but rather to "cover a wide geographic field" that treats "tendencies, rather than personali-ties" (n. pag.). He continues: "It is not expected that the works reproduced in the Original Section will in every case be regarded as the 'best' of the year's work" ("Preface" n. pag.). Thus, "though sometimes not as 'accomplished' as works more reminiscent of other days and other schools," these works "should be of interest to Canadians as symptomatic of the activity all around them produced by artists alive to our own new and particular conditions" ("Preface" n. pag.).

The anthology is divided into a "Review Section" and an "Original Sec-tion," and is copiously illustrated. In his general introduction, "When We Awake!," Brooker defines the artist as someone who is able "to concentrate his experiences into unities and universalities" (5), as, one would assume, an anthologist would likewise seek to do. But for the Canadian artist (and anthologist) there are immense difficulties, because Canada is "not unified geographically"; "not unified racially"; has "a history that centres about a few picturesque personalities and events, failing to unify for us our past as a people"; has "a population too small to provide an adequate audience"; "a general conception of art that lacks any hint of national consciousness, but clings instead to old notions of connoisseurship borrowed from feudal times and countries"; has experienced "a disruption of the settling process, which might have unified some aspects of Canadian life, by the mechanization of civilization all over the world"; and, finally, has undergone "a destruction of ethical-philosophic-religious stability by the encroaching skepticism of a science-ridden age" (5). These would appear to be hard odds to overcome.

Brooker advances the thesis that it is the critical function that can find unity in this chaos. He makes a distinction between the "universals" that are in fact "the art-shibboleths of two or three centuries of European culture" (8), and the universals of art itself:

> The Canadian critic, as a rule, is not only unfamiliar with the art of Greece and China (the little he knows about an art as recent and accessible as that of Russia is usually only sufficient to make him detest it), he seems to be also unfamiliar with the broad historical fact that the aims of artists in certain countries and in certain ages have differed very greatly and that to judge the art of one by the standards of another is to ignore those 'universal' standards he often postulates but rarely knows how to apply. (8)

What the Canadian critic has to recognize is the universal that extends across space rather than through time. In doing so, the critic will produce an environment in which a universal art can exist. This critic will not ignore the past but will make the past present as a platform for addressing the future.

The speed-up of time (a constant theme in art of this period, emphasized by the *moderne* curve, in which time appears to be curving back into space, as Einstein suggested it would do) is emphasized in the first essay of the "Review Section," in which William Arthur Deacon proclaims that the "centennial" of Canadian literature has in fact occurred in 1929 (even though Canada had been founded only sixty-two years before), since it was one hundred years earlier that Joseph Howe had "published the first book of Thomas Chandler Haliburton, *An Historical and Statistical Account of Nova Scotia*" (23). Pelham Edgar takes the time question in a different direction, arguing that the "cult of primitivism"—that is, localism—threatens to defeat the larger aspirations of Canadian literature. Here, the local is defined as the representation of "peasants, negroes, and pile-drivers" who constitute, for Edgar, "a vanishing race" (41–42). The progress associated with modernity thus also has elements of class and race: to progress is to attain racial purity and capitalist plenitude. But Brooker's notion that modernity had made us *all* primitives in our confrontation with an utterly new social context produced by the new technologies of communication moves in a different direction: "it is most natural that a genuine 'modern' to-day should react 'primitively' to his surroundings ... for we are, in the strictest sense *primitives*, the first men of a new civilization whose implications are incalculable" ("When We Awake!" 12). This movement backwards in time reflects the poetic and the political anxieties of the period, when (as Klein puts it in *The Second Scroll*) there was an urgency to find "the unique, the autochthonous, the primal seed" (104), to be "more aboriginal than the aborigines" (100). Arthur Lismer takes up this strand to argue that the arts of the native "were derived from his environment and he has left us more than merely outward forms" (68), a notion that Marius Barbeau extends to contemporary music in Canada. For Eric Arthur, in his survey of "Architecture in Canada," the "outstanding buildings in the west are certainly the grain elevators. There is a grandeur about them that would have thrilled Piranesi" (107), a comment captured in the photograph of a grain elevator taken by John Vanderpant and included in the section of reproductions.

The "Original Section" of the *Yearbook* comprises "reprints and reproductions of short stories, essays, poems, sculpture, paintings, drawings, architecture and music" selected on the basis of having "figured in the year's news" or because they are "believed to be significant of recent developments" (Brooker, *Yearbook* 141). Among these essays, Lawren Harris's "Creative Art and Canada" invokes the spiritual theme, but this time infused with theosophical mysticism, which enables Harris to make the pronouncement that the "creative faculty being spiritual ... is universal and without Time" (179). For Harris, the "national" is the "immediate." The artist achieves the universal through the particular: "the world moves into new relationships in space and into new impingements that elicit a somewhat new way of seeing" (180), just as two dimensions can suggest a third, and three dimensions a fourth.[13] Roy Mitchell extends this dynamic notion of artistic expression with his thesis that "literature comes into the theatre only as a servant of motion" (189). His criteria are thus formal and not canonical: "*goingness*"; a "vortex"; "dynamo"; "vital coil"; "dynamic energies" (190). These must come to constitute "canons of to-and-fro motion" (191) such that the dramatic work be understood as "a vortex of vortices" (194). The allusion to Vorticism makes clear the extent to which Brooker's volume as a whole seeks to declare its modernist allegiances, and these are evident as well in the majority of photographs of artworks in the volume.

Klein's narrator in *The Second Scroll* declares himself "bound to the country of [his] father's choice, to Canada" (20), while at the same time finding himself connected affectively to "the Palestine whose geography was as intimately known as the lines of the palm of [his] hand" (20). This connection to Palestine is the basis on which the narrator's publisher asks him "to produce, after sojourning in the land, a volume of translations of the poems and songs of Israel's latest nest of singing birds" (20–21). The "founding" literature of Israel, in this way, becomes a pretext for the representation of Canadian literature. Melech figures this new literature as a "re-membering" (as "re-membered bones" [34]), that is, as a putting together again of what had been dismembered, an activity congruent with the making of an anthology. Like the calligraphy the narrator sees in Casablanca, the art of the anthology is a spatial art, "an art of traceries and fretwork," of "both space and space filled," an "art of alternations and changes" (69). Such an art does not aim for wholeness; it will always and by definition be incomplete, as, indeed, the narrator's quests—for Melech and for the poetry—remain incomplete. Melech's gloss on the Sistine Chapel, likewise incomplete, will be incorporated as the first entry in the narrator's anthology (55), even though not "couched as Hebrew" (55) and containing a good deal of Latin (135). Here, the memorial quality of the forget-me-not (flower and anthology) emerges in the context of a mourning that must remain unfinished—"[n]ot tranquil recollection of event" but "[t]he strength and vividness of nonage days" (126). As Melech gazes at the ceiling of the Chapel, it becomes an allegory of the Holocaust—the "sistine limepit" (140). But to complete the mourning, in the way suggested by Freud in "Mourning and Melancholia," would paradoxically annihilate the subject who is mourned,[14] and thus it is the narrator who is in his turn placed "within the degree of mourning," intoning the Kaddish for his uncle in "a mourner's Magnificat which does not mention death" (Klein 120–21).

Our Sense of Identity: A Book of Canadian Essays (1954) disavows its status as an anthology from the outset: "This is not an anthology of fine writing" (front jacket flap).[15] Like Brooker's *Yearbook*, Ross's book seeks "to catch and hold some sense of the variety and vitality of the Canadian mind" (front jacket flap). It seeks to "destroy the myth of 'Canadian provincialism and timidity'" and to reveal the "unconventional, experimental and even perverse strands in our make-up" (front jacket flap), a statement that gains significant weight in the context of Ross's role in establishing The New Canadian Library, an imprint of publisher McClelland and Stewart presenting classic works of Canadian literature. Far from jacket puffery, however, this tone is maintained in Ross's "Introduction" to the volume, where he again denies that it is an anthology. What drops out of the equation from the beginning is the "chronological" (vii) element, as well as the essay; instead, Ross focuses on the "'sketch'"; the "'article'"; the "'paper'"; the "'column'"; and the "'spoken essay,'" a form that responds to "a new medium of communication" and represents "a return to the oral tradition" (vii).

As this comment indicates, the introduction is written very much in the wake of "the brilliant speculative leap of the late Harold Innis" and "the cosmopolitan time-and-space insights of Northrop Frye and Marshall McLuhan" (vii). Ross quotes from McLuhan's landmark essay, "The Later Innis" (1953), in which McLuhan argues that Innis's vast panoramas of communications histories in his last books were less interested in developing a point of view than with being "an intellectual radar screen" (viii), or producing, as Ross puts it, a "bi-focalism" (ix), which reflects the fact that "we have been restlessly (and self-critically) in motion" (ix). This leads Ross to posit that "[i]rony is the key to our identity" (x),[16] the "collision of opposites" (x) that produces a "multi-dimensional structure, an openness to 'the larger mosaic,' to the vivid themes of A. M. Klein's Jewish heritage, to the fine rich Slavic interlacings of Winnipeg and the prairies"—the "diversity of the full Canadianism" (xi). Hence the importance of "the eager openness of a Marshall McLuhan to the world-loosening, world-binding potential of the new mass media—and to the foreshadowings of a new Promethean age of the technological, foreshadowings which threaten with extinction the parochial, self-centered, encrusted sense of identity of the older nations" (xi–xii).

At first reading, this mosaic spirit does not seem to be immediately in evidence. However, it soon becomes clear that the import of these pieces is in their juxtaposition. Thus, Susanna Moodie can proclaim the fundamental humanity of the colonial subject, while Hugh Kenner can rail against the Canadian's "pathological craving for identification with the sub-human" (203). Goldwin Smith can produce a polemic against granting aristocratic titles to Canadians, while S. J. Duncan can assert her "latent loyalty" (53) to the Crown. W. E. Walsh proclaims (ironically) the "importance of being English" (28), while Bruce Hutchison reminds us (with no irony at all) that to "set the Scotsman or the Welshman against the Englishman" is to "observe the startling diversity and contrast of British life" (40). Morley Callaghan urges Toronto on us; Hugh MacLennan, Montreal. As Ross states, "[o]urs is not, can never be, the 'one hundred per cent' kind of nationalism. We have always had to think in terms of 50–50" (xi).

Written in the wake of the 1951 Massey Report, *Our Sense of Identity* confronts another binary, that of colonialism versus continentalism. Frank Underhill speaks directly to this issue in his "Notes on the Massey Report," stating that the "Commissioners seek a national Canadian culture which shall be independent of American influences" (37), influences that they deem "alien." Underhill argues, however, that "we live on the same continent as the Americans, and ... the longer we live here the more are we going to be affected by the same continental influences which affect them" (37). In fact, Underhill continues, "[t]hese so-called 'alien' influences are not alien at all; they are just the natural forces that operate in the conditions of twentieth-century civilization" (37). Those "natural" forces are the mass media; "[i]f *Maclean's Magazine* achieved its ambition, and American competition were shut out from its constituency, it would continue to be what it is now, only more so, i.e., a second-rate *Saturday Evening Post* or *Colliers*. It is mass-consumption and the North American continental environment which produce these phenomena, not some sinister influences in the United States" (38). Underhill lambastes Vincent Massey's assumption that "with the help of some government subventions, we can become another England" (38); in fact, he states, what the report should have studied much more carefully is American culture, which provides the paradigm for mass culture generally.

Innis takes up these issues as well in an excerpt from *Empire and Communications* that closes the volume. Like Underhill, Innis is aware that Canadian culture cannot be understood apart from the fact that Canada is "located so near a centre which has been the heart of an economic empire" (336), adding that "[i]t is an advantage ... to emphasize these dangers [of being on the edge of an empire] ... so that we can at least be alert to the implications of this type of bias" (336), a bias that manifests itself as an "[o]bsession with economic considerations" (336). At this point, Innis articulates what can be taken as the keynote of the volume: "Civilizations can survive only through a concern with the limitations of their institutions" (336). The remainder of the essay is a paean to the oral tradition, and one cannot help but assume that Innis means this as a contrastive element to the written culture of the United States, as exemplified by what was understood as the mass media in the 1950s. In this he would be closer to the position of the Massey Report than McLuhan was. But Innis is also pointing toward the connection between print culture and nationalism, an idea that McLuhan would develop in *The Gutenberg Galaxy* (1962), as, subsequently, would Benedict Anderson in *Imagined Communities* (1983; 1991). It is surely for this reason that the "nationalism" question has devolved consistently upon print, even though, as Innis suggests, there are other domains of cultural expression—I write as Canada mourns Rita MacNeil, as, earlier this year, it mourned Stompin' Tom Connors, for whom flags flew at half mast for a week here in Vancouver.

McLuhan's contribution to the volume brings a number of these points together. His focus on "The Comics and Culture" is meant, first of all, to undermine the canonical concerns of the Massey Report (as McLuhan did far more polemically in 1954's *Counterblast*). Following Innis, though in a way Innis could not have predicted and of which he surely would not have approved, McLuhan argues that comics are "time binders" (240), suggesting that they are the "'songs'" of a post-literate culture, a culture in which "the photo [has] diminished the power of the word," binding in time the "breadth of geographic perception" (241) that the newspaper affords. McLuhan reminds his readers that "[p]rinting fostered nationalism" (241), and as mass media move away from the printed word, nationalism would follow, the "non-literary Canadian"[17] being "untrammeled by any sense of bookish or colonial inferiority" (242). In this scenario, "pictorial communication" would regain the ascendancy it had before the book, especially as fuelled by "the mechanization of the spoken word and of bodily gesture (cinema and TV)" (242). McLuhan emphasizes that the poetics of this "'verbivocovisual'"[18] world are juxtapositional, and we see in Ross's volume that these poetics are political as well, "linking past and present, distant racial memories and current politics" (243) in a "dynamic process of *becoming*" (245).

As the narrator of *The Second Scroll* prepares to land in Israel, he listens to a fellow passenger's musings on the paradox of a placeless nation and a discarnate[19] people, "[w]ithout home, yet everywhere; without language, yet echoed in all speech; without polity, yet the inspiration and basis of all social contract" (87). While the narrator finds the man's argument to be a "counterpoint" (89) to his own, he surprises himself by thinking of Montreal as he steps off the plane in Lydda. He sees his uncle everywhere and finds him nowhere; similarly, he begins to realize the folly of the task his publisher has set him, "as if it were going to be a simple flower-picking foray" (99). It would not be a matter merely of selecting from contemporary poems with their "insularity" and their "reactionary mottoes," a "retort to Europe, couched in Europe's language" (100), their theme "a continual backward-glancing to the past and their technique a pedantry of allusiveness."[20] Nor was it possible to find "a completely underivative poet" (104). Where the narrator does find the poetry for which he has been searching is all around him, "[i]n the streets, in the shops," spoken by "the fashioning folk, anonymous and unobserved" (106), who are "giving new life to the antique speech" (107). One hears in this Eliot's "purify the dialect of the tribe" (Eliot 57);[21] however, it is not purity that the narrator seeks but the complexities of a multifarious tribe made possible by what an elder calls "the curtailment of the route": a route "which but yesterday was long and arduous suddenly becomes short and speedy" (Klein 114), the route by which the narrator arrived in Israel.

The narrator's quest for his uncle fails—Melech dies a victim of sectarian violence—as does his quest for the poetry of Israel. This mournful note has been read by Heike Härting as "an affect of racialized colonial violence and modernity" (177). Terming literature a "legitimizing discourse of citizenship" (178), Härting asks how that discourse can obtain purchase in the postnational diaspora of globalization. Rejecting Hardt and Negri's account of a disembodied and deracialized subject, as developed in *Multitude* (2004), Härting proposes that embodiment is the anchor of the discursive practices of globalization. These tensions are evident in *The Second Scroll*. Israel represents in that work the complexities of diaspora and nation as figured in Melech, who is at once Wandering Jew and writer of the prime entry in the narrator's anthology. However, as Härting notes, the novel opens with "the prohibition to speak the uncle's name, symbolizing an originary and violent erasure of the text's diasporic signature" (183), resulting in "a narrative of incomplete mourning that seeks to cope with the ways in which the Israeli nation-state necessitates the death of the diaspora while remaining haunted by what it represses, its diaspora" (183). It is for this reason that the narrator must return to Canada: paradoxically, it is in Canada that the diaspora remains active, though at the price of national identity. What the novel proposes instead is "global rather than national citizenship" (Klein 197). The novel's *refusal* of narration[22] constitutes its most radical rejection of the colonialist understanding of diaspora. As Härting puts it, "in contrast to the time and place of the diaspora, the time and place of the nation remain static" (189). It is a refusal of that stasis that marks the end of "Deuteronomy," with its reference to "new moons, festivals, and set times" (Klein 121).

If literature is one of the ways in which citizenship is legitimized, as Härting suggests, how is that role performed by literary works *outside* the national narrative of citizenship? This is the question raised by *Sexing the Maple: A Canadian Sourcebook*, edited by Richard Cavell and Peter Dickinson.[23] It seeks to shift the ground on which that question is addressed by positing sexuality as one of the constitutive elements of nationality, albeit outside the traditional discourse of nationhood. If, as the editors suggest, "what connects sexual discourse with national discourse is the question of identity" (xiii), the connection is rendered problematic by the essentializing tendencies associated with identity politics in the sexual sphere. But this problematic points to a larger one—the essentializing tendencies inherent in positing a national literature *tout court* in an era of increasing globalization. While adding sexuality to the understanding of "nation" does not eliminate nationhood as the basis of literary inquiry, it does inflect it to a certain significant degree.

To put it another way, this focus opens up the notion of the literary to that of discourse, and it opens discourse onto sexuality, proposing thus that nations constitute themselves through discourses, one of which is literature and another of which is sexuality. This notion is at the heart of Homi Bhabha's concept that nation and narration are intimately connected. The presence of minority discourses in the national narrative—including sexual minorities—however, shifts the "story" told by that narrative from outside to inside. As Bhabha puts it, "[o]nce the liminality of the nation-space is established, and its 'difference' is turned from the boundary 'outside' to its finitude 'within,' the threat of cultural difference is no longer a problem of 'other' people. It becomes a question of the otherness of the people-as-one" (31). In this formulation, to posit a Canadian national narrative is to produce an essentialist discourse that is belied by the multiplicity of nations in Canada. This multiply-authored narrative of many discourses contests "originality" with the "secondary" status of narratives that are outside the narrative of national singularity. It is precisely this "original secondariness" that the anthology embodies. To put it another way: the anthology must *always* fail to represent the nation because there is no nation to represent. It is in this context that the full import of the appropriation of "nation" by queers, or lesbians, or aboriginals becomes apparent. These terms represent an involution of the concept of nationhood—both a withering and a reconstituting through inversion. In response to our anthem's invocation of "true patriot love," these "nations" remind us of Jacques Lacan's statement that "[l]ove is a sign that we are changing discourses" (301).

The complexities of these relationships are apparent in Alice Munro's story (the first in the sourcebook), "Family Furnishings." While the story's *point de repère* is a childhood memory of church bells pealing at the end of the First World War, this forget-me-not turns out to be the repository of a sexual *méconnaissance* that completely undermines the patriarchal narrative of that national coming-of-age. The Canada that is memorialized is one that never existed. Nor does Munro allow us to gain our bearings in the story, rewriting it three times in an astonishing tour de force, each rewriting telling a different story, none producing a narrative consistent with the others. Rather, what emerges is a will to power on the part of the narrator-protagonist: "This was what I wanted, this was what I thought I had to pay attention to, this was how I wanted my life to be" (Munro 25), the four "I"s suggesting the multiple narratives that obtain even in a single person, let alone a nation.

The notion of multiple narratives is ideally suited to an anthology, but belies the violence that configures it as a single narrative. This notion emerges powerfully in selections such as Trish Salah's "Surgical Diary," about transgender surgery ("Why this cut, here?" [153]), and the excerpt from John Colapinto's *As Nature Made Him* (173–91), where a grim irony centres on the violence necessary to produce a "natural" male body for David Reimer in response to a botched phalloplasty. The phallogocentrism implied by this project (biology as a discourse of masculinity; "true patriot love" as a discourse of nation) is at the core of anthologies that seek to represent nationhood through what Derrida has called the "violence of the letter" (101). This is the violence that seeks to represent "the dream of a full and immediate presence closing history" (115), such that the "ideal profoundly underlying this philosophy of writing is therefore the image of a community immediately present to itself, without difference" (136). This is the myth produced by the anthology—and its deconstruction.

Northrop Frye, in his "Preface to an Uncollected Anthology" (1957), suggests, like Brooker, that "[c]ertain critical principles are essential for dealing with Canadian poetry" (165), one of which is that "[i]t is not a nation but an environment that makes an impact on poets" (166). The Canadian environment that Frye sketches is one of absence: no Atlantic seaboard; existing in one dimension; divided by two languages and much wilderness; a circumference rather than a boundary; unseen by most of its people; a series of railway stops; "unhumanized isolation" (166), and "less an inhabited centre than an episode of communication" (166). This environment reveals Frye's anthology to be an act of mourning; it is a poetry of what is not there—*ca nada*, in the dubious Portuguese phrase he was fond of quoting.[24] This poetry's "tone is nostalgic" and its dominant theme "pain, loss, loneliness, or waste" (174); the greatest of these poems is one with the telling title "The Truant" (175), whose theme is that "the great Panjandrum of nature is fundamentally death" (175). Like the anthology of Klein's narrator, this one must remain uncollected, its mournful tone a sign of its becoming something other.

NOTES

1 "For those with eyes, who know in their hearts that terror is mutual, then this hard community has a beauty of its own." "Why Commands Are Obeyed," in *Flowers for Hitler* (Toronto: McClelland and Stewart, 1964).

2 In addition to the sources on anthologies cited in this chapter, I have consulted the following: Peggy Kelly, "Anthologies and the Canonization Process," *Studies in Canadian Literature* 25.1 (2000): 1–9; Frank Davey, "Canadian Canons," *Critical Inquiry* 16.2 (Spring 1990): 672–81; Carole Gerson, "Anthologies and the Canon of Early Canadian Women Writers," *Re-(Dis)covering Our Foremothers: Nineteenth-Century Canadian Women Writers*, ed. Lorraine McMullen (Ottawa: U of Ottawa P, 1989), 55–76; Robert Lecker, ed., *Canadian Canons: Essays in Literary Value* (Toronto: U of Toronto P, 1991); Robert Lecker, "The Canonization of Canadian Literature: An Inquiry into Value," *Critical Inquiry* 16.2 (Spring 1990): 656–71; George Elliott Clarke, "Let Us Compare Anthologies: Harmonizing the Founding African-Canadian and Italian-Canadian Literary Collections," Web.

3 Robert Lecker, "Nineteenth-Century English-Canadian Anthologies and the Making of a National Literature," *Journal of Canadian Studies* 44.1 (2010): 95.

4 Frederic Shoberl, ed., *Forget-Me-Not: A Christmas and New Years [sic] Present for 1823* (London: Ackermann, 1822).

5   Jacques Derrida, "The Violence of the Letter: From Lévi-Strauss to Rousseau," *Of Grammatology*. Trans. G. Spivak (Baltimore: Johns Hopkins UP, 1976) 101–40. I return to this text below.

6   This term figures in Geoffrey Winthrop-Young's discussion of McLuhan's place in German media theory. See "Cultural Studies and German Media Theory," *New Cultural Studies: Adventures in Theory*, ed. Gary Hall and Clare Birchall (Edinburgh: Edinburgh UP, 2006), 91.

7   This notion is developed by Homi Bhabha in "DissemiNation: Time, narrative, and the margins of the modern nation." I will return to this essay below.

8   Dean Irvine puts this relationship justly: "Although it would be overreaching to assert precise homologies between Klein's conceptions of diasporic and Israeli cultures and of cosmopolitanism and nativism in Canadian modernism, there is no doubt that these defining literary and cultural narratives of the period are contiguous in his mind." See "Dialectical Modernisms: Postcoloniality and Diaspora in A. M. Klein," *Modernism/Modernity* 18.3 (2012): 597–615; this quote 599.

9   The "Review Section" of the book has articles by William Arthur Deacon; Pelham Edgar; Carroll Aikins; Merrill Denison; Arthur Lismer; Fred S. Haines; Frederick B. Housser; Emanuel Hahn; Bertram Brooker; Eric R. Arthur; Campbell McInnes; Marius Barbeau; Augustus Bridle. The "Original Section" has selections by Will E. Ingersoll; Leslie Gordon Barnard; Lawren Harris; Roy Mitchell; Bliss Carman; Wilson Macdonald; Duncan Campbell Scott; E. J. Pratt; Martha Ostenso; Frederick Philip Grove; J. E. H. MacDonald; Louise Morey Bowman; Joseph Easton McDougall; John Linnell. The "Plates" are of works by Emanuel Hahn; Henri Hébert; Elizabeth Wyn Wood; Sylvia d'Aoust; Florence Wyle; Frances Loring; Tait McKenzie; Prudence Heward; L. Torrance Newton; M. Emily Carr; F. H. Varley; L. Lemoine Fitzgerald; Charles F. Comfort; Walter J. Phillips; A. Y. Jackson; George D. Pepper; Bess Housser; Gordon Weber; Lawren Harris; Arthur Lismer; Clarence Gagnon; A. H. Robinson; Frank Carmichael; A. J. Casson; F. H. Bridgen; Fred S. Haines; Horatio Walker; L. A. C. Panton; Yvonne McKague; Kathleen Munn; Bertram Brooker; Carl Schaefer; Thoreau MacDonald; Lowrie Warrener; Peter Haworth; J. E. H. MacDonald; Edwin H. Holgate; Chapman and Oxley; Ross and MacDonald; John M. Lyle; H. L. Fetherstonhaugh; Murray Brown; Marani, Lawson and Paisley; George, Moorehouse and King; A. T. Galt Durnford; Mathers and Haldenby; J. Vanderpant; Ernest MacMillan; Healey Willan.

10 On the gift book tradition in Canada, see Robert Lecker, *Keepers of the Code: English-Canadian Literary Anthologies and the Representation of Nation* (Toronto: U of Toronto P, 2013), 26–27.

11 Contributors include Sir George Arthur; Maurice Baring; Max Beerbohm; Clive Bell; Hilaire Belloc; Lord Berners; Edmund Blunden; Ivor Brown; Godfrey Childe; Cyril Connolly; Bernard Darwin; Richard Elwes; Tyrone Guthrie; Ian Hay; Father Ronald Knox; Shane Leslie; Robert Lynd; Rose Macaulay; Denis Mackail; Raymond Mortimer; Harold Nicolson; Naomi Royde-Smith; Elizabeth Ryan; E. Sackville-West; V. Sackville-West; Siegfried Sassoon; Christopher Scaife; Edward Shanks; J. C. Squire; Christopher Sykes; Lord Thomson; H. M. Tomlinson; Philip Tomlinson; The Marquis of Tweeddale; John van Druten; Hugh Walpole; George Wansbrough; Dorothy Wellesley; R. H. Wilenski.

12 On Brooker and space see Richard Cavell, *McLuhan in Space: A Cultural Geography* (Toronto: U of Toronto P, 2002) 15. See also Adam Lauder, "'Trade Routes of the Mind': A Brief History of Information Art in Canada," *H& IT ON*, ed. Adam Lauder, introduction by Richard Cavell (Toronto: YYZ Books, 2012), 11–47.

13 Fourth-dimensional thought was all the rage among the Theosophists; see Cavell, *McLuhan* 58–61.

14 I elaborate this position, drawing on Derrida and Judith Butler, in "Jane Rule and the Memory of Canada," *Unruly Penelopes and the Ghosts: Narratives of English Canada*, ed. Eva Darias-Beautell (Waterloo: Wilfrid Laurier UP, 2012): 157–81.

15 The book contains contributions by Susanna Moodie; Joseph Howe; Goldwin Smith; Sara Jeannette Duncan (2); W. E. Walsh; Frank H. Underhill (2); Bruce Hutchison; P. D. Ross; W. H. Blake; James A. Roy; W. E. Collin; Vincent Massey; Thomas Chandler Haliburton; William Lyon Mackenzie; A. M. Klein; H. A. Kennedy; Emily Carr; Morley Callaghan; Hugh MacLennan; J. D. Robins; Pelham Edgar; G. G. Sedgewick; A. R. M. Lower; Harry Henderson; E. K. Brown; Thelma Lecocq; Hugh Kenner; William Arthur Deacon; A. J. M. Smith; A. Y. Jackson; Barker Fairley; Lister Sinclair; Marshall McLuhan; Northrop Frye; J. A. Corry; Gerald B. Phelan; B. K. Sandwell; J. S. Woodsworth; Arthur L. Phelps; Stephen Leacock; A. S. P. Woodhouse; H. A. Innis.

16 Lister Sinclair's essay "The Canadian Idiom" makes the same point, arguing that the Canadian idiom is characterized by "*irony*, the jiu-jitsu of literature" (240).

17 McLuhan does not mean this negatively; his example is Norman McLaren.

18 The reference is to James Joyce, *Finnegans Wake*.

19 Klein refers to "Discarnation"; "discarnate" was a key term for McLuhan, representing the body extended by electronic media.

20 I explore a number of these themes in "'The Nth Adam': Dante in Klein's *The Second Scroll*," *Canadian Literature* 106 (1985): 45–53.

21 The implied critique of Eliot is present also in the novel's allusions to James Joyce's *Ulysses*, Klein's Melech figuring Joyce's Bloom.

22 It is in terms of an understanding of narration, or its absence, that my reading differs from Härting's, which tends to elide the complexities of the novel's textuality, attributing, for example, "Gloss Gimel" to the narrator, rather than to Uncle Melech. "Gloss Gimel" will be *incorporated* as the lead text of the narrator's anthology.

23 The sourcebook includes contributions by Alice Munro; Ivan E. Coyote; Gertrude Pringle; Michael Bliss; Mariana Valverde; Irving Layton; Persimmon Blackridge; Nicole Markotic; Marshall McLuhan and George B. Leonard; Katherine Monk; Derek McCormack; Trish Salah; Patricia Baird; John Colapinto; Dorothy Livesay; Jane Rule; Daphne Marlatt; Lyndell Montgomery; Roberta Hamilton; SKY Lee; Ian Iqbal Rashid; Gregory Scofield; Martin Cannon; Karen Dubinsky and Adam Givertz; Timothy Findley; Leonard Cohen; Margaret Atwood; Nancy Christie; Iain A. G. Baird; Michael Turner; Lynn Crosbie; Gary Kinsman; Stan Persky and John Dixon.

24 See Northrop Frye, *The Modern Century* (Toronto: Oxford UP, 1967).

Publication, Performances, and Politics

The "Indian Poems" of E. Pauline Johnson / Tekahionwake (1861–1913) and Duncan Campbell Scott (1862–1947)

Margery Fee

The title of Sherman Alexie's short-story collection, *Lone Ranger and Tonto: Fistfight in Heaven,* makes a tempting analogy for anyone comparing the "Indian poems" of E. Pauline Johnson and Duncan Campbell Scott in the twenty-first century.[1] After all, Johnson was a Mohawk, a Status Indian, and a ward of the state. In 1913, the year Johnson died, Scott became the highest non-elected official in the Department of Indian Affairs, a post he held for the next two decades. Comic-book binaries are dangerous, yet the poems of these two authors on Indigenous themes conveyed different messages and affects. And the literary institution received these poems differently.

Even if one quibbles about which poems or anthologies to count, in the forty-four national anthologies published between 1887 and 2008 that I surveyed for this essay, Scott's poems on Indigenous topics were anthologized more than twice as often as Johnson's. Although Charles G. D. Roberts, among others, admired and promoted her writing,[2] the rise of modernist tastes meant her work was rarely anthologized between 1940 and 1990 (see appendix 1, 2). Carole Gerson and Peggy Kelly have shown that this was the fate of women poets more generally; in fact, Johnson fared better than most (Gerson, "Anthologies" 166). To isolate the effect of Scott's and Johnson's different representations of Indigenous people in this history is difficult, if not impossible. Still, those of her poems that depicted strong and virtuous Indigenous women and directly criticized colonial power were anthologized less often and later than her others. Looking at how anthologists received Johnson's and Scott's Indian poems illuminates some of the complex web connecting political viewpoints, representations, and literary canonization.

Their careers began in similar ways. Both published in Goldwin Smith's *The Week*. W. D. Lighthall's *Songs of the Great Dominion* (1889) contained two poems by each of them, although none was on an Indigenous subject. They both participated at the Toronto reading that launched Johnson's fifteen-year career as a "Mohawk Indian poet-reciter" in 1892 (Strong-Boag and Gerson 105). She recited "A Cry from an Indian Wife," with "As Red Men Die" as an encore (Keller 58); Scott read a prose sketch (Bentley, *Confederation* 255). Their few professional contacts were cordial. As members of the same small, elite group, they worked in the same field of cultural production, producing similar symbolic goods for the same market (Bourdieu 176).

Much of this chapter is an excursus on a point made by Carole Gerson: "The canon has allowed the poetry of Duncan Campbell Scott to represent

Table 1   "Indian Poems" by Johnson and Scott, Anthologized between 1893 and 2008

JOHNSON TITLES	YEARS ANTHOLOGIZED	SCOTT TITLES	1ST YEAR ANTHOLOGIZED / TOTALS[a]
"As Red Men Die"	1893, 1916, 1922, 1926	"The Forsaken"	1913 / 21 times
"The Indian Corn Planter"	1902, 1922	"The Half-breed Girl"	1913 / 11 times
"Lullaby of the Iroquois"	1907, 1913, 1922, 1973, 1974, 1994	"Lines Written in Memory of Edmund Morris"	1916 / 4 times
"The Pilot of the Plains"	1916, 1926	"On the Way to the Mission"	1935 / 9 times
"The Corn Husker"	1922, 1935, 1954, 1974, 1978, 1994, 2007, 2008	"Watkwenies"	1942 / 7 times
"The Legend of Qu'Appelle Valley"	1922	"At Gull Lake: 1810"	1943 / 14 times
"The Ballad of Yaada"	1928, 1930	"The Onondaga Madonna"	1946 / 20 times
"The Cattle Thief"	1945, 2007, 2008	"Indian Place-names"	1952 / 2 times
"Silhouette"	1974, 1978, 1990, 1994, 2002	"Night Hymns at Lake Nipigon"	1960 / 7 times
"Ojistoh"	1982	"Powassen's Drum"	1960 / 3 times
"A Cry from an Indian Wife"	1990, 2002, 2007, 2008	"The Height of Land"	1960 / 11 times
		"Scenes at Lake Manitou"	2000 / 1 time

a For the years of Scott's subsequent anthology appearances, see Appendix 1.

Native concerns in early Canadian literature, while ignoring Johnson's advocacy in 'The Corn Husker'" ("Recuperating" 180–81). To expand on this point, I counted their poems on Native themes in forty-four anthologies (including several editions of a few) published between 1887 and 2008 (listed in appendix 2). Although their intended audiences varied, these anthologies all claim a national scope. Neither poet published many poems on Indigenous subjects. Johnson published only twenty, all of them between 1884 and 1898.[3] Of these, only eleven appeared in the anthologies I surveyed. (The others are "The Avenger," "Brant: A Memorial Ode," "Dawendine," "The Death Cry," "The Happy Hunting Grounds," "The Quill Worker," "The Reinterment of Red Jacket," "A Request," and "Wolverine.") Scott wrote twelve poems that qualify,[4] all of which appear at least once. He published the first, "The Onondaga Woman and Her Child," in 1894;[5] all but three had appeared in one of his books by 1916; these ("At Gull Lake: 1810," "Powassen's Drum," and "Scenes at Lake Manitou") appeared in *The Green Cloister*, 1935. Johnson's "The Corn Husker" is indeed completely routed by Scott's "The Onondaga Madonna." And Johnson's resistant poems either do not appear at all ("Brant: A Memorial Ode," "The Reinterment of Red Jacket," "A Request," "Wolverine"), or were late to appear ("The Cattle Thief," "A Cry from an Indian Wife," "Ojistoh," "Silhouette"). Johnson recited many of these poems in her hundreds of performances, indicating the importance she attached to them.[6] Significantly, although Johnson chose "A Cry from an Indian Wife" for her performing debut, it appeared in the anthologies I surveyed only after 1990. She offered it to W. D. Lighthall for inclusion in *Songs of the Great Dominion* (Gray 120–21), but for the "Indian" section of the anthology only translations and poems by non-Indigenous Canadian men, including himself, were chosen. Most depicted the Indian as definitively vanishing. Yet the Seneca activist Arthur C. Parker quotes a large section of "A Cry from an Indian Wife" in 1915 in the *American Indian Magazine*, indicating that he admired it and thought his readers would too. Colonial beliefs do appear to have affected Canadian anthologists, at least until recently.

Johnson held that Indigenous people were the intellectual, social, and political equals of other Canadians. "Canadian Born" was the title poem of her second collection, published in 1903. It declares that "we, the men of Canada, can face the world and brag / That we were born in Canada beneath the British flag" (125–26). On the title page an inscription concludes: "White Race and Red are one if they are but Canadian born," making "explicit her vision of an egalitarian nation" (Gerson and Strong-Boag xix). Unfortunately, her forthright inscription is usually omitted by anthologists, allowing the poem to be read as a celebration of white settler nationalism.[7]

Scott, however, like most non-Indigenous Canadians, believed fervently in assimilation, whether by intermarriage or education. For him, the primitive cultures of Indigenous nations had to be replaced by those of a superior civilization (see Salem; Titley). In 1920, testifying before a parliamentary committee in support of mandatory school attendance for Indigenous children, he said, "Our objective is to continue until there is not a single Indian in Canada that has not been absorbed into the body politic and there is no Indian question, and no Indian Department" (qtd. in Titley 50). Critics argue about the closeness of the connection between his political views and his literary work (see Salem-Wiseman). Obviously, a speech like this and a poem like "The Forsaken" differ at the generic, formal, and aesthetic levels. However, both poets' political views can be connected to their poetry; I argue that these views, however mediated, ultimately affected both poets' canonization.

The canon, as John Guillory reminds us in *Cultural Capital: The Problem of Literary Canon Formation,* is an "imaginary totality" that exceeds those works actually found in anthologies and curricula (30). Nonetheless, canonicity is usually extended to works valued by important critics and anthologists and taught in schools and universities. Access to these works is regulated by education in ways that distribute cultural capital unevenly. In Johnson's time, status in the dominant society was enhanced by the ability to read and write Standard English, to recite canonical poems, and to create highly valued literary forms. Indigenous children sent to segregated schools were not given access to these goods. Clifford Sifton, Minister of the Interior and Scott's superior between 1896 and 1905, commented, "we are educating these Indians to compete industrially with our own people, which seems to me a very undesirable use of public money—it has to be carefully considered how far the country can be properly burdened with the cost of giving them superior advantages" (qtd. in Barman, *West* 172). Johnson spent two years at a reserve school, but her cultural capital was gained at home and during two years at the Brantford Collegiate Institute (Keller 29–30). Indeed, she performed a paradox: Indigenous people were supposedly primitive, innately unable to compete with the civilized; she not only competed, she excelled. Certainly, without cultural capital, she would not have been able to enter the canon. But she used this privilege to make political arguments that countered those of the mainstream.

Before turning to the poems, I should acknowledge some of the limitations of this study. Critics recruit poems and poets to different—sometimes radically different—causes. Assuming stable meanings or categories is naive. Counting poems barely scratches the surface of how these anthologies frame individual poets and their work with photographs, introductions, and biographies. Nor, Glenn Willmott argues, can Johnson's recent return to the canon be explained in terms of formerly popular notions of absolute quality:

> It is not that her work is suddenly considered as good as that of Roberts, Lampman, Carman, and Scott. The comparison to a normative good is mistaken. Where we speak of literary value, the good has not simply changed, it has multiplied. The good is multiple and relative, a matter of perspective and position within a given social and institutional horizon. Every good is historical, invented, imaginary, ephemeral, and material, nothing but the fluttering flag of one interpretive community seeking to fly above the others. (n. pag.)

We keep running up our flags, nonetheless. In "Paddled by Pauline," Willmott makes a claim for Johnson's skill in a close reading of "Shadow River (Muskoka)": "This poet is no mere imitator, as I hope to have demonstrated, but a compelling and crafty contributor to the aestheticist tradition" (n. pag.). What he calls her "shadow writing" enacts her own insistent destabilizing of the binary between Mohawk woman and British lady in her writing and performances. Here, my focus on those poems with *explicit* Indigenous content reinforces the distinction between white and Indigenous that she worked to undermine. "Shadow River" *is* an Indigenous poem, a meaning carried by its subtitle, "Muskoka": "What this word refers to, from the subject perspective of Shadow River, is both less concretely real, and more political, than we might ever have suspected" (Willmott n. pag.). Willmott makes the case for refusing to divide "the feather from the flint," or Johnson's aestheticist "shadow writing" from her more politically engaged dramatic and narrative work (n. pag.).[8] Similarly, Rick Monture considers "The Song My Paddle Sings," which can easily be read as a "nature poem," as cleverly using the canoe to symbolize both her difficulties as an Iroquois person of mixed ancestry as well as the dangers faced by Iroquois society in a time of tumultuous change (102–4). He sees the metaphor found in the famous Two-Row Wampum, which represents white and Iroquois in their separate canoes, each holding to their own course, as central to any reading of this poem, although this message is "covert, ... invisible, and ironic" (104).

So here I proceed tentatively to examine the anthologists' choices. Before Johnson's death, her Indian poems were more anthologized than Scott's, perhaps reflecting her connections with Roberts and other prominent literati. Anthologists also selected those of her poems that supported the narrative of the Canadian love of nature and canoes, the latter deemed to be "a symbol uniting Natives and whites" (Lecker 53).[9] Given that most national anthologies were compiled by Romantic nationalists, it is hardly surprising that "The Cattle Thief," "A Cry from an Indian Wife," and "Silhouette" were late to appear, since they all explicitly criticize Canadian settler society for its bad treatment of Indigenous people. Although "The Corn Husker" mentions "might's injustice," which Gerson sees as "advocacy" ("Recuperating" 180–81), its elegiac tone softens the impact of these words. Scott's Indian poems became more popular over time, perhaps because of his increasing public prominence. Modernism's move to appropriate the "primitive" also supported his continuing importance. It also became clear after the First World War that Indigenous people were not about to vanish or assimilate voluntarily, despite the intense regulation of their lives. Since the main purpose of mainstream nationalist anthologies has been, at least until recently, to assimilate readers to a singular national imaginary, Scott's Indian poems served double duty: exalting the virtues of what Daniel Coleman has aptly named "white civility," while rationalizing the dispossession and assimilation of Indigenous peoples. Some of these poems simply represent Indigenous peoples as primitive and vanishing: "Indian Place Names" begins "The race has waned and left but tales of ghosts" (36), while "Night Hymns on Lake Nipigon" comments on the incongruity of the "noble Latin" as it is "married" with the "uncouth and mournful" Ojibwa (35). "Lines Written in Memory of Edmund Morris" is not only an elegy for Scott's friend, the painter, but also for the Indigenous men he painted. In "Powassen's Drum" a shaman, "parched with anger / And famished with hatred" (85), drums relentlessly, conjuring up the Gothic apparition of a headless Indian in a canoe.

Johnson's gender and both poets' deployment of gendered representations loom large in this history. Women and babies often represent Indianness or symbolize contact between Indigenous and white cultures. Scott published "The Onondaga Woman and Child" in *Atlantic Monthly* in 1894 (he retitled it for his second collection). This poem, like Johnson's "Ojistoh," was perhaps too sexy for early canonization, since it did not appear in these anthologies until 1946, in John D. Robins's *A Pocketful of Canada*. Certainly, this is where I first encountered it—inside the cover of my copy is written "Margery Fee, 8G." "The Onondaga Madonna" had much the same effect on me as did the "savage and superb, wild-eyed and magnificent" African woman of Joseph Conrad's *Heart of Darkness* (129). I encountered *her* in grade 13, as did every other grade 13 student in Ontario that year. Clearly, the Onondaga madonna and this African woman were intended as contrasts to the *real* madonna (pure, white, and virginal) and Conrad's portrait of Kurtz's Intended (ditto). I was able to articulate my unease with the whole setup only after my encounter with feminism a few years later. (The students I taught last year, however, were quick to identify the Onondaga madonna as a vampire!) As D. M. R. Bentley points out, despite Scott's reasoned position that assimilation was possible through education and intermarriage, his poetry shimmers with "late Victorian fears of the irruption of the irrational, the instinctual [and] the primitive" ("Shadows" 754). The madonna's blood is "mingled," her baby "paler than she"—but *this* assimilation is obviously the result of her uncivilized depravity. She is, quite simply, a danger to white men. Technically, the poem is a tour de force, condensing a radioactive sexuality into a Petrarchan sonnet. The Onondaga madonna is "of a weird and waning race" and her baby the "latest promise of her nation's doom." These references to the vanishing Indian still suggest a continuing threat, given the "primal warrior gleaming" from the baby's eyes (14). The poem exemplifies the ways in which stereotypes justify colonization. Indigenous women in particular have been discursively constructed as temptresses, prostitutes, or sexual prey rather than as potential wives, peers, or co-workers, a shift that happened quickly once white settlement began (see Barman, "Taming"). This shift served to exclude Indigenous people from public life and the economic benefits reserved for white settlers. Unsurprisingly then, Scott's poems consistently depicted the children of "mixed" relationships—like Johnson, whose mother was English— in negative terms. The Onondaga madonna's sulky and restless baby contrasts with the baby in Johnson's pretty, rhythmic, and popular "Lullaby of the Iroquois," observing its surroundings with "wonder-black eyes" (120). The title character of Scott's "The Half-breed Girl" is, as Bentley puts it, "so conflicted as to render her little short of insane and suicidal" ("Shadows" 758). What Scott represented as the disastrous results of miscegenation Johnson refuted in her work, including hundreds of embodied performances.

Johnson's romantic poems focus on lovers parted by death, a common sentimental theme. "Legend of the Qu'Appelle Valley," for example, explains the origins of the valley's name in an Indian man's premonition of his lover's death. However, "The Ballad of Yaada" and "The Pilot of the Plains" are distinguished from hundreds of other contemporary effusions about lovelorn Indian maidens because of their support for inter-ethnic romance.[10] In the latter poem, Johnson depicts a white man faithful to his Yakonwita, countering the stereotype of the suicidal Indian maiden helplessly in love with a white man who spurns or ignores her, a stereotype that is the subject of her sarcasm in her newspaper article "A Strong Race Opinion." Scott's "At Gull Lake: 1810" depicts just such a woman, Keejigo, the daughter of a French hunter and a Saulteaux woman. The third wife of a Saulteaux chief, she offers herself with "an abject unreasoning passion" to an Orkney trader who rejects her overtures. Her jealous husband burns her face with a "live brand" and then his older wives "dragged her away / And threw her over the bank / Like a dead dog" (98). Although Johnson's poems were roundly criticized by modernists for being sentimental, melodramatic, and didactic, nothing she wrote beats this.

Scott's highlighting of polygamy foregrounds the dangers of the exotic and primitive customs of Indigenous people. Sarah Carter's *The Importance of Being Monogamous* details the difficulties that polygamy in the prairie provinces, including that of Mormons, posed to government. Indigenous partners were generally free to leave their relationships without penalty: "no marriage needed to be for life, as divorce was easy to obtain and remarriage was accepted and expected" (Carter 5). But the insistence on legally regulated or Christian marriage meant that Indian Status could be stripped from women who married non-Status men, assumed to be assimilated by marriage (see "Bill C-31" n. pag.). Further, dominant Christian notions made it difficult for authorities to see Indigenous sexual and gender relations as anything but chaotic licentiousness. Keejigo, like the Onondaga madonna, is eroticized as a dangerous attraction to susceptible white men, and thus as a blameable victim. The moral hero of the poem is the Orkneyman. And the stereotype of the unrestrained sexuality of Indigenous women has been used to excuse rape and worse (see Barman, "Taming").[11] As in colonial situations in South Asia and elsewhere, to paraphrase Gayatri Spivak, Canadian authorities set themselves up as the rescuers of red women from red men (287)—but also as the protectors of white men from red women. Indeed, the Canadian government, by treating Indigenous people as wards rather than citizens, pretended to an even broader role as moral guardian. Scott's poems certainly would have appealed to Romantic nationalist anthologists because of their representations of Indigenous people as in need of the Canadian civilizing mission.

The sentimental and moralizing focus on women and children in danger marks Scott's "The Forsaken," a nameless "Chippewa woman" who finds herself and her baby at risk of starving in a blizzard (37). The first part of the poem describes the mother catching fish on a hook baited with her own flesh; in the second part, when she is old, her children, including the son she saved, abandon her. In the first half, the woman makes it back to the fort after three days: "And then she had rest" (38). In the second half, old and forsaken, she sits in the forest for two days; on the second night she is covered with a "crystal shroud" of snow, but when morning comes, she is still alive, "a column of breath" marking "a sign of the spirit." That night "all light was gathered up by the hand of God and hid in his breast"—the last line repeats, "Then she had rest" (39). The woman is described three times as "Valiant, unshaken." The echoes of Christ's betrayal by his disciples, bodily sacrifice, and resurrection on the third day need not be emphatic for a Christian reader. The woman is a noble savage: she stoically accepts her fate and the primitive customs of her people.[12] Her children, on the other hand, who "slunk away," are neither noble nor assimilated (38), and clearly in need of moral correction.

"On the Way to the Mission" depicts a Montagnais trapper pulling a loaded toboggan. He is dogged by two white men, twice described as "servants of greed," who hope to rob him of his furs (38). Eventually they shoot him, only to find that what he is drawing on his sled is his dead wife. He planned to bury her at the mission. In the end, "The moon went on to her setting / And covered them with shade." Christian, married, and dead, the wife can safely be sentimentalized:

> There in the tender moonlight,
> As sweet as they were in life,
> Glimmered the ivory features,
> Of the Indian's wife. (39)

Here Christian values have clearly ennobled—even whitened—the Montagnais, but the fate of this couple also demonstrates the need to protect good Indigenous people against exploitation by bad white people. Scott saw them as "a savage or a semi-savage race," while the white savagery depicted in this poem is, apparently, exceptional (qtd. in Titley 176).

Compared to "On the Way to the Mission" and some of her own more sentimental poems, Johnson's "The Corn Husker" and "The Indian Corn Planter" represent Indigenous people as ordinary rather than exotic. "The Corn Husker," despite its protest against the dispossession of the old woman's people by "might's injustice," can easily be read as an elegy. Her people are now "unheeded" like "the dead husks that rustle through her hands" (121). Nonetheless, Monture sees this poem as "culturally subversive" in its metaphorical use of corn, which the Haudenosaunee view as a spiritual gift, and in its depiction of the old woman's resilience (87). "The Indian Corn Planter," which looks to the future, is harder to read as an elegy. Although the Haudenosaunee were farmers, plains peoples had to shift from buffalo hunting to farming. Despite the need to turn from the "hunter's heaven" to the "grim / Realities of labouring for bread," the planter adapts, supported by his "simple pagan faith" (124–25). The soil "true as God" rewards him, and "mothers every grain" (125). The planter, despite drastic disruption, moves into a new economy while holding fast to his cultural beliefs. Further, he and the corn husker are depicted as hard workers, contrary to the stereotype of the idle Indian.[13] "The Indian Corn Planter" was anthologized less often than "The Corn Husker," perhaps because of its celebration of the pagan, a position Johnson takes further in her newspaper article "A Pagan in St. Paul's Cathedral" and elsewhere.

Unlike Scott's Indian women, Johnson's women are active and often articulate, reflecting the power of Mohawk women, particularly the hereditary clan mothers like Johnson's grandmother, Helen Martin Johnson. "A Cry from an Indian Wife" reflects the need to negotiate among conflicting loyalties that Johnson (and Indigenous peoples generally) faced in promoting their claims. The wife, speaking as a member of one of the plains tribes during the second Riel Resistance in 1885, shifts between the loyalty affirmed in treaties ("Revolt not at the Union Jack"), sympathy for the young and inexperienced white troops ("this stripling pack / Of white-faced warriors"), and an understanding of the national government's "well-meant" if forgetful "new rule and council" (14). In the last four lines, however, she urges her husband to fight, voicing outrage at the imposition of rule by force: "By right, by birth, we Indians own these lands" (15). This assertion quickly turns to resignation: her "starved, crushed, plundered" nation will once again be defeated (15). Published in *The Week* in June 1885 while events were still unfolding (Strong-Boag and Gerson 149), the poem gets some of the facts wrong, but the general point is clear.[14] The might of colonial domination did not make right. One account of Johnson's first performance of this poem testified to its effect: "complaisant white intellectuals were startled" (qtd. in Strong-Boag and Gerson 107). Despite Johnson's attempt at balancing sympathies in this poem, it first appeared in the anthologies surveyed only in 1990, when Indigenous literature first began moving into anthologies and classrooms in Canada.

"The Cattle Thief" is even more forthright about the mistreatment of the plains peoples than "A Cry from an Indian Wife." Although an excerpt appeared in Margaret Fairley's *The Spirit of Canadian Democracy* in 1945, it did not appear in any other anthology until 2007. A Communist, Fairley saw "literary modernism in Canada as just another project of American cultural imperialism" and preferred a literature native to Canada: "Canadian and aboriginal" (Irvine 254). The poem starts with desperate riders, "their British blood aflame" (97), pursuing a Cree cattle thief. He comes out to face them "unarmed" (97); they shoot him and "rush like a pack of demons on the body," which they propose to cut up and leave for the wolves (98). Then his daughter appears and stands them off "with a courage beyond belief": she says in Cree "If you mean to touch that body, you must cut your way through *me*" (98) and indignantly continues:

> What have you left to us of land, what have you left of game,
> What have you brought but evil, and curses since you came?
> How have you paid us for our game? how paid us for our land?
> By a *book*, to save our souls from the sins *you* brought in your other hand....
> When *you* pay for the land you live in, *we'll* pay for the meat we eat. (98–99)

Johnson takes up the theme of starvation on the plains again in "Silhouette," where a gaunt "Indian Chief ... looks towards the empty west / to see the never-coming herd of buffalo" (104–5). This poem waited until 1974 for inclusion in a national anthology.

Finally, we come to "Ojistoh." Night after night Johnson recited Ojistoh's story of her kidnapping by a vengeful Huron warrior in retaliation for her husband's victories. The Huron carries her off behind him on his galloping horse, providing a hugely evocative image of the sexually wild and violent savage. Facing rape, Ojistoh seduces the Huron into unbinding her. Then (spoiler alert) she stabs him with his own knife and rides back to her husband on her captor's horse. Monture points out that although this scene "depicts a courageous and strong female figure at a time when few such images circulated, it can also be interpreted as perpetuating the sensationalized image of a highly sexual and violent Native woman" (88). This poem works, as did "The Cattle Thief," by evoking familiar racist and sexist stereotypes and then reversing them ("Wolverine" works the same way). "Ojistoh" ends with a ringing declaration refuting the stereotype of the sexually promiscuous Indian woman as its heroine gallops home:

> My hands all wet, stained with a life's red dye,
> But pure my soul, pure as those stars on high—
> My Mohawk's pure white star, Ojistoh, still am I! (116)

"Ojistoh" was first anthologized in 1982 by Margaret Atwood in *The New Oxford Book of Poetry*; she was at this point working on *The Handmaid's Tale*, a novel about institutionalized patriarchal rape. Despite Ojistoh's fidelity to husband and nation, she retains a phallic agency that Atwood reserves for her most powerful women characters. One might speculate that this poem is still rarely anthologized because—as Monture suggests—Ojistoh cannot easily be seen as a good or bad woman, even in a modern context. How can we reconcile her shift from innocent victim, through calculating seductress and efficient murderess, to faithful wife? Her behaviour is at odds with dominant notions of femininity even today.

"Ojistoh" can be usefully read against Scott's sonnet "Watkwenies." This Mohawk's "valiant name" means "The Woman who Conquers." Scott fronts the notion, also found in Johnson's "Avenger," that "[v]engeance was once her nation's lore and law" (13). As a young woman, Watkwenies surprises a white soldier, a "tired sentry": "Her long knife flashed, and hissed, and drank its fill" (13). In the sestet, she has been tamed by old age and government money: "She weighs the interest-money in her palm" (13).[15] The implication of the poem is that the Mohawk are both untrustworthy and ungrateful. Although both "Ojistoh" and "Watkwenies" deploy the same tropes of Mohawk violence, Ojistoh remains loyal to her husband,[16] while Watkwenies is still weighing the price of loyalty to the Crown. And, as with the Onondaga madonna's frowning baby, the threat evoked by the hiss of her knife continues as the whooping boys play snow-snake at the end of the poem. Here the Mohawk are figured as potential betrayers, rather than as "Feathered Loyalists" who were granted their land in Canada to reward them for their service as British allies during the American Revolution. .

Despite the ways in which Scott's and Johnson's poems differ in their relation to stereotypical discourses of women and Indigenous people more generally, Johnson's disappearance from the canon between 1940 and the mid-1970s cannot be explained simply by her position in national debates about Indigenous peoples. As part of an international movement, modernist critics drove Johnson—and most other women poets—out of the canon. They described her poetry as "meretricious," "elocutionist-fodder," "not important to Canadian literature," "cheap, vulgar, and almost incredibly bad" (qtd. in Gerson and Strong-Boag 126–30). A. J. M. Smith says of *Flint and Feather* that "responsible criticism" (i.e., his) cannot say that it is "genuine poetry" or the "true voice" of the North American Indian (21). Johnson, he writes, is "likely to be remembered for one or two graceful lyrics which make no claim to racial or national significance. In the theatrical and once popular ballads of Indian life, her rhythm is heavy, her imagery conventional, her language melodramatic and forced" (21). Here, Smith makes good use of the notion of an elite poetry uncontaminated by politics or popular approval (Chater n. pag.). However, Smith praises Scott for his

> remarkable poems of Indian life, from "The Half-breed Girl" in his first volume of 1893 to his tragic masterpiece "At Gull Lake: 1810." ... As an interpreter of the Indian, Duncan Campbell Scott is deserving of more serious consideration than is the widely acclaimed poet Pauline Johnson. But Miss Johnson had special advantage: she was a real Indian princess, a genuine half-breed girl. (21)

Smith scoffs at the idea that Johnson's knowledge could equal Scott's, acquired in his "lifework as an administrator" (20)—what Scott himself called in 1931 "my fifty year imprisonment with the savages" (qtd. in Dragland, Introduction xiv). Scott's sneering last sentence suggests that Johnson was neither princess nor Mohawk. Clearly, Indigenous people could not represent themselves; they required others to do it. As a result of such critical judgments, Scott's racist, sexist, and sentimental poetry about Indigenous people remains securely in anthologies, the curriculum, and the canon.

Modernists attacked sentimentality first and foremost. The use of sentimental tropes became dominant in literature by both men and women during the nineteenth century. The period's focus on women's duty to home, husband, children, and God was clearly gendered: women who took up this stance were already breaching its conventions by daring to hold a pen. Men were the ultimate beneficiaries of sentimentalism, given its support for women who devoted themselves to husband, home, and family. Mary Chapman and Glenn Hendler point out in their introduction to *Sentimental Men: Masculinity and the Politics of Affect in American Culture* that many well-known male writers deployed sentimental tropes. However, sentimentality was more and more argued to be a purely feminine failing. As a result, male writers, whose sentimental writing was not seen as such, stayed in the canon (Chapman and Hendler 2–5).

In the early part of Johnson's career, the New Woman and the suffragists began to appear on platforms and in the pages of newspapers, magazines, and books. Paula Bernat Bennett traces this history in *Poets in the Public Sphere: The Emancipatory Project of American Women's Poetry, 1800–1900*. She makes clear that sentimentalism had exhausted its political force by 1850 for majority women activists, who turned to fighting for social and political equality with men. Minority women, however, continued to find the politics of empathy promoted by sentimentalism useful. After all, their cultural difference resided precisely in their homes, husbands, children, customs, and communities. To abandon sentimentalism was to move away from a focus on difference to a focus on equality, but this meant, in effect, aspiring to become middle class and white: "The vast majority of nineteenth-century U.S. minority women had no way to separate their political progress from both assimilation and genteelization" (Bennett 81). White women could claim equality with white men without losing their cultural affiliations,[17] while minority women were fighting precisely to keep the affiliations that marked their communities as distinctive. They were forced to appeal to the sympathy of majority readers to make the point that this difference was worth preserving. As Bennett notes, Indigenous activist writers such as Johnson and Zitkala-Ša did not use their writing to inspire their own people to embrace social mobility or assimilation, but rather to "make those who oppress aware of what they do" (83). Thus they wrote primarily for mainstream audiences using sentimental tropes designed to promote sympathy for their cause.

This made them sitting ducks for modernist critics. Two of Johnson's poems were included in an American anthology, *The Path on the Rainbow: An Anthology of Songs and Chants from the Indian of North America* (1918): "The Lost Lagoon" and "The Song My Paddle Sings." Most of the collection

consisted of translations or imitations of Indigenous songs by non-Indigenous writers. The introduction, by Mary Austin, an American poet, explains
the book's importance:

> it becomes appropriate and important that this collection of American Indian
> verse should be brought to public notice at a time when the whole instinctive
> movement of the American people is for a deeper footing in their native soil.
> It is the certificate of our adoption, that the young genius of our time should
> strike all unconsciously on this ancient track to the High Places. (xiii)

Modernism, in moving to appropriate Indigenous cultural forms for the
national culture, to get a "certificate of adoption," was making a literary land
claim. What was wanted was a direct "unconscious" connection by the young
American "genius," not with contemporary Indigenous people or concerns,
but with "the ancient track to the High Places." This move sidestepped any
need to deal consciously with a violent and continuing colonial history.
Instead of writing about Indigenous people, white (and implicitly male) poets
were to take their place.

In a review of this collection, T. S. Eliot seems reluctant to endorse Austin's idea at first: "suddenly, egged on by New York and Chicago intelligentsia,
the Chippeway bursts into the drawing room ..." (1036). But then he goes on
to argue for the poet as uniquely positioned to transform primitive culture
into the modern: "for the artist is, in the impersonal sense, the most conscious of men ... the first person to see how the savage, the barbarian, and the
rustic can be improved on" (1036). This idea explains how Scott's "The Height
of Land" becomes an "Indian poem," as Sarah Krotz argues (86), although it
mentions Indians only once: "Now the Indian guides are dead asleep" (Scott
52). In this poem, Scott produces the Canadian version of Austin's "young
genius" at the end of the "ancient track to the High Places" (xiii). Wrapped in
his "poetic mantle," he stands overlooking vast territories. Although the poem
does not mention it, Scott bases this scene on trips he made in the summers
of 1905 and 1906 to negotiate Treaty Nine. In the daytime, he is in charge of
claiming the land from people he did not believe could understand the terms
being offered: "What could they grasp of the pronouncement on the Indian
tenure which had been delivered by the law lords of the Crown?" (qtd. in
Titley 74).[18] After a day of bad-faith negotiations, Scott imagines a poet of the
future, even more civilized than his persona, one who will see his own "ideal
hope and promise" to be as crude as "the pictograph / Scratched on the cave
side by the cave dweller / To us of the Christ-time" (55). Nonetheless, in the
present, Scott is the best person to appropriate culture and land from people
who are, like the Indigenous people in many of his poems, depicted as dying

or dead. Ten anthologists, at least, agreed with Stan Dragland's assertion that "The Height of Land" is "near the core of the Canadian imagination" (*Floating* 229). If I believed there was a single Canadian imagination, I might agree too. Krotz describes the poem as a "poetic appropriation of space" (87): it certainly rationalizes the appropriation of land, a central concern of Canadian nationalist discourse.

Eliot also saw the modernist poet as objective, as "the last person to see the savage in a romantic light, or to yield to the weak credulity of crediting the savage with any gifts of mystical insight or artistic feeling that he does not possess himself" (1036). Already, one can see how Johnson's poems would be positioned by modernists. Louis Untermeyer's review of the collection in *The Dial* is more doubtful than Eliot's about the possibilities of the primitive, but he is seriously disappointed to find in the collection "jingles like Pauline Johnson's 'The Song My Paddle Sings,' which is neither original nor aboriginal," and "time-dusty ... rhymed sweetmeats" like "The Lost Lagoon" (240). Johnson's aestheticist lyrics and her monologues written for oral recitation were no longer in fashion; Scott's use of "primitive" styles and interior monologue, however, provided a useful bridge between the Canadian Romantics and Modernists.

In a review article in 1950, Northrop Frye calls Scott "one of the ancestral voices of the Canadian imagination" (247). Speaking of "the impact of the sophisticated on the primitive, and vice versa," he uses the "dramatic example" of Scott,

> working in the department of Indian Affairs in Ottawa. He writes of a starving squaw baiting a fish-hook with her own flesh, and he writes of the music of Debussy and the poetry of Henry Vaughan. In English literature we have to go back to Anglo-Saxon times to encounter so incongruous a collision of cultures. (221)

Frye uses the word "squaw" without a blink; nor does he consider that a real Chippewa woman might have baited her fishhook with something less demonstrative of her primitive indifference to pain. His reference to "Anglo-Saxon times" grounded Canadian poetry in an epic past, just as British literature was grounded in poems like *Beowulf*. A proper national literature evolved from the primitive to the modern, just as its people did.

After 1940, with minor exceptions, Johnson was effectively written out of anthologies, and thus the canon, until 1990. This raises the question of whether she can be considered to have been canonized before 1940. She became one of Canada's first literary celebrities, but as Gerson points out, "achieving celebrity is not the same thing as enjoying canonicity" (*Canadian*

Women in Print 196). And as Lorraine York makes clear in *Literary Celebrity in Canada*, popular success is usually antithetical to canonical status (35–36). *Flint and Feather* made the bestseller list in 1914 (Gerson, "Unique" 227). However, I do argue Johnson was canonized before 1940 because her poems would have been read by, and in all likelihood taught to, not only school-children but also university students.

University courses in Canadian literature became securely institutional-ized only in the 1960s; however, in the 1920s, courses were taught at Acadia, Bishop's, British Columbia, Dalhousie, Manitoba, Mount Allison, Queen's, and Western. McGill and Toronto included Canadian literature as part of courses on American literature in 1907 and 1934 respectively (Fee 22–23). Any Canadian anthology these courses used would have contained some of Johnson's poems. Robert Lecker notes that Watson and Pierce's *Our Cana-dian Literature* (1922) was "the first Canadian anthology to gain wide usage in Canadian classrooms" (75). It went through several editions. E. K. Broadus, head of the English Department at the University of Alberta, and his wife, Eleanor, produced two editions of a survey anthology, *A Book of Canadian Prose and Verse* (1923; 1934). Norman Shrive notes an upswing in Johnson's reputation in the 1920s, when her work was "assured space in a large num-ber of text-books and anthologies" recruited to serve Canadian nationalism (37); her resistant Indian poems were not included. "The Song My Paddle Sings" and "In the Shadows" were memorized by schoolchildren as part of "an indoctrination program, by which the maple leaf, the beaver and Jack Canuck became almost holy symbols" (37).

After the modernist turn, Klinck and Watters's *Canadian Anthology* (1955, 1966, 1974)—containing nothing by Johnson—held sway for a long time as a mixed-genre teaching anthology. (I used it in the first course I taught in Canadian literature, at the University of Toronto in 1974–75.) After a flurry of activity in the mid-to-late 1970s, with Douglas Daymond and Leslie Monkman attempting to bring both literature in French and Johnson into the canon, Bennett and Brown's two-volume *Anthology of Canadian Liter-ature in English* (Oxford UP, 1982)—containing nothing by Johnson—dom-inated through the 1980s. Only with the 1990 revision and abridgement of the two-volume edition did this anthology include her "A Cry from an Indian Wife," "Silhouette," and four other poems. After this, Johnson was back.

This shift during the 1990s came out of debates—called the "canon wars" in the United States and the "appropriation of voice" controversy in Can-ada—that revisited established national literary traditions. New national teaching anthologies emerged that attempted a broader inclusion of writers who were not white men. In the United States, this pitted the dominant

Norton anthologies (first two-volume edition 1979; now in its eighth edition; one-volume sixth ed. 2003) against the *Heath Anthology of American Literature* (two-volume edition first published in 1989; now in its eighth edition; one-volume edition 2003) and others. Although Johnson did not appear in the Heath anthology, two of her poems—"The Song My Paddle Sings" and "As Red Men Die"—appear in another revisionist textbook, *The Harper Anthology of American Literature* published in 1987 (McQuade et al.).

Now, Johnson's work is being reappropriated to many canons, some overlapping, since she appears in anthologies of Canadian and American literature, as well as anthologies of women's and Indigenous writing in both countries (see appendix 3). How Scott, still a major figure in Canadian anthologies, will fare in the future remains to be seen.

APPENDIX 1

Comparing Representation in Anthologies of the Poems of E. Pauline Johnson/Tekahionwake and Duncan Campbell Scott

	ANTHOLOGY AUTHOR, SHORT TITLE	PUB. YEAR	JOHNSON	SCOTT
1	Seranus, *Cdn Birthday Bk*	1887	1	0
2	Lighthall, *Songs of the Great Dominion*	1889	2	2
3	Wetherall, *Later Cdn Poems*	1893	Red Men +4	12
4	Rand, *Treasury of Cdn Verse*	1900	5	9
5	Caswell, *Cdn Singers & Their Songs*	1902	Corn Planter	1
6	Hardy, *Sel. from Cdn Poets*	1907	Lullaby +3	3
7	Burpee, *Flowers from a Cdn Garden*	1907	0	6
8	Campbell, *Oxford Book of Cdn Verse*	1913	Lullaby + 4	Forsaken, Half-breed +8
9	Garvin, *Cdn Poets*	1916	Pilot, Red Men +5	Half-breed, Morris (part) +6
10	Garvin, *Cdn Poets of the Great War*	1918	0	3
11	Dickie, D. J. *Cdn Poetry Book*	1922	Corn Planter, Husker, Lullaby, Qu'Appelle, Red Men +3	0
12	Watson & Pierce, *Our Cdn Lit* 3rd ed.	1923	5	6
13	Broadus, *Bk of Cdn Prose & Verse*	1923	3	0
14	Stephen, *Voice of Canada*	1926	Qu'Appelle	2
15	Garvin, *Cdn Poets*	1926	Pilot, Red Men + 4	Half-breed, Morris +6
16	Stephen, *Golden Treasury of Cdn Verse*	1928	Yaada +1	Half-breed +3
17	Garvin, *Cdn Verse for Boys and Girls*	1930	Yaada + 1	2
18	Broadus, *Bk of Cdn Prose & Verse*	1934	3	1
19	Carman & Pierce, *Our Cdn Lit*	1935	Husker +5	Forsaken, Half-breed, Mission +8
20	Brown, *Poetry* (Chicago)	1941	0	1
21	Gustafson, *Anth of Cdn Poetry*	1942	0	Half-breed, Watkwenies +3

Short titles are given for Indigenous-themed poems (for full titles see Table 1, page 52); the numbers indicate how many poems on other topics are included.

ANTHOLOGY AUTHOR, SHORT TITLE	PUB. YEAR	JOHNSON	SCOTT
22 Smith, *Bk of Cdn Poetry*	1943	1	Gull +4
23 Fairley, *Spirit*	1945	Cattle Thief (part)	0
24 Robins, *Pocketful of Canada*	1946	Husker	Onondaga
25 Smith, *Bk of Cdn Poetry*	1948	1	Gull +6
26 Dudek & Layton, *Cdn Poems 1850–1952*, 2nd ed.	1952	0	Place-Names +1
27 Carman, Pierce, Rhodenizer, *Cdn Poetry*	1954	Husker +3	Forsaken, Half-breed, Mission +5
28 Klinck & Watters, *Cdn Anth*	1955	0	Forsaken, Half-breed, Onondaga +8
29 Smith, *Bk of Cdn Poetry*	1957	1	Gull +1
30 Gustafson, *Penguin Bk of Cdn Verse*	1958	0	Onondaga, Watkwenies +5
31 Smith, *Oxford Bk of Cdn Verse*	1960	0	Gull, Night +5
32 Ross, *Poets of Confederation*	1960	0	Forsaken, Gull, Half-breed, Height, Mission, Onondaga, Powassen's +13
33 Klinck & Watters, *Cdn Anth*	1966	0	Forsaken, Half-breed, Height (part), Morris (part), Night, Onondaga + 5
34 Green & Sylvestre, *Century of Cdn Lit*	1967	1	1
35 Gustafson, *Penguin Bk of Cdn Verse*	1967	0	Onondaga, Watkwenies +5
36 Edwards et al., *Evolution Cdn Lit* Vol. 2	1973	Lullaby +4	Forsaken, Gull, Half-breed, Height, Onondaga, Powassen's +4
37 McLay, *Cdn Lit*	1974	Husker, Lullaby, Silhouette + 11	Forsaken, Gull, Half-breed, Mission, Night, Onondaga +8
38 Lochhead & Souster, *100 Cdn Poems*	1974	0	7

cont'd

	ANTHOLOGY AUTHOR, SHORT TITLE	PUB. YEAR	JOHNSON	SCOTT
39	Klinck & Watters, *Cdn Anth*	1974	0	Forsaken, Gull, Height, Onondaga +7
40	Weaver & Toye, *Oxford Anth*	1974	0	1
41	Pacey, *Sel. of Major Cdn Poets*	1974	0	Forsaken +5
42	Gustafson, *Penguin Bk of Cdn Verse*	1975	0	Onondaga, Watkwenies +5
43	Daymond & Monkman, *Lit in Canada*	1978	Husker, Silhouette +2	Forsaken, Gull, Height, Mission, Watkwenies +5
44	Colombo, *Poets of Canada*	1978	0	Forsaken
45	David & Lecker, *Cdn Poetry*	1982	0	Forsaken, Gull Mission, Night, Onondaga +2
46	Bennett & Brown, *Anth Cdn Lit* 1	1982	0	Forsaken, Height, Onondaga + 6
47	Atwood, *New Ox Bk of Cdn Verse*	1982	Ojistoh	Forsaken, Gull, Mission + 2
48	Gustafson, *Penguin Bk of Cdn Verse*	1984	0	Onondaga, Watkwenies +5
49	Lecker & David, *New Cdn Anth*	1988	0	Forsaken, Gull, Mission, Onondaga
50	Brown, Bennett, and Cooke, *Anth* rev. and abr. ed.	1990	Cry, Silhouette +4	Forsaken, Height, Onondaga +2
51	Gerson & Davies, *Cdn Poetry*	1994	Husker, Lullaby, Ojistoh, Silhouette +6	Forsaken, Gull, Height, Onondaga, Watkwenies +9
52	Ware, *Northern Romanticism*	2000	0	Forsaken, Gull, Height, Manitou, Mission, Morris, Night, Onondaga, Watkwenies +13
53	Bennett & Brown, *New Anth*	2002	Cry, Silhouette + 4	Forsaken, Height, Night, Onondaga +3
54	Lecker, *Open Country*	2007	Cattle Thief, Cry, Husker, Ojistoh, Pilot +1	Forsaken, Gull, Height, Mission, Onondaga +2
55	Sugars & Moss, *Cdn Lit in English*	2008	Cattle Thief, Cry, Husker +3	Onondaga, Place-names, Powassen's +2

Appendix 2
List of Canadian National Anthologies Surveyed for Table 1 and Appendix 1

Atwood, Margaret, ed. *The New Oxford Book of Canadian Verse*. Toronto: Oxford UP, 1982.

Broadus, Edmund Kemper, and Eleanor Hammond Broadus, eds. *A Book of Canadian Prose and Verse*. 1923. 2nd ed. Toronto: Macmillan, 1934.

Brown, E. K., ed. Canadian Number. *Poetry* (Chicago) 58.1 (1941).

Brown, Russell, and Donna Bennett, eds. *An Anthology of Canadian Literature in English*. Vol. 1. Toronto: Oxford UP, 1982.

———, eds. *A New Anthology of Canadian Literature in English*. Toronto: Oxford UP, 2002.

Brown, Russell, Donna Bennett, and Nathalie Cooke, eds. *An Anthology of Canadian Literature*. Rev. and abr. ed. Toronto: Oxford UP, 1990.

Burpee, Lawrence, ed. *Flowers from a Canadian Garden*. Toronto: Musson, 1909.

Campbell, W. W., ed. *The Oxford Book of Canadian Verse*. Toronto: Oxford UP, 1913.

Carman, Bliss, and Lorne Pierce, eds. *Our Canadian Literature: Representative Verse, English and French*. Toronto: Ryerson, 1935.

Carman, Bliss, Lorne Pierce, and V. B. Rhodenizer, eds. *Canadian Poetry in English*. Toronto: Ryerson, 1954.

Caswell, Edward S., ed. *Canadian Singers and Their Songs: A Collection of Portraits and Autograph Poems*. Toronto: McClelland, 1902.

Colombo, John Robert, ed. *Poets of Canada*. Edmonton: Hurtig, 1978.

David, Jack, and Robert Lecker, eds. *Canadian Poetry*. Toronto: New, 1982.

Daymond, Douglas, and Leslie Monkman, eds. *Literature in Canada*. Vol. 1. Toronto: Gage, 1975.

Dickie, D. J. *The Canadian Poetry Book*. London: Dent, 1922.

Dudek, Louis, and Irving Layton, eds. *Canadian Poems, 1850–1952*. 2nd ed. Toronto: Contact, 1952.

Edwards, Mary Jane, et al., eds. *The Evolution of Canadian Literature in English: 1867–1914*. Vol. 2. Ed. George L. Parker. Toronto: Holt, Rinehart and Winston, 1973.

Fairley, Margaret, ed. *Spirit of Canadian Democracy: A Collection of Writings from the Beginning to the Present Day*. Toronto: Progress, 1946.

Garvin, John W., ed. *Canadian Poems of the Great War*. Toronto: McClelland, 1918.

———, ed. *Canadian Poets*. 1916. Rev. ed. Toronto: McClelland, 1926.

———, ed. *Canadian Verse for Boys and Girls*. Toronto: Nelson, 1930.

Gerson, Carole, and Gwendolyn Davies, eds. *Canadian Poetry: From the Beginnings through the First World War*. Toronto: McClelland, 1994.

Green, H. Gordon, and Guy Sylvestre, eds. *A Century of Canadian Literature / Un siècle de littérature canadienne*. Toronto: Ryerson, 1967.

Gustafson, Ralph, ed. *Anthology of Canadian Poetry*. Harmondsworth, UK: Penguin, 1942.

———, ed. *The Penguin Book of Canadian Verse*. Harmondsworth, UK: Penguin, 1958. 3rd ed. 1975. 4th ed. 1984.

Hardy, E. A. *Selections from the Canadian Poets*. Toronto: Macmillan, 1907.

Klinck, C. F., and R. E. Watters, eds. *Canadian Anthology*. Toronto: Gage, 1955. 2nd ed. 1966. 3rd ed. 1974.

Where two or more editions of anthologies are listed, each edition was surveyed. *cont'd*

Lecker, Robert, ed. *Open Country: Canadian Literature in English.* Toronto: Thomson Nelson, 2007.

Lecker, Robert, and Jack David, eds. *New Canadian Anthology: Poetry and Short Fiction in English.* Scarborough: Nelson, 1988.

Lighthall, W. D., ed. *Songs of the Great Dominion.* London: Walter Scott, 1889.

Lochhead, Douglas, and Raymond Souster, eds. *One Hundred Poems of Nineteenth-Century Canada.* Toronto: Macmillan, 1974.

McLay, Catherine M., ed. *Canadian Literature: The Beginnings to the 20th Century.* Toronto: McClelland, 1974.

Pacey, Desmond, ed. *Selections from Major Canadian Writers: Poetry and Creative Prose in English.* Toronto: McGraw-Hill, 1974.

Rand, Theodore. H., ed. *A Treasury of Canadian Verse.* Toronto: Briggs, 1900.

Robins, John D., ed. *A Pocketful of Canada.* Toronto: Collins, 1946.

Ross, Malcolm, ed. *Poets of Confederation.* Toronto: McClelland, 1960.

Seranus [Harrison, Susan Frances], ed. *The Canadian Birthday Book.* Toronto: Robinson, 1887.

Smith, A. J. M. *The Book of Canadian Poetry: A Critical and Historical Anthology.* Chicago: U of Chicago P, 1943. 2nd ed. 1948. 3rd ed. 1957.

———, ed. *The Oxford Book of Canadian Verse.* Toronto: Oxford UP, 1960.

Stephen, A. M., ed. *The Golden Treasury of Canadian Verse.* Toronto: Dent, 1928.

———, ed. *The Voice of Canada: A Selection of Prose and Verse.* Toronto: Dent, 1926.

Sugars, Cynthia, and Laura Moss, eds. *Canadian Literature in English: Texts and Contexts.* Vol. 1. Toronto: Pearson Longman, 2009.

Ware, Tracy, ed. *Northern Romanticism: Poets of the Confederation.* Ottawa: Tecumseh, 2000.

Watson, Albert Durrant, and Lorne Pierce, eds. *Our Canadian Literature: Representative Prose and Verse.* 3rd ed. Toronto: Ryerson, 1923.

Weaver, Robert, and William Toye, eds. *The Oxford Anthology of Canadian Literature.* Toronto: Oxford UP, 1973.

Wetherall, James E., ed. *Later Canadian Poems.* Toronto: Copp Clark, 1983.

APPENDIX 3

The Representation of E. Pauline Johnson's Poems in Selected Anthologies

Anthologies of Indigenous Literature		
Cronyn, *Path on the Rainbow*	1918	2
Petrone, *First People, First Voices*	1983	Lullaby, Red Men
Moses & Goldie, *Anth of Cdn Native Lit* (same sel., 2nd ed. 1998, 3rd ed. 2005, 4th ed. 2013)	1992	Cattle Thief, Husker +2
Kilcup, *Native American Wmn's Writing, 1800–1924*	2000	Cattle Thief, Corn Planter, Husker, Lullaby, Quill Worker, Wolverine +13
Ramsey & Burlingame, *In Beauty I Walk*	2008	Cry, Husker Ojistoh, Quill Worker, Red Men +6
Anthologies of Women's Writing		
Sullivan, *Poetry by Cdn Women*	1989	Husker, Ojistoh, Wolverine +1
Kilcup, *Nineteenth-Century American Women Writers*	1997	Corn Planter, Husker +4
Campbell, *Hidden Rooms: Early Cdn Women Poets*	2000	Cry, Husker, Ojistoh, Silhouette, Yaada +15
Gilbert & Gubar, *Norton Anth of Lit by Women*, 3rd ed.	2007	1

Appendix 4

List of Anthologies Surveyed for Appendix 3

Campbell, Wanda, ed. *Hidden Rooms: Early Canadian Women Poets.* London, ON: Canadian Poetry, 2000.

Cronyn, George W., ed. *Path on the Rainbow: An Anthology of Songs and Chants from the Indians of North America.* New York: Liveright, 1918. Sacred-texts.com. Web. 15 May 2013.

Gilbert, Sandra M., and Susan Gubar, eds. *Norton Anthology of Literature by Women.* 3rd ed. Vol. 1. London: Norton, 2007.

Kilcup, Karen L., ed. *Native American Women's Writing, 1800–1924.* London: Blackwell, 2000.

———. *Nineteenth-Century American Women Writers.* Cambridge, MA: Blackwell, 1997.

Petrone, Penny, ed. *First People, First Voices.* Toronto: U of Toronto P, 1983.

Ramsey, Jarold, and Lori Burlingame, eds. *In Beauty I Walk: The Literary Roots of Native Writing.* Albuquerque: U of New Mexico P, 2008.

Sullivan, Rosemary, ed. *Poems by Canadian Women.* Toronto: Oxford UP, 1989.

NOTES

1 "Indian" is the term that they both used; I prefer either national labels or, if an over-arching term is needed, Indigenous or Native. The term "Indian" was legislated in the Indian Act, 1876; the term "Aboriginal" in the Constitution Act of 1982. I use "Indian" to refer to the stereotype or representation.

2 Gerson notes that "he always viewed Johnson as an equal," including her in what he called "the 1860 group" ("Recuperating" 171).

3 Some are "Indian" only tangentially or by allusion: "The Archers," "La Crosse," "The Train Dogs," and "The Wolf." "The Ballad of Lalloo" was posthumously published.

4 Scott told E. K. Brown that "Night Burial in the Forest" was about loggers (Adams n. pag.).

5 He retitled the poem "The Onondaga Madonna" for its first book publication in 1898.

6 For example, she recited "As Red Men Die," "Avenger," and "A Cry from an Indian Wife" in 1892 in Toronto; "The Cattle Thief" and "Ojistoh" in Winnipeg in 1898; "Wolverine" in 1899 in Winnipeg; "The Cattle Thief" and "A Legend of the Qu'Appelle Valley" in 1904 in Vancouver (Johnson Fonds, Box 6, File 6, Mills Memorial Library, McMaster University). Detailed records do not exist for all her performances.

7 The disconnect between the poet herself and "we, the men of Canada" is striking: most women born in Canada would wait until 1918 for the federal vote; Native men and women waited until 1960.

8 Indeed, the aestheticist move to "art for art's sake" was not a simple resistance to politics per se, but a resistance to treating language as a functional code, an approach that takes language as literal and discounts wordplay, wit, ambiguity, and desire.

9 Indeed, Lighthall's anthology depicted the reading of his anthology as a canoe voyage: "the paddles are ready, let us start!" (Introd. xxxvii).

10 Johnson also canvassed this topic in "Dawendine" and many of her prose pieces, including "My Mother," about her own parents' happy marriage. Her point was not that all mixed marriages were happy, but that they could be, although social prejudice hindered this outcome (as in her "A Red Girl's Reasoning").

11 Indigenous literary works often tackle this subject, e.g., Marie Clements's play *The Unnatural and Accidental Women* (2000) and Tomson Highway's novel *Kiss of the Fur Queen* (1998). Several poets memorialize Helen Betty Osborne, whose brutal murder by four white men went unpunished for sixteen years (Manitoba).

12 Such abandonment does feature in Indigenous stories, as in European ones, and evoked similar disquiet. In the Nipmuck story "The Useless Grandfather," the boy ordered to abandon his grandfather brings back half the blanket he was told to wrap him in. His father asks why, and the boy replies it is for the father when *he* becomes old (Legends). Who left the old woman in "Hansel and Gretel" in the forest to fend for herself?

13 In 1931, Marius Barbeau of the National Museum of Canada wrote this on the pre-contact Indian: "Formerly they idled away their existence in squalor and crass ignorance" (qtd. in Donald B. Smith 161); he collaborated with Scott (Dragland, *Floating* 259).

14 Johnson revised the conclusion after its first publication to make her point even clearer (Strong-Boag and Gerson 150). The poem overstates Indigenous involvement in what was, essentially, a Métis resistance. Nonetheless, Big Bear and Poundmaker were convicted of treason. See Stonechild and Waiser.

15 The land granted to the Iroquois in Canada by Governor Haldimand in 1784 replaced their territories lost to the United States, compensation for the Mohawk's vital military support during the American Revolution. The history of the reduction of the grant to only 5 percent of the original is complex and disputed. Although much of it

was leased or sold to provide funds for the benefit of the Iroquois, few leases were paid, and large sums from land sales were either stolen by corrupt officials or allocated to other government purposes. What money was paid out was rigidly controlled (Catapano 263). See also Six Nations Lands and Resources.

16 Ojistoh's trajectory differs from that of two of Johnson's other poetic heroines, Dawendine and Yaada, who abandon their people for an enemy warrior. However, neither is married, and their love for the enemy man saves their people from further war.

17 They did lose touch with their feminist tradition, however; first-wave feminists had to be recuperated in the 1960s and 1970s by the second wave, having been repudiated by modernists, men and women alike. As Dean Irvine shows, the many women modernists who edited important literary magazines were written out of literary history too.

18 See Long for an account of the differences between the treaty commissioners' oral promises and what was written in the treaty.

WORKS CITED

Adams, John Coldwell. "Confederation Voices: Seven Canadian Poets." *Canadian Poetry*. London, ON: U of Western Ontario P, n.d. Web. 9 May 2013.

Austin, Mary. Introduction. *Path on the Rainbow: An Anthology of Songs and Chants from the Indians of North America*. Ed. George W. Cronyn. New York: Liveright, 1918. xii–xxii. Web. 5 May 2013.

Barman, Jean. "Taming Aboriginal Sexuality: Gender, Power and Race in British Columbia: 1850–1900." *BC Studies* 115/116 (1997/98): 237–66. Print.

———. *The West beyond the West: A History of British Columbia*. Rev. ed. Toronto: U of Toronto P, 1996. Print.

Bennett, Paula Bernat. *Poets in the Public Sphere: The Emancipatory Project of American Women's Poetry, 1800–1900*. Princeton: Princeton UP, 2003. Print.

Bentley, D. M. R. *The Confederation Group of Canadian Poets, 1880–97*. Toronto: U of Toronto P, 2004. Print.

———. "Shadows in the Soul: Racial Haunting in the Poetry of Duncan Campbell Scott." *University of Toronto Quarterly* 75.2 (2006): 753–70. Print.

"Bill C-31." *First Nations Studies Program*. U of British Columbia, 2009. Web. 21 August 2013.

Bourdieu, Pierre. *The Field of Cultural Production: Essays on Art and Literature*. Ed. Randal Johnson. Cambridge: Polity, 1993. Print.

Carter, Sarah. *The Importance of Being Monogamous: Marriage and Nation Building in Western Canada to 1915*. Edmonton: U of Alberta P, 2008. Print.

Catapano, Andrea Lucille. "The Rising of the Ongwehònwe: Sovereignty, Identity, and Representation on the Six Nations Reserve." Diss. Stony Brook University, 2007. Web. 2 April 2013.

Chapman, Mary, and Glenn Hendler. Introduction. *Sentimental Men: Masculinity and the Politics of Affect in American Culture*. By Chapman and Hendler. Berkeley: U of California P, 1999. 1–13. Print.

Chater, Nancy. "Technologies of Remembrance: Literacy Criticism and Duncan Campbell Scott's Indian Poems." MA thesis. University of Toronto, 1999. Web. 22 May 2013.

Coleman, Daniel. *White Civility: The Literary Project of English Canada*. Toronto: U of Toronto P, 2006. Print.

Conrad, Joseph. *Heart of Darkness*. 1899. 2nd ed. Ed. D. C. R. A. Goonetilleke. Peterborough: Broadview, 1999. Print.

Dragland, Stan. *Floating Voice: Duncan Campbell Scott and the Literature of Treaty 9*. Concord: Anansi, 1994. Print.

———. Introduction. *Duncan Campbell Scott: Addresses, Essays, and Reviews*. Ed. Leslie Ritchie. London: Canadian Poetry, 2000. xi–xlii. Print.

Eliot, T. S. "War-paint and Feathers." Rev. of *The Path on the Rainbow*. *Athenaeum* 4668 (1919): 1036. Web. 16 May 2013.

Fee, Margery. "Canadian Literature and English Studies in the Canadian University." *Essays on Canadian Writing* 48 (1992–93): 20–40. Print.

Frye, Northrop. *The Bush Garden: Essays on the Canadian Imagination*. Toronto: Anansi, 1995. Print.

Gerson, Carole. "Anthologies and the Canon of Early Canadian Women Writers." *New Contexts of Canadian Criticism*. Ed. Ajay Heble, Donna Palmateer Pennee, and J. R. (Tim) Struthers. Peterborough: Broadview, 1997. 146–67. Print.

———. *Canadian Women in Print, 1750–1918*. Waterloo: Wilfrid Laurier UP, 2010. Print.

———. "Pauline Johnson and Celebrity in Canada: 'The Most Unique Fixture in the Literary World of Today.'" *Women Writers and the Artifacts of Celebrity in the Long Nineteenth Century*. Ed. Ann R. Hawkins and Maura Ives. Farnham: Ashgate, 2012. 219–32. Print.

———. "Recuperating from Modernism: Pauline Johnson's Challenge to Literary History." *Women and Literary History: "For There She Was."* Ed. Katherine Binhammer and Jeanne Wood. Newark: U of Delaware P, 2003. 167–86. Print.

Gerson, Carole, and Veronica Strong-Boag, eds. Introduction. *E. Pauline Johnson / Tekahionwake: Collected Poems and Selected Prose*. By Gerson and Strong-Boag. Toronto: U of Toronto P, 2002. xiii–xliv. Print.

Gray, Charlotte. *Flint and Feather: The Life and Times of E. Pauline Johnson*. Toronto: Harper Flamingo, 2002. Print.

Guillory, John. *Cultural Capital: The Problem of Literary Canon Formation*. Chicago: U of Chicago P, 1993. Print.

Irvine, Dean Jay. *Editing Modernity: Women and Little-Magazine Cultures in Canada, 1916–1956*. Toronto: U of Toronto P, 2008. Print.

Johnson, E. Pauline / Tekahionwake. *E. Pauline Johnson / Tekahionwake: Collected Poems and Selected Prose*. Ed. Carole Gerson and Veronica Strong-Boag. Toronto: U of Toronto P, 2002. Print.

Keller, Betty. *Pauline: A Biography of Pauline Johnson*. Vancouver: Douglas & McIntyre, 1981. Print.

Kelly, Peggy. "Anthologies and the Canonization Process: A Case Study of the English-Canadian Literary Field, 1920–1950." *Studies in Canadian Literature* 25.1 (2000): 73–94. Print.

Krotz, Sarah. "Shadows of Indian Title: The Territorial Underpinnings of 'The Height of Land.'" *Canadian Literature* 204 (2010): 85–101. Print.

Lecker, Robert. *Keepers of the Code: English-Canadian Literary Anthologies and the Representation of Nation*. Toronto: U of Toronto P, 2013. Print.

Long, John. *Treaty No. 9: Making the Agreement to Share the Land in Far Northern Ontario in 1905*. Montreal: McGill-Queen's UP, 2010. Print.

Manitoba. "The Death of Helen Betty Osborne." Aboriginal Justice Implementation Commission. *Report of the Aboriginal Justice Inquiry of Manitoba*. November 1999. Web. 20 August 2013.

McQuade, Donald, et al., eds. *The Harper American Literature*. Vol. 2. New York: Harper, 1987.

Monture, Rick. *We Share Our Matters: Two Centuries of Writing and Resistance at Six Nations of the Grand River*. Winnipeg: U of Manitoba P, 2014. Print.

Parker, Arthur C. "A Certain Important Element of the Indian Problem." *American Indian Magazine* 3.1 (1915): 24–38. Print.

Salem, Lisa. "'Her Blood Is Mingled with Her Ancient Foes': The Concepts of Blood, Race and 'Miscegenation' in the Poetry and Short Fiction of Duncan Campbell Scott." *Studies in Canadian Literature* 18.1 (1993): n. pag. Web. 28 April 2013.

Salem-Wiseman, Lisa. "'Verily, the white man's ways were the best': Duncan Campbell Scott, Native Culture and Assimilation." *Studies in Canadian Literature* 21.2 (1996): 120–42. Web. 28 April 2013.

Scott, Duncan Campbell. *Selected Poetry*. Ed. Glenn Clever. Ottawa: Tecumseh, 1974. Print.

Shrive, Norman. "What Happened to Pauline?" *Canadian Literature* 13 (1962): 25–38. Print.

Six Nations Lands and Resources. *Land Rights: A Global Solution for the Six Nations of the Grand River*. n.d. Web. 24 May 2013.

Smith, A. J. M. Introduction. *The Book of Canadian Poetry: A Critical and Historical Anthology*. By Smith. 2nd ed. Chicago: U of Chicago P, 1948. Print. 1–36.

Smith, Donald B. *From the Land of Shadows: The Making of Grey Owl*. 1990. Vancouver: Douglas & McIntyre, 1991. Print.

Spivak, Gayatri. *A Critique of Postcolonial Reason: Toward a History of the Vanishing Present*. Cambridge: Harvard UP, 1999. Print.

Stonechild, Blair, and Bill Waiser. *Loyal till Death: Indians and the North-west Rebellion*. Calgary: Fifth House, 1997. Print.

Strong-Boag, Veronica, and Carole Gerson. *Paddling Her Own Canoe: The Times and Texts of E. Pauline Johnson*. Toronto: U of Toronto P, 2000. Print.

Titley, E. Brian. *A Narrow Vision: Duncan Campbell Scott and the Administration of Indian Affairs in Canada*. Vancouver: U of British Columbia P, 1986. Print.

Untermeyer, Louis. "The Indian as Poet." *The Dial* 66.7 (8 March 1919): 240. Print.

"The Useless Grandfather." *Legends of the Nipmuck People: The Story of the Pine Hawk*. n.p., n.d. Web. 16 May 2013. http://ab.mec.edu/pinehawk/legends/grandfather.html

Wilmott, Glen. "Paddled by Pauline." *Canadian Poetry* 46 (2000): n. pag. Web. 6 May 2013.

York, Lorraine. *Literary Celebrity in Canada*. Toronto: U of Toronto P, 2007. Print.

The Poetry of the Canoe

William Douw Lighthall's *Songs of the Great Dominion*

D. M. R. Bentley

I
GENESIS AND DEVELOPMENT

> *"It is doubtful whether any first-class canoe is the result of any one person's study. The builder's shop is the mill, he is the miller. The ideas of others are grists ..."*
> —J. H. Rushton[1]

Sometime in 1887, as he was in the process of mustering the Confederation group of poets—Bliss Carman, Archibald Lampman, William Wilfred Campbell, Frederick George Scott, Duncan Campbell Scott, and himself—Charles G. D. Roberts apparently wrote to William Sharp, the editor of the Canterbury Poets Series of the London publisher Walter Scott, urging him to commission an anthology of Canadian poetry.[2] According to Roberts, he also wrote, perhaps early in 1888, to the editor of Walter Scott's Camelot Series, Ernest Rhys, declaring his willingness to "undertake" such an anthology "whenever called upon," an offer that Rhys accepted, for on 7 May 1888 Roberts told another correspondent that "Rhys has just written ... asking if I would edit a volume of Canadian verse" (*Collected Letters* 77). In the meantime, on 21 April, the Montreal lawyer, philosopher, novelist, and poet William Douw Lighthall had been inspired by seeing a copy of Douglas Sladen's *Australian Ballads and Rhymes: Poems Inspired by Life and Scenery in Australia and New Zealand* (1888) in the Canterbury Poets series to send a proposal for such a volume to Walter Scott.[3] This was duly forwarded to Sharp, who had independently conceived of a Canadian equivalent of Sladen's anthology that he intended to offer to Roberts;[4] however, on 19 June, "after careful consideration," he commissioned the volume from Lighthall for both the Canterbury Poets series and for Walter Scott's larger-format Windsor series.[5] It was a decision to which Roberts gladly acceded, ostensibly because he was "overwhelmingly busy" with his writing, his work as a professor at King's College in Windsor, Nova Scotia, and his editing of another anthology, *Poems of Wild Life* (1888),[6] for the Canterbury Poets series, but probably also because, as the widely acknowledged leader of a new generation of Canadian poets, he hoped to influence Lighthall's conception of the anthology and choice of its contents. So began *Songs of the Great Dominion: Voices from the Forests and Waters, the Settlements and Cities of Canada*, "selected and edited by William Douw Lighthall, M.A., of Montreal"[7] and released by Walter Scott in the spring of 1889, the most important Canadian anthology of the Confederation period and arguably the most editorially vexed and problematic anthology in the history of Canadian literature.

That Roberts was indeed intent on influencing Lighthall's conception of *Songs of the Great Dominion* as well as its content is evident even in the letter of 23 May 1888 in which he gracefully bows out of the project and states that he "will write to Professor Rhys, Mr Scott, and my friend Mr Sharp, emphasizing ... [Lighthall's] fitness for the undertaking" (*Collected Letters* 77).[8] Immediately following this gesture (the wording of which was surely intended to display his own superior stature in the literary world of the metropolitan centre to Lighthall), Roberts suggests that the anthology "should aim to show *the best* as well as the most Canadian, of our poetry! It should not, I think, be a *specialized* collection" (*Collected Letters* 77). What he meant by this is evident from his statement earlier in the letter that "*Poems of Wild Life* ... is a thoroughly cosmopolitan collection, though it contains Canadian poems. There is no clash here!": in making his selections, Lighthall should not focus only on manifestly Canadian subjects and themes; rather, he should include poems of high quality on any subject or theme, be it, say, a classical myth, an Arthurian Legend, or a philosophical abstraction—all of which, of course, are abundantly present in Roberts's *Orion, and Other Poems* (1880) and *In Divers Tones* (1886). "[L]et me say a word concerning that perpetual injunction to our verse-writers to choose Canadian themes only," Roberts had written in "The Beginnings of Canadian Literature" (1883), adding with an eye surely on his own work: "[i]t is true we have much poetical wealth unappropriated in our broad and magnificent landscapes, in our seasons that alternate so swiftly between gorgeousness and gloom, in the stirring episodes scattered so abundantly through parts of our early history; but let us not think we are prohibited from drawing a portion of our material from lands where now the very dust is man" (*Selected* 258–59).[9] As for Canadian poets, so for the anthologists of Canadian poetry: *Songs of the Great Dominion* could be thoroughly Canadian *and* contain "cosmopolitan" poems; it should reflect the presence of both types of poetry and their corresponding literary stances within Canada's national space.

As soon as Lighthall had contacted him with the news that he would be editing *Songs of the Great Dominion*, Roberts began to press upon him the merit of Carman's work. "Did you see his 'Low Tide on Grand Pré' in the *Atlantic* about a year ago?" he asked on 23 May, and on 30 September, probably in response to the biographical note on Carman that Lighthall had by then written for the anthology (which describes him as "[p]erhaps the most original of Canadian lyrists" [449]): "Carman *is* the most original *lyric* genius we have produced"; "Low Tide on Grand Pré" is "exquisite" and "those strange, fresh & Canadian poems, 'First Croak,' & the 'Red Swan,'" are also admirable (*Collected Letters* 77, 87). No doubt in part because of Roberts's advocacy, Carman's lyricism is well represented in *Songs of the Great Dominion* by "In Apple Time," "Carnations in Winter," and "In Lyric Season," as well as "Low Tide on Grand Pré" and "The Wraith of the Red Swan," which occupies no fewer than six pages and is glossed by a note repeating almost verbatim the information provided by Roberts that refers to Carman's "favourite birch bark canoe, so named by him from the phenomenal rosiness of its bark material" (157; see *Collected Letters* 87 and 89). "Carman has earned special honour for the originality and finish of his lyrics," observes Lighthall in the introduction to the anthology, but his final word on the poet in the "Notes Biographical and Bibliographical" that conclude the volume may well be the principal reason behind his inclusion: despite the appearance of his poems in the "*Atlantic Monthly* and *Century*," "[h]e is enthusiastically patriotic" (xxx; 449).

That Lighthall had no intention whatsoever of deviating from his own patriotic agenda for *Songs of the Great Dominion* is fully evident in a printed letter dated 2 July that he circulated to a large number of Canadian poets and cognoscenti. Giving as his goal "to make up a book *thoroughly representative of, and to be a credit to Canada, in England and throughout the world*," the letter states with equal emphasis that "[w]hat are most desired are (besides the best literary bits) pieces and passages *distinctive of Canada*" (Lighthall, "Correspondence" Carton 1). As telling here as Lighthall's italics of emphasis is his relegation of literary quality to parentheses, for the hierarchy thus typographically reinforced flies in the face, not merely of Roberts's cosmopolitanism, but of Sharp's insistence in accepting his proposal on 8 May that he should "aim" for "[v]ariety, representativeness, and *quality*—but not quantity *per se*— ... *quality* above all" (Lighthall, "Correspondence" Carton 1; Sharp's emphasis). As will soon become apparent, Lighthall's failure to follow

Sharp's instructions in this and in other respects would radically alter the anthology that that was dispatched to Walter Scott on 22 September and, after forwarding, acknowledged by Sharp on 11 October.

Among the first to respond to Lighthall's printed letter was Roberts. "I approve of your plan of making the vol[ume] distinctively Canadian," he wrote on 7 July, and then used the opportunity once again to urge Lighthall to broaden his criteria for inclusion in the anthology:

> but [I] feel at the same time that it would fail to represent fully the develop-ment of Canadian song if it *absolutely* excluded such work as is, like much of the best English & American work, *cosmopolitan*! Will you consider this point, & tell me what you think of it? I should like my own poetry to [be] rep-resented in the collection chiefly by such work as "The Tantramar Revisited," "On the Brink," "In the Afternoon," "Canada" and so forth.... But I would like my work on more *general* subjects not to go *entirely* unrepresented. (*Collected Letters* 84)

Lighthall's reply has not survived, but on the evidence of *Songs of the Great Dominion* he was unmoved: all thirteen of Roberts's poems in the anthology are "distinctively Canadian," including the two pieces from the *Orion* volume, "The Maple" and "To Winter." "I *agree* with your selection," Roberts would eventually tell Lighthall on 30 September; "moreover, heartily, seeing that you desire to make the collection Canadian in tone throughout" (*Collected Letters* 87). Lighthall did not leave Roberts's cosmopolitan work entirely unrecog-nized, however: "[h]is pure Hellenic poems must be dismissed from consid-eration here," runs a passage in the introduction to the anthology, "but ... it [is] proper to say of them that they have obtained for him a growing rec-ognition in the ranks of general English literature; and that his feeling for beauty of colour and form is so really artistically correct as well as rich, that he deserves a permanent place in the Gallery of *Word-painters*" (xxiv).

Nor did Roberts waste the opportunity in responding to Lighthall's printed letter of 7 July to engage in some further nepotism. Drawing Lighthall's attention to the fact that his younger sister, Jane Elizabeth Gost-wyck Roberts, is also a poet, he promises to "submit ... some of her MSS" to him for consideration (*Collected Letters* 84). He then introduces "*Barry Stratton*," a cousin of his and Carman's, saying only that he is "a Fredericton youth, with a fine ear for melody & a deficient education" who has "pub-lished a volume called *Lays of Love* [1884]" and "some better things in the *University Monthly*, in Fredericton." In both cases, Lighthall acceded to his friend's advocacy: the former has a substantial poem, "In the Golden Birch," in *Songs of the Great Dominion* and is said to "write ... verse with good 'body,' and of a tone curiously reflecting the family likeness" (461), and the latter has no fewer than four poems in the anthology, including one, "A Dream Fulfilled," that runs to over two pages and two others that run to two pages each—in all one fewer poem and page than Lampman. Stratton's response to the anthology is unknown, but the other members of the clan who benefited from Roberts's good offices were delighted, and if he himself was residually dismayed by Lighthall's "distinctively Canadian" emphasis when he saw the published anthology, he showed it only by omitting to comment. "*Songs of the Great Dominion* came to hand on Saturday, and we are all in delight over it," he told Lighthall on 10 June 1889. "Carman ... & Janie ... send regards & many congratulations. They think the editing is admirable, & the material fine. For me, I cannot thank you. What you say [in the Introduction and "Notes Biographical and Bibliographical"] gratifies me so deeply that I know not how to speak of it; but I shall try to deserve it in the future" (Roberts, *Collected Letters* 109).

In addition to his remarks on his sister and cousin in his letter of 7 July, Roberts's specific suggestions for poems to include are contained in "A Partial List of Canadian Verse-Writers, from most of whom ... [Lighthall] will perhaps wish to make selections" (*Collected Letters* 84). While several of the poets named—John Reade, Charles Mair, Lampman, and probably Campbell—were known personally or through correspondence to Roberts, others appear to have been known to him only through their work: Kate Seymour MacLean had published *The Coming of the Princess, and Other Poems* in 1881; Isabella Valancy Crawford had published *Old Spooks's Pass, Malcolm's Katie, and Other Poems* in 1884; Phillips Stewart had published *Poems* in 1887; and Mary Morgan had published *Poems and Translations* in the same year. In accordance with Roberts's view that most of his "best [material] will come from our younger writers," most of the poets on his list are more or less contemporary, if not always young (others include Arthur Weir, Charles Weir, John Hunter-Duvar, Agnes Maule Machar ["Fidelis"], and Susie Frances Harrison ["Seranus"]), but several come from the period that he tropes as the "night" before the "dawn" of Canadian poetry: Charles Heavysege, Joseph Howe, Charles Sangster, Alexander McLachlan, and Charles Pelham Mulvaney (*Collected Letters* 82).

Between 2 July and 22 September Lighthall worked like a frenetic beaver at assembling the contents of *Songs of the Great Dominion*.[10] Within two weeks of the date of his printed letter, he had replies not only from Roberts, but also from, among others, Sangster, McLachlan, Machar, MacLean, William Kirby, James Bain, William Ryan, and Arthur John Lockhart ("Pastor Felix"). In the ensuing two months, submissions and suggestions came from a host of other poets, including Stratton, Mair, Hunter-Duvar, John Henry

Brown, Nicholas Flood Davin, William Wye Smith, Hiram Ladd Spencer, Sir Daniel Wilson, E. Pauline Johnson, and, of course, Campbell, Carman, and belatedly—on 14 September—Lampman. Besides being among the very earliest to respond to Lighthall's call, Lockhart was also the most indefatigable in his suggestions for poets and poems for consideration: in July alone he sent no fewer than five lengthy and detailed letters, and a letter of 9 August contains a list of fifty-seven poets for consideration. Very clearly, Lockhart served—or at least saw himself—as a key advisor in the selection of poets and poems for the anthology. Perhaps in part as a reward for his labours, two of his poems are included in *Songs of the Great Dominion*, and an excerpt from his *The Masque of the Minstrels* (1887) serves as its poetic preface.

Throughout the fall of 1888—long after Lighthall had sent the manuscript to Sharp—the continuing epistolary conversation about Canadian poetry between him and Roberts is indicative of what, as will be seen, his correspondence with Sharp confirms: he was continuing to send poems and suggestions for poems to be included in *Songs of the Great Dominion* long after its general editor's work was well advanced. "I should feel some doubt as to [George] Martin's 'Marguerite'! Is it not weak & prosaic?" wrote Roberts on 18 November, adding: "I should not question anything else but *Jephthah's Daughter*. Meseems Heavysege were better represented by *Saul* alone. What think you? Why not put in [Hunter-] Duvar's *Enamorado*? Has good poetry in it. So glad you like Lockhart! What of Evan McColl[11] & [George Frederick] *Cameron?*" (*Collected Letters* 96). The published volume reveals that, once again, he accepted parts of Roberts's advice and ignored others: *Songs of the Great Dominion* includes an excerpt from Martin's *Marguerite* (1887) and a poem from Cameron's *Lyrics of Freedom, Love and Death* (1887), but, presumably because Lighthall was steadfast in his resolve to select "Canadian" rather than "cosmopolitan" material, Heavysege is represented by three nature sonnets from *Jephthah's Daughter* (1865) and Hunter-Duvar by excerpts from *De Roberval* and "The Emigration of the Fairies" (both published in 1888).

As important a factor in shaping *Songs of the Great Dominion*, in securing Roberts's eventual agreement with Lighthall's emphasis on the distinctively Canadian, and in fostering the friendship between the two men that burgeoned during its genesis was a shared commitment to Canadian nationalism and in due course "Canadianism"—a term variously defined in 1888 and 1889 as a "love for Canada" that is stronger than loyalty to Britain and "the natural feature of every literary product of a Canadian pen" (Bentley 92, 321). The writer who defined "Canadianism" simply as "love for Canada" was Watson Griffin, the author of a novel unpromisingly entitled *Twok* (1887), a fervent anti-annexationist, and a friend of Lighthall. "Count me in with you & the author of *Twok*. *Of course* I'm into it," Roberts told Lighthall on

6 October 1888 in what may well be a statement of solidarity with fellow believers in Canadianism, which is present in all but name in Roberts's next letter to Lighthall on 20 October: "[y]ea, indeed, let us who are true Canadians ever strengthen each others' hands, and unite to keep pure our ideals. The difficulty I feel is to keep sane & dignified in my tone when I speak of Canada. The name thrills me, and I have difficulty in keeping foolish tears out of my eyes when I am talking to my classes of Canadian possibilities & aspirations" (*Collected Letters* 90). Some two weeks later Roberts does use "*Canadianism*" in a letter to Lighthall, albeit only in connection with his hope to secure a professorship at the University of Toronto. Some two weeks later still, the word appears in a literary context, specifically in connection with Roberts's presidency of a society at King's College named in honour of Thomas Chandler Haliburton: "[t]he Society includes all the students but three or four, most of the Professors, many town men, & some outside members. I talk *Canadianism* all the time to the members. We have a literary programme, of Canadian color" (*Collected Letters* 92, 96). Before, between, and after these letters, Roberts's comments in letters to Lighthall about his own literary ambitions—a "Quebec ... work ... a series of Canadian idylls ... a narrative poem of Acadian life"—and about his friend's "Canada Not Last," "The Battle of Chateauguay," and *The Young Seigneur* (1888)—"pure Canadianism, & it took hold beautifully" (*Collected Letters* 99, 97, 102, 98) at the Haliburton Society—leave no room to doubt that Canadianism played a major role not merely in their friendship, but also in the conception and construction of *Songs of the Great Dominion*. While the anthology was making its way through the editing process, Lighthall published a long letter on the "The Sentiment of Nationality" in the 10 November issue of the *Montreal Daily Witness* and received confirmation that on 1 December he had been elected a member of the Haliburton Society.[12] Closer to home, the 23 January 1889 roster of members of the newly formed Society for Canadian Literature in Montreal included Lighthall, Griffin, and several of the poets in *Songs of the Great Dominion* (Lighthall, "Correspondence" Carton 3).[13] Clearly, the imminent publication of the anthology encouraged Lighthall to become a public advocate of Canadian nationalism and gave added impetus to his commitment to the production and promulgation of Canadian literature.

No less important than nationalism in the structure and content of the *Songs of the Great Dominion* was imperialism, a concept that gained momentum and credibility in the aftermath of the first Colonial Conference, which was convened in London in 1887 at the request of the Imperial Federation League and with the aim of strengthening the ties between Britain and her colonies. While the preliminary plan for the volume that Lighthall sent to Sharp on 6 June 1888 includes a section entitled "Nationality," this is not

complemented as it is in the published anthology by one on "The Imperial Spirit" (Lighthall, "Correspondence" Carton 1). Nevertheless, Lighthall
assured Sharp in the same letter that imperialism would be the "key-note"
of his proposed introduction, and while soliciting poems he apparently let it
be known that the anthology would have an imperial component—at least,
that is what Sarah Anne Curzon conveyed to Mair, who told Lighthall on
23 July that, such "being the case," "it is my duty to serve your purpose"
(Lighthall, "Correspondence" Carton 1). In fact, by early June, imperialism
was already an important part of the conversation between Lighthall and
Roberts with regard to the three alternatives that have traditionally faced
Canada: annexation to the United States, complete independence from Britain, or continuation within the British Empire. As Carl Berger has long since
shown in *The Sense of Power: Studies in the Ideas of Canadian Imperialism, 1867–1914*, the spectre of annexation during the post-Confederation
period led increasingly to the recognition by many Canadian nationalists
that Canada's future as a nation would be better guaranteed, not by independence, but by remaining within a federated empire. One such Canadian was
Roberts, who concluded his letter of 2 June with a position statement that
again appears to be a response to comments by Lighthall: "[a]s to Canada's
destiny, though primarily an Independent, I have Federation sympathies.
Am intensely anti-annexationist. Federation on *certain lines* would suit me
thoroughly. But Canadian autonomy would have to be absolutely secured.
England should be simply *Primus inter pares* [first among equals]" (*Collected
Letters* 82). "Annexation ... I believe would be bad for both countries," he
told the American poet Richard Watson Gilder on 16 July; "Imp[erial] Fed-
[eration] is just now making the best stand against it, so I'll help Imp[erial]
Fed[eration]. Federationists & Independents need to join their forces just now
in Canada" (*Collected Letters* 86). Here was the soil from which the "mutually
strengthening" (Smith 6) combination of Canadianism and imperialism in
Songs of the Great Dominion sprang. By helping to consolidate the nation
and align it with the Empire, the anthology would help to protect it against
the threat of annexation.

Also part of that soil from which *Songs of the Great Dominion* grew was
what Lighthall called "New Utilitarianism" or "Spiritualized Happiness Theory," a philosophy that he first expounded at length in 1888 in his *Sketch
of the New Utilitarianism*, which he sent to Roberts in September or early
October of that year (see *Collected Letters* 89). Derived in large measure from
a marriage of Hegelian historicism to the neo-Kantianism of the English philosopher and political theorist T. H. Green, whose 1883 and 1886 books on
ethics and political obligation place emphasis on rights and responsibilities
over and against individualism in the advancement of societies and nations,

"New Utilitarianism" is a form of evolutionary idealism centred on the belief that a supreme directive force—the "Mysterious Power"[14]—is willing all life to progress upwards toward a condition of happiness measured by quality rather than, as is the case with Utilitarianism per se, quantity. It was a way of thinking that meshed very well with Canadianism and Imperial Federation, which are installed in tandem in the opening pages of *Songs of the Great Dominion* well before the two sections entitled "The Imperial Spirit" and "The New Nationality," the first with two lines from Frederick George Scott's "In Memoriam" for "*Those Killed in the North-West, 1885*" that appear on the anthology's title page—"All the future lies before us / Glorious in that sunset land"—and the second with Lighthall's lengthy dedication of the anthology "TO THAT SUBLIME CAUSE. THE UNION OF MANKIND, WHICH THE BRITISH PEOPLES, IF THEY ARE TRUE TO THEMSELVES AND COURAGEOUS IN THE FUTURE AS THEY HAVE BEEN IN THE PAST, WILL TAKE TO BE THE REASON OF EXISTENCE OF THEIR EMPIRE; AND TO THE GLORY OF THOSE PEOPLES IN THE SERVICE OF MAN."[15] As a participant in the twofold *telos* thus announced, *Songs of the Great Dominion* is a contribution to national and imperial progress that will end in a post-national and post-imperial sublime.

Arguably, all anthologies that seek to represent the work of a diverse body of writers however small or large must adhere to an aesthetic of variety within unity, but this is perhaps especially true of a volume guided by nationalism, Imperial Federation, and New Utilitarianism. A conspicuous way in which Lighthall draws together the various poets and poems in *Songs of the Great Dominion* is by grouping them in nine sections: after "The Imperial Spirit" and "The New Nationality" come "The Indian," "The Voyageur and Habitant," "Settlement Life," "Sports and Free Life," "The Spirit of Canadian History," "Places," and "Seasons." Within each of these thematic groups, pieces by different poets, from different parts of Canada and from different racial and linguistic groups, including some French and a few Native Canadians, enter into interdependent and mutually modifying relationships whereby, ideally, their different images, themes, forms, tones, and tropes interact so as to convey the impression of a unified sensibility and perspective: the "Voices from the Forests and Waters, Settlements and Cities of Canada" of the anthology's subtitle become a chorus whose members have been brought together to sing a series of variations on themes in a harmonious manner and, in so doing, make the nation's geographically, racially, and linguistically diverse character apparent and legible. By thus reflecting and reinforcing communal spirit and commonality, *Songs of the Great Dominion* serves the agendas of all three strains of Lighthall's thought: whether they were in England or Canada, its readers were asked to imagine a state of variety within a unity that can and will progress and extend teleologically from Canada to a federated empire (and, ultimately, by Lighthall's lights, to the "Union of Mankind," a collectivity conducive to "Spiritualized Happiness").

II
CONTENTION AND SLAUGHTER

1: 1888

> *"It is not possible to put too much quality into a pleasure craft, or indeed into any craft that floats."*
> —Walter Dean

In the letter of 22 September accompanying the manuscript of *Songs of the Great Dominion* to England, Lighthall assured Sharp that "no *first-class* names ... and no second-class names of those who have written anything 'distinctively Canadian'" have been omitted from the anthology, and that he has "tried to keep as possible to the suggested ... 450 pages of Canterbury size of page (35 ll), exclusive of the Introduction and appendices," adding: "I enclose a few additional pieces separate in case you think any of them ought [to] go in or replace some of the others" (Lighthall, "Correspondence" Carton 1). On receipt of the manuscript on 11 October, Sharp replied that he "may not write again until the proofs are ready, but will then ... do so fully," and then registered an ominous first impression of its size: "[t]here is, I fancy, an excess of matter" (Lighthall, "Correspondence" Carton 1). Four days later, after he had "just glanced thro' copy," Sharp reiterated his misgiving: "[t]here seems to me to be too much, but perhaps I am mistaken. In any case that can be remedied. Altogether the book seems to me to be an admirable one, and is sure to attract great attention. The Preface [Introduction] and Appendices are most interesting" (Lighthall, "Correspondence" Carton 1). A closer look at what Lighthall had sent would confirm Sharp's initial impression, precipitate an angry exchange between the two men, and result in a wholesale revision of the anthology.

Despite his misgivings, that closer look did not happen until after Sharp had sent the manuscript to be typeset. By 22 November, however, his first impressions were confirmed and resulted in a lengthy letter to Lighthall in which politeness gives way to anger. After a plea to Lighthall not to "send ... any more MSS, or suggestions, as the book has been sent to the printers, and no further alterations can be made," Sharp focuses on the larger problem of which Lighthall's supplements and suggestions are a part:

You will, I know, regret to hear that you have been very far out in your "close estimate"—and that in consequence I have been caused an infinitude of trouble (having had to work ... on [your] MSS at much loss of valuable time—and health—to myself)—while the appearance of the book has been considerably delayed. So much thrown out indeed has everyone been that a few days ago it was almost decided to postpone the book till the winter of 1889. However, I have managed to arrange matters.

As you yourself stated, you fully understood, the *maximum* length of the text of the book was to be 450pp. After lineal estimate, the matter was found to occupy exactly 800 pages!! ...

The only course open to me (after mastering the contents of the book) was to preserve and delete in strict accordance with poetic value. There were many poems which it was nothing but gain to lose[;] still there are no doubt, some excellent productions among the pile of discarded MSS representing 350 pages. If you saw the book now you would shudder at the wholesale slaughter. (Lighthall, "Correspondence" Carton 1)

Sharp concludes by speculating that the abbreviated anthology will be better received in England but perhaps not in Canada, regretting the loss of unspecified appendices and the reproaches that Lighthall will receive from slaughtered authors, and castigating him once again for causing so much "trouble."

Lighthall's response to this in a note of 8 December occasioned further harsh words from Sharp, who describes it as "written very inadvisedly," dismisses Lighthall's "tone of resentment" as "not at all called for," and expresses "indifference" as to whether or not he is perceived as "'touchy and peremptory'" (Lighthall, "Correspondence" Carton 1). After reiterating yet again that the anthology has "cost ... [him] much trouble and thought" and would have been returned "had it not been for the disappointment of many of the contributors," Sharp asserts that Lighthall has "overstepped the mark" in his last letter, urges him to "modify the dictatorial tone" that he "occasionally adopts," and advises him to keep "strictly to the point in future" if he cannot control his rhetoric. Sharp's rancour did not last long, however: on 15 January of the new year he assures Lighthall that his Introduction will not require augmentation and observes regretfully that the revision of it and the "Notes Biographical and Bibliographical" "will cause ... [him] some trouble, owing to the numerous excerptions from the original" that were necessary to reduce it from 800 to 434 pages. Lighthall obviously harboured no ill feeling, for in May 1889 he invited Sharp to visit and stay with him in Montreal, an invitation that Sharp happily accepted on 23 May (see Lighthall, "Correspondence" Carton 1).

Just how much "trouble" the "excerptions" caused Lighthall is apparent in the changes to one of the three sets of proofs that were sent to him by

Walter Scott on 21 February 1889. In addition to page proofs of the preliminary materials and the poems themselves, the proofs consist of galleys that,
as Sharp explained, had not been "made up into pages on a/c [account] of
the deletions and additions ... [Lighthall] may deem necessary" (Lighthall,
"Correspondence" Carton 1). Predictably, the "deletions and additions" to the
"Notes Biographical and Bibliographical" that resulted from Sharp's drastic
cuts necessitated some adjustments in the Introduction. Thus, the deletion
of excerpts from Oliver Goldsmith's *The Rising Village* from the anthology
resulted in the deletion of a sentence in the Introduction that links the poem
and the poet to *The Deserted Village* of the Anglo-Irish Oliver Goldsmith,
and a plea by Lighthall for recognition that he has "spared no necessary trouble" (xxxvi) in compiling the anthology, and, on the contrary, "gone pretty
thoroughly over the field" and "exercised at least not unreasonable discre-
tion" (Lighthall, "Correspondence") is replaced by a paragraph that is at once
face-saving for Lighthall, mollifying to deleted poets, and inaccurate:

> The editor regrets to say that through an accidental cause unnecessary to
> explain, more MSS. were sent to the publishers than the volume required. As
> no time could be lost the general editor had no recourse except to undertake
> the difficult task of cutting down the matter, which he did in accordance with
> his best judgment, but guided by the sole criterion of the symmetry of the
> work. Some good poetry originally included has not found a place owing to
> the necessary reduction, and apology is tended where unintentional injustice
> has resulted. (xxxvi–xxxvii)

In the proofs, the paragraph is written and crossed out by Lighthall, and
below it, in a later form of his handwriting, is a "Memo" that reads: "[t]his
'accident' was really an oversight of the General Editor of the series, William
Sharp, by which he asked for too many pages. W. D. L."
    Most of the changes in the poems themselves in the proofs are correc-
tions of a minor nature, three notable exceptions being the replacement of
Machar's "Father Couture" with Hunter-Duvar's "Adieu to France" (104), the
reduction of Susanna Moodie's "Indian Summer" from five stanzas to two so
that it occupies one page rather than two (396), and the addition immediately
after it of "Indian Summer" (397–98) by Isidore G. Ascher. Of course, by
far the most extensive and radical changes appear in the "Notes Biographical and Bibliographical." From these, it can be deduced that, in addition to
Goldsmith, a dozen poets and their poems were deleted by Sharp, while
only one—Ascher—was added at Lighthall's request. Most of the slaughtered
poets were extremely minor figures such as John Murdoch Harper, Gustavus
W. Wicksteed, and Lockhart's brother Burton Wellesley Lockhart, whose

absence would go unnoticed even in Canada, but others were writers of considerable stature, including four of the most prominent or promising female writers of the post-Confederation period: Morgan, MacLean, Alice Maude Ardagh ("Espérance"), and Agnes Ethelwyn Wetherald ("Bel Thistlewaite"). Canadian reviewers would notice, and would not be pleased.

2: 1893

The volume that reviewers saw in 1889 was in the Windsor rather than the more prestigious Canterbury Poets series, a demotion occasioned perhaps by Sharp's perception that the anthology needed further deletions and revisions. Before that happened, it went through two further printings in 1892 as *Canadian Poems and Songs* and *Canadian Songs and Poems*, the latter co-published by Walter Scott and W. J. Gage and Co. of Toronto. On 23 May 1889, Sharp had told Lighthall that the "Canterbury volume" would "probably" be published in the spring of 1890 (Lighthall, "Correspondence" Carton 1); however, *Canadian Poems and Lays: Selections of Native Verse, Reflecting the Seasons, Legends, and Life of the Dominion* did not appear until the late summer of 1893. In its new incarnation, the anthology is leaner by sixty poems, with omissions falling heavily in the final two sections, "Seasons" (20) and "Places" (15) (where, however, Lockhart's "The Vale of Gaspereau" has been added at Lighthall's request [see Proof]). Many of the deletions are poems by minor poets such as Stratton, Kate B. Simpson, and Charles Edwin Jakeway, but others are by Crawford, Carman, Lampman, Roberts, and, probably at his own request, Campbell, whose "Indian Summer" had been moved to replace Moodie's poem of the same title. Other notable victims of this second slaughter were poems by Sangster, McLachlan, and Lighthall himself, and, in "The Indian" section, the translations of two "Wabanaki Song[s]" that Lighthall had erroneously attributed to Charles Leland.[16] (Curiously, Roberts is deprived of the authorship of "Tantramar Revisited," which is listed as "Anonymous" on the Contents page and not attributed to him in the body of the text.)

Other changes between *Songs of the Great Dominion* and *Canadian Poems and Lays* are by turns obvious and subtle. The epigraph from F. G. Scott's "In Memoriam" is omitted, Lighthall's lengthy dedication is replaced by a poem by him on the imperial theme ("To history's vastest Brotherhood"), and the volume contains neither the "Notes Biographical and Bibliographical" nor the appendices. While Lighthall's Introduction remains substantially the same, it too is shortened in places; for example, the sentence referring to Roberts's "Hellenic poems" and skill as a *"Word-painter"* (xxv) is gone, an account of Sangster's career is similarly abbreviated, and Emily McManus's "Manitoba," which is quoted in its entirety in *Songs of the Great Dominion,* is reduced from four stanzas to two. Machar's "Canada to the Laureate" and the sentences framing it in the earlier anthology are entirely omitted, as are comments on "Chanson literature" that refer to a now absent appendix, and there is no longer an acknowledgement of the help of "many kind persons" in assembling the volume (xxxvi–xxxvii). Almost imperceptibly, "The Editor regrets ..." (xxxvi), which introduces the apologia for the now twofold reduction of the volume, becomes "Both Editors regret ..." (*Canadian Poems and Lays* xxxiii)—a gesture that makes explicit the fact that the anthology is indeed what it always reluctantly was for both Lighthall and Sharp: a collaborative effort.

III
LIGHTHALL'S INTRODUCTION

> "When a man is part of his canoe, he is a part of all that canoes have known."
> —Sigurd F. Olson

Lighthall begins his Introduction by reiterating and elaborating upon the "Voices" of the subtitle, identifying them as "cheerful with the consciousness of young might, public wealth, and heroism" and expressing the hope that, "[t]hrough them, taken together, ... [the reader] may catch something of great Niagara falling ... the crack of the rifle in the haunts of the moose and caribou, the lament of vanishing races singing their death-song ..., proud traditions of contests with the French" (xxi), and other sights, sounds, and events that he regards as quintessentially and formatively Canadian. The phrase "taken together" already counterbalances the impression of plurality conveyed by the references to various ethnic groups and historical conflicts that follow, as, indeed, does Lighthall's assertion that the "tone" of all the voices is "*courage*" and their "undertone" "the virility of fighting races" (xxi). Later in the introduction, he will build upon the masculinist conception of Canada that is implicit in the word "virility" and becomes explicit in his assertion that "*courage*" is the unifying tone of the anthology because "to hunt, to fight, to hew out a farm, one must be a man!" (xxii).[17] Initially, however, he turns to another time-sanctioned stereotype—the personification of a nation as female (as in Britannia, for example, or Marianne)—in order to trope Canada's relationship with Britain and, perhaps, to counteract Roberts's earlier Independentist personification of the Dominion in "Canada" (1885) as a male "Child of Nations, giant-limbed" that must outgrow his "ignoble sloth" and callow dependence on "greatness not ... [his] own" and manfully "bear / A nation's franchise, a nation's name" (18). Given the immense popularity of "Canada," an anthology of Canadian voices without it would have been unthinkable, so it duly appears in "The New Nationality" section of *Songs of the Great Dominion*, as do Roberts's "Collect for Dominion Day" and "An Ode for the Canadian Confederacy" (1888), which was written after he turned to Imperial Federation and concludes with a clarion call to Canadians to "Let flame your loyalty forth ... Till earth shall know the Child of Nations by her name!" (31). In "his 'Canada' and 'Ode for the Canadian Confederacy,'" observes Lighthall later in the Introduction, Roberts "has struck the supreme note of Canadian nationality" (xxiv).

As conceived and personified by Lighthall in a paragraph that A. J. M. Smith considers a "remarkable piece of prose" that rises to the level of "poetry" (6–7), Canada is the "Eldest Daughter of Empire," "the full-grown of the family," and "the Empire's completest type," which is to say, the child that most fully exhibits and exemplifies the sterling characteristics of Britain (xxii). Moreover, Canada is "Imperial in herself," he continues, citing as evidence the sheer size and wealth of the country: each of her provinces is "not less than some empire of Europe"; "[s]he stands fifth among the nations in the tonnage of her commercial marine"; "the Colony of the Maple Leaf is about as large as Europe" (xxii). As if this were not enough, "Canada is also Imperial in her traditions" on both the French and the English sides, an assertion duly supported by references to several figures and groups in the history of the *ancien régime* (Cartier, Champlain, the Jesuits ...), all framed and contained by references to the Loyalists, whose withdrawal from the United States is extravagantly characterized as "the noblest migration the world has ever seen" and as the seminal event for "[e]xisting English Canada": "from that to the present there has been a steady unfolding of power and culture" (xxii–xxiii). It would appear that the Loyalists were an especially influential vehicle for the supreme directive force that wills all life to progress upwards toward "Spiritualized Happiness."

Between arguing that the overall tone of Canadian poetry is manly "*courage*" and presenting Canada as the youthful female embodiment of all things imperial, Lighthall draws upon contemporary notions of environmental determinism[18] to claim that "[t]he delight of a clear atmosphere runs through ... [Canadian] poetry," and the "rejoicings of ... [Quebec's Winter Carnival[,] which is only possible in the most athletic country in the world" (xxii). This last claim might seem a risible aside, but its import becomes clearer with Lighthall's assertion, again with an eye on environmental determinism—and now with the aim of distinguishing Canadian poetry from the poetry of the other settler colony with which it was increasingly being compared—that life in Australia has generated "a poetry of the *horse*" but life in a "Northern atmosphere" has given Canadian poetry a "special flavour" and made it "a poetry ... of the *canoe*" (xxiii). And it becomes even clearer with his characterization of the "foremost name in Canadian song at the present day"—Roberts, of course—as a "poet, canoeist, and Professor of Literature, the very embodiment of feeling, action, and intellect" (xxiv). Who could be a fitter conductor of the canoe of the "daughter-nation of the West" than the evidently "athletic" author of "Birch and Paddle" and "On the Creek" (both of which are included in the "Sports and Life" section of the anthology)—a man whose "virility" and priapic escapades were well on the way to becoming notorious and whose "youth ... can scarcely be called over" (xxxiv–xxv). (In fact, as Lighthall concedes in his "Notes Biographical and Bibliographical," Roberts was twenty-nine when the anthology went to press [460].) "The personal quality of his poetry is distinguished, next to richness of colour and artistic freedom of emotional expression, by manliness," continues Lighthall: "Roberts is a high-thinking, generous man. He speaks with a voice of power and leadership.... This manliness and dignity render him particularly fitted for the great work which Canada at present offers her sons" (xxv). Little wonder that Roberts was at a loss for words to thank Lighthall for his remarks.

Most of the remainder of Lighthall's Introduction consists of commentaries, in decreasing order of magnitude, on the other poets in the anthology. Next comes Sangster (Canada's "first important national poet"), who is allotted a little less space than Roberts, and then Crawford (the author of "the most striking volume of poetry next to those of Roberts—indeed more boldly new than his"), who is allotted a little more (xxv–xxvii). While Lighthall's comments on both are curtailed and largely appreciative, they nevertheless contain some acute insights: Sangster's lack of formal education "mak[es] a good deal of his poetry the curious spectacle of inborn striving after perfect ideals driven to expression abstractions rather than concrete clothing of colours and forms"; the "names in the title of *Old Spooks's Pass, Malcolm's Katie, and Other Poems* "were against it" but "the passage [in *Malcolm's Katie*] from the 'Shanties grew,' down to its glorious climax in the song 'O Love will build his lily walls' ... seems to us ... the most effective known use of a lyric introduced into a long poem" (xxv–xxxii). After Sangster and Crawford come McLachlan, Kirby, and Reade with a brief paragraph each of commentary, then Heavysege with over a page and Mair with another paragraph. Very brief comments on several other poets, including Carman, Campbell, Lampman, and Cameron, follow before the Introduction becomes little more than a list of other authors and then, with a shift in focus, first a two-paragraph enumeration of "lady singers" that reenacts in small the pattern of the previous pages and then reiterates the anthology's overall emphasis on nation and empire by quoting McManus's "Manitoba" and Machar's "Canada to the Laureate" (xxxii, xxxiii–iv). Next comes a one-paragraph nod toward "[a] curious Indian song" ("Caughnawaga Song") that Lighthall has had translated by John Waniente Jocks, "the son of a Six-nation chief" on the Caughnawaga Reservation near Montreal (xxx–xxxiv). Not until near the end of the Introduction does Lighthall make a "bow" toward the selection of French-Canadian *chansons* and the specimens of four French-Canadian poets (Louis-Honoré Fréchette, J. O. Chauveau, Benjamin Sulte, and Pamphile Le May) that he has placed in two appendices. To all appearances, in matters of gender and race *Songs of the Great Dominion* mirrors the patriarchal and fraternal assumptions and hierarchies of the Anglo-Scottish establishment to which Lighthall belonged: poems by women occupy only slightly more than 19 percent of the pages allotted to poetry in the volume, poems by French Canadians in the appendices and the text proper approximately half that, and translations of poems by Natives a meagre three pages. As is now known, however, a good deal of the responsibility for what is omitted from and retained in the anthology must rest with Sharp.

Yet appearances and statistics do not tell the entire story of the representation of gender and race in *Songs of the Great Dominion*. True, Canadian poetry's manly head canoeist is allotted the greatest number of pages (28) in the anthology (both he and Campbell have 13 poems but the latter only 17 pages). Nevertheless, Crawford's regrettably named volume is described, it will be recalled, as "more boldly new than those of Roberts," a judgment that is reflected not merely in the number of poems (7) and pages (22) given to her, but also in the fact that the "Settlement" section begins with a song from *Malcolm's Katie* and contains two further excerpts from the poem, as well as "The Farmer's Daughter Cherry," the net result being that Crawford dominates the section both in the quality and in the number of her poems in it.[19] Two other sections of the anthology—"The New Nationality" and "The Voyageur and the Habitant"—also begin with poems by women, the former with "Dominion Day" by Machar and the latter with "The Old Régime" by Harrison. Surely it is to Lighthall's credit that he gave some prominence to women poets (in J. E. Wetherell's *Later Canadian Poets* [1893] they are relegated to a "Supplement"), that he included some examples of French-Canadian poetry both in translation and in the original, and that he sought out, and in one instance commissioned, three translations of Native songs. To some twentieth-century sensibilities all this may seem woefully inadequate, but Lighthall—and Sharp—should not be harshly castigated for failing to apply as yet undreamed-of standards of equity to the anthology, let alone for failing to anticipate the hard-eyed epistemologies of feminism and postcolonialism.

In addition to Lighthall's "bow" to French-Canadian poetry, the final pages of *Songs of the Great Dominion* contain "[a] few general remarks" that include a further apology for its necessarily limited nature that seems to be addressed directly to Roberts (to "illustrate ... the country and its life *in a distinctive way* ... the subjective and unlocal ... [had to be] passed over," as did "poems whose merit lies in perfection of finish") and an admission that the anthology's nine sections provide "merely ... a sketch of the complete range of the[ir] subjects" rather than a full picture (xxiv, xxxv). Lighthall also glances back at the anthology's antecedents and positions it in relation to them: Harrison's *Canadian Birthday Book* (1887) "affords a miniature survey of the chief verse-writers, French and English" and Edward Hartley Dewart's *Selections from Canadian Poets* (1864) is "antiquated" and its contents are "apologetic and depressed" in comparison with those of *Songs of the Great Dominion*, which are "far better" as poetry and imbued with "a tone of exaltation ... celebration" and "hopefulness" (xxxv). In the final paragraph comes the apologia for the anthology's abbreviated form that, implicitly and eventually explicitly, identifies it as a collaborative effort. Lighthall was entirely responsible for the Introduction, however, including the jaunty invitation to read on that brings it to a contrived and juvenile close: "[a]nd now, the canoes are packed, our *voyageurs* are waiting for us, the paddlers are ready, let us start!"[20]

At the very end of *Songs of the Great Dominion*, after the two appendices and the "Notes Biographical and Bibliographical" for each poet in the anthology, Lighthall acknowledges and thanks all the people and institutions that have assisted him in one way or another—or, as far as can be told, all but one: conspicuous by his absence is Roberts. Nor was this an oversight. "*Of course* you should not acknowledge any assistance I may be to you in your work," Roberts had told Lighthall on 9 August 1888: "[t]he assistance is almost infinitesimal, anyway; but it would be [by] no means judicious to say anything about it" (*Collected Letters* 86). It would not have been "judicious" because, almost needless to say, it would have laid Roberts open to the charge of using Lighthall and the anthology to further and enhance his own reputation, which was very likely true and certainly consistent with Roberts's manipulative practices at the time and later. In the fall and winter of 1888–89, he called upon Lighthall, Campbell, Griffin, Lampman, and perhaps others to exercise what "pull" they could to assist him in his bid for a professorship at the University of Toronto (*Collected Letters* 91; see 90–106). Meanwhile, he was writing anonymous and commissioning favourable reviews of their work; for example, on 16 November he promised Lampman that he would review *Among the Millet, and Other Poems* in the St. John *Progress* and arrange for it to be reviewed in several other Maritime newspapers, and on 21 November he asked Lighthall to send material for an article about him in the *King's College Record* (which his brother Goodridge Roberts edited), saying "I'll do the rest, under a *nom de plume!*" (*Collected Letters* 93, 97). (The article, signed "Stanley F. W. Symonds," eventually appeared in November 1889.) The term for this is "log-rolling"—that is, "mutual assistance" and "mutual puffing in literary productions" ("Log-rolling" *OED*)—and it would shortly flow publicly, venomously, and corrosively from the pen of a poet who knew full well what Roberts had been up to: Campbell.

IV
RECEPTION

1: 1889

> *"Are we quite sure that there is no feeling in the 'heart of oak,' no sentiment under bent birch ribs; that a canoe, in fact, has no character?"*
> —John MacGregor

The reception of *Songs of the Great Dominion* after it appeared in May 1889 was polite and mixed. In England, the poet and man of letters Theodore Watts-Dunton gave it a lengthy review in the 28 September 1889 number of the prestigious and influential *Athenaeum* that is as much a meditation prompted by the anthology as a review of it. Although he criticizes some unnamed poets in the volume as "too ready" to "pipe" and doubts the truth of Lighthall's claim that the migration of the Loyalists was "'the noblest ... the world has ever seen,'" Watts-Dunton sees the volume as evidence of Matthew Arnold's statement that "'the future of poetry is immense,'" especially, he adds, in the burgeoning English-speaking world (411). Attributing the tone of "hope—almost of exaltation" in the anthology to the "secrets and ... wealth" of nature in Canada, he singles out for praise and quotation Campbell, Carman, Machar, McLachlan, Lighthall himself, one of the Indian songs, and, above all, Johnson and Crawford, "the most interesting English poetess now living" (Johnson) and "the Emily Bronte of Canada" (Crawford) (412, 413). The piece concludes by quoting the first stanza of John Talon-Lespérance's "Empire First" as an example of "verses whose loyalty to the empire and affection for the mother country cannot but touch every English heart" (413). Roberts is not so much as mentioned, let alone quoted. (In a letter of 4 July 1889 from Arthur Symons to Carman he fares better: the "only good things in the book," in Symons's view, are poems by Roberts, Lampman, and Carman himself, "the Indian songs," and "a few other pieces here & there" [qtd. in Ware 44].)

In Canada, reviewers and commentators laboured hard to balance praise for Lighthall himself and for some aspects of *Songs of the Great Dominion* with dismay at others, especially, in the latter category, the exclusion of poems that do not "illustrate ... the life of the country and its life *in a distinctive way*" (411). At the beginning of a substantial review in the 7 June 1889 number of *The Week*, G. Mercer Adam states that the anthology "must meet with well-nigh unqualified approval," but only within the restrictions placed upon it by "the space at the editor's disposal and having regard to the limitations of his aims in making the selections"—namely, his decision to include only "objective verse dealing with the many and rich phases of Canadian life and scenery" (421). As if in disbelief, Adam repeats this reservation and its corollary again and again so that "the omission ... of verse of a subjective and introspective character" and "subjective verse and the larger class of poems of an introspective character" seems almost as heinous as a failure to allow women into the lifeboats of a sinking ship. Nor does he blame all of Lighthall's omissions on the limitations of space and the "distinctively Canadian" "character of the volume"; rather, he names seventeen poets without whose work any "volume of Canadian verse ... will scarcely give satisfaction to a wide and catholic taste" (421). Especially irksome to him is the omission of poems by Wetherald, the lack of space accorded to Crawford and Johnson, and the relatively weak representation of female poets in general, a series of criticisms that is somewhat weakened by the fact that Adam and Wetherald were coauthors of *The Algonquin Maiden* (1886) and by the fact that most of the poets, both male and female, whose absence he laments—for example, Ardagh, Sarah Jeannette Duncan, Frederick Augustus Dixon, and Edward Burrough Brownlow ("Serepta")—were fellow contributors to *The Week* who had not published—and in most cases never would publish—a collection of poetry. Adam's unreservedly positive comments later in his review are not for the anthology itself but for what it promises: "higher and richer notes" from Roberts, Lampman, Campbell, Carman, William McLennan, and Lighthall himself, and a future "store of verse more worthy" of Canada" (421). "No Canadian patriot will regard Mr. Lighthall's volume as a poetic totality, but will see in it the promise of better things yet to come," concludes Adam; "[f]or what is in it all will at present be thankful, and we trust that the work will meet with such a reception as to make it the forerunner of still weightier and more generous volumes of Canadian song" (421).

Most of the same weaknesses and limitations are mentioned by Edward William Thomson in a similarly substantial commentary on *Songs of the Great Dominion* in the 5 July 1889 issue of the Toronto *Globe*: Lighthall did not intend "to give the world the best possible selection from Canadian poetry.... [T]he plan of his work excluded verses not illustrating in some way the peculiarities of things Canadian.... His purpose was to set forth in one volume a number of verses having Canadian color.... The pursuance of such a plan involved the exclusion of a great deal of Canadian verse as meritorious, or more so, than any to be found in the volume" (Thomson 4).

Wetherald's absence is again lamented, as is that of Robert Kirkland Kernighan ("The Khan"). At the heart of Thomson's commentary, however, lies a fulsome paean to Lampman as "the foremost of the young poets of America" that anticipates the laudatory review of *Among the Millet, and Other Poems* in the 10 August 1889 issue of the *Globe* that led to the close friendship of the two men, and a more muted endorsement of Campbell, whose "Indian Summer" is quoted in its entirety as an "admirable rendering of … [the] spirit of the season" (4). Crawford and McLennan are also singled out for praise, as is John E. Logan's "A Blood-Red Ring Hung Round the Moon." No other poets are mentioned, including Roberts.

Adam's reservations are loudly echoed in the brief review of the anthology that appeared ten days later in the 17 June issue of the *Ottawa Daily Citizen*. Lighthall is given "credit for preserving many of the productions of promising writers" and for the displaying the "public spirit" needed to "encourage … native Canadians in the field of literature," but the remainder and the bulk of the review is devoted to naming writers omitted from it: McColl, Wicksteed, Martin Griffin, Jonathan J. B. Plumb, and "one of Montreal's most gifted writers" (n. pag.). Predictably, the longer review that had appeared in the 8 June issue of the *Montreal Gazette* was more positive than Adam's, Thomson's, or the *Ottawa Citizen's*. Granting that Lighthall's decision to "confine … his choice" to Canadian subjects and themes "may" make the "book … defective from a purely literary point of view" and expressing the hope that "[a]n anthology, based solely on literary merits may, perhaps, come later," the review compliments the physical appearance of volume ("handsome … well printed and tastefully bound, with emblematic cover")[21] and bestows guarded praise on its contents ("interesting, and, on the whole, a meritorious collection of poetry"). It also mingles warm admiration for Lighthall with a sympathy that is difficult not to share:

> The task of preparing it was not easy. It required taste, judgement and discrimination and it also called for no little firmness. Whether all the poets of Canada will be satisfied with the tender mercy that Mr. Lighthall has shown them, we cannot say. He has evidently discharged what he deemed a patriotic duty—virtually a labor of love—with a full consciousness of its responsibility and with a sincere desire to be fair to all, and above all to be just to Canada. As yet we have only had time to glance through these well filled pages, but, from what we have seen, we believe that we can conscientiously congratulate Mr. Lighthall on his editorial success.[22]

2: 1892, 1896

Evidently the response to *Songs of the Great Dominion* was sufficiently positive for, as has been seen, Walter Scott repeatedly reissued it in its original and
then a re-edited form in the early 1890s.[23] This time, however, the response
was even less positive than before. Despite his near parity with Roberts in the
original anthology, Campbell felt that he had not been properly represented
in it, and in his *At the Mermaid Inn* column in the 3 December 1892 number
of the Toronto *Globe* he vented his spleen. Claiming not to be disparaging
Lighthall himself, whom he describes as "a sincere and high-minded patriot ...
of lofty ideals," he warms to his subject by asserting that "not more than a
dozen of the sixty names mentioned in his anthology have ever laid serious
claim to real poetical achievement, and ... certainly not more than half that
number have any title to lengthy remembrance even in Canada" (203). But
those are not his "serious objections" to the anthology; rather, these are that

> true Canadian literature as it now exists is neither represented nor even fore-
> shadowed in its pages, and that Canada is represented as a crude colony,
> whose literature, if it could be called by such a name, is merely associated
> with superficial canoe and carnival songs, backwoods and Indian tales told
> in poor rhyme, and all tied together by pseudo-patriotic hurrahs, which are
> about as representative of our true nationality as they are of literature.... As
> far as Canada is concerned, Mr. Lighthall's anthology might even at this day
> be regarded as obsolete.... But when we remember that this work is being
> sold in England and goes into the hands of cultured English men and women
> as representative of our best work and our claim for rank in the literature of
> the day, we cannot help but feel that we are being imposed upon ... (203–4)

An intimation of the personal grievance against Lighthall that Campbell had
been harbouring for some three years can be apprehended in his subsequent
remark that the reputation of a young writer can be "seriously injur[ed]" when
he is "represented by his poorest work," as Lighthall has done by making his
selections on the basis of "subject matter" alone (204).[24] Campbell's final and
least credible charge is that Lighthall's description of Roberts as a "'poet and
canoeist'" casts "the fact that he is a professor in a college ... altogether into
the shade" (204). If it ever existed, such concern for Roberts's reputation on
Campbell's part had long been on the wane, however; indeed, references a
week later in his *At the Mermaid Inn* column to literary "cliques" of writers
whose reputation "may depend largely on the booming qualities of ... personal friends" (204) and to critics who judge Canadian poets by such criteria
as their "patriotism" indicate that the charge of log-rolling that Campbell
would lay at the door of Roberts, Carman, Lampman, Duncan Campbell

Scott, and others in August 1895 was already well on the way to being full blown. Clearly, *Songs of the Great Dominion* was among the causes of the "War among the Poets" that signalled the imminent disintegration of the Confederation group.[25]

A year later, the anthology—specifically the 1892 edition co-published with Gage—provoked one of the most sustained and witty satirical attacks on writers in Canadian literary history: *The Poetical Reviews: A Brief Notice of Canadian Poets and Poetry* (1896) by Alexander Charles Stewart, a "tunnel and bridge contractor at Fort William, Ontario" (Wallace). Explaining in the Preface to his Popean poem that "[t]he authors ... under review are those who willingly, or unwillingly, contributed" to what he describes as a "lilliputian tower of Babel," "A glorious supplement to Mother Goose," and "a literary sty / Where ... [Lighthall] and his shall unlamented lie," Stewart characterizes "Attorney Lighthall" as a jack of all literary trades and the "Accoucher-general to the labouring scribes" whose own "doggerel lacks ... common sense" (70–73). Bouquets are tossed to Crawford, Johnson, McLachlan, Thomas D'Arcy McGee, and a few others whose work satisfies Stewart's criteria of "Simplicity and truth" (Stewart 88), but the members of the Confederation group and several others are subjected to an almost unrelenting barrage of brickbats. Carman and Lampman get off lightly: the former's "rising strain / Shows power" but his canoe "is not worthy of the wind" he has "waste[d] on it" and the latter "rant[s] of ... white and dusty ways" in "Heat" but will "outgrow his present rhyme / And soar to stellar heights, alone sublime" (70–83); however, Roberts is the perpetrator of "Tantramarian nonsense" who "succumbs to poetical hysterics at the sight of a *pumpkin*";[26] Campbell "makes a poetry of wild pretense ... And deems his jingle constitutes a song" (70–83); Duncan Campbell Scott should be wary of taking liberties with the sleeping woman of his "Isabelle"; and Frederick George Scott should "never hence vent mutilated verse" (70–83). Log-rolling and self-promotion are roundly condemned, as is the failure of Canadian poets to use their work to attack "those degraded, vicious, and mercenary boodlers" in political office "who are a blot upon this age and country" (76, 87). Stewart lands some palpable hits and he has a keen eye for unintentional humour (for example, he simply quotes Lighthall's description of Roberts as "poet, canoeist, and Professor of Literature" and allows it to satirize itself). Moreover, many, though by no means all, of his assumptions and arguments have a strangely modernist flavour that would be at home in extended versions of F. R. Scott's "Canadian Authors Meet" (1927) and A. J. M. Smith's "Wanted—Canadian Criticism" (1928).

In fact, by 1896 literary tastes were already shifting, as were attitudes to empire. Arnold, Tennyson, and Robert Browning were dead. William Butler

Yeats, Joseph Conrad, and Stephen Crane had published books that signalled the arrival of modernism. The Jameson Raid and the Boer War would soon multiply doubts about the wisdom and cost of imperialism. By the time Duncan published *The Imperialist* in 1904, Imperial Federation was for all practical purposes dead. *Songs of the Great Dominion* and *Canadian Poems and Lays* are saturated with the assumptions, ideals, and hopes of their author and of an era that was fast on the wane. As a result, they were largely ignored until generously treated by Smith in "Canadian Anthologies, New and Old" (1942)[27] and later revived by literary historians in the years surrounding the Centennial, when Roy Daniells, writing in the *Literary History of Canada* (1965), dubbed them "landmark[s] of cultural publication" in "a high colonial culture" and remarked with some truth and more wishful thinking that "Lighthall's introduction and his choice of poems have a firmness of stance which gave his readers the shock of recognition and his book a wide regard" (197). It is tempting to speculate that Lighthall came to regret his decision to exclude "cosmopolitan" poems from the book, but he seems to have remained true to his commitment to the "*distinctively Canadian*": in 1898 he published *The False Chevalier*, a historical romance about the son of a Quebec merchant in the court of Louis XVI, and in 1908 he returned to the same genre with *The Master of Life: A Romance of the Five Nations and of Prehistoric Montreal*; from 1900 to 1903 he was mayor of Westmount and in 1901 he cofounded the Union of Canadian Municipalities, which, some twenty years after his death in 1954 became the Federation of Canadian Municipalities. That might have been enough for the fervent advocate of Canadianism whose idealism had led him to champion Imperial Federation as a stage in human progress toward the "Union of Mankind" and "Spiritualized Happiness."

NOTES

1 The quotations that serve as epigraphs to this essay are the words of master canoe builders in Ted Moore's and Marilyn Mohr's *Canoecraft*, 20, 8, 12, and 6.

2 Roberts's proposal was prompted by hearing that Douglas Sladen was editing *Australian Ballads and Rhymes: Poems Inspired by Life and Scenery in Australia and New Zealand* (1888) for Walter Scott (see Roberts, *Collected Letters* 79).

3 The date of Lighthall's letter and the information that his proposal was prompted by Sladen's anthology is based on the copy of the letter in the folder entitled "Lighthall: Correspondence with William Sharp and Others, ca. 1888–1889" in the Lighthall Papers in Rare Books and Special Collections at McGill University. Sharp's response to the letter on a postcard franked 8 May 1888 is also in the Lighthall Papers.

4 So at least Sharp claimed in a letter to Lighthall of 12 August 1888 in which he also states that he suggested the idea of *Poems of Wildlife* to Roberts (Lighthall, "Correspondence" Carton 1). In the bound copy of the proofs of *Songs of the Great Dominion* at McGill University, hereafter cited as Proof, a later handwritten note by Lighthall

confirms that seeing Sladen's anthology was indeed the inciting moment for his proposal to Sharp.

5   "Immediately on receiving your postcard," Sharp wrote to Lighthall on 6 June 1888 with reference to a stage in their discussion of the project, "I wrote, as you suggested, to Prof. Roberts ... sending him my copy of my letter to you & a memo of your reply" (Lighthall, "Correspondence" Carton 1).

6   In a letter to Lighthall on 12 August 1888, Sharp states that he was "entirely responsible ... for ... 'Poems of Wild Life' which, having thought out, I suggested to Prof. Roberts" (Lighthall, "Correspondence" Carton 1).

7   Unless otherwise indicated, all quotations are from *Songs of the Great Dominion*.

8   On June 2, Roberts reiterated and expanded his offer, asking: "[s]hall I write to Mr Sharp & Professor Rhys to enter into correspondence with you? Telling them, at the same time, that I shall be on hand to furnish all the aid & advice you may desire, and answering for your qualifications?" (*Collected Letters* 82).

9   For a detailed discussion of Roberts's "cosmopolitanism," see Bentley, *The Confederation Group*, 59–69 and elsewhere.

10   "The book was wanted in September, so that I put it together in great haste, most of the work being done in a three weeks' vacation," Lighthall would later confess; "[t]he unique collection of several hundred volumes in the Toronto Public Library was 'done' in about three hours. By that time I could see at a glance what was *not* wanted" (presumably, that is, poems that were not "distinctively Canadian") (Proof).

11   McColl was to have been included in the volume, but was later omitted for reasons of space to be discussed above. In responding to Lighthall's call, he exposed one of the weaknesses of the criterion set out in the printed letter of 2 July: "such of my rhymes as may be considered 'distinctive of Canada' are far from being among the best of my productions" (Lighthall, "Correspondence" Carton 1).

12   See also *Collected Letters* 96 and 97 for Roberts's invitation to Griffin as well as Lighthall to join the Society.

13   See also Lighthall, "Correspondence" Carton 3 for the flyer dated 17 January 1889 stating the purposes of the Society, which include "examination of our national literature, English and French [and] the acquirement and diffusion of a knowledge of our best ... writing."

14   This term, which Lighthall defines in the second section of his *Analysis of the Altruistic Act in Illustration of a General Outline of Ethics* (1885), is one of a number that he later used to describe and clarify the concept.

15   It is in keeping with Lighthall's imperialism that the only non-Canadian poem that he mentions in his Introduction is "Locksley Hall" (1842), in which Tennyson of course envisages a "Parliament of man" and "the Federation of the world" (128).

16   See Lighthall, "Correspondence" Carton 1 for the letter of 28 June 1889 in which Mrs. H. Wallace Brown chides Lighthall for crediting her translations to Leland.

17   For a thorough discussion of the theme of masculinism in early Canadian writing, see Aaron J. Schneider's "Total Man!: Literature, Nationalism, and Masculinity in Canada."

18   See Bentley 145–76 for a discussion of the environmental ideas of the period as they are registered in the work of the poets of the Confederation group.

19   No doubt this is in part a reflection of Sharp's admiration of Crawford's work. In a letter to Lighthall on 15 October 1888, he declares himself "much struck by the appendical and other extracts from Isabella Valancy Crawford. She seems to me to be distinctly the premier poet of all whom you mention" (Lighthall, "Correspondence" Carton 1).

20 In one of his handwritten notes in Proof, Lighthall admits that he "gauged" the "assertive style" of his Introduction on that of Sladen in *Australian Ballads.*

21 This may have been based on a "rough sketch for the design of the cover" that Lighthall sent to Sharp 16 August 1888 (Lighthall, "Correspondence" Carton 1).

22 Understandably, responses to the anthology in letters to Lighthall—at least those that he kept—were largely positive. On 12 June 1889, Lockhart wrote that, despite "some little disappointments ..., on the whole it satisfies" (Lighthall, "Correspondence" Carton 3), and on 18 June Mair wrote that, although he agreed "in the main" with Adam's review, "[t]he book is a great gain to our literature" (Lighthall, "Correspondence" Carton 1). A month later Edward Burrough Brownlow ("Serepta"), whose poems were deleted by Sharp, "congratulate[d]" Lighthall on his "success," "sympathize[d]" with the loyal & patriotic spirit" of the volume, pronounced its "arrangement into divisions very happy," and regretted the lack of space in it for more work (Lighthall, "Correspondence" Carton 1; and see also Thomson's positive response in a letter of 12 July). "The book is a delightful one," Marshall Saunders would write on 14 November 1894, "and I take great pride in it" (Lighthall, "Correspondence" Carton 1).

23 In *The Walter Scott Publishing Company: A Bibliography*, John R. Turner, in the entry on *Songs of the Great Dominion,* indicates that, in addition to being published in the Windsor series, it was published in the company's Brotherhood, Emerald, Half-roan, Library of Poetry, Oxford, and Reward series. The entry on *Canadian Songs and Poems* lists only the edition co-published in 1892 by Walter Scott and W. J. Gage and Company and fails to note that it appeared in the Canterbury Poets series. See also the listings in Robert Lecker's *English-Canadian Literary Anthologies.*

24 When Campbell sent Lighthall a "collection" of his "poems classified ... into *Lake Lyrics, Patriotic Poems*, and other verse" on 9 August 1888, he requested him "not to draw from one clan alone" because he would "like to be represented by each" (Lighthall, "Correspondence" Carton 1). Later in the month, on 28 August, he chided Lighthall for not wanting to include "Burnaby," asking: "would not a poem on an English subject by a Canadian be of interest to an Englishman?" In letters of 17 and 21 January 1889 he demanded with increasing vehemence that "Vapor and Blue" be removed from the anthology (it was not) and in a letter of 6 February he demands "*a list* of ... [his] poems included" (Lighthall, "Correspondence"). Other letters express resentment at Roberts's success while also denying any feeling of resentment because of it: he has merely "[a]dvertised more than the rest of us. I do not say that with any bitterness" (28 August); "I hope you don't think I have any bad feeling against Roberts. I ... only think he has been over promoted" (30 August [Lighthall, "Correspondence" Carton 1]); "[I wrote] in slightly bitter spirits of Roberts' success" (7 December [Lighthall, "Correspondence" Carton 1]).

25 See Bentley 273–90.

26 The reference is to Roberts's "The Pumpkins in the Corn," which is obviously not in the anthology because it was published in *Songs of the Common Day* (1893).

27 "Lighthall's book is not unreasonably cluttered up with fake Canadiana," writes Smith, "and is a real testimony to the compiler's taste and literary accomplishment that it remained by and large the best anthology until we come to ... [Ralph] Gustafson's" *Anthology of Canadian Poetry* (1942) (9).

WORKS CITED

Adam, G. Mercer. "A New Anthology." Rev. of *Songs of the Great Dominion*, ed. William Douw Lighthall. *The Week* 6.27 (1889): 421. Print.

Bentley, D. M. R. *The Confederation Group of Canadian Poets, 1880–1897*. Toronto: U of Toronto P, 2004. Print.

Berger, Carl. *The Sense of Power: Studies in the Ideas of Canadian Imperialism, 1867–1914*. Toronto: U of Toronto P, 1970. Print.

Campbell, William Wilfred, Archibald Lampman, and Duncan Campbell Scott. *At the Mermaid Inn: Wilfred Campbell, Archibald Lampman, Duncan Campbell Scott in The Globe 1892–93*. Ed. Barrie Davies. Toronto: U of Toronto P, 1976. Print.

Daniells, Roy. "Confederation to the First World War." *Literary History of Canada*. Ed. Carl F. Klinck. 1963. Toronto: U of Toronto P, 1965. 191–207. Print.

Lecker, Robert. *English-Canadian Literary Anthologies: An Enumerative Bibliography*. Teeswater, ON: Reference, 1997. Print.

Lighthall, William Douw, ed. *Canadian Poems and Lays: Selections of Native Verse, Reflecting the Seasons, Legends, and Life of the Dominion*. London: Walter Scott, 1893. Print.

———. *Canadian Songs and Poems. Voices from the Forests and Waters, the Settlements and Cities of Canada*. London: Walter Scott; Toronto: W. J. Gage, 1892. Print.

———. "Correspondence with William Sharp and Others, ca. 1888–1889." *Papers and Proof*. Rare Books and Special Collections, McGill University. Montreal, Canada. Archival.

———. "The Sentiment of Nationality." Letter. *Montreal Daily Witness*. 10 Nov. 1888: n. pag. Print.

———. *Songs of the Great Dominion. Voices from the Forests and Waters, the Settlements and Cities of Canada*. London: Walter Scott, 1889. Print.

"Log-rolling." *Oxford English Dictionary*. http://www.oed.com. Online.

Moores, Ted, and Marilyn Mohr. *Canoecraft: A Harrowsmith Illustrated Guide to Fine Woodstrip Construction*. Buffalo, NY: Camden House, 1983. Print.

"New Books." Rev. of *Songs of the Great Dominion*, ed. William Douw Lighthall. *Ottawa Daily Citizen*. 17 June 1889: n. pag. Print.

Roberts, Charles G. D. *Collected Letters*. Ed. Laurel Boone. Fredericton, NB: Goose Lane Editions, 1989. Print.

———. *Selected Poetry and Prose*. Ed. W. J. Keith. Toronto: U of Toronto P, 1974. Print.

Schneider, Aaron J. "Total Man!: Literature, Nationalism, and Masculinity in Canada." Diss. University of Western Ontario, 2011. Print.

Smith, A. J. M. "Canadian Anthologies, New and Old." *On Poetry and Poets: Selected Essays*. Toronto: McClelland and Stewart, 1977. 1–18. Print.

Stewart, A. C. *The Poetical Review: A Brief Notice of Canadian Poets and Poetry*. Ed. D. M. R. Bentley. *Canadian Poetry: Studies, Documents, Reviews* 1 (1877): 66–88. Print.

Tennyson, Alfred Lord. *Poems*. Ed. Christopher Ricks. London: Longman; New York: Norton, 1969. Print.

Thomson, E. W. "Literary Notes." *Globe* (Toronto). 5 July 1889: 4. Print.

Turner, John R. *The Walter Scott Publishing Company: A Bibliography.* Pittsburgh, PA: U of Pittsburgh P, 1997. Print.

Wallace, W. Stewart. *Macmillan Dictionary of Canadian Biography.* Toronto: Macmillan, 1945. Print.

Ware, Tracy. "Two Unpublished Letters from Arthur Symons to Bliss Carman." *English Language Notes* 28.3 (1991): 42–46. Print.

Watts-Dunton, Theodore. Rev. of *Songs of the Great Dominion.* Ed. William Douw Lighthall. *Athenaeum* 28.3231 (1889): 411–13. Print.

Excerpts of Exploration Writing in Anthologies of English-Canadian Literature

Cheryl Cundell

Anthologies of English-Canadian literature that include excerpts of exploration writing elucidate some of the negotiations underpinning literary canonization. These anthologies are elucidating because including excerpts of exploration writing involves them in a paradox of place: "place" denoting both literary situation and geographical delineation. Paradox of place refers to the simultaneously canonical and non- or anti-canonical status conferred upon exploration writing as a result of negotiations needed in transferring sixteenth- through early-nineteenth-century non-Canadian non-fiction concerning the geographical space that would become Canada to the English-Canadian literary canon. The paradox of place points to one principle of canonizing, for although anthologies either implicitly or explicitly debate questions concerning the "who," "what," "when," "how," and "why" of English-Canadian literature, "where" typically functions as a foregone conclusion or rear-view vision—from sea to sea to sea.

To identify anthologies that include exploration writing, I use Robert Lecker's "Anthologizing English-Canadian Fiction" chapter of *Making It Real* (1995), in which, searching for a "recognizable canon of Canadian fiction" (114), Lecker analyzes "65" (115) anthologies (including different editions) for the period 1922 to 1992. Noting not only fiction but also exploration writing, which he categorizes as "travel literature" (137), Lecker says, "[t]o the best of my knowledge, this database includes all anthologies of Canadian literature that represent themselves as being national" (115), although he adds, "[b]ecause a number of anthologists who call their collections 'modern' insist that this modernity is in fact representative of some kind of Canadian tradition, I have included their work" (124). Exploration writing occurs in ten of Lecker's sixty-five anthologies, and to these ten I add four, from 1993 to 2008, to my discussion.[1]

Given the anthologies that focus exclusively on the modern period and the interest that Lecker has in fiction, the "ten to sixty-five" ratio says little— except that, if canonization is a process of selection and repetition, then at least some anthologizers think that the genre of exploration writing should be canonized. The modern focus, however, says much about the negotiations involved in canonizing that impinge upon exploration writing. One of these negotiations involves the "why" of, or rationales for, anthologizing, the most obvious of which is to collect works of literary value. In this case, if "modern" is taken to mean either recent or modernist, the focus might reflect an evaluative perspective that rejects early literature as being of poor quality and refuses to engage with changing perceptions of literary value over time. This evaluative perspective contributes to exploration writing's simultaneously canonical and non- or anti-canonical status, for while changing perceptions of literary value have to do with changing ideas about what constitutes *good* literature, they also have to do with distinctions between fiction and prose, or between *belles lettres* and *lettres pratiques*: that is, the first question of literary value is the question of what constitutes literature. Because exploration writing has a documenting or empirical function, the phrase "non-fictional exploration writing" is a redundancy. The expectation is that exploration writing deals—or *should deal*—in facts, and it is because of the matter of fact, understood as "datum of experience" ("Datum" *OED*), that exploration writing suffers from a paradoxical literary status. Although it appears in literary anthologies because it is valued, exploration writing is frequently devalued as literature because of habits of reading that read its non-fictional status—by transposition—as a *non-literary* status. Thus, it becomes canonical non-literature.

If the "modern" of the modern focus of some of the anthologies is taken to mean recent rather than modernist, then the focus highlights another negotiation involved in canonizing that impinges upon exploration writing. The focus provides an answer to the question "When is Canada?" In this case, "modern" takes into account the historical process of nationhood, and the answer to the question is "Canadian literature begins after Newfoundland joins Confederation." While exploration writing preceding the process of Confederation seems safely not Canadian (if not safely *not literature*), it is, nonetheless, included in some English-Canadian literary anthologies because the process of Confederation presents both a problem and an opportunity for determining when Canadian literature begins. The operating logic is as follows: if Canada has no "defining moment," then any moment might do.

Certainly there are preferred "defining moments," some of which are pre-Confederation moments. Although anthologies rarely acknowledge historical events as the basis for selecting exploration writing, their selections nevertheless point to specific events, not the least of which is European arrival at various points in North America. Three of the fourteen anthologies under discussion include exploration writing dating from the sixteenth century; the other eleven begin with exploration writing pertaining to late-eighteenth-century exploration. Although the preponderance of selections suggesting that Canada begins in the late eighteenth century might be the result of convenience, with the more recent anthologies modelling the selections of the less recent, the choice of selections can also be seen to follow the logic of the earliest North American literary histories. The choice might reflect distinctions between the United States of America and British North America following Ray Palmer Baker's *A History of English-Canadian Literature to the Confederation* (1920), which, for example, assumes that there *is* a pre-Confederation English-Canadian literature but that it "does not begin until the close of the American Revolution" (7). More likely, given the great French–English divide and the anthologies' English-Canadian focus, the choices reflect the logic of either J. D. Logan and Donald G. French's *Highways of Canadian Literature* (1924), which begins with the 1760 "Fall of Montreal" (20), or Lorne Pierce's *An Outline of Canadian Literature* (1927), which begins with the 1763 "Peace of Paris" (1) and the cession of New France to Britain.

As for the anthologies beginning with sixteenth-century exploration writing—William Toye's *A Book of Canada* (1962), Douglas Daymond and Leslie Monkman's *Literature in Canada* (1978), and Cynthia Sugars and Laura Moss's *Canadian Literature in English* (2008)—their Canada includes New France, in translation. All three anthologies excerpt from French explorer Jacques Cartier, who explored the St. Lawrence River; from the seventeenth century, Toye's and Sugars and Moss's anthologies excerpt from another St. Lawrence River explorer, Samuel de Champlain; and Toye's anthology excerpts from Pierre-Esprit Radisson, who explored around Hudson Bay. Given that these anthologies also include excerpts from late-eighteenth-century British explorer–fur traders, the decision to begin with the French seems to follow Harold A. Innis and Donald Creighton's Laurentian thesis. Innis and Creighton, both economic historians, see Canada's origins in the westward expansion of the St. Lawrence fur trade of the late-eighteenth-century North West Company, which later became part of the northern (truly northern?) monopoly of the Hudson's Bay Company. Innis argues that "[t]he Northwest Company was the forerunner of Confederation" because, upon "[t]he work of the French traders and explorers and of the English who built upon foundations laid down by" the French, it "had built up an organization which extended from the Atlantic to the Pacific" (265).

While Sugars and Moss keep their sixteenth- through late-eighteenth-century selections within the limits of the Laurentian thesis, Toye and

Daymond and Monkman push those limits. In a nod to Newfoundland, they push farther east than the mouth of the St. Lawrence River and include selections on Sir Humphrey Gilbert's 1583 voyage: Toye offers an excerpt from Edward Haies's report of the voyage; Daymond and Monkman offer, in full (and in translation from the original Latin), Stephen Parmenius's "Letter to Richard Hakluyt" (4), British compiler of exploration writing. Anomalous among all of the anthologies, all of which excerpt from eighteenth-century exploration writing, Daymond and Monkman include a selection from George Vancouver, whose *A Voyage of Discovery to the North Pacific Ocean* (1798) does not pertain to the trade in beaver furs. Selecting Vancouver for his focus on geography, Daymond and Monkman excerpt from his survey of Burrard Inlet, for along the southern shore of the inlet lies the City of Vancouver, with Gastown, the original city site, just south of the "island" (Daymond and Monkman 65)—not an island and now known as Stanley Park (Lamb 581 n.1)—that Vancouver passes while surveying.

Being so obviously about location, this Vancouver selection highlights one reason for including exploration writing in the English-Canadian literary canon: that is, in answer to the question "What constitutes Canadian literature?" it provides the further question "What is printed about the geographic space that would become Canada?" This is the rear-view vision that opens up the field to retroactive CanLit. Leon Surette explains the logic of retroactive CanLit when he traces the importance of territory to English-Canadian conceptions of the national literature. Coining the term "topocentrism" to indicate the tendency to imagine cultures geographically, Surette observes that "[t]opocentrism dominates critical perspectives on Canadian literature, because no other means of establishing its boundaries are available" (51). Surette is not himself of the mind that there are no options for defining Canadian literature other than a backward-looking geographic *fait accompli*, but he observes that although "the Canadian political entity might provide some literary borders as it does geographical ones," "critics and imaginative writers of the anglophone community are unanimous in their conviction that the Canadian political entity is too vague in outline and pale in hue to enter into the literary imagination" (51).

Topocentrism is at work in some of the early literary histories that attempt to determine who qualifies as a Canadian author. Although both Baker's and Logan and French's histories address some exploration writing as Canadian literature, Baker's excludes "visitors" from qualifying as Canadian authors while admitting "those of European birth and education who became identified with [Canada's] development" (6), whereas Logan and French are more inclusive of authors but more precise in regards to these authors' relationship to Canada. They use "'Incidental'" (21) to describe literature "written in or about Canada by British authors, visiting or sojourning in Canada" (20) and "'Nativistic'" (21) for the pre-Confederation literature of writers who were born in or emigrated to what would become Canada—both of which are distinguished from the post-Confederation "'Native or National'" (21) literature. In another one of the early literary histories, *Appraisals of Canadian Literature* (1926), Lionel Stevenson muses on what exactly defines a "Canadian author":

> the effort to treat Canadian literature systematically and categorically is immediately beset by the difficulty of striking a basis of definition among the various writers who might demand inclusion—Canadian-born authors domiciled elsewhere and not using Canadian themes, authors born outside of Canada but genuinely interpreting the country, and so on. (vi)

Although Stevenson's definition of literature excludes exploration writing, his reference to those writers who are "genuinely interpreting the country" (vi) reveals a common rationale for anthologizing that permits explorers among Canadian authors and, thus, transforms "incidental" into "national."

While Baker's and Stevenson's literary histories reveal how explorers get to become Canadian authors, and Logan and French's history reveals how exploration writing gets to become Canadian literature, Reginald Eyre Watters's *A Check List of Canadian Literature and Background Materials 1628–1950: In Two Parts* (1959) reveals more about the paradox of place that produces exploration writing's uncertain literary status. Like Stevenson, Watters too muses on what defines a "Canadian author," but, unlike Stevenson, his musings end in a definition:

> [t]he definition of "Canadian author" was ... deliberately left very broad.... Canadian birth alone was not considered an adequate claim for persons who left Canada in early childhood and apparently never returned. On the other hand, persons who came to Canada in maturity to reside here and then commenced or continued as authors are normally included, whether or not they later left the country. (vii–viii)

Unlike Stevenson, who remains open to "Canadian-born authors domiciled elsewhere," Watters suggests, both for the Canadian- and foreign-born, that to qualify as a Canadian author one must be influenced by Canada as a geographic construct: that is, there is implicit in Watters's musings the idea of a residency requirement. And while according to Watters's definition some of the explorers may count as Canadians, whether they fully qualify as *authors of literature* may be debated given that their texts appear not in "Part I," which deals with "the recognized forms of poetry, fiction, and drama," but in "Part II," which "is a more or less selective listing of books by Canadians which seem likely to be of value to anyone studying the literature or culture of Canada" (vii). Surette notes that there is a "tendency to write cultural history when observing Canadian literature" (44), and one can see how it might be that, when these "books" that are of "value to anyone studying the literature or culture" (Watters vii) are considered as *Canadian Literature* and not just *"Background Materials,"* the tendency would be strengthened.

Dermot McCarthy sees topocentrism as one of the problematic perspectives on Canadian literature that arises because "[f]rom its beginnings in the nineteenth century, the writing of Canadian literary history has been organized around the extra-literary concept of the 'nation'" (32). Given that any national literary history is necessarily a nationalist project, however, the real problem seems to be that, where Canadian literature is concerned, "nation" is opposed to "evaluation"—or one might say that there is a distinction to be made between the value of literature and literary evaluation. So instead of a canon representing works judged on the basis of literary criteria, McCarthy argues that the result is "the canonical privileging of only those works or oeuvres which express the 'spirit of the place' or 'the spirit of the people'—these being, for all intents and purposes, one and the same" (32).

While I agree with McCarthy's remark, I believe that it captures only half of the canonical-privileging equation, for anthologies are interested in both the essence and substance of the nation. This interest produces what I like to think of as a Spirit and Image ethos, in acknowledgement of Stevenson, who has some interesting ideas about literature and geography. Beginning figuratively, Stevenson argues that there is a "Canadian quality sufficiently distinctive to warrant the acceptance of Canadian literature as a separate entity in the intellectual geography of the world" (viii). He then creates a literal geographical distinction between poetry and narrative prose by saying, "[p]oetry is a less localised affair than prose narrative" (x) because the poetry best "exemplifying the essential Canadian spirit" deals with "universal poetic themes" (x), whereas "writers of prose ... have been content with the superficial distinctiveness which Canadian settings and events provide" (xii). Not only does Stevenson subscribe to topocentrism to remark upon the distinctiveness of Canadian literature and mark distinctions between literary valuations of poetry and prose, but he also uses topocentrism to justify talking about Canadian literature at all: although he makes "no extravagant claims for the excellence of Canadian literature" (xiii), the literary works that he discusses are valuable because they either capture "the elusive national quality" or "depict the real life of the country" (xiii). Stevenson's perspective suggests that the problem is not that there is no literary evaluation in attempts to define the canon, but rather that the value attributed to the canon might be the result of an initial devaluation of the literature. Perhaps worse than always indicating an initial devaluation, however, the Spirit and Image ethos, which values "the nation," neither confirms nor denies literary value.

The Spirit and Image ethos is evident in Edmund Kemper Broadus and Eleanor Hammond Broadus's *A Book of Canadian Prose and Verse*, the first anthology on Lecker's list in which exploration writing appears (in both its 1923 and 1934 editions). In this anthology, the editors' declared intention is "to create, with its proper setting, a picture of Canadian life, past and present," and their rationale for neglecting texts that do not contribute to this "picture" is that "much of the best of Canadian literature has been either directly inspired by the Canadian scene or has reflected the effort to recreate the historic past" (1923, vii). The editors admit that, as a result of their intention, their anthology "falls short of being representative in the larger sense of the word" and, because of their logic, "much that is excellent has been lost" (vii). Because the editors positively evaluate texts included in and excluded from their anthology, their admission highlights the distinction between selecting literary texts to represent the nation and selecting texts representative of the literature produced by the nation. While the distinction speaks to the struggle to answer the question "What is Canadian?" the distinction is not a problem of using a "concept of the 'nation'" (McCarthy 32) as a criterion for selection but a problem of selection itself, for there might also be a distinction between selecting the best of the nation's literature and selecting texts representative of the literature produced by the nation.

The sole explorer Broadus and Broadus excerpt is Alexander Mackenzie, trader and partner in the North West Company, whose *Voyages from Montreal* (1801) begins by providing a history of the fur trade that includes a generalized voyage "from Montreal" to Fort Chipewyan. The remainder of the text is devoted to Mackenzie's one failed attempt to reach the Pacific Ocean, during which he reached the Arctic, and his one successful attempt. In the "THE PEOPLE" (xiv) section of the anthology, the excerpt is from the final leg of Mackenzie's successful Pacific-going voyage, and it finishes by describing the "Bella Coola" (Mackenzie 368) or Nuxalk totems. Offered as a piece of ethnography, the excerpt takes on another meaning with respect to its introduction, which quotes Mackenzie's Pacific arrival:

> I now mixed up some vermillion in melted grease, and inscribed, in large characters, on the South-East face of the rock on which we had slept last night, this brief memorial—"Alexander Mackenzie, from Canada, by land, the twenty-second of July, one thousand seven hundred and ninety-three."
> (Broadus and Broadus 160; Mackenzie 378)

Although the quotation is given as evidence of Mackenzie's "plain prose" (160) style, the editors' choice for evidence of style celebrates Mackenzie's territorial assertion. Often appropriated as Canadian national symbols, the totems of the excerpt thus become icons of the fur trade stretching, in the words of Mackenzie's book title, "from Montreal ... to the ... Pacific."

John D. Robins's *A Pocketful of Canada* (1946) and Toye's *A Book of Canada* (1962) also have a Spirit and Image ethos, but the editors' aims are not literary. Carole Gerson notes that Robins's is a "collection of visual, cultural, and political materials" (65), and "Robins took pains to state that the volume 'is not intended as an anthology, it makes no claims to be a repository of the best Canadian writing'" (Robins xiii; qtd. in Gerson 65–66). Gerson also notes, however, that "the Canadian Council of Education for Citizenship," which "issued" (65) the volume, in its "own later publicity would describe the volume as 'An anthology of Canadian poetry, prose and art, selected in a successful attempt to capture the spirit of Canada and its people'" (qtd. in Gerson 66). She argues that, with 1948 and 1952 editions, "the reduction of the non-literary sections further implies that the publisher regarded the book principally as a literary commodity" (72).

Robins offers selections from Mackenzie's text and David Thompson's *David Thompson's Narrative of His Explorations in Western America, 1784–1812* (1916), edited from Thompson's manuscript by J. B. Tyrrell for the Champlain Society of Canada, the first to publish the full text. Both selections are in the anthology's section titled "*THE BUSH*" (81), although neither offers solely verbal landscape portraits. The Mackenzie selection excerpts from the fur trade history including the generalized trip, the part "*between Montreal and the mouth of the French River on Georgian Bay*" (83). Although Thompson too was a trader (for both the Hudson's Bay Company and the North West Company), the Thompson excerpt makes no mention of the trade. From the "Trip to Lake Athabasca" chapter, near the end of one of Thompson's surveying trips, it narrates Thompson's plunge down a waterfall on the Black River.

Boasting "51 photographs" (title page), Toye's anthology is advertised as one of the "Collins National Anthologies" (prefatory matter) devoted to the nations of the British Isles (among which is "A BOOK OF LONDON") and Britain's former settler colonies. The boast of photos is suggestive of the anthology's intent, which is to present a picture—historical, geographical, cultural—of Canada. This picture begins with European arrival, as Toye introduces his text saying, "Canadiana came into being when [the land] [...] impelled explorers, colonizers, missionaries, settlers, and even tourists to penetrate its mysteries and write about what they saw" (15). Here the Europeans are cast in not only the imperial but also the *empirical* mould, as "those assiduous, inquisitive note-takers," and the "explorers and fur traders," specifically, as those "who doggedly reduced momentous journeys to laconic diary entries" (15). Using empiricism to characterize the arriving Europeans, Toye transforms the empirical function into not only a necessary outcome of travel and curiosity but also a general literary thematic: he continues, "Canada Observed was a tirelessly repeated theme for over three centuries" (15).

Besides selections from Cartier, Gilbert, Champlain, and Radisson, Toye offers a selection from Samuel Hearne's *A Journey from Prince of Wales's Fort in Hudson's Bay, to the Northern Ocean* (1795)—possibly because he is inspired by the contemporaneous publication of Farley Mowat's truncated edition, *Coppermine Journey* (1958). Composed of three distinct sections in its first edition, Hearne's text covers his two failed attempts and his one successful journey to reach the Arctic Ocean, "A short Description of the Northern Indians, also a farther Account of their Country, Manufactures, Customs, & c." (304) pertaining to the Chipewyan with whom he travelled, and descriptions of the plant and non-human animal life of the Hudson Bay area. The excerpt, taken from near the turning point of the successful journey, is from Hearne's chapter 6, the descriptive heading of which begins "Transactions at the Copper-mine River" (145). Toye titles the excerpt "The Coppermine Massacre" (73) because it concerns Hearne's Chipewyan companions massacring a group of Inuit living near the mouth of the Coppermine River at the Arctic Ocean, at a section of which Hearne later denominates "Bloody Falls" (166). Given that the excerpt includes little but the massacre, it seems chosen for its dramatic horror. Notably, it ends with Hearne, who remained, as he explains, "neuter in the rear" (Toye 74; Hearne 153) during the attack, "shedding tears" (75; 155) in remembrance of the event, a symbol of civilized man confronting "barbarity" (74; 153).

While the Broadus and Broadus anthology might be said to be a literary anthology with a national perspective, and the Robins and Toye anthologies might be said to be national anthologies with literary interests, all three anthologies commingle literature and nation in such ways as to elide distinctions between the two. Part of the commingling arises from arrangement, for the anthologies do not organize their contents in strict chronology but, rather, into sections, using titles to indicate what the selections therein reveal of the nation. Although Toye uses chronological arrangement in the section "*The Passage of the Years*" (5), in which the exploration writing selections appear, the title of the section and the selections included suggest that its purpose is to outline national history. The absence of strict chronology in the three anthologies suggests that they neither formulate nor are formulated upon literary history, and, thus, they promote or contribute to cultural history views of literature.

If Surette is correct that perspectives on English-Canadian literature have a markedly topocentric, cultural history orientation and that English-Canadian critics and writers reject the Canadian polity as an organizing principle for Canadian literary history because they desire "a *Canadian* story or myth" (52), then exploration writing is the crux of English-Canadian literary history. The logic holds because exploration writing's uncertain status has it serving various functions: it provides a geographic view, it outlines history in document form, and it allows for the land to function as a literary influence. Finally, a compelling candidate for retroactive CanLit, exploration writing offers the possibility of an originary story complete with travelling heroes.

Northrop Frye sees the possibility when, musing on the inadequacies of English-Canadian literature in his "Conclusion" to the first edition of *Literary History of Canada* (1965), he remarks that "[t]he literary, in Canada, is often only an incidental quality of writings which, like those of many of the early explorers, are as innocent of literary intention as a mating loon" (822). Loon notwithstanding, what seems like an offhand simile is a calculated move in Frye's strategy whereby he justifies *Literary History*'s first three chapters on exploration writing by using the genre to explain both English-Canadian literature's poor quality and its prospects for improvement. Disparaging the literary in Canada and exploration writing in general while hinting at an aesthetic hierarchy of "literary" over "writing," Frye's remark also elides distinctions between writings Canadian and non-Canadian. The remark is essential given that *Literary History* narrates the development of English-Canadian literature, which not only improves but also becomes more Canadian with time. In Frye's words, *Literary History* "has its own themes of exploration, settlement, and development," and "these themes relate to a social *imagination* that explores and settles and develops," an imagination that "has its own rhythms of growth as well as its own modes of expression" (822). Therefore, as both the text's final part and the happy result of the imagination's growth and development, there is "The Realization of a Tradition"—national, Canadian.

After mentioning the accidental literariness of exploration/Canadian writings, Frye shores up the developmental narrative by arguing that the inadequacies of Canadian literature arise because

> the Canadian sensibility has been profoundly disturbed, not so much by our famous problem of identity, important as that is, but by a series of paradoxes in what confronts that identity. It is less perplexed by the question "Who am I?" than by some such riddle as "Where is here?" (826)

The much-cited, much-alluded to "'Where is here?'" (826) is a question of convenience for which exploration writing has the answer. If Canadian literature has a problem of geography, then geographic knowledge is the solution. Enter exploration writing. Exploration writing *must be* the nation's earliest literature because without its observations, maps, and directions—without its arrival—Canadian literature would be lost. Thus, Frye addresses literary evaluation and national definition with a myth of origins.

Surveying views of exploration writing, Roger Leonard Martin notes the "strange coincidence" (60) of the date of publication of the first edition of *Literary History* (1965) and A. J. M. Smith's literary anthology *The Book of Canadian Prose* (1965). (Perhaps the editors were hoping to make good on the upcoming centennial?) Martin argues that the views espoused by Frye and Smith in these texts suggest that Canada's "national prose epic" or "creation myth could be informed by documentary rather than predominantly mythological values" (63). The trick is, the documents provide the myth, and if Frye does not say as much, Smith does.

The Book of Canadian Prose, Volume 1: Early Beginnings to Confederation (1965) covers what Smith refers to in his "Preface" as "our colonial period" (xi). Thus, like some of the earlier anthologists and literary historians, he believes that there *is*, if not a Canadian literature before Confederation, at least a Canadian-ness expressing itself in literature. In Smith's opinion, "in the period from about 1870 to 1910, few Canadian writers seemed able to escape from a genteel English tradition that was unmistakably literary" and, as a result, produced writing that "seems weak, derivative, and ... thoroughly colonial" (xiii), whereas "the practical, amateur writers" (xiii) like "the explorers" "created a literature simply by minding their own business and writing out of the immediate experience of the world around them" (xiv). Going further than Toye's thematic "Canada Observed" (15), Smith believes that this "amateur" writing best captures Canadian literature's "individuality" (xiii). The irony is not only that this "amateur" writing is not amateur but also that this *distinctly Canadian* writing is *thoroughly colonial*. If the shared publication date of *Literary History* and *The Book of Canadian Prose* is coincidental, then perhaps also coincidental is the similarity of *vision* in Frye's "Conclusion" and Smith's "Introduction," particularly in Frye's idea that the Canadian environment is "the immediate datum of ... imagination" (827) and Smith's idea that "the explorers" wrote from their "immediate experience" (xiv).

Smith selects Hearne, Mackenzie, and Thompson, and in his introduction to the Hearne selection, he quotes Tyrrell's assessment that Hearne's text "'is chiefly valuable'" as a work of "'ethnology'" (qtd. in Smith 53). Following Tyrrell's assessment and Toye's precedent, Smith excerpts for "ethnological" interest at the same time that he tries to preserve some sense of the whole of the third and successful exploration of the *Journey* by excerpting important moments leading up to, including, and following the massacre. Smith does not end with Hearne's tears but rather with the Chipewyan purification ritual following the massacre and, thus, maintains "ethnological" interest. Indicating that James George Frazer's 1935 text on comparative religion influenced his selection, Smith notes, "[t]he elaborate purification ceremonies ... [are] quoted at length in *The Golden Bough*" (53).

While Hearne remains the "ethnologist," Mackenzie is the epic hero, as Smith speaks of Mackenzie's crew members "whose names are recorded like an Homeric list of heroes" (86). Celebrating Mackenzie's heroism but preferring plain prose, Smith is not fond of the text's "literary artifice," which he attributes to (if not blames upon) Mackenzie's "ghost writer, William Combe" (87). Like Robins, Smith excerpts from Mackenzie's fur trade history, but he selects different details and does not include any part of the generalized trip. He also excerpts from the beginning of the explorer's successful Pacific voyage, the part that includes the list of crew members to which he refers, and, like Broadus and Broadus, he excerpts from near the voyage's end. Smith concludes the selection with Mackenzie's inscription, which he also quotes in his introduction and describes as "a single sentence of monumental grandeur" and the "greatest stylistic achievement" of the "amateur writers" (xv). Thus, a territorial marker transforms into a sentence of literary value.

Finally, following Tyrrell's assessment of Thompson, "one of the greatest geographers of the world" (Tyrrell xix), but expanding upon it, Smith selects excerpts that reveal some of Thompson's variety. Thompson is astronomer, raconteur, naturalist, and ethnographer. Smith begins his selection with an excerpt that includes some of Thompson's comments on "practical astronomy" (Smith 103–4; Thompson, *Narrative* 89), and he follows this excerpt with a naming-legend told to Thompson "by an old Canadian" (Smith 108; Thompson 139). The following excerpt, titled "'TWO DISTINCT RACES OF BEINGS—MAN AND THE BEAVER'" (108), is Thompson's pre- and post-discovery story of Canada showing aboriginal peoples (as "man") living in balance with the natural world ("the beaver") until the arrival of Europeans with their demand for beaver furs and their "articles of iron" (Smith 110; Thompson 152) offered in trade. This excerpt reveals the influence of Innis, who introduces his *The Fur Trade in Canada* (1930) with a brief chapter titled "The Beaver," in which he quotes from Thompson. Smith excerpts from that part of Thompson's text that is the source of two of the three quotations in Innis: one detailing "the average weight" and taste of "a full grown male" (Smith 110; Innis 2) beaver and another detailing how beaver "became an easy prey to the Hunter" (Smith 110; Innis 4) because of improvements in weapons technology.

Smith draws a parallel between the excerpt "'Two Distinct Races of Beings'" and the epic genre by describing the passage as having "an almost

Homeric freshness of vision" (103). Instead of conflating "epic hero" with "writer of epic," as he does in Mackenzie's case, Smith here subordinates the hero to the writer. Appropriate for the hero, however, the final excerpt, following one of ethnological description, is from Thompson's trip through the Rockies. It describes Thompson's exhilaration when he notes that his party's location has "all the appearance to the height of land between the Atlantic and Pacific Oceans" (Smith 118; Thompson 321), which suggests that they have reached the Great Divide. Looking west, Thompson exclaims, "a new world was in a manner before me" (322), and, thus, he serves as a visionary, evoking Canada's first motto: *a mari usque ad mare*.

Following Smith's anthology is Robert Weaver and William Toye's *The Oxford Anthology of Canadian Literature* (1973), with an offering from Hearne. Like Smith, Weaver and Toye allude to Tyrrell's assessment and excerpt details pertaining to the Coppermine massacre—but to a lesser degree than does Smith. Although Toye's *A Book of Canada* excerpted Hearne earlier, the editors excerpt "like Smith" because, unlike *A Book of Canada*, they include the purification rituals quoted in the *Golden Bough*. Thus, if Smith observes precedent, then he also sets precedent. In the case of Weaver and Toye, however, the precedent is the excerpt and not the developmental perspective. More interested to "convey a real sense of a community of writers" (xiv) than to relate literary history, the editors provide "cross-references": here, Hearne with "John Newlove's 'Samuel Hearne in Wintertime'" (1966) (xiv). Weaver and Toye also eschew the Spirit and Image ethos, as they organize their authors alphabetically and explain "it is somehow liberating to view our writing apart from categories" (xiii). *Reading/Writing Canada: Short Fiction and Nonfiction* (2005), edited by Judith Maclean Miller, also arranges alphabetically but selects Thompson and, following no precedent, begins at the beginning with the fourteen-year-old Thompson leaving London for Hudson Bay and describing the difficulties he has adjusting to the "circumstances" (388; Thompson, *Travels* 67) of his new home.

Published nine years after his *Book of Canadian Prose*, Smith's *The Canadian Experience: A Brief Survey of English-Canadian Prose* (1974) includes excerpts from Hearne and Thompson but not Mackenzie. Preserving his 1965 introductions to the excerpts in the 1974 text, Smith reduces his selections from Hearne and Thompson. In Hearne's case, he goes the way of "The Slaughter of the Esquimaux" (26) or the Coppermine massacre—although he preserves his original excerpts in full and, thus, retains their "ethnological" interest. In Thompson's case, Smith offers only the "Two Distinct Races of Beings" (35) excerpt, which emphasizes Thompson's fur-trade interests rather than his cartographic achievements. The absence of excerpts from Mackenzie's text is the result of a volume-reducing necessity that reflects

Smith's negative opinion of the text's style; the persisting reference to Mackenzie's text and the quotation of Mackenzie's inscription in the anthology's introduction, however, maintain the text's literary value—which is that it is exploration inscribed.

Daymond and Monkman (1978) include, along with their less-than-usual excerpts from Cartier, Parmenius, and Vancouver, excerpts from Hearne and Thompson. The Hearne excerpt is "The Coppermine Massacre" (53), and they end it, as Toye does in *A Book of Canada*, with Hearne's tears. The Thompson excerpt follows the latter portion of Smith's "Two Distinct Races of Beings" and continues somewhat beyond, with Thompson musing on the beaver scarcity resulting from supplying the demands of the fur trade.

R. G. Moyles's *"Improved by Cultivation": An Anthology of English-Canadian Prose to 1914* (1994) is motivated by an observation like Lecker's regarding the practice of anthologizing literature that is "modern" (124) as representative of "Canadian." Following the Spirit and Image ethos of the earlier anthologies, Moyles explains that the aim of his anthology is "to rediscover [the earlier] literature and the Canada it portrayed" (11). Perhaps also following the earlier anthologies (and because his anthology's end date excludes Thompson's 1916 text), Moyles includes Hearne and Mackenzie. Titled "Transactions at the Coppermine River" (33), the Hearne selection begins with Hearne and his companions arriving at the Coppermine River, continues through the day of the massacre, and ends with Hearne's tears. The Mackenzie selection is from several days before Mackenzie writes his inscription, from before Mackenzie and his crew depart from "Friendly Village" (Mackenzie 390), when Smith's final 1965 excerpt begins.

An Anthology of Canadian Literature in English, Volume I (1982), edited by Russell Brown and Donna Bennett, and the "Revised & Abridged Edition" (title page) of *An Anthology of Canadian Literature in English* (1990), edited by Brown, Bennett, and Nathalie Cooke, share selections from Hearne and Thompson. Sounding like Frye and Smith in their introduction to the first edition, Brown and Bennett explain that texts of exploration writing "are significant pieces of early *writing* in their own right, as well as important influences on the *literature* that followed" (1st ed. xi; emphasis added). Perhaps justifying the presence of exploration writing in their anthology of "*Literature*," certainly attempting to explain why this "writing" is "significant," the editors note that some early "writers ... expressed concern over the lack of an indigenous mythology" and explain that writers like Hearne and Thompson "are interesting to read not only because they record the first stages of this quest for a viable myth but because they provide the source material for later writers; that is, they themselves have become myth-makers and even mythic figures" (1st ed. xii). Transforming exploration from a quest

for geographical facts to a quest for myth, the editors offer a remedy for a
"concern" that is, simultaneously, a denial of indigenous mythologies and an
ambition to supplant them.

With introductory remarks quoting from Hearne's second set of "Orders
and Instructions" (1770), which command him to go "*in quest of a North West
Passage*" and "*Copper Mines*" (1st ed. 23, typescript following Hearne 64), the
selection strives for narrative unity by focusing on the idea of the north. New
to Hearne selections, an excerpt from the second (failed) journey emphasizes
the physical conditions of travel in the far north and acts as a context for the
third journey. Although the editors echo Smith quoting Tyrrell by saying
that the text is "valuable to ethnographers" (1st ed. 24), the final excerpt,
which is of the massacre, ends with Hearne's "tears" (1st ed. 32, 155). At
the end of the excerpts, the tears are not, however, the end of the selection,
which reiterates "north" by quoting Hearne's conclusion to his third journey:
"[t]hough my discoveries are not likely to prove of any material advantage"
they have "put a final end to all disputes concerning a North West Passage
through Hudson's Bay" (Hearne 303).

Noting Tyrrell's involvement with the first edition of Thompson, the editors roughly quote Tyrrell's assessment of Thompson as "the greatest practical
land geographer that the world had produced" (1st ed. 32). The reference to
Tyrrell seems to arrive via the influence of Smith because, for the conclusion to their introduction, the editors quote from Smith's 1965 "A Night in
the Mountains" (117) and, thus, end their introduction with Thompson's
exhilarated "*a new world was in a manner before me*" (1st ed. 33). Also, the
excerpts from Thompson are taken from the chapter from which Smith takes
his excerpt on "practical astronomy" (Smith 103–4; Thompson, *Narrative*
89), part of which is included.

A New Anthology of Canadian Literature in English (2002), edited by Bennett and Brown, borrows much from the Hearne and Thompson selections in
the first edition and includes one new explorer: Sir John Franklin. The selection from Franklin's *Narrative of a Journey* (1823) speaks of resurging interest in the Canadian Arctic following the formation of Nunavut on April 1,
1999, and interplays with the Hearne selection because, in their remarks
prefatory to the selection, the editors quote Franklin as he describes coming
upon the place where the massacre occurred. In their prefatory remarks
to the section "Exploration Narratives" (27), the editors evoke the developmental perspective, saying "[a] desire to observe the environment closely, to
map physical and relational space, to document the details of one's milieu,
and to discover the source of events has been evident in Canadian writing"
(27). This "desire," however, has not simply "been evident" but is, rather, a
"habit of mind" that "has manifested itself as an imperative to record the

objective details of experience" (27); moreover, this "habit of mind ... has shaped the early non-fiction" (27). Employing originary myth in service of reverse logic, the editors reveal their own desires, which are to define English-Canadian literature as empirical and to make exploration writing express a pre-national national habit. The originary myth takes a curious turn, however, with the editors' attempt to recover an aboriginal voice. Added—as the anthology's first selection and not within the "Exploration Narratives" section—is Thompson's pages-long transcription-translation of the oral history told to him by "Nahathaway" (72) or Cree elder Saukamappee (Thompson's spelling).

Sugars and Moss's "Narratives of Encounter" section of *Canadian Literature in English* (2008) offers tribute to Frye in its "Introduction: Who/What/Where Is Here?" (15) and in its idea of the "development of Canadian literature" (xiv) being solely a print phenomenon: "[t]o present oral narratives [of Aboriginal Peoples] at the beginning of a collection of Canadian writing in English would suggest a formative influence on the subsequent development of Canadian literature that would be historically inaccurate" (xiv). Although the editors acknowledge that "[b]eginning with the period of European exploration is admittedly problematic" (xii), they overlook the developmental perspective when sequencing Cartier, Champlain, Hearne, Thompson, and Franklin, for Thompson's printed text belongs to the twentieth century. Moreover, they justify including Cartier and Champlain by appealing to the Spirit and Image ethos, saying "[i]t is impossible to paint an historical picture of the early European encounter with North America without them" (xiv). Different from others, the Thompson selection includes an excerpt from the added "Chapter IIA: The Saskatchewan" (37) in Richard Glover's 1962 edition. The selection also incorporates excerpts from the early part of the first Bennett and Brown (2002) selection including, in full, Smith's "practical astronomy" (103–4). Modelled on and yet different from Bennett and Brown (2002), the Hearne selection excerpts from Hearne's first "Orders and Instructions" (1769) (xxxv) and, following Brown and Bennett (1982), from the second journey. The final selection concerns the Coppermine massacre. It offers an expanded narrative with excerpts following Smith (1965) and Brown and Bennett (1982), but it ends, as Toye's (1962) does, in tears.

If the canonization of exploration writing is a process of selection and repetition, then it includes convenience, precedent, and attempts to be different. It offers variations on familiar excerpts and introduces new ones. It is an ongoing conversation—involving power and privileging. The ghostly apparition of fur trade history haunts its process. Frye and Smith exert their influence. Cartier has some say, and Franklin may be a contender, but the late eighteenth century holds sway. Mackenzie gives way to Thompson and his variety, and Thompson does double duty, as ideas about what constitutes "Canadian" shift. Then there is Hearne, Hearne, Hearne—and the massacre.

I. S. MacLaren calls the massacre a "purple patch" ("Exploration" 58; "Notes" 24) and notes that printed editions of the text "contain an element— torture—that one cannot find in the two surviving versions of Hearne's field notes" ("Notes" 21). MacLaren argues that the "element of torture" was added to the text because of the popularity of "the gothic novel" (24) coincident with its production. Thus, it may be that the massacre is canonized because, besides being the climax of the *Journey*, it is the part that most conforms to conceptions of the literary. Or perhaps a cultural history perspective elucidates the national value of the excerpt as a form of wish fulfillment: a tableau of one aboriginal group massacring another—and a European (or is that a proto-Canadian?) bystander in tears over the whole bloody thing.

NOTE

1 Chronological Listing of Anthologies: The ten from Lecker's *Making It Real*: Edmund Kemper Broadus and Eleanor Hammond Broadus, eds., *A Book of Canadian Prose and Verse* (Toronto: Macmillan, 1923 and 1934); John D. Robins, ed., *A Pocketful of Canada* (Toronto: Collins, 1946); William Toye, ed., *A Book of Canada* (London: Collins, 1962); A. J. M. Smith, ed., *The Book of Canadian Prose, Volume 1: Early Beginnings to Confederation* (Toronto: Gage, 1965); Robert Weaver and William Toye, eds., *The Oxford Anthology of Canadian Literature* (Toronto: Oxford UP, 1973); A. J. M. Smith, ed., *The Canadian Experience: A Brief Survey of English-Canadian Prose* (Agincourt, ON: Gage, 1974); Douglas Daymond and Leslie Monkman, eds., *Literature in Canada*, Vol. 1 (Toronto: Gage, 1978); Russell Brown and Donna Bennett, eds., *An Anthology of Canadian Literature in English*, Vol. 1 (Toronto: Oxford UP, 1982); Russell Brown, Donna Bennett, and Nathalie Cooke, eds., *An Anthology of Canadian Literature in English*, Revised & Abridged (Toronto: Oxford UP, 1990). The additional four: R. G. Moyles, ed., *"Improved by Cultivation": An Anthology of English-Canadian Prose to 1914* (Peterborough, ON: Broadview, 1994); Donna Bennett and Russell Brown, eds., *A New Anthology of Canadian Literature in English* (Don Mills, ON: Oxford UP, 2002); Judith Maclean Miller, ed., *Reading/Writing Canada: Short Fiction and Nonfiction* (New York: Norton, 2005); Cynthia Sugars and Laura Moss, eds., *Canadian Literature in English: Texts and Contexts*, Vol. 1 (Toronto: Pearson, 2008).

WORKS CITED

Baker, Ray Palmer. *A History of English-Canadian Literature to the Confederation: Its Relation to the Literature of Great Britain and the United States*. Cambridge: Harvard UP, 1920. Print.

Bennett, Donna, and Russell Brown, eds. *A New Anthology of Canadian Literature in English*. Don Mills, ON: Oxford UP, 2002. Print.

Broadus, Edmund Kemper, and Eleanor Hammond Broadus, eds. *A Book of Canadian Prose and Verse*. Toronto: Macmillan, 1923. Print.

Brown, Russell, and Donna Bennett, eds. *An Anthology of Canadian Literature in English*. Vol. 1. Toronto: Oxford UP, 1982. Print.

"Datum." Def. 1. a. *The Oxford English Dictionary*. 20 April 2015. http://www.oed.com.

Daymond, Douglas, and Leslie Monkman, eds. *Literature in Canada*. Vol. 1. Toronto: Gage, 1978. Print.

Frye, Northrop. Conclusion. *Literary History of Canada*. 1st ed. Ed. Carl F. Klinck. Toronto: U of Toronto P, 1965. 821–49. Print.

Gerson, Carole. "Design and Ideology in *A Pocketful of Canada*." *Papers of the Bibliographic Society of Canada* 44.2 (2006): 65–85. Print.

Hearne, Samuel. *A Journey from Prince of Wales's Fort in Hudson's Bay to the Northern Ocean. Undertaken by Order of the Hudson's Bay Company, for the Discovery of Copper Mines, a Northwest Passage, &c. In the Years, 1769, 1770, 1771, and 1772*. London: A. Strahan and T. Cadell, 1795. Print.

Innis, Harold A. *The Fur Trade in Canada: An Introduction to Canadian Economic History*. New Haven: Yale UP, 1930. Print.

Lamb, W. Kaye. Introduction. *A Voyage of Discovery to the North Pacific Ocean and round the World 1791–1795*. Ed. W. Kaye Lamb. London: Hakluyt Society, 1984. Vol. 1. 2–269. Print.

Lecker, Robert. *Making It Real: The Canonization of English-Canadian Literature*. Concord, ON: Anansi, 1995. Print.

——, ed. *Canadian Canons: Essays in Literary Value*. Toronto: Toronto UP, 1991.

Logan, J. D., and Donald G. French. *Highways of Canadian Literature: A Synoptic Introduction to the Literary History of Canada (English) from 1760 to 1924*. Toronto: McClelland & Stewart, 1924. Print.

Mackenzie, Alexander. *Voyages from Montreal, on the River St. Laurence, through the Continent of North America, to the Frozen and Pacific Oceans; in the Years 1789 and 1793*. 1801. *The Journals and Letters of Sir Alexander Mackenzie*. Ed. W. Kaye Lamb. Cambridge: Cambridge UP, 1970. 57–418. Print.

MacLaren, I. S. "Exploration/Travel Literature and the Evolution of the Author." *International Journal of Canadian Studies* 5 (1992): 39–68. Print.

——. "Notes on Samuel Hearne's *Journey* from a Bibliographic Perspective." *Papers of the Bibliographic Society of Canada*. 31.2 (1993): 21–45. Print.

Martin, Roger Leonard. "(Pre-)Texts of Exploration: 'Re-Exploration Narrative,' Meta-historiography and Contemporary Canadian Prose." Diss. Queen's University, 1995. Print.

McCarthy, Dermot. "Early Canadian Literary Histories and the Function of a Canon." *Canadian Canons: Essays in Literary Value*. Ed. Robert Lecker. Toronto: U of Toronto P, 1991. 30–45. Print.

Miller, Judith Maclean, ed. *Reading/Writing Canada: Short Fiction and Nonfiction*. New York: Norton, 2005. Print.

Moyles, R. G., ed. *"Improved by Cultivation": An Anthology of English-Canadian Prose to 1914*. Peterborough, ON: Broadview, 1994. Print.

Pierce, Lorne. *An Outline of Canadian Literature (French and English)*. Toronto: Ryerson, 1927. Print.

Robins, John D., ed. *A Pocketful of Canada*. Toronto: Collins, 1946. Print.

Smith, A. J. M., ed. *The Book of Canadian Prose, Volume 1: Early Beginnings to Confederation*. Toronto: Gage, 1965. Print.

———. *The Canadian Experience: A Brief Survey of English-Canadian Prose*. Agincourt, ON: Gage, 1974. Print.

Stevenson, Lionel. *Appraisals of Canadian Literature*. Toronto: Macmillan, 1926. Print.

Sugars, Cynthia, and Laura Moss, eds. *Canadian Literature in English: Texts and Contexts*. Vol. 1. Toronto: Pearson, 2008. Print.

Surette, Leon. "Here Is Us: The Topocentrism of Canadian Literary Criticism." *Canadian Poetry* 10 (1982): 44–57. Web. 28 May 2013.

Thompson, David. *David Thompson's Narrative 1784–1812*. Ed. Richard Glover. Toronto: Champlain Society, 1962. Print.

———. *David Thompson: Travels in Western North America, 1784–1812*. Ed. Victor G. Hopwood. Toronto: Macmillan, 1971. Print.

Toye, William, ed. *A Book of Canada*. London: Collins, 1962. Print.

Tyrrell, J. B. Preface. *David Thompson's Narrative of His Explorations in Western America 1784–1812*. Ed. J. B. Tyrrell. Toronto: Chaplain Society, 1916. xv–xxi. Print.

Watters, Reginald Eyre. *A Check List of Canadian Literature and Background Materials 1628–1950: In Two Parts*. Toronto: U of Toronto P, 1959. Print.

Weaver, Robert, and William Toye, eds. *The Oxford Anthology of Canadian Literature*. Toronto: Oxford UP, 1973. Print.

Anthologies and the Canonization Process

A Case Study of the English-Canadian Literary Field, 1920–1950

Peggy Lynn Kelly

> "*What is commonly called literary history is actually a record of choices.*"
> —Louise Bernikow[1]

Literary critics' contestations of the traditional canon have led to discussions, in literary discursive communities, of multiple canons. Among the many canons considered by critics who work in materialist and cultural-studies fields are the traditional canon, the feminist canon, and the curricular or institutional canon. Drawing on American critic Alistair Fowler's categories of canons, Alan C. Golding discusses three canons related to the literary marketplace: the potential canon constitutes the entire archive of literary production, the accessible canon includes those works that remain in print, and the selective canon is made up of accessible literature that is deemed to be of the highest quality (Golding 279). However, as Golding points out, "selection precedes as well as follows the formation of the accessible canon, affecting the form that 'accessibility' takes" (279). For instance, publishers, whose decisions are determined by market factors, have a major role in the construction of the accessible canon. In addition, editors of anthologies and literary histories have enormous influence not only on the shape and content of their own projects, but also on the shape and content of the traditional and curricular canons.

Canonization is a complex process of construction, a process that articulates with race, ethnicity, class, institutional power struggles, differential evaluations of popular and canonical literature, and gender. As Robert Lecker claims, the traditional canon of Canadian literature has been racialized white and gendered male, and "the canonizers can demonstrate their liberalism by admitting a few token savages" (669). Paul Lauter sees similar exclusionary and segregating practices in the United States (438–39, 445, 451). John Guillory views the canon as a middle-class enterprise because being represented in the canon, and thereby acquiring cultural capital, means little to those who seldom read (38). Frank Davey correctly points to state institutions as important players in the canon-making process (678). For example, the Canada Council funds high art, works that are independent of the marketplace, and refuses to fund organizations such as the Canadian Authors Association (CAA) that are perceived to be driven by commercial concerns. Through its control over the administration of federal funds, the Canada Council has the power to perpetuate the view of the CAA as a forum of writers who are attached primarily to the marketplace, that is, at the popular literature end of the lowbrow–highbrow continuum. Furthermore, educational institutions, in their roles as marketplaces for textbook publishers, have the power to create canons through the development of syllabi. Canadian cultural nationalists of the 1920s, such as the members of the CAA and publishers Lorne Pierce and Hugh Eayrs, were instrumental in the production of historical and literary textbooks based on English-Canadian perspectives. The history of the curricula in which these textbooks appear reveals one of the many processes through which non-canonical works become canonical (Guillory 51).

The production of English-Canadian poetry anthologies between 1920 and 1950 exemplifies the process of canonization that is defined by struggles over the evaluation of the potential canon. My choice of dates derives from a larger project, a Canadian cultural history in which I examine the negotiations made by Dorothy Livesay and Madge Macbeth in the English-Canadian literary field. Relations between the social, political, and cultural forces of this period are vibrant and volatile. The economic upheaval of the Great Depression, the political turmoil of two World Wars, technological and social innovations, waves of high nationalism, and fierce debates within the English-Canadian literary community mark this time period as one of immense importance and change. For instance, the copyright amendments of the 1920s were points of great contention between Canadian cultural producers and Canadian printers, and the nationalist fervour among Canadians of the period motivated a conscious development of the traditional canon. Literature was seen as a means of nation-building and of developing national unity. The CAA, a volunteer, non-profit, and nationalist organization, began to publish its members' poetry in 1925, according to CAA historian Lyn Harrington (249). Originally formed in 1921 by male and female professional Canadian writers to lobby against the federal copyright law, the CAA instituted Canada Book Week, the Governor General's Literary Awards, the *Canadian Poetry Magazine*, and the *Poetry Year Books*, many of which were organized with a nationalist purpose. In E. J. Hobsbawm's terms, this period of the twentieth century constitutes a "crucial moment" in the history of Canadian nationalism, because nationalism became a mass movement in Canada at this time (12).[2]

However unique and fascinating the 1920 to 1950 time period is, it also resembles other historical moments in Canada through its practice of systemic discrimination on the bases of class, race, sex, and ethnicity. These systemic biases affected the choices made by publishers, editors, and curriculum developers. Their politically based decision-making perpetuated the distinctly Anglo-Saxon, white, and masculine traditional canon that had been developing since the arrival of European settler-invaders. Furthermore, definitions of quality in literature depend on the evaluator's gender, class, race, age, and position in the literary field. If systemic discrimination was a factor in the power relations of Canadian society during this period, the literary archive should contain evidence of the exclusion of writers on the bases of class, race, ethnicity, and sex. To test my hypothesis, and following Carole Gerson's methodology in "Anthologies and the Canon of Early Canadian Women Writers," I conducted a survey of forty-eight English-Canadian anthologies published between 1920 and 1950, concentrating on the two factors that appear repeatedly in the research material: gender and ethnicity.

The eastern-European, Irish, African, and Asian diasporas of the eighteenth, nineteenth, and twentieth centuries brought waves of immigrants to Canada between 1750 and 1950.[3] Upon arrival, these new Canadians were faced with French and Anglo-Saxon imperialist discourses of assimilation, often couched in patronizing and benevolent terms. For example, J. S. Woodsworth's 1909 text *Strangers Within Our Gates* represents the Anglo-Protestant ideology of Christian service to the nation and the British Empire, an imperialist ideology that dominated Canadian public discourse of the early twentieth century. Furthermore, English-Canadian literary discourse of the 1920–50 period was dominated by anti-feminine evaluations; for instance, *virile* was an adjective frequently used by critics of both sexes to compliment an author's work. In such a discourse community, the adjective *feminine* becomes an epithet. The work of William Arthur Deacon, Archibald MacMechan, J. D. Logan, E. K. Brown, and E. J. Pratt, professional writers and critics of the period, attest to their gendered views of the literary field of production.[4] In addition, these critics, most of whom were academics, had important material effects on the publication records of both male and female writers. For example, E. J. Pratt held a veto over the publication of Canadian poets who submitted their work to Macmillan Canada in the 1930s, a period during which Pratt acted as reader and advisor to Macmillan's president, Hugh Eayrs. As Gerson explains in "The Canon between the Wars," the work of Doris Ferne, a member of the female collective that founded the first *Contemporary Verse*,[5] was rejected by Eayrs because Pratt criticized her manuscript for lack of virility (54). Many other examples of exclusionary practice suggest that female writers of the period faced barriers that male writers did not face. For instance, Dorothy Livesay, a published and active modernist writer of the period, was excluded from *New Provinces* (1936), the only anthology of modernist poetry to be published during the 1930s (Kelly, "Politics" 56).

I began to compile the database for my study by turning to Reginald Watters's important *A Checklist of Canadian Literature and Background Materials 1628–1960* (1972), which is arranged by genre and alphabetically by author or editor within each category. Due to the economic collapse of 1929 and the Great Depression of the 1930s, only a small number of anthologies from the 1920–50 period appear in Watters's *Checklist*. Although a few anthologies in my database contain both prose and poetry, I looked mainly for Canadian anthologies of Canadian poetry by Canadian editors. Watters's *Checklist*, which represents the potential canon, directed me to both canonical Canadian literary anthologies, such as A. J. M. Smith's *The Book of Canadian Poetry*, and to popular literature, such as the anthologies produced by the CAA and the Writers' Craft Club.[6] The latter publications do not appear in evaluative bibliographies such as Smith's, which also served as a source for my survey list. The forty-eight anthologies that make up my study fall into two major groups: anthologies produced by individual editors and anthologies produced by associations. The individual editors were mainly academics or professional writers whose anthologies were produced by established publishing companies; I refer to them as the academic-professional group. The CAA's and the Writers' Craft Club's anthologies make up the association category. My analysis is based on tabulation of the number of male and female writers in each anthology, as well as the number of pages allotted to each sex. The results of this process appear in tables 1, 2, and 3.

The association anthologies represent a complex position in the field. On the one hand, in comparison to the academic-professional anthologies, which were the products of private negotiations between the publisher and the editor, the association anthologies were produced through a more public and bureaucratic process. Most of the association volumes, twenty-seven of twenty-eight, were published by branches of the CAA. The poems in these volumes were drawn from the results of national or regional poetry competitions held annually by local CAA branches. Two levels of "gatekeepers" operated in this competitive process: the editors and the judges, both of whom made decisions concerning the anthology before it reached the printer (Gerson, "Anthologies" 57). The association anthologies' editors shaped the anthologies by setting guidelines for submissions and appointing judges, and the judges finalized the anthologies by selecting the contents. Both associations in this survey, the CAA and the Writers' Craft Club, acted as publishers. In the academic-professional category, on the other hand, the editors both judged and edited the anthologies, and negotiated with the publisher, the second gatekeeper in this category. Although most editors in both groups of anthologies were male, association anthologies were edited by both women and men, whereas the poetry submitted to the association anthologies came overwhelmingly from women writers and was adjudicated, in most cases, by male judges. However, in the case of the *Alberta Poetry Year Books*, there were only three editors in fifty years, 1930–80, all of whom were female (Harrington 249–51). During the same period, the judges who chose the contents of the Year Books were mainly male, according to June Fritch, one of the long-term editors of the *Alberta Poetry Year Book* (qtd. in Harrington 250). The division of labour for the Alberta CAA's poetry publications follows the gendered divisions within masculinist systems of power. Judging a poetry contest consisting of hundreds of entries is a difficult task, but it places the judge in a more powerful position than that of editor, a position that involves repetitive work similar to housework, a feminine domain. As Fritch comments, "the most devoted woman wearies of this expenditure of her time and talent" (qtd. in Harrington 250). In addition, the volunteer work of the judges is acknowledged in print in the association anthologies, usually in a preface or foreword, but most editors remain unnamed. *Border Voices*, edited by Carl Eayrs in 1946, and *Voices of Victory* (1941), a publication of the CAA's Toronto branch, constitute the two exceptions to this rule. The editorial board of *Voices of Victory* consisted of three men and one woman, and all of its judges were male.[7]

The association volumes garner slight cultural capital, are deemed to be vanity publishing, and have little hope of entering the traditional canon (Kelly "Is Poetry Contest an Oxymoronic Term?"). Almost no critical attention was paid to these publications when they appeared. Only three reviews were published in Canada: two favourable and one unfavourable. In the *Canadian Poetry Magazine*, organ of the CAA, Clara Bernhardt praised *Voices of Victory* as "a collection which every Canadian, for reasons patriotic or aesthetic, will want upon his bookshelf" (44).[8] *Voices of Victory* was also the subject of the unfavourable review, published a month earlier in *Saturday Night* and written by Robertson Davies. "It would be dishonest and unfair to the cause of poetry in this land to pretend that this volume is any very significant addition to its literature," Davies asserted (24). Moreover, F. R. Scott criticized the CAA's poetry contests for encouraging "old and decrepit" "Canadian poetasters" to write poetry that is ideologically nationalist and imperialist, formally "orthodox," and humourless ("New Poems for Old II" 338, 337). Both Scott and Davies, unlike Bernhardt, have since become canonical figures in the Canadian literary field.

The devaluation of association anthologies is closely connected to the feminization of both popular literature and traditional Victorian stylistics,[9] as well as to Pierre Bourdieu's concept of the upside-down economic character of the literary field. First, the marginalization and exclusion of feminine, emotional, domestic art forms and the idealization and centralization of masculine, abstract, public art forms defines such a cultural field; furthermore, the popular end of the continuum is feminized within masculinist ideology. As Andreas Huyssen puts it, "The problem is rather the persistent gendering as feminine of that which is devalued" (53). Second, Bourdieu refers to the economic aspect of literary fields as upside-down because most writers assume that literary writing is above remuneration. Even those who object to connections between money and art garner financial benefits in the long run, through the symbolic capital and symbolic power that literary awards bring to an award winner (Bourdieu, *Field* 29–73). In Bourdieu's model, poetry belongs to the restricted field of literary production, where writers write for each other and literature is not expected to garner financial rewards; however, female authorship, feminine content, and traditional stylistics devalue the poetry published by the associations. As Guillory asserts, "The distinction between serious and popular writing is a condition of canonicity," one that keeps most women outside the canon because their work is often labelled popular or frivolous (23). Ironically, editors of some association anthologies hoped to support the production of poetry in Canada by offering prizes of ten to twenty-five dollars and the publication of the winning poems. The monetary prizes were meant to contribute to the professionalization of the literary vocation, and this professionalization was seen to be a necessary step in the development of a national literature. In his "Preface" to the 1928–29 *Poetry Year Book*, published by the Montreal Branch of the CAA, Leo Cox mentions the difficulty of "earning a living" and writing at the same time (iii). The CAA's Ottawa branch also wanted "to provide one more outlet for Canadian writers" by publishing *Profile: A Chapbook of Canadian Verse* in 1946 (v). However, all poetry publication in Canada of this time period, whether written by men or women, amounted to vanity publishing, including those volumes that were published by established publishing companies, such as Macmillan Canada or Ryerson Press. Therefore, the prizes awarded by some association anthologies carry little weight in the masculinist literary field of the period. Contradictorily, the academic-professional anthologies that were published as textbooks stood to earn profits for their publishers, and the writers included in these textbooks also earned cultural capital by entering the canon through the curriculum.[10] This contradiction in the field rests on a complex foundation marked by gender and artistic generations, and perpetuated through the artificial binary of popular versus serious writing and the constructed canon. The mostly female writers who were published in the association anthologies were excluded from more widely distributed, more canonically powerful poetry anthologies. This anti-feminine foundation of the Canadian literary field of 1920–50 is nicely illustrated by Scott's comment on the position of modernist poetry in the Canadian literary field of the 1930s: "Violent hostility has ceased in educated communities, though in Canada the modernist still has to endure the derision of ageing critics as well as the indifference of the bourgeoisie of poetry readers who pull up their *Golden Treasury* skirts and pass him by on the other side" ("New Poems for Old: I" 297). In this passage, Scott feminizes the bourgeoisie, popular literature, and earlier literary generations at the same time as he masculinizes poets, modernism, and his own literary generation. The implication is that only young, cosmopolitan, upper-class, British-educated, and anti-capitalist males like himself are enlightened enough to admit modernist poetry into the literary canon. Scott attended Oxford University as a Rhodes Scholar. His devaluation of non-modernist positions through the tactic of feminization constitutes one of his literary generation's successful strategies to create a prominent place for itself in the Canadian literary field.

When the association and academic-professional groups of anthologies in my study are considered separately, a gender-based dichotomy is clearly evident. The percentage of women writers included in the academic-professional anthologies, 27 percent, is less than half of the corresponding figure for the association anthologies, 70 percent. Furthermore, the amount of space given to women writers in each group of anthologies indicates an even wider discrepancy. Women's writing fills 18 percent of academic-professional anthologies and 67 percent of association anthologies (see table 3). The space assigned to female poets by the association anthologies ranges from 27 to 90 percent of pages, while women's writing in the academic-professional anthologies occupies from 4 to 34 percent of the total number of pages (see tables 1 and 2). For example, 14 percent of the writers published in the academic-professional anthology *A Book of Canadian Prose and Verse* (Broadus 1923) are female, yet the writing of these four women occupies only 7 percent of the text (see table 2). The much larger amount of textual space allotted to women in association anthologies suggests that when women have control of the material resources necessary for literary production, their published work reflects their numbers, even when positions of power, such as adjudication, are held by men. In the 1943 and 1948 editions of Smith's canonical *Book of Canadian Poetry*, women writers constitute from 21 to 27 percent of the total number of writers, and Smith allots only 14 to 16 percent of the texts' pages to these writers. Gerson has shown that, after the first edition appeared, Smith gradually eliminated early Canadian women writers from successive editions of *The Book of Canadian Poetry*, until only two of seven remained ("Anthologies" 61). She also notes, drawing on Anne Dagg's research, that "In English Canada, from the beginnings to 1950, women have represented 40 per cent of the authors of books of fiction and 37 per cent of the authors of books of poetry" ("Anthologies" 57).

Only two of the twenty academic-professional anthologies in my survey are edited by women, while the male editor of a third was assisted by a woman (see table 2). Ethel Hume Bennett's anthology, *New Harvesting*, allocates 34 percent of its pages to women writers, while Margaret Fairley's *Spirit of Canadian Democracy* allots only 10 percent, one of the lowest percentages of women authors in the entire group of anthologies. This vast difference may be explained by the nature of each woman's anthology. Fairley's is a collection of poems and excerpts from the prose of writers in Canada from 1632 to 1945. Besides the long timeline, Fairley's collection focuses on politics, a masculine field that excluded most women during the time periods covered in her collection. Furthermore, Fairley draws from a wide range of textual material, including letters, political manifestos, autobiography, fiction, journalism, essays, and poetry, a range that tends to overwhelm genres that have been gendered as feminine, such as the novel, the diary, and the memoir. Bennett's anthology, on the other hand, covers a much shorter time period, 1918–38, and is restricted to poetry, which is gendered masculine and deemed to be high art, that is, of more value than popular literature because it is supposedly independent of the marketplace. Finally, Alan Creighton, editor of *A New Canadian Anthology*, lists Hilda M. Ridley, a member of the Toronto branch of the CAA, as his assistant. Among the academic-professional anthologies, this male-female collaboration contains a relatively high proportion of female poets, 75 percent. The lack of women editors among academic-professional anthologies in this survey is evidence of both systemic discrimination on the basis of sex and the power of the symbolic violence of gender, factors that relate to a gendered imbalance of financial and cultural power.

Ethnic anthologies, narrowly defined here as anthologies that publish non-English-language writing, hardly appear at all in this group of anthologies. Two association anthologies and two academic-professional anthologies are the exceptions. In the academic-professional category, *A Book of Canadian Prose and Verse* (1923) contains six untranslated poems by Louis Fréchette, occupying eight pages. Fréchette's work is followed by a poetic tribute from John Reade, titled "To Louis Fréchette / On the occasion of his poems being crowned by the French Academy" (49). In his poem, Reade describes French Canadians and English Canadians as "one great race to be," because both descend from Bretons and Normans (49). In keeping with the nationalist view of the role of literature in nation-building, verse is used by Reade to call for the unity of two ethnicities, based on similarities in gene-alogical histories. In addition, the poet's reference to the French Academy gestures simultaneously toward the acceptance of European cultural values by their former colonies and to the importance of language as a marker of an ethnic group. Also in the academic-professional category, Bliss Carman and Lorne Pierce's *Our Canadian Literature* presents an eighty-three-page section of French-Canadian poetry. Sandra Campbell explains that Pierce's self-proclaimed goal was to unify the French and English sectors of Canada through cultural exchanges; he read French-Canadian literature and met the authors during the course of his work as literary editor of Ryerson Press (138–39). Pierce's rationale for a bilingual edition of a poetry anthology is similar to the assumptions underlying Reade's poem. Pierce writes, in the foreword to *Our Canadian Literature*: "The golden age of letters in France and England was born of a common source. In Canada the two traditions again meet, and the roots are buried deep in a common soil" (x). Pierce also encourages other anthologists to create bilingual anthologies: "To speak of Canadian verse without including Canadian poetry written in French is a common fault among us, and one that can no longer be condoned" (x). Writ-ing from "'La Ferme,' York Mills," Pierce belongs, physically and ideologically, to the traditional centrist view of Canada's history, a view that recognizes only two founding nations as responsible for Canada's development (x).

Profile: A Chapbook of Canadian Verse* (1946) and the *Manitoba Poetry Chapbook* (*MPC* 1933) provide the other two examples of attention to eth-nicity among the forty-eight anthologies surveyed. *Profile* was produced by the Ottawa branch of the CAA, and it contains one French-Canadian poem, by Marie Sylvia. The *Manitoba Poetry Chapbook*, on the other hand, is much more extensively an attempt to represent the ethnic diversity among Cana-dian writers of the period; it includes poems in French, German, Ukrainian, Swedish, and Yiddish. The Manitoba branch of the CAA held a poetry contest that was open to Manitoban poets of all languages. All three of the judges were male, English-Canadian academics, and the winning poems were writ-ten in English and Icelandic. In the "Preface," Watson Kirkconnell, who also served as a judge of the entries, emphasizes the difficulties of publishing a small volume in several languages and the importance of cooperation to the success of the project. According to Kirkconnell, Winnipeg's "foreign language presses," including the anthology's publisher, the Israelite Press, worked together to produce the volume (4). Kirkconnell concludes: "The result is a volume quite unique in the history of Canadian poetry. Manitoba is a province of fifty languages, and we hope that this chapbook may convey to other parts of the Dominion some hint of the rich and varied potentialities inherent in this mingling of cultures throughout the years to come" (4). Kirkconnell's statement contrasts pointedly with Pierce's assumption of two founding nations in Canada. However, as in E. K. Broadus and E. H. Broadus's *A Book of Canadian Prose and Verse* (1923), Kirkconnell assumes the existence of an unproblematized mosaic or the desirability of a unified nation. Throughout his academic career, poet-translator Kirkconnell worked toward widespread acceptance of northern- and eastern-European immigrants by Anglo-Saxon Canadians. His translations of poetry by Icelandic, Swedish, Hungarian, Italian, Greek, Ukrainian, and French Canadians into English were designed to promote a recognition among English-speaking Canadians of the variety of ethnic cultural groups in the Canadian literary field, a variety that extends far beyond the two founding nations (Craig 598). According to N. F. Dreisziger, Kirkconnell "anticipated the concept of government-supported multicultural programmes by some four decades" (94).

In spite of Kirkconnell's avowed opposition to assimilation, the production of the *Manitoba Poetry Chapbook* may be used by the state to support its claims that multicultural equality exists in Canada. In such a case, a federal state's interest in a unified nation is advanced by the work of employees of the postsecondary educational system, which is funded by federal and provincial governments. Both Kirkconnell and Edmund Broadus were university professors. According to Terrence Craig, Kirkconnell wrote *Canadians All: A Primer of Canadian National Unity* (1941) in order to "reassure Canadians of the loyalty of these immigrants in wartime" (598).[11] Kirkconnell's major role in the production of the *Manitoba Poetry Chapbook* must be considered in relation to this project, to which he dedicated himself only seven years later, and which Craig describes in terms that juxtapose a homogeneous group of white Anglo-Saxon Canadians to a homogeneous group of immigrants (598). The slight number of anthologies in this survey containing non-English writing suggests that, although a few members of the English-Canadian literary field addressed Canada's ethnic diversity, their efforts were anomalies. Furthermore, the predominance of white Anglo-Canadian writers in this field creates a power imbalance in which non-white, non-Anglo writers function as exotic Others, just as women function as Others in masculinist societies. Such a representation of ethnicity both stems from and perpetuates racialization. At the same time, these anthologies challenge the aspirations to ethnic and racial homogeneity within English-speaking Canada. However, the hope of Broadus and Broadus that their anthology will contribute to understanding and unity among Canada's regions suggests that assumptions concerning the desirability of homogeneity are not far below the surface of their rhetoric (viii).

The ideological conflict between nationalism and internationalism appears in both the association and academic-professional anthologies. Many association anthologies were produced with nationalist aims. For instance, the *Alberta Poetry Year Book* of 1930–31, one of the few in which the majority of the judges are female,[12] begins with an introduction by Evelyn Gowan Murphy in which she foregrounds nationalism and regionalism:

> The motive which prompted the Edmonton Branch of the Canadian Authors' Association to sponsor a poetry competition among the residents of Alberta was a desire to inspire Canadian writers to make use of the vast wealth of western Canadian material which lies before them and to awaken in Canadians, through the medium of verse, a deeper patriotism and interest in their own country. ("The Prize Contests" 5)

Murphy was disappointed "that the percentage of poems with a distinctive Canadian motif or background were much in the minority" (5) among the submissions. The nationalist motivation of these anthologies is grounded in the nineteenth-century notion of the importance of a national literature to a nation's strength. Moreover, the organization, by a predominantly female association, of national or regional poetry contests around a patriotic theme exemplifies one way in which women fulfill their assigned role of cultural arbiters and conduits. As Anne McClintock points out, nationalist ideology employs the metaphor of the nation as a family to mobilize, in the public sphere, masculinist divisions of labour that already operate within families (357–58). Just as capitalism depends on women to reproduce the worker, nationalist ideology expects women to maintain and reproduce a legacy of cultural traditions that are learned in private and practised in public. The conjunction of nationalism with gendered stereotypes of women as cultural reproducers naturalizes the unpaid production of nationalist poetry *Year Books* by voluntary organizations as a feminine activity. The paradoxical corollary to this gendering of literary spaces lies in the delegitimization that feminization entails, a double standard that marks the Canadian literary field as masculinist and undermines the recognition of nationalist cultural products.

Systemic discrimination on the basis of sex was practised in the English-Canadian literary field in the decades between 1920 and 1950. Not only do the academic-professional anthologies include fewer women, they allow even less space to their women writers than is implied by the male-female ratio of these editors' choices. In addition, the popular–serious dichotomy delegitimizes the literary production of writers who contribute to popular association anthologies and elevates those writers whose work appears in academic-professional anthologies. Moreover, within this group of English-Canadian anthologies, the ethnicity of Canadian writers is virtually ignored. Finally, these markers of the process of anthologization are perpetuated by the inclusion of academic-professional anthologies in the literary and curricular canons, and the concurrent exclusion of association anthologies. Thus, the production of anthologies impacts on the formation of a canon, in this case by perpetuating the Anglo-Saxon, masculine nature of the traditional, selective English-Canadian canon, which is maintained by the reliance of later anthology editors on the earlier productions (Gerson, "Anthologies" 63). Theories concerning relations between accessibility and canonicity are grounded in material conditions and practices, including archival practices. The CAA's *Alberta Poetry Year Books* are stored off-site, in the University of Alberta's closed stacks, the Book and Record Depository (BARD). Examination of the volumes in this study required ordering them a few days in advance, whereas every edition of Smith's *The Book of Canadian Poetry* was readily available on the library shelves. Many academic-professional anthologies are also stored in BARD, but only when a second copy is available; the first copy is in the open stacks. Accessibility to editors and readers impacts the frequency of a book's use, the possibility of republication, and the place of a text in both the canon and cultural memory.

In conclusion, analysis of canons is mandatory for educational discursive communities that value self-knowledge. As Lauter states, discussions of canons assist in "reconstructing historical understanding to make it inclusive and explanatory instead of narrowing and arbitrary" (456). Lauter's point resonates with Catharine Stimpson's description of the three articulated zones within which canon debates occur: "At the first level is the opening up the canon to include works that have been irresponsibly excluded; at the second level is the study of the process of canon formation, for example, the kind John Guillory does; and the third is the questioning of greatness and universals ..." (qtd. in Brooks et al. 387).

The female and ethnic writers whose work was excluded from or published in anthologies of the first half of the twentieth century provide instances of the first two steps; the particulars of their experiences deserve further attention from researchers. My survey of forty-eight anthologies provides statistical material for debating the third step, "the questioning of greatness and universals," in one historical moment of the English-Canadian literary field (Brooks et al. 387).

Table 1 Association Anthologies

TITLE	SEX OF EDITORS AND/OR JUDGES	TOTAL WRITERS	TOTAL WOMEN	WOMEN AS % TOTAL WRITERS	TOTAL PAGES	PAGES BY WOMEN	WOMEN'S PAGES AS % TOTAL
Alberta Poetry Year Book	2 F; 1 M	1930: 18	11	61	25	16	64
	Male	1931: 25	9	36	29	8	27
	Female	1932: 25	20	80	28	23	82
	Male	1933: 25	14	56	28	15	53
	Male	1934: 24	19	79	27	18	66
	Male	1935: 39	29	74	30	23	76
	Male	1937: 35	26	74	28	19	68
	Male	1938: 26	22	84	29	24	82
	Male	1939: 37	30	81	37	31	84
	Unknown	1940: 61	49	80	44	36	82
	Male	1941: 53	39	73	43	34	79
	Male	1942: 68	52	76	45	32	71
	Female	1943: 55	43	78	39	27	69
	Male	1944: 34	25	73	47	33	70
	Male	1945: 84	63	75	51	41	80
	Female	1949: 69	54	78	56	38	68
Border Voices	Male	10	9	90	48	43	89
Canadian Poems	Male	35	17	48	41	24	58
MPC	Male	26	11	42	32	11	34
Poetry Year Book	Male and Female	1928: 30	1928: 18	1928: 60	1928: 50	1928: 25	1928: 50
		1929: 31	1929: 22	1929: 71	1929: 43	1929: 31	1929: 72
		1930: 40	1930: 28	1930: 70	1930: 49	1930: 36	1930: 73
		1936: 34	1936: 27	1936: 79	1936: 44	1936: 35	1936: 79
		1939: 32	1939: 18	1939: 56	1939: 41	1939: 20	1939: 49
		1940: 24	1940: 18	1940: 75	1940: 34	1940: 23	1940: 67
Profile	Unknown	26	19	73	47	25	53
Sheaf of Verse	Unknown	18	16	89	20	18	90
Voices of Victory	3 Male 1 Female	67	35	52	94	47	50

Table 2 Academic-Professional Anthologies

TITLE	SEX OF EDITOR	TOTAL WRITERS AND ARTISTS	TOTAL WOMEN	WOMEN AS % TOTAL	TOTAL PAGES	PAGES BY WOMEN	WOMEN'S PAGES AS % TOTAL
ACP	Male	56	14	25	114	15	13
BCP	Male	1943: 76	1943: 21	1943: 27	1943: 432	1943: 72	1943: 16
		1948: 5	1948: 14	1948: 21	1948: 462	1948: 67	1948: 14
BCPV	M &F	29	4	14	390	27	7
CA	Male	23	3	13	142	14	10
CP	Male	75	29	38	530	143	27
CVO	Male	54	16	29	147	29	20
GTCV	Male	25	10	40	146	29	20
MCP	Male	20	6	30	227	54	24
NCA	M&F	99	75	78	236	73	31
NH	Female	45	19	42	192	66	34
NTWP	Male	106	25	23	261	45	17
OC	Male	18	4	22	112	12	10
OCL	Male	116	40	34	329	84	25
PC	Male	108	21	19	421	46	11
Poetry	Male	13	5	38	33	11	33
SCD	Female	174	15	8	281	28	10
Unit Five	Male	5	1	20	87	14	16
Yearbook of Arts	Male	1929: 77	1929: 12	1929: 15	1929: 307	1929: 12	1929: 4
		1936: 144	1936: 30	1936: 21	1936: 256	1936: 72	1936: 28

Table 3 Summary

TYPE	NO. OF VOLUMES	TOTAL WRITERS	TOTAL WOMEN	WOMEN AS % TOTAL WRITERS	TOTAL PAGES	PAGES BY WOMEN	WOMEN'S PAGES AS % TOTAL
Association	28	1051	743	70	1129	756	67
Academic-Professional	20	1328	364	27	5105	913	18

Notes to Tables

- In most anthologies, editors are unidentified, and judges are identified by name and professional title. In some anthologies, neither is identified.
- All numbers over .75 have been rounded off to the next-highest number.
- The total number of pages was calculated by counting only pages on which poetry appears. Title pages and pages of illustrations have not been included.
- Following are the full titles for abbreviations used in tables 1 to 3:

  ACP: Anthology of Canadian Poetry
  BCP: Book of Canadian Poetry
  BCPV: Book of Canadian Prose and Verse
  CA: Canadian Accent
  CP: Canadian Poets
  CVO: Canadian Voices and Others
  F: Female
  GTCV: Golden Treasury of Canadian Verse
  M: Male
  MCP: Modern Canadian Poetry
  MPC: Manitoba Poetry Chapbook
  NCA: New Canadian Anthology
  NH: New Harvesting
  NTWP: New Treasury of War Poetry
  OC: Other Canadians
  OCL: Our Canadian Literature
  PC: Pocketful of Canada
  SCD: Spirit of Canadian Democracy: A Collection of Canadian Writings from the Beginnings to the Present Day

NOTES

1 From Louise Bernikow's 1974 publication *The World Split Open: Four Centuries of Women Poets in England and America 1552–1950.* Qtd. in Gerson, "Anthologies," 65.

2 For information on the many volunteer and nationalist organizations that were formed in the English-Canadian cultural field during this time period, see historian Mary Vipond (1980).

3 The first Irish arrived in Nova Scotia in 1780, and a full-scale Irish diaspora occurred in the 1850s, when thousands of Irish immigrated to Ontario. See Power's *The Irish in Atlantic Canada, 1780–1900* (1991). See Peter S. Li's *Chinese in Canada* (1998), Marlene NourbeSe Philip's *Frontiers: Selected Essays and Writings on Racism and Culture, 1984–1992* (1992), and John Boyko's *Last Steps to Freedom* (1998).

4 See E. K. Brown's "Canadian Poetry" in the *Yearbook of the Arts in Canada 1936,* Ed. Bertram Brooker, 206–7; W. A. Deacon's *Poteen: A Pot-Pourri of Canadian Essay* (1926), 160, 169, 174–76; J. D. Logan's *Highways of Canadian Literature,* 195–208, 220; Archibald MacMechan's *Headwaters of Canadian Literature,* 118. In a letter dated 26 June 1944, E. J. Pratt described Livesay's poetry as "muscular." See the Dorothy Livesay Papers in the Bruce Peel Special Collections Library, University of Alberta, Collection 96–69, Queen's Box 2, File 24.

5 *Contemporary Verse* was founded in 1941 by Doris Ferne, Dorothy Livesay, Anne Marriott, and Floris McLaren. Alan and Jean Crawley edited the journal until it ceased publication in 1952. *Contemporary Verse II* was founded once again in 1975 by Dorothy Livesay; it is edited by a collective at the University of Manitoba.

6   *Sheaf of Verse* (Ryerson, 1929), the only volume I have examined by the Writers' Craft Club, offers the poetry of sixteen women and two men. One of the women is Hilda Ridley, who "assisted" Alan Creighton in the editing of the academic-professional text *A New Canadian Anthology* (1938). (See Titles of Anthologies Included in Survey.)

7   The judges were A. M. Stephen, Watson Kirkconnell, E. J. Pratt, E. A. Hardy, S. Morgan-Powell, and V. B. Rhodenizer. The editorial board consisted of Nathaniel Benson, W. A. Deacon, John M. Elson, and Amabel King.

8   Berhnardt's own poetry appeared in another association anthology, the *Alberta Poetry Year Book* in 1940 and 1943, and in the *Canadian Bookman* between 1933 and 1935.

9   Victorian stylistics of the period are characterized by archaic diction, Romantic values, and a focus on nature. Both popular literature and Victorian poetry was devalued by modernists of the period, who turned to new forms, a focus on urban concerns, modern language, and, perhaps, political content. See David Arnason's "Canadian Poetry: The Interregnum," in *CVII: A Quarterly of Canadian Poetry Criticism* 1.1 (Spring 1975): 28–32.

10   Surveyed anthologies that self-identify as textbooks are Robins's *A Pocketful of Canada* (1946) and Stephens's *The Golden Treasury of Canadian Verse* (1928) and *Canadian Voices and Others* (1943).

11   Kirkconnell was the chair of the Writers' War Committee, a group organized by the CAA in 1943 to provide the Wartime Information Board with reports on Canadians' attitudes to rationing, price control, and other wartime issues. Kirkconnell was also the national president of the CAA from 1942 to 1944. See the CAA Collection in the National Archives of Canada, MG28 I2, Volumes 2 and 3.

12   It is significant that the foreword to this *Alberta Poetry Year Book* was written by Emily Murphy (1868–1933), feminist, reformer, judge, politician, and writer.

TITLES OF ANTHOLOGIES INCLUDED IN SURVEY

Alberta Poetry Year Book. Edmonton: CAA, 1930–35, 1937, 1938–45, 1949.

Anthology of Canadian Poetry. Ed. Ralph Gustafson. Toronto: Penguin, 1942.

The Book of Canadian Poetry (1st and 2nd eds.). Ed. A. J. M. Smith. Toronto: Gage, 1943, 1948.

A Book of Canadian Prose and Verse. Ed. E. K. and E. H. Broadus. Toronto: Macmillan, 1923.

Border Voices: A Collection of Poems. Ed. Carl Eayrs. Windsor: CAA, 1946.

Canadian Accent: A Collection of Stories and Poems by Contemporary Writers from Canada. Ed. Ralph Gustafson. New York: Penguin, 1944.

Canadian Poems. Calgary: CAA, 1937.

Canadian Poets. Ed. John W. Garvin. Toronto: McClelland & Stewart, 1926, 1930.

Canadian Voices and Others: Poems Selected for the Classroom. Ed. A. M. Stephen. Toronto: Dent, 1934.

The Golden Treasury of Canadian Verse. Ed. A. M. Stephen. Toronto: Dent, 1928.

Manitoba Poetry Chapbook. Ed. Watson Kirkconnell. Winnipeg: Israelite Press and the CAA, 1933.

Modern Canadian Poetry. Ed. Nathaniel A. Benson. Ottawa: Graphic, 1930.

A New Canadian Anthology. Ed. Alan Creighton, Hilda M. Ridley. Toronto: Crucible Press, 1938.

New Harvesting: Contemporary Canadian Poetry 1918–1938. Ed. Ethel Hume Bennett. Toronto: Macmillan, 1938.

New Provinces: Poems of Several Authors. Ed. F. R. Scott and A. J. M. Smith. Toronto: Macmillan Canada, 1936.

New Provinces: Poems of Several Authors. Ed. Michael Gnarowski. Toronto: University of Toronto Press, 1976.

The New Treasury of War Poetry: Poems of the Second World War. Ed. George Herbert Clarke. Freeport, NY: Books for Libraries Press, 1943.

Other Canadians: An Anthology of the New Poetry in Canada 1940–1946. Ed. John Sutherland. Montreal: First Statement Press, 1947.

Our Canadian Literature: Representative Verse, English and French. Revised Edition. Ed. Bliss Carman and Lorne Pierce. Toronto: Ryerson Press, 1935.

A Pocketful of Canada. Ed. John D. Robins. Toronto: Collins, 1946.

Poetry (Chicago) Canadian Number 58.2 (April 1941). Ed. E. K. Brown.

Poetry Year Book. Montreal: CAA, 1928, 1929, 1930, 1936, 1939, 1940.

Profile: A Chapbook of Canadian Verse. Ottawa: CAA, 1946.

A Sheaf of Verse. Ed. The Writers' Craft Club. Toronto: Ryerson, 1929.

Spirit of Canadian Democracy: A Collection of Canadian Writings from the Beginnings to the Present Day. Ed. Margaret Fairley. Toronto: Progress, 1945.

Unit of Five. Ed. Ronald Hambleton. Toronto: Ryerson, 1944.

Voices of Victory: Representative Poetry of Canada in War-time. Ed. CAA Toronto. Toronto: Macmillan, 1941.

Yearbook of the Arts in Canada 1928–1929, and 1936. Ed. B. Brooker. Toronto: Macmillan, 1929, 1936.

WORKS CITED

Bernhardt, Clara. Rev. of *Voices of Victory: Representative Poetry of Canada in War-Time*. Ed. Canadian Authors' Association. *Canadian Poetry Magazine* 6.1 (Dec. 1941): 43–44. Print.

Bernikow, Louise. *The World Split Open: Four Centuries of Women Poets in England and America 1552–1950*. New York: Vintage, 1974.

Bourdieu, Pierre. *The Field of Cultural Production: Essays on Art and Literature*. Ed. Randal Johnson. New York: Columbia Press, 1993. Print.

Boyko, John. *Last Steps to Freedom: The Evolution of Canadian Racism*. Winnipeg: J. Gordon Shillingford Publishing, 1998.

Broadus, E. K., and E. H. Broadus, eds. *A Book of Canadian Prose and Verse*. Toronto: Macmillan, 1923. Print.

Brooks, Cleanth, Gertrude Himmelfarb, Wilson Moses, and Lionel Abel. "Remaking of the Canon." *Partisan Review* 58.2 (1991): 350–87. Print.

Brown, E.K. "Canadian Poetry." *Yearbook of the Arts in Canada 1936*. Ed. Bertram Brooker. Toronto: Macmillan, 1936. 206–7.

Campbell, Sandra. "Nationalism, Morality, and Gender: Lorne Pierce and the Canadian Literary Canon, 1920–60." *Papers of the Bibliographical Society of Canada* 32.2 (Fall 1994): 135–60. Print.

Clarke, George Herbert. Introduction. *The New Treasury of War Poetry: Poems of the Second World War.* Ed. George Herbert Clarke. Freeport, NY: Books for Libraries P, 1943. xxxiii. Print.

Cox, Leo. Preface. *Poetry Year Book.* Montreal: CAA, 1928–29. Print.

Craig, Terrence. "Watson Kirkconnell." *The Oxford Companion to Canadian Literature.* 2nd ed. Ed. E. Benson, W. Toye. Toronto: Oxford UP, 1997. 597–98. Print.

Davey, Frank. "Canadian Canons." *Critical Inquiry* 16 (Spring 1990): 672–81. Print.

Davies, Robertson. "The Trumpets Falter in Their Sound." Rev. of *Voices of Victory.* Ed. Canadian Authors' Association. *Saturday Night* 22 Nov. 1941, 24. Print.

Deacon, W. A. *Poteen: A Pot-Pourri of Canadian Essays.* Ottawa: Graphic Press, 1926.

Dreisziger, N. F. "Watson Kirkconnell and the Cultural Credibility Gap Between Immigrants and the Native-Born in Canada." *Ethnic Canadians: Culture and Education.* Ed. Martin L. Kovacs. Regina: Canadian Plains Research Center, 1978. 87–96. Print.

Gerson, Carole. "Anthologies and the Canon of Early Canadian Women Writers." *Re(Dis)covering Our Foremothers: Nineteenth-Century Canadian Women Writers.* Ed. Lorraine McMullen. Ottawa: University of Ottawa P, 1989. 55–76. Print.

———. "The Canon Between the Wars: Field-notes of a Feminist Literary Archaeologist." *Canadian Canons: Essays in Literary Value.* Ed. Robert Lecker. Toronto: U of Toronto P, 1991. 46–56. Print.

Golding, Alan C. "A History of American Poetry Anthologies." *Canons.* Ed. Robert von Hallberg. Chicago and London: U of Chicago P, 1984. 279–307. Print.

Guillory, John. *Cultural Capital: The Problem of Literary Canon Formation.* Chicago: U of Chicago P, 1993. Print.

Gustafson, Ralph. Preface. *Anthology of Canadian Poetry.* Ed. Ralph Gustafson. Toronto: Penguin, 1942. 5. Print.

Harrington, Lyn. *Syllables of Recorded Time: The Story of the Canadian Authors Association 1921–1981.* Toronto: Simon & Pierre, 1981. Print.

Hobsbawm, E. J. *Nations and Nationalism since 1780: Programme, Myth, Reality.* Cambridge: Cambridge UP, 1990. Print.

Huyssen, Andreas. *After the Great Divide: Modernism, Mass Culture, Postmodernism.* Bloomington and Indianapolis: Indiana UP, 1986. Print.

Kelly, Peggy. "Politics, Gender, and *New Provinces*: Dorothy Livesay and F. R. Scott." *Canadian Poetry* 53 (Fall/Winter 2003): 54–70. Print.

———. "Is *Poetry Contest* an Oxymoronic Term?: An Enquiry into the *Alberta Poetry Year Book* Series, 1930–1955." History of the Book in Canada's Open Conference for Volume III (1918–2000). Simon Fraser University, Vancouver, BC. November 15, 2001. Paper Presentation. http://www.hbic.library.utoronto.ca/vol3kelly _en.htm. Web.

Kirkconnell, Watson. Preface. *Manitoba Poetry Chapbook.* Ed. Watson Kirkconnell. Winnipeg: Israelite Press and the Canadian Authors' Association, 1933. 4. Print.

Lauter, Paul. "Race and Gender in the Shaping of the American Literary Canon: A Case Study from the Twenties." *Feminist Studies* 9.3 (Fall 1983): 435–63. Print.

Lecker, Robert. "The Canonization of Canadian Literature: An Inquiry into Value." *Critical Inquiry* 16 (Spring 1990): 656–71. Print.

Li, Peter S. *Chinese in Canada.* 2nd ed. Don Mills, ON: Oxford UP, 1998.

Logan, J. D., and Donald G. French. *Highways of Canadian Literature: A Synoptic Introduction to the Literary History of Canada (English) from 1760 to 1924.* Toronto: McClelland & Stewart, 1924.

MacMechan, Archibald. *Headwaters of Canadian Literature.* Toronto: McClelland & Stewart, 1974.

McClintock, Anne. *Imperial Leather: Race, Gender, and Sexuality in the Colonial Contest.* London and New York: Routledge, 1995. Print.

Murphy, Evelyn Gowan. "The Prize Contests." *Alberta Poetry Year Book.* Edmonton: Canadian Authors' Association, 1930. 5. Print.

Pierce, Lorne. Foreword. *Our Canadian Literature.* Ed. Bliss Carman and Lorne Pierce. Rev. ed. Toronto: Ryerson, 1935. ix–x. Print.

Philip, Marlene Nourbese. *Frontiers: Selected Essays and Writings on Racism and Culture, 1984–1992.* Stratford, ON: Mercury Press, 1992.

Power, Thomas P. *The Irish in Atlantic Canada, 1780–1900.* Fredericton: New Ireland Press, 1991.

Reade, John. "To Louis Frechette." *A Book of Canadian Prose and Verse.* Ed. E. K. and E. H. Broadus. Toronto: Macmillan, 1923. 49. Print.

Scott, F. R. "New Poems for Old: I. The Decline of Poesy." *Canadian Forum* 11.128 (May 1931): 296–98. Print.

———. "New Poems for Old: II. The Revival of Poetry." *Canadian Forum* 11.129 (June 1931): 337–39. Print.

Stephen, A. M. Introduction. *The Golden Treasury of Canadian Verse.* Ed. A. M. Stephen. Toronto: Dent, 1928. vii–ix. Print.

Tory, H. M. Introduction. *A Pocketful of Canada.* Ed. John D. Robins. Toronto: Collins, 1946. 5. Print.

Vipond, Mary. "The Nationalist Network: English Canada's Intellectuals and Artists in the 1920s." *Canadian Review of Studies in Nationalism* 7 (1980): 32–52.

———. "The Canadian Authors' Association in the 1920s: A Case Study in Cultural Nationalism." *Journal of Canadian Studies/Revue d'études canadiennes* 15.1 (Printemps 1980 Spring): 68–79.

Voices of Victory: Representative Poetry of Canada in War-time. Ed. Canadian Authors' Association of Toronto. Toronto: Macmillan, 1941. Print.

Watters, Reginald Eyre. *A Checklist of Canadian Literature and Background Materials, 1628–1960.* 2nd ed. Toronto: U of Toronto P, 1972. Print.

Woodsworth, J. S. *Strangers Within Our Gates, or Coming Canadians.* 1909. Toronto: U of Toronto P, 1977. Print.

Nation Building, the Literary Tradition, and English-Canadian Anthologies

Presentations of John Richardson and Susanna Moodie in Anthologies of the 1950s and 1960s

Bonnie Hughes

Anthologies of English-Canadian literature are found throughout university classrooms and play an important role in the study of the nation's literature, as they offer overviews, introductions, critical analyses, and suggestions for further reading. Many students' first exposure to this body of literature is through the anthology, suggesting that both the content and the format of the anthology play an important, influential role in presentations and understandings of the nation's writing. Despite this, the anthology as a genre is not often scrutinized, and the manner in which the contents, format, and introductions influence presentations and understandings of the literature is not often discussed. Further, the part that the anthology plays in defining the nation's literature, shaping the Canadian canon, and articulating visions of national identity is rarely analyzed.

To contribute to a conversation on the function, development, and traits of the anthology, this essay examines anthologies of English-Canadian literature and studies one specific stage of anthology development. General anthologies of English-Canadian literature, defined as collections that contain both poetry and prose and claim to be representative of the nation (rather than a particular region or group), developed in distinct stages, and there are clear connections between dominant critical trends and the guiding interests of the various phases of anthology development. As critical and pedagogical tools, anthologies both reflect and contribute to defining views of the nation and its literature. There are links between a phase of anthology development and an author's reception, inclusion, and presentation, and anthologies serve many functions, including recovering overlooked authors, addressing oversights, reflecting new areas of critical interest, and defining and preserving the national literary tradition. The ways in which authors are treated in anthologies also reveal the effect of larger critical concerns, such as alignment with dominant visions of the nation, considerations of genre, and reassessments of past views. To illustrate more clearly the relationship between anthologization and these other factors, this essay discusses the roles and functions of anthologies, outlines the phases of development of English-Canadian literary anthologies, and then details and compares the receptions of John Richardson and Susanna Moodie within a specific stage of anthology development, the literary nationalistic, to illustrate the links between prevailing critical interests, anthology development, and views of the nation. These two authors are among the nation's most widely recognized early writers, and their treatment in collections reveals much about the influences and goals of anthologists of the time and speaks more broadly to the process of anthology compilation.

ROLE OF THE ANTHOLOGY

The connection between a national literary tradition and collections of literature was established early in Canadian literature. Edward Hartley Dewart, in his introduction to *Selections from Canadian Poets; With Occasional Critical and Biographical Notes, and an Introductory Essay on Canadian Poetry* (1864), asserts that

> [a] national literature is an essential element in the formation of national character. It is not merely the record of a country's mental progress: it is the expression of its intellectual life, the bond of national unity, and the guide of national energy. It may be fairly questioned, whether the whole range of history presents the spectacle of a people firmly united politically, without the subtle but powerful cement of a patriotic literature. (xxii)

In his view, a unified, independent, and intelligent nation requires a distinct national literature. *Selections from Canadian Poets*, recognized as the first major Canadian poetry anthology,[1] thus asserted the existence of a distinct, valuable national literature. Dewart's remarks connect cultural nationalism, the literary tradition, and the anthology format, creating associations that have since remained a critical element of anthologization. His claims and approach influenced later anthologies, and anthologists of English-Canadian literature have frequently quoted his introduction. In particular, his emphasis on national traits and patriotism has continued to preoccupy anthologists, as anthologies of English-Canadian literature both reflect and participate in shaping an understanding of the nation and its literature. Historical context and critical trends influence anthologists' choices, and tracing these factors reveals how they have changed ideas of Canada and Canadian literary culture over time.

Since the publication of *Selections from Canadian Poets*, numerous anthologies of Canadian literature have been published,[2] focusing on a range of genres, themes, groups, regions, and periods. The variety of collections that have been produced suggests the many functions of the anthology: it preserves valued works, outlines a tradition, and introduces a subject through its contents and textual apparatus, which include introductions, headnotes, bibliographies, and suggestions for further reading. The pedagogical role of the anthology is one of its key purposes, and several anthologists have noted that their anthologies were created to meet the demands of the classroom.[3] While anthologies most often collect previously published works, they are sometimes the impetus for the creation of a work, demonstrating what Jeffrey R. Di Leo terms the "generative power of anthologies" (16). Anthologies are also tools of recovery. As J. R. Struthers points out, "Anthologies [...] can be ways of demonstrating the range and strength of areas of interest that conventional pedagogy or literary history has marginalized or ignored. Such works come into existence because of a perceived need, an editor and publisher having imagined alternatives to whatever options currently exist" (31). Anthologies can thus address perceived oversights through the inclusion of material that was never included or was removed from collections. Anthologies, then, both establish and revise traditions.

In order to create collections that meet these many needs and requirements, numerous decisions and evaluations must be made. A multitude of factors affect anthology compilation, including economic and material considerations such as budget, including permissions fees, page count, paper type, and publishing technologies and options, to name only a few. Previously published anthologies, personal preference, and dominant critical trends further determine the shape of an anthology. Critics have noted that anthologies are inevitably influenced by a range of factors and are not compiled solely on the basis of literary value. Paul Lauter, a prominent anthologist and editor of *The Heath Anthology of American Literature*, notes that the anthology is "a problematic cultural construction shaped by a variety of motives and demands" (38). Lauter values the anthology genre but cautions against uncritical acceptance. Struthers takes a similar approach in determining the worth of the anthology, pointing out that while the anthology format is not without complications, it ultimately has much to offer: "Despite all the intrinsic limits of the anthology form—among them the inevitable bias of selectivity and the perennial indeterminacy of the idea of balance—its invitation to read the word and the world against a multiplicity of contexts is its potential strength" (35). While there are many difficulties associated with anthology compilation, the anthology plays a vital role in the development of Canadian literature, and this analysis outlines some of the trends that determine the forms of anthologies and their contents.

STAGES OF ANTHOLOGY DEVELOPMENT

Anthologies of Canadian literature are distinct from other collections of English-language literature in a number of ways. One of these is the stages through which Canadian literary anthologies have developed. In *Canons by Consensus*, Joseph Csicsila divides the evolution of the American literature anthology into three distinct phases: literary historiography, occurring from 1919 to 1946; the New Critical, ranging from 1947 to the mid-1960s; and the multicultural, taking place from 1967 to the present (xx). English-Canadian anthologies have followed a similar though not identical path, and four distinct stages of anthology development have occurred to date: the literary historical, from 1922 to the late 1940s; the literary nationalistic, from the 1950s to the late 1960s; the thematic, occurring throughout the 1970s and into the early 1980s; and the pluralistic, from the early 1980s to the present.[4] Not all anthologies fit neatly into these categories and there is some overlap between stages, yet these divisions show how anthologies have been shaped and revised, and they illustrate the connection between dominant critical practices and the form of anthologies.

The main concern of the first stage of general anthology development, the literary historical, was asserting the existence and parameters of a national literature. Editors sought to increase awareness of Canadian literature, make literature widely accessible, and preserve works that risked otherwise being forgotten. Since they felt that Canadian literature was undervalued and frequently overlooked, editors were primarily concerned with ensuring that readers had access to as much material as possible: this emphasis on quantity meant that literary quality was a secondary consideration. Anthologies of this time are characterized by broad coverage, short excerpts, brief critical analyses, and an interest in articulations of national identity. The main impulses evident throughout the stage were to preserve, historicize, and nationalize Canadian literature, and throughout the phase an image of a nation with a rich, varied culture and past was created.

In the literary nationalistic phase of anthology development, questions of national identity and the aesthetic worth of Canadian literature became central areas of interest. While these concerns had emerged in the earlier literary historical phase, anthologists now turned their attention more fully to aesthetic quality. Anthologists asserted the value of the nation's writing and applied more strident critical guidelines in their evaluations than they had in the past. They promoted Canadian writing as worthy of academic study, a view reflected in the format of the anthology: introductions included critical evaluations of writers, and editors wrote more detailed headnotes. Authors were granted more pages and excerpts were longer. The process of anthologization became more scholarly, particularly as editors became interested in the study of Canadian literature at the university level. Anthologists moved away from the broad inclusiveness of the previous phase and selected a smaller number of authors, increasing the number of works by each individual author. An earlier emphasis on political and sociological writing was discarded, and poetry and prose became the primary focus. These changes to the anthology were spurred by the desire to assert the value of Canadian writing; the broad contours of a national literature had been established in the previous phase, and anthologists turned to determining its unique features and aesthetic quality.

Interest in the notable features of the nation's literature escalated in the thematic stage, which was characterized by the dominance of a single, thematic approach to texts—a determination to find certain ideas and attitudes in the literature—and a drive toward more detailed examinations. This phase was strongly influenced by Northrop Frye's concept of the "garrison mentality" (842); anthologists identified the struggle to survive as a distinctly Canadian preoccupation and emphasized the new understandings of the nation's literature and people that emerged as a result. Literature celebrating once popular ideas—such as a close, rewarding connection with nature— was re-evaluated through the more focused lens of thematic criticism, and critical attention shifted from the beauty of the land, climate, and northern geography to an emphasis on the destructive effects of the physical environment. Foreign influence, particularly American culture, was considered a threat to the evolution of the Canadian identity. The aboriginal presence, which was aligned with nature in the literary historical phase, was now seen in one of two ways: as a threatening "instrument of Nature the Monster" or as a "variant [...] of the victim motif" (Atwood, *Survival* 102). Due to the focus on negative themes and discord, Canadian identity was most frequently portrayed as governed by the garrison mentality and characterized by tension, fear, uncertainty, and hopelessness. Despite this often negative characterization of the Canadian psyche, however, thematic assessments of this phase demonstrate an increasing confidence in the value of the nation's literature as a record of Canadian identity and the movement toward a clear and unified vision of the Canadian literary tradition.

Near the end of the thematic phase, anthologists, like critics, began to resist the narrow and sometimes restrictive focus of thematic criticism by exploring new approaches to canonical texts and considering works previously overlooked or undervalued. Anthologies from the early 1980s on show a renewed interest in literary and social history and a move away from notions of nation, nationality, and unity toward considerations of gender, sexuality, region, and cultural plurality. These considerations reflect the rise of multiculturalism, feminism, and postcolonial theory and an overarching concern with inclusiveness and diversity. Interest in alternative and subversive views of the nation, issues of race, and the inclusion of marginalized voices became dominant areas of critical inquiry and emphasis, marking a major departure in selection criteria. Anthologists at this time emphasized the diversity of Canada and viewed the multiplicity of voices and perspectives as an integral element of Canada's literary heritage.

All four stages of development speak in specific and interesting ways about the nation's literary tradition, and key traits emerge in each. The literary nationalistic phase, however, is distinct in its intent focus on the distinguishing traits of both the nation and its literature. While only a small number of anthologies were published in this period, they marked a clear move away from a broad inclusiveness and interest in the existence of a national literature toward a more critical examination of the nation's writing and the claim that the nation had a literature worthy of scholarly study. During this time, interest in cultural distinctiveness and value grew, and the anthology came to be seen as playing a central role in defining the nation. Throughout the literary nationalistic phase, editors were concerned with the question of literary value and chose authors whose works they believed were of high quality and worthy of study, particularly in the university. With its greater concern for unique cultural elements and the assertion of the value of Canadian writing, this phase reveals key changes in the anthology genre at a point when the nation's literature was beginning to receive greater critical and scholarly attention.

More specifically, Richardson's and Moodie's inclusion in anthologies in the literary nationalistic phase shows that the anthology is a carefully constructed, culturally valuable work that both responds and contributes to literary critical trends, asserts the existence and value of a national literature, and works to define the nation, and, further, is a genre worthy of careful scrutiny. This focus on a single phase illustrates how anthologies accommodate dominant social and cultural influences, as well as the connections between a specific stage of anthology development and views of the nation. Further, while Richardson and Moodie were treated in a fairly similar manner within this phase, their inclusion in anthologies after this stage has been markedly different, and focusing on key commonalities illustrates how contemporary critical approaches impact critical reception and literary reputations.

RICHARDSON IN THE LITERARY NATIONALISTIC PHASE

John Richardson (1796–1852), the author of *Wacousta; or, the Prophecy: A Tale of the Canadas* (1832), was consistently included in the anthologies of this phase, and his writing was viewed as central to Canadian history and tradition. Richardson's skills as a writer were reassessed at this time, as editors began to promote more strident critical standards, asserting the importance of both a strong national identity and high literary standards. While earlier anthology editors were primarily concerned with outlining the contours of Canadian literature, editors of this stage focused on evaluation of both identity and aesthetics. This change is evident in Richardson's representation, for the works anthologized in the 1950s and 1960s are presented as being of high quality in addition to informing the reader of some aspect of the nation. This stage of the anthology illustrates increased confidence in, or at least patriotic promotion of, the worth of the nation's writing. Writing by Richardson that had been excluded from earlier collections was now anthologized, demonstrating editors' broader knowledge of Richardson's body of writing and higher estimation of its literary merits.

The re-evaluation of Richardson's quality as a writer began in the 1950s, which is evident in the first anthology of this phase, Carl F. Klinck and Reginald E. Watters's *Canadian Anthology* (1955). Like editors before them from the literary historical phase, Klinck and Watters focus on Richardson's personal history, stressing the connections between his life and significant events in the nation's history. In the headnotes, they highlight Richardson's lifelong interest in and involvement with the military and with aboriginal people. And in the introduction to Richardson's selections, the editors refer specifically to the War of 1812, showing that in the literary nationalistic phase war gained perhaps even greater recognition as a defining event in Canadian history and national identity. Richardson's familiarity with the events he incorporated into his literature is emphasized, positioning him as an informed, reliable source of information regarding early Canada.

But Richardson's personal knowledge of historical events alone was not the focus of Klinck and Watters's analysis; the editors also turned to the question of aesthetic merit and determined that the sequel to *Wacousta*, *The Canadian Brothers; or, the Prophecy Fulfilled* (1840), offered both high literary quality and a convincing representation of Canadian history. They argue that Richardson's skill improved throughout his career, noting that "the realism of *Ecarté* and of his historical narratives had toned down the

melodrama of *Wacousta*" (17). They excerpted parts of chapters 2 and 3 of
The Canadian Brothers, which describe the beginnings of the War of 1812
and introduce the Grantham brothers, the novel's protagonists. Their criticism of the "melodrama of *Wacousta*" shows a lack of interest in plot twists
and dramatic revelations; rather, the editors seek to present Richardson as a
witness to important historical events who created authentic depictions of
the time. Choosing *The Canadian Brothers* emphasizes the realistic aspects
of Richardson's writing, thus presenting him as a skilled author with valuable
insight into the past.

Presentations of Richardson shifted slightly in the late 1960s as editors
focused more intently on the question of literary value and gave greater consideration to his non-fiction works. In the second edition of their anthology,
published in 1966, Klinck and Watters included an excerpt from Richardson's
body of non-fiction writing. They retained the headnotes from their earlier
edition, maintaining a focus on Richardson's personal history, but in place
of an excerpt from *The Canadian Brothers*, they chose a passage from *War
of 1812* (1842), Richardson's memoir of his war experience. The selection
is fairly short, consisting of only a few pages describing the deaths of two
prisoners in Tecumseh's camp. Modifying their presentation of Richardson
places greater emphasis on the War of 1812 and on Richardson's firsthand
knowledge of the events; it may also suggest that they had reconsidered their
positive assessment of *The Canadian Brothers*. The editors' increased interest in the war is also apparent in other additions made to the collection:
they included two anonymously authored ballads of the War of 1812, "Come
All You Bold Canadians" and "The Battle of Queenston Heights," before the
excerpt from Richardson. By substituting a non-fiction passage from *War
of 1812* for the excerpt from *The Canadian Brothers*, the editors decisively
shifted their emphasis away from Richardson's status as a novelist and toward
his status as a credible reporter recounting crucial events of Canadian history.

Other editors in the later part of the literary nationalistic stage also
focused on Richardson's non-fiction. A. J. M. Smith in *The Book of Canadian Prose: Early Beginnings to Confederation* (1965) contrasts Richardson's
fiction and non-fiction, finding the latter superior. He discusses the qualities
of *Wacousta* that prevent him from including the novel:

> Some of the descriptions and many of the pictures of Indian fighting are
> vivid and forceful, but the characterization, particularly that of the 'females'
> is melodramatic or weak and the rather rambling plot is not free of sensation-
> alism. Neither this novel nor its sequel, *The Canadian Brothers* (1840) [...] can
> compare with the works of the explorers and fur-traders in the presentation
> of the Indian. The literary professional romanticizes and sentimentalizes; the
> practical amateur puts down exactly what he sees. (123)

Smith values the documentary aspect of early writing, arguing that Richardson's fiction is sentimental while the accounts of explorers and fur-traders are objective and accurate. Despite his misgivings concerning the novel's style, Smith admits its value to the literary tradition: "*Wacousta*, however, stands as the first of a long series of historical romances that includes Kirby's *The Golden Dog* and Sir Gilbert Parker's *The Seats of the Mighty*" (123). His emphasis on the worth of *Wacousta* to the history and development of a particular genre suggests that the novel is significant only for its influence on other work in this tradition. Smith's critique also suggests that he is aware of the inclusion of *Wacousta* and *The Canadian Brothers* in earlier collections and that his evaluation of Richardson is a deliberate revision of earlier assessments.

Having determined that the literary value of Richardson's novels is quite low, Smith then discusses a work he admires, the non-fiction account *War of 1812*. In his general introduction, he identifies the War of 1812 as a pivotal event in the development of Canadian national identity and growth: "The war did more to unite the Canadas and turn the thoughts of the people toward an eventual union of all the British North American colonies than any other event before the American Civil War, when the complex relations between the Canadian colonies, the warring powers in the United States, and Great Britain, was seen by Canadians as a threat to the very existence of the colonies" (xix). Smith links the war with national unity, positioning it as a pivotal event in the nation's history and upholding earlier assessments of the connections between war, national identity, and affiliation with Britain.[5] Building on this assertion, Smith excerpts Richardson's *War of 1812* and includes a section called "The Battle of Moraviantown and Death of Tecumseh," which details the defeat of the British at Lake Erie on September 10, 1813, and the death of Native American leader Tecumseh. He writes that it is in Richardson's "historical writing of a more sombre sort that [his] true merit is to be found. His most valuable book is his fine military history, *The War of 1812* [*sic*], published in 1842, from which we have selected the dramatic narrative of the death of Tecumseh" (123). Here, Smith reveals his New Critical stance, as he emphasizes vividness and drama and rejects melodrama and sensationalism. His interest in historical events and veracity shows that he valued writing that realistically depicted elements of the past. This combination of modernist principles and celebration of authenticity corresponds with the literary nationalistic stage of anthology development, which promoted Canadian writing as a literature of high aesthetic worth while also promoting Canadian distinctiveness.

Throughout the literary nationalistic phase, then, Richardson was included because several of his works supported both the narrative of national advancement and the assertion of high aesthetic value. While he had been included in earlier anthologies because editors valued the documentary elements of his writing and viewed him as having unique insights into the nation's past, editors in the 1950s and 1960s began to champion the literary value of his writing. He also became valued for creating a body of work that articulated a unique vision of the nation.

MOODIE IN THE LITERARY NATIONALISTIC PHASE

Susanna Moodie (1803–85) is one of the most widely recognized and studied authors of Canadian literature. Moodie, a British emigrant, was the author of numerous sketches, poems, essays, and books; her best-known work is *Roughing It in the Bush; or, Forest Life in Canada* (1852), an account of her early experiences as a settler in Upper Canada. In the literary historical phase, editors built on earlier views of Moodie's work as an accurate and entertaining account of settler life and continued to praise *Roughing It*; they also began to draw attention to her other works, situating her as a skilled and prolific author with specific knowledge of Canada in the nineteenth century. While editors of the literary nationalistic phase were clearly familiar with Moodie's biography, they began to shift attention toward the literary value of her writing. They agreed that *Roughing It* was an important book, yet their presentations of Moodie aimed to bring greater exposure to her other works. The changes in interest in Moodie's work and life reflect the transition from the literary historical to the literary nationalistic phase and illustrate how various aspects of an author's creativity are valued at different points.

Emphasis on the literary culture of Canada became apparent in presentations of Moodie beginning in the 1950s. In *Canadian Anthology* (1955), Klinck and Watters note that Moodie was

> a leading contributor of both prose and verse to *The Literary Garland* of Montreal [...] *Roughing It in the Bush* (1852) is not only her masterpiece, but a work which has a secure place in Canadian literary history as a vigorous, accurate, and humorous account of frontier conditions in Upper Canada. It is currently available in a modern reprint. *Life in the Clearings* (1853) is perhaps not as remarkable, but it deserves to be better known than it now is. (49)

The reference to the reprint of *Roughing It* indicates that the editors believed that Moodie's book was widely read.[6] Their interest in broadening knowledge of Moodie's other works is also evident in their selections: they chose a passage from *Life in the Clearings versus the Bush* (1853) and the introduction to *Mark Hurdlestone; or, the Goldworshipper* (1853). By including excerpts from Moodie's lesser-known books and mentioning Moodie's involvement with a prominent Canadian literary magazine, the editors sought to position her as an important contributor to the growth and development of the nation's literature.

The excerpt from *Life in the Clearings* is from the first chapter of the book and offers a more optimistic image of Canada than most of *Roughing It*. The selection describes the clothing and appearance of the Canadian lady, as well as members of the "lower class" who "are not a whit behind their wealthier neighbours in outward adornments" (50). In this passage, Moodie argues that poor emigrants may obtain a level of comfort, status, and prosperity in Canada that would not have been possible in their home countries. The second part of the selection, also taken from the first chapter, describes a group of French-Canadian lumbermen at work and focuses on the dangers of spring thaw and a dramatic incident Moodie witnessed following the collapse of a bridge. The selection describes several aspects of the Moodies' lives in Belleville and the tone is pleasant; while certain environmental, social, and cultural challenges are depicted, the passage is quite lighthearted and offers a positive view of the area and the opportunities available to new Canadians.

The second excerpt, "Early Canadian Periodicals," was taken from the introduction to *Mark Hurdlestone*; it discusses the difficulties of writing in Canada in the late 1800s and outlines the history of Canadian periodicals. With this selection, the editors present an example of the criticism of the time, thereby asserting and highlighting the existence of a developing literary culture. Moodie discusses *The Literary Garland*, which was published for twelve years until it could no longer compete with American periodicals, namely *Harper's Magazine* and the *International*. Moodie was a frequent contributor to *The Literary Garland* and laments the end of its publication, writing that it is "much to be regretted that a truly Canadian publication should be put to silence by a host of foreign magazines, which were by no means superior in literary merit" (58). She then briefly recounts the publication histories of a number of other periodicals published at roughly the same time as *The Literary Garland*, including one that she and her husband edited for a year, *Victoria Magazine*. Through her summary of these periodicals, Moodie asserts that there was a valuable literature in Canada as well as an appreciative readership, affirming that Canadian literary culture existed and flourished in the early to mid-nineteenth century. Inclusion of such an essay is an attempt to verify the existence and worth of a literature, aligning with the literary nationalistic tendency to promote a distinct culture. The excerpt also shows an expanded understanding of Moodie as an author, adding literary criticism to the genres in which she wrote. The selection of this excerpt reveals the tendency of editors during the literary nationalistic phase to highlight the contributions of authors to a unique national literature.

Even more than the 1955 edition, the revised 1966 edition of Klinck's and Watters' *Canadian Anthology* forcefully promoted Moodie's status as a central figure of the nation's literature. In the second edition of the anthology, Klinck and Watters made some changes to their presentation of Moodie, selecting two essays and a poem, all first published in *The Literary Garland*. They also altered the headnotes, placing greater emphasis on her personal life, noting, for instance, that her literary career was more successful once she and her family moved to Belleville and that she was a frequent contributor to Canadian literary magazines. They stressed that her best work stemmed from her Canadian experiences, remarking that "her poetry is generally undistinguished and her fiction (in which she avoids Canadian settings) is imitative of the sentimental and melodramatic popular fiction of the day in England. When she draws upon her personal experiences in Canada, however, she is at her best" (58). The editorial concern with asserting the aesthetic worth of Moodie's writing, especially her writing about Canada as she had experienced it, a core trait of the literary nationalistic phase, demonstrates that the editors were deliberately working to position Moodie as a skilled author who should be recognized for her body of work overall, not only her first Canadian book.

Their first selection in the revised edition is an essay entitled "A Word for the Novel Writers." As they note, the piece was first published in *The Literary Garland* in August 1851. They chose to republish the essay "as a period piece of Canadian literary criticism and as a statement of Mrs. Moodie's theory and practice in the serialized fiction that she wrote for *The Literary Garland*" (58). Although this selection discusses British literature, not Canadian, Moodie's literary activities are significant as evidence of Canada's extant literary culture. The essay is a defence of novels against those who argue that only works of "religious, historical, or scientific subjects" (58) are worthy of study. It gives a sense of Moodie's view of literature and approach to criticism, and its significance therefore lies in what it reveals about Moodie and her authoritative position as an arbiter of culture.

The second selection, "Early Canadian Periodicals," is the same excerpt from *Mark Hurdlestone* chosen for their first edition, and the presentation is unchanged. As does the first excerpt, this selection emphasizes Moodie's literary critical activity and positions her as an engaged contributor to early Canadian writing. Unlike "A Word for Novel Writers," this selection focuses on Canadian writing and the difficulties authors face in Canada. The editorial decision to retain this essay suggests that the piece was viewed as a strong example of Moodie's criticism.

The final selection Klinck and Watters included in their first edition is a poem, "The Indian Fisherman's Light," first published in *The Literary Garland* in February 1843. The poem was later included in *Roughing It* and is found at the end of chapter 15, "The Wilderness and Our Indian Friends." As the editors remark in the headnotes, they do not hold her verse in high regard; the inclusion of the poem, then, suggests their interest in showing the reader the range of Moodie's writing and giving some sense of the style of the poems in *Roughing It*.

A different view of Moodie's work emerges in Smith's edition of *The Book of Canadian Poetry: A Critical and Historical Anthology* (1957).[7] Smith selected Moodie for all three editions of the anthology and kept the same headnotes and selections in each. He chose two poems from *Roughing It*, "The Canadian Herd-Boy" and "The Fisherman's Light," both describing features of life in the colony. He comments on the quality of the poems, noting that while the lyrics in the book "are not without some historical interest[,] ... the conventionality of most of the verse is in sharp contrast to the vigorous, witty, and homely prose" (60). He finds that the greatest value of Moodie's poetry is instead found in its descriptions of settler life: "Mrs. Moodie is very much the cultured Englishwoman—superior, strong-minded, humorous, energetic, and, when necessary, courageous. Her book, because of these qualities, is the most vivid and authentic account we have of the conditions under which the English settlers opened up the frontier in Upper Canada" (60). In his poetry anthologies, Smith makes it clear that he values Moodie's book primarily for its documentary focus, and his emphasis on the accuracy of her writing reveals an interest in detailing national history and unique traits, which were key elements of the earlier literary historical phase. Smith's unchanging presentation of Moodie suggests that he did not reassess the value of her poetry and considered its value to be historical rather than aesthetic.

Smith's inclusion of Moodie in *The Book of Canadian Prose* (1965), then, shows a significant change in his evaluation and positioning of Moodie and her writing. In this collection, he excerpted *Roughing It*, and his anthology shows an interest similar to Klinck and Watters's in presenting Moodie as a skilled, significant author. Smith comments on Moodie's personal life to a greater degree than did earlier editors of this phase, and than he did in his poetry anthologies. He remarks that *Roughing It* was published twenty years after her emigration, when she was settled in Belleville, "prosperous, well-established, and reconciled to her new country" (159), suggesting that the discomfort and unhappiness with Canada expressed in her book had disappeared. Although he continues to find the descriptions of early settler life to be a distinguishing feature of the book, he also highlights Moodie's writing skills, an emphasis that sets him apart in his representation of Moodie from editors of the literary historical phase. He praises both *Roughing It* and *Life in the Clearings* while also finding aspects of the two works problematic:

> Because of the vigor of the narrative, the vividness of the descriptions, and the often humorous characterizations, these books stand apart from the generally undistinguished poetry and fiction of Mrs. Moodie. The story they tell is a representative and significant one, and what gives them a special interest for the social historian is the quite unselfconscious sense of superiority based on class, sex, and race which they reveal on every page. (159)

Smith's characterization of Moodie as superior reveals a more negative view of the author than he'd expressed earlier, and more negative than anything expressed by other anthology editors, thus revealing the impact of changing critical interests. He begins the later trend to view Moodie as an archetypal pioneer figure whose struggles to adapt to the rugged Canadian environment symbolize the clash between Old and New World values.

Smith chose two excerpts from *Roughing It*: a selection from the introduction and the sketch "Uncle Joe and His Family," abridged. The introduction is a warning to British citizens of the challenges and hardships of emigration. Smith's assertion that Moodie ultimately accepted Canada sharply contrasts the introduction; his interest in the ways that she and her views of her new home changed indicates a preoccupation with the author as a person not evident in earlier anthologies. The second excerpt is more lighthearted and supports Smith's assertion that Moodie's writing is humorous, vivid, and vigorous, as well as proving his assertions about her class snobbery and ethnocentrism. Moodie describes Uncle Joe's "jolly red face, twinkling black eyes, and rubicund nose" and notes that "Yankee he was by birth, ay, and in mind, too; for a more knowing fellow at a bargain never crossed the lakes to abuse British institutions and locate himself comfortably among the despised Britishers" (163). Similarly, Moodie's description of Uncle Joe's daughters' visits to the Moodie home emphasizes the differences she saw between American and British settlers:

> Fine strapping girls they were, from five years old to fourteen, but rude and unnurtured as so many bears. They would come in without the least ceremony, and, as young as they were, ask me a thousand impertinent questions; and when I civilly requested them to leave the room, they would range themselves upon the door-step, watching my motions, with their black eyes gleaming upon me through their tangled uncombed locks. Their company was a great annoyance, for it obliged me to put a painful restraint upon the thoughtfulness in which it was so delightful to me to indulge. Their visits were not visits of love, but of mere idle curiosity, not unmingled with malicious hatred. (171)

As the sketch describes the Moodies' interactions with their American neighbours, it reveals aspects of Moodie that position her as an irritable and supercilious pioneer whose connection to the Old World and inability to adapt to new conditions represent the worst of British colonialism. Smith thus stresses Moodie's condescension and her upper-middle-class persona in a way no one had previously done.

In sum, presentations of Moodie changed notably in the literary nationalistic phase, as editors began to insist on the literary worth of her works. Klinck and Watters laboured to make readers aware of her lesser-known works and to show the value of her contributions to early criticism, and Smith maintained his earlier view of her poetry and argued that her prose presented a fuller, more nuanced view of Moodie and was worthy of further study. In general, editors of this phase offered critical evaluations of her work and asserted that while her prose and literary criticism were of high quality, her poetry was not noteworthy. Greater interest in Moodie's critical activities emerged and editors sought to bring awareness to the diversity of her writing and the variety of genres in which she wrote. Additionally, less-flattering aspects of Moodie's viewpoint and responses were highlighted, offering a new perspective on *Roughing It* and challenging earlier, uniformly positive presentations. The treatment of Moodie in this phase reveals growing confidence in the value of early Canadian writing and interest in articulating the history of the nation's writing.

CONCLUSIONS

Throughout the literary historical phase, both Moodie and Richardson were viewed as authors whose voices and works were central to articulations of the nation and the establishment of the country's literature. In the literary nationalistic phase, editors reassessed the value of Richardson's and Moodie's writing, finding that each had made valuable contributions to the literary tradition. Further, the inclusion of their writing was linked with the genres of their works and connections that anthologists saw between literature and views of the nation. The issue of genre is particularly important to a discussion of Richardson, for several traits of his best-known novel and the fluctuations in his critical reception are related to genre. *Wacousta* is firmly situated in the tradition of the historical romance, and critics have frequently noted the influence of the Gothic tradition on this novel. More central to its inclusion in anthologies, however, is the specific way in which it uses its historical material, and its role in defining a national identity. As Carole Gerson notes in *A Purer Taste: The Writing and Reading of Fiction in English in Nineteenth-Century Canada*, throughout the nineteenth century, writers and critics held a "reverence for history based on the assumption that history was objective, factual, one of the classical pursuits, and therefore unquestioningly superior to 'mere works of fiction'" (92). Richardson used events from Canadian history as the basis of his novel, and while the work is not entirely factual, history forms the core of the work. The incorporation of historical material was also regarded highly because it was a means to foster a sense of national identity: writers of the time "promote[d] the historical romance as the genre which would develop a national identity by popularizing and mythologizing Canada's neglected history" (Gerson 91). Further, historical fiction was popular in Europe, which "fortified Canadians' interest in indigenous material and reinforced their view that the development of a recognizable literary tradition was inseparable from the establishment of a distinctive historical identity" (Gerson 94). Generally, the historical novel in Canada was seen to elevate the nation's sense of identity and value of its writing: "No critic questioned the importance of history and most presumed a direct correspondence between a country's awareness of its past and the quality of its imaginative literature" (Gerson 94). Historical material is an essential aspect of *Wacousta* and the novel was written at a time when historical fiction was regarded as a means to define the country and its literature and elevate the status of both. Since the historical romance is tied closely to views of the nation, Richardson's novel was particularly appealing in the first phase of anthology development.

However, as anthologies of English-Canadian literature continued to develop, Richardson's body of work became less interesting to anthologists, as their interests and views of the nation shifted to other areas and concerns. Changes in contemporary criticism and the notion of authenticity have had an impact on the reception of Richardson's writing. Early on, his work was valued for its association with his personal participation in warfare and with his relatives who had participated in earlier conflicts; he was also praised for his presumed knowledge of aboriginal life on the frontier. Later, his haunting Gothic accounts of the darkness of the New World were central to anthologies of the thematic phase. However, in the pluralistic stage, Richardson's accounts have come to be regarded as Eurocentric and biased, and anthologies of this phase ignore his writing and instead offer accounts of another kind, namely those of fur-traders, explorers, and aboriginal people themselves. He has been excluded due to a preference for aboriginal perspectives and genuine eyewitness exploration accounts. Richardson's vision of the nation is no longer considered important enough to include, and other views that more closely align with current critical interests have been selected instead. The changes in Richardson's status from a central author to one who is marginalized in anthologies reveals the impact of changing critical values and assessments.

Moodie's inclusion in the literary nationalistic phase was similar to Richardson's, as anthologists found her body of work appealing in terms of style, alignment with views of nation, and incorporation into a broader tradition. While Richardson's genre and view of the nation fell out of favour with anthologists in later phases, Moodie's writing has been consistently included. On closer examination, *Roughing It*'s own heterogeneous genre has significantly impacted its inclusion. One of the aspects of the book that has allowed for its frequent selection is that its form makes it easy to excerpt and it is adaptable to various editorial agendas for anthologies. Editors and critics have categorized and studied it as travel writing, autobiography, emigrant guide, novel, and a collection of sketches; the many classifications of the work speak to its diversity and wealth of material. In their discussion of nineteenth-century guidebooks, Cynthia Sugars and Laura Moss note, "The literature of the period is thus a mixture of many genres: satires, travel and adventure stories, and emigrant guides" (111); as critics have remarked, *Roughing It* is an excellent example of such generic multiplicity. Its mixing of genres has contributed to the book's frequent inclusion, as the variety of writing, generically and thematically, provides ample selection for editors and support for a range of approaches.

Moodie's treatment also offers valuable insight into the process of anthologization, for the consistency with which she has been included in anthologies, as well as the sustained and evolving critical interest in her work, demonstrates that some authors have been and continue to be valued consistently even as critical interests shift. While her inclusion in anthologies has been nearly uninterrupted, anthologists have presented her essays, sketches, poems, and books in various ways, showing the impact of considerations of genre on an author's presentation. Early anthologists selected both her prose and poetry but placed them in different sections, clearly distinguishing the genres. When excerpts from *Roughing It* were selected, their format, in which poems appeared at the beginnings and ends of sketches, was altered so that prose and poetry were separate. In later anthologies, a shift away from Moodie's poetry was evident. Later editors valued Moodie primarily as a prose writer, and although a number of critics have analyzed her poetry, her prose has received more attention in general. Thus, Moodie's reception is linked with assessments and views of the genres of her writing, and the various ways anthologists view and organize genre demonstrate how various elements of a single work may be foregrounded at different times.

The inclusion of Richardson and Moodie in anthologies of the 1950s and 1960s thus reveals much about critical interests of the time, as well as the value of analyzing the correlations between the content and focus of anthologies with dominant critical trends and views of the nation. Both Richardson and Moodie were viewed as authors who were central to the nation's literary culture, and their works were presented as aesthetically valuable and able to withstand critical scrutiny. The ways that their treatment has since differed shows that the anthology plays a role as a cultural document, and the format, contents, and guiding interests of anthologies have much to tell about the development of the nation's literature and interpretations of the country. These two cases provide important insight into the process of anthologization and the correlations among anthologies, prevailing critical trends, and the national literary tradition.

NOTES

1   Robert Lecker in "Nineteenth-Century English-Canadian Anthologies and the Making of a National Literature" notes that "Dewart is usually seen as Canada's first true literary anthologist" (97).

2   In his introduction to *Open Country: Canadian Literature in English*, Lecker notes that more than 3,000 anthologies have been published since Dewart's (xxii).

3   Carl Klinck, Reginald Watters, Donna Bennett, and Russell Brown all note that their anthologies were compiled for the university classroom.

4   For a further examination of these stages, consult Bonnie Hughes's *"[T]he subtle but powerful cement of a patriotic literature": English-Canadian Literary Anthologies, National Identity, and the Canon* (unpublished doctoral dissertation).

5   Lorne Pierce, in his introduction to the prose section of the first general anthology of Canadian literature *Our Canadian Literature: Representative Prose and Verse* (1922), establishes a link between war and national identity. He connects the emergence of an original national literature with the end of the American War of Independence, asserting that Canadian literature truly began after 1776, for the American Revolution resulted in a "great influx of loyalists into Canada" and that the "literary output after this change of residence" was notably improved (125). He further argues that the next pronounced change in Canadian writing occurred as a result of the War of 1812: "The process which had been operating after the war of 1776 reached a culmination in the war of 1812. English, Scotch, Irish and French were welded together against one common foe. However, once the emergencies of the war were removed the old lines of demarkation [*sic*] began again to assert themselves, though not as clearly or as persistently as before. There might be unity on occasion, but not union. Nevertheless the episode did show that their likes were stronger than their dislikes, and their similarities than their dissimilarities" (126). These connections between war and identity are a critical part of Watson and Pierce's presentation of Richardson in their anthology.

6   Their selections also reflect adherence to the guidelines for inclusion that Klinck and Watters outlined in the preface: "Whenever equally valuable alternatives were available, we have endeavoured to avoid using excerpts from long works such as novels, or from familiar and comparatively accessible books. Our intention throughout has been, not to substitute a part for a whole, but to supplement the known and stimulate exploration" (xv).

7   Smith edited three editions of *The Book of Canadian Poetry: A Critical and Historical Anthology* (1943, 1948, 1957), as well as *The Book of Canadian Prose: Early Beginnings to Confederation* (1965). Although the poetry and prose anthologies were published separately, they were intended as complementary collections. Smith writes in the

preface to the 1965 edition of *The Book of Canadian Prose* that the anthology "forms a companion to the poetry in the earliest sections of *The Book of Canadian Poetry.* The two books together will provide the reader with a broad picture of the literature of our colonial period" (Preface xi). Smith's anthologies therefore have been included in this study and are considered collectively as editions of general anthologies.

WORKS CITED

Atwood, Margaret. *Survival: A Thematic Guide to Canadian Literature.* Toronto: Anansi, 1972. Print.

"Battle of Queenston Heights." Klinck and Watters, rev. ed. 31. Print.

Brown, Russell, and Donna Bennett. Introduction. *An Anthology of Canadian Literature in English.* Ed. Russell Brown and Donna Bennett. 2 vols. Toronto: Oxford UP, 1982–83. xi–xiv. Print.

"Come All Ye Bold Canadians." Klinck and Watters, rev. ed. 30–31. Print.

Csicsila, Joseph. *Canons by Consensus: Critical Trends and American Literature Anthologies.* Tuscaloosa: U of Alabama P, 2004. Print.

Dewart, Edward Hartley, ed. Introduction. *Selections from Canadian Poets; With Occasional Critical and Biographical Notes and an Introductory Essay on Canadian Poetry.* By Edward Hartley Dewart. Montreal: Lovell, 1864. ix–xix. Print.

Di Leo, Jeffrey R. "Analyzing Anthologies." *On Canons: Politics and Pedagogy.* Ed. Jeffrey R. Di Leo. Lincoln: U of Nebraska P, 2004. 1–27. Print.

Frye, Northrop. Conclusion. *Literary History of Canada: Canadian Literature in English.* Ed. Carl F. Klinck. Toronto: U of Toronto P, 1965. 821–52. Print.

Gerson, Carole. *A Purer Taste: The Writing and Reading of Fiction in English in Nineteenth-Century Canada.* Toronto: U of Toronto P, 1989. Print.

Hughes, Bonnie. "'[T]he subtle but powerful cement of a patriotic literature': English-Canadian Literary Anthologies, National Identity, and the Canon." Diss. University of Ottawa, Ottawa, 2012. Print.

Klinck, Carl F., and Reginald E. Watters, eds. *Canadian Anthology.* Toronto: Gage, 1955. Print.

———, eds. *Canadian Anthology.* Rev. ed. Toronto: Gage, 1966. Print.

———. Preface. Klinck and Watters, 1955 ed. xv. Print

Lauter, Paul. "Taking Anthologies Seriously." *MELUS* 29.3–4 (Fall/Winter 2004): 19–39. Print.

Lecker, Robert. "Nineteenth-Century English-Canadian Anthologies and the Making of a National Literature." *Journal of Canadian Studies* 44.1 (Winter 2010): 91–117. Print.

———. Preface. *Open Country: Canadian Literature in English.* Ed. Robert Lecker. Toronto: Nelson, 2008. xxi. Print.

Moodie, Susanna. "The Canadian Herd-Boy." *Book of Canadian Poetry.* Ed. A. J. M. Smith. 3rd ed. 74–75. Print.

———. "Early Canadian Periodicals." Klinck and Watters, 1955 ed. 56-60. Print.

———. "Early Canadian Periodicals." Klinck and Watters, rev. ed. 63–66. Print.

———. "The Fever of Immigration (from the Introduction)." *The Book of Canadian Prose: Early Beginnings.* Ed. Smith. 161–63. Print.

———. "The Fisherman's Light." *The Book of Canadian Poetry.* Ed. Smith. 3rd ed. 75–76. Print.

———. "The Indian Fisherman's Light." Klinck and Watters, rev. ed. 66. Print.

———. "from *Life in the Clearings versus the Bush.*" Klinck and Watters, 1955 ed. 50–55. Print.

———. *Roughing It in the Bush: or, Life in Canada.* London: Bentley, 1852. Print.

———. "Uncle Joe and His Family." *The Book of Canadian Prose: Early Beginnings.* Ed. Smith. 163–72. Print.

———. "A Word for the Novel Writers." Klinck and Watters, rev. ed. 58–63. Print.

Pierce, Lorne Albert. Introduction to Prose Section. *Our Canadian Literature: Representative Prose and Verse.* Ed. Albert Durrant Watson and Lorne Pierce. Toronto: Ryerson, 1922. 123–29. Print.

Richardson, John. "The Battle of Moraviantown and Death of Tecumseh." *The Book of Canadian Prose: Early Beginnings.* Ed. Smith. 124–31. Print.

———. "from *The Canadian Brothers, or the Prophecy Fulfilled.*" Klinck and Watters, 1955 ed. 18–24. Print.

———. *The Canadian Brothers; or, The Prophecy Fulfilled.* Montreal: Armour and Ramsay, 1840. Print.

———. *Wacousta; or, the Prophecy: A Tale of the Canadas.* London: Cadell, 1832. Print.

———. "from *War of 1812.*" Klinck and Watters, rev. ed. 32–35. Print.

Smith, A. J. M., ed. *The Book of Canadian Poetry: A Critical and Historical Anthology.* Toronto: Gage, 1943. Print.

———, ed. *The Book of Canadian Poetry: A Critical and Historical Anthology.* Rev. ed. Toronto: Gage, 1948. Print.

———, ed. *The Book of Canadian Poetry: A Critical and Historical Anthology.* 3rd ed. Toronto: Gage, 1957. Print.

———, ed. *The Book of Canadian Prose: Early Beginnings to Confederation.* Toronto: Gage, 1965. Print.

———. Introduction. *The Book of Canadian Prose: Early Beginnings.* Ed. Smith. xiii–xxii. Print.

Struthers, J. R. "Anthologies." *Encyclopedia of Literature in Canada.* Ed. W. H. New. Toronto: U of Toronto P, 2002. 31–35. Print.

Sugars, Cynthia, and Laura Moss, eds. *Canadian Literature in English: Texts and Contexts.* Vol. 1. Toronto: Pearson, 2009. Print.

Anthology on the Radio

Robert Weaver and CBC Radio's *Anthology*

Joel Deshaye

How does our concept of the anthology change when an anthology orig-inates on the radio? The answers obviously depend partly on media. The media of radio and print have such physical differences, more so than radio and television, or television and film, that the contrast verges on a fascinating incompatibility. Stuart McLean's recent anthology *The Vinyl Cafe Notebooks* (2010) originated on the radio and alludes to mixed media in its title, referring not only to books and the title of McLean's popular radio show but also to vinyl records—three media and plenty of nostalgia. But the main precedent for this in Canada—an anthology with an origin on air—is CBC Radio's *Anthology*, a literary program started by Robert Harlow and Robert Weaver in 1954 that became one of the network's longest-running shows and contributed greatly to the boom in Canadian literature in the 1960s and '70s. It was Harlow's idea but Weaver's product to create and promote. Although *Anthology* was a new way of "retailing literature" (Locke 117) to a new and larger public created by mass media, it had an old way about it—a role in the very conservative, preservative tradition of anthologization associated with small readerships in Canada and elsewhere.

Radio of course is a technological "advance" over print, but until the age of the Internet listeners could not expect to access archived broadcasts on demand. Even now such access is spotty. So to allow listeners to "listen" again to what had already been aired, radio had to devolve to print. When excerpts from *Anthology* appeared in print in *The Anthology Anthology: A Selection from Thirty Years of CBC-Radio's "Anthology"* (1984) a full thirty years after the broadcast's launch, Weaver wrote in the preface that his pro-gram—despite the ephemerality of radio broadcasts—had surprising "staying power" (xi). He was referring to the longevity of the program but did not mention that the following year, 1985, would mark his retirement and the program's not coincidental end. On the one hand, any change to our concept of the anthology that resulted from *Anthology* on radio might have been symbolically cancelled by *The Anthology Anthology* in print. On the other, the amusing title of the book hinted at the duality of the broadcasts. Weaver used *Anthology*, and the CBC that his career helped to define, to reconcile the sometimes oppositional cultures of mass media and literature. By putting an anthology on the radio, he helped to suggest that the anthology as a concept integrates these cultures by matching their scope, in this case at the national level—bringing literature up into bigger markets and, at the same time, addressing publics as the nation.

From the beginning of his work at the CBC, Weaver had a dual interest in publishing and broadcasting, and the scope of his achievements in the related media offers clues to the relationships between the media and their associated cultures. Weaver wrote that the CBC provided writers with "a form of publication through readings broadcast over its radio network" (Preface xi). Barry Callaghan said of *Anthology*, "It was a radio show, but it was a literary magazine" (qtd. in Naves 107). More accurately, it was a radio show based on the format of a literary magazine, though Weaver didn't start publishing his own magazine, the *Tamarack Review*, until 1956, a couple of years after *Anthology* had begun broadcasting. *Anthology* presented short stories, poems, plays, interviews, and literary criticism. Mark Everard explains that "[Weaver's] main concern was not to develop radio as a medium, but to promote literature through the medium of radio" (10). And how well did he "promote literature" on air? Ultimately, "while not attracting the mass audiences of the magazine-style current affairs shows, [in 1984 *Anthology* had] an average listenership somewhere in the area of 50,000, a number far larger than the combined readership of all the literary periodicals in the country" (Everard 4)—a claim that Elaine Kalman Naves later echoes (44). Indeed, the circulation of the *Tamarack Review* "would never rise above 2,000" (Naves 56) in its twenty-six years, while Weaver's anthologies of short stories published by Oxford University Press sold "hundreds of thousands of copies" (Naves 81). Why did the circulation of *Tamarack* not increase as a spinoff effect of his involvement in national network radio and major publishing ventures? One answer is that the modes of production were not always compatible or commensurable; a little magazine run by volunteers, with limited production capacity, is unlikely to gain tremendously from even a tremendous positive influence from the outside.[1] But, regardless of this limitation, Weaver was successful for almost three decades in both the restricted and large-scale fields of cultural production. Twenty-six years of independent literary publishing is a long time, and hundreds of thousands of copies are big numbers, and thirty-one years of weekly radio programming amounts to many episodes and far more listeners.

Notably, the public of *Anthology* was established very quickly in the program's first year or two, for reasons that were partly monetary. Weaver had had an earlier success with a similar program, *Canadian Short Stories*, which led in 1952 to the first of a series of anthologies based on it. The series eventually sold very well. The first edition of *Canadian Short Stories* "was by no means a trivial accomplishment, inasmuch as it was the first collection of radio stories, and one of a very few short story anthologies of any kind, to be published in this country" (Everard 16). This accomplishment might not have been possible if Weaver had remained oblivious to the fact that he had to compete financially with "large American magazines" (Everard 13) and other sources of greater income for Canadian writers. As the government increased its funding to the CBC in the 1950s, *Anthology* could afford to spend more on its writers—even to the point of inspiring Callaghan to claim retrospectively that "Bob was prepared to waste money in the interest of supporting in a general sense a writer, or a group of writers" (qtd. in Naves 113). Callaghan's potential irony here is not easy to assess; Weaver was probably *not* wasteful in having a positive effect on the self-confidence, reputation, and finances of many writers of Canadian literature (and criticism), perhaps most recognizably Alice Munro and Mordecai Richler. Nevertheless, asserting that Weaver was open to any kind of writing from any school or style, Callaghan also said that Weaver "would buy anything" (qtd. in Naves 108).

No evidence that I have found is directly against the spirit of Callaghan's assertion, but even someone as open as Weaver had to deal with the material limitations of anthologization. In the introduction to *Open Country* (2008) and throughout *Keepers of the Code* (2013), Robert Lecker implicitly and explicitly writes about a tension between "open" and "closed" anthological practices. Although each individual anthology is restricted and each individual anthologist is restrictive, in theory anything can go into the book: any writer or artist, any printable and relatively short or small art form, any genre, from any time and place. In practice, however, anthologies tend to be thematically or chronologically ordered, and they have various closures due to the anthology's material limitations, such as the number of pages and the budget for the publication. Radio has no page limit, no spatial limitation except the range of the waves, but it has time limits—minutes per broadcast, broadcasts per year, years per program—and so in either medium limitations require editors to reveal their explicit preferences or unspoken biases about content, often both.

When Weaver proposed *Anthology* to the management at CBC, he stated: "We aren't aiming at anything precious [...] but rather at a varied and interesting program of good literary quality" (qtd. in Everard 20). Although he joked that he was "a good American" and had "more curiosity than taste" (Weaver, "Broadcasting" 104), he was a man of taste by all other accounts, and it's impossible not to read those accounts in an academic context without thinking Bourdieuian thoughts. As a cultural production, *Anthology* reflected a statement by Eugene Hallman, one of Weaver's contemporaries at the CBC: "the CBC should be committed to certain values which are not necessarily mass" (qtd. in Locke 117). In other words, not the cheap products of mass culture but something rarer, something of tasteful quality. The authors of the two book-length studies of Weaver—Everard and Naves—both repeatedly quote Weaver and others who say that "quality" was the main item on his agenda. So what did this quality mean? It meant, for example, the broadcasting of poems by Earle Birney, Kildare Dobbs, Louis Dudek, Peter Garvie, Irving Layton, James Reaney, Raymond Souster, A. J. M. Smith, Gael Turnbull, Phyllis Webb, and Anne Wilkinson—and these from the first two years alone, plus short fiction and criticism (Lecker, *Keepers* 193). *The Anthology Anthology* has selections by Margaret Atwood, Morley Callaghan, Gwendolyn MacEwen, Alice Munro, Al Purdy, Phyllis Webb, and many others—almost all of this latter group still widely known today, and known at least for occasional quality if not consistency. (See Purdy's 1978 lyric "On Realizing He Has Written Some Bad Poems" for further thoughts on this.) In her review of *The Anthology Anthology*, Donna Bennett writes:

> if some of the works in this volume do not meet a reviewer's literary standards, it is not because they try to do so and fail, but because they do not really attempt to be "literary" at all, at least not in the strictest sense of the term.
>
> And yet we are accustomed to thinking of the radio programs that Weaver produced for CBC as bastions of cultural quality. If the works he broadcast do not exhibit—seem not to have been chosen for—literary merit, then what kind of beasts are they? Has *Anthology* after all been merely another example of mass culture? (121)

Her answer to the latter question is "no." For Bennett, "the modernist split between 'high' and 'low' culture seems to be less severe in Canada than in a country like the US" (125). The texts in *The Anthology Anthology* are "neither failed art nor pap for the mass taste" (Bennett 122). She calls it "populist" and "'middle' writing" (122, 125),[2] and she invokes the prediction of Leslie Fielder that, after modernism, high and low cultures would reunite. They did—for a time, regardless of whether modernism was over or had begun a new phase. Quality and quantity came together.

Postwar literary and popular cultures were indeed remarkably aligned, especially in the 1960s. The national radio service was gaining a major partner in television, which was being established in Canada faster than anywhere else on the planet (McKay 65; "Canadian Broadcasting Corporation"), and together they reinforced each other, with shows such as *Fighting Words* appearing in both media, just as broadcasters sometimes worked in both. Although the CBC seems always to have appealed to both highbrow and mass cultures, from the mid-1950s to the 1970s the two cultures were far more mixed than at other times. There were objections, of course, from populists who resented the popularity of figures of elite society such as Leonard Cohen, and from elites in the academy who disapproved of the incursion of celebrity into the field of poetry. The alignment was not permanent, however. In one example from my book, *The Metaphor of Celebrity: Canadian Poetry and the Public, 1955–1980* (2013), we can see in Layton's career that, after success across cultures in the 1960s, his topicality in the mass media increased as his book sales decreased and literary reviews worsened. By the end of the 1970s, in poetry anyway, high and low cultures had diverged again. There are many reasons for this. At least in Layton's case, high-cultural critics seemed to lose patience with his careless self-promotional poems, and in the field there seemed to emerge an increasingly theoretical, academic, experimental style.

Experimentation, however, has not always been unpalatable to the popular taste. Think now of Christian Bök's bestselling *Eunoia* (2001). And in the 1950s, experimentation—but with realism—was an aspect of what Weaver meant by the "good literary quality" that he helped to popularize. He claimed to want "unorthodox" (qtd. in Everard 25) works, nothing, according to Everard, "sentimental" or "melodramatic" (42). Lecker writes in *Keepers of the Code* that "[i]t seems odd to hear anthologists like [Desmond] Pacey or Weaver talk about the need to support 'experimental' writing while they devoted themselves to promoting realism. But it's not such a contradiction: in Canada, in 1947, realism *was* experimental, and it remained so well into the 1950s, as Weaver's selections [in his 1952 anthology *Canadian Short Stories*] make clear" (194). Lots of readers and moviegoers today would have difficulty imagining how realism could be experimental rather than a constant. But this is because what we interpret as "realism" is usually melodrama, the "realism" being "superficial" (Williams 42), an argument made by Linda Williams in the context of American popular movies that is perhaps surprisingly applicable here. In the same context, Christine Gledhill explains that in cultural studies "tragedy and realism became cornerstones of 'high' cultural value, needing protection from mass, 'melodramatic' entertainment" (qtd. in Williams 43). Although Weaver was trying to popularize Canadian writing, he was also

trying to minimize the "sentimental" and "melodramatic" while re-introduc-
ing and preserving the "'high' cultural value" of realism. Why?

Arguably, there was an aspect of this new realism that was as old as one
of the first Canadian literary anthologies, Edward Hartley Dewart's *Selections
from Canadian Poets* (1864): nationalism. One of Lecker's contentions is that
even anthologies "that embraced experimentalism found themselves caught
in the nationalist-mimetic net" (*Keepers* 195). According to Naves, Weaver
was twenty-seven years old when he "decided [that] his overarching objective
was the advancement and development of Canadian literature" (35). Nevertheless, Weaver demurred when his work was associated with nationalism,
and in his preface to *The Anthology Anthology* he asserts: "Most of the material broadcast on *Anthology* has been by Canadian writers and performers,
but we have tried not to ignore the rest of the world even during that period
when cultural nationalism was fashionable in this country" (xii). The "quality"
of *Anthology* was unobtrusively nationalistic. I recall nothing on *Anthology*
as overt as the works collected by Purdy in *The New Romans* (1968), but *The
Anthology Anthology* arguably represents a subtle vision of Canada from the
1950s to the 1980s: cosmopolitan yet aware of our native land, international
but yoked neither to Britain nor the United States, typically plainspoken and
not too self-reflexive, and generally serious in tone. Many Canadian writers of
the era saw things differently, through different kinds of experimental lenses,
but they weren't really represented in *The Anthology Anthology*. As a cultural
production, *Anthology* was establishing a mainstream that wasn't concerned
with being "fashionable" as much as classic. Weaver seemingly wanted it to
be popular for the sake of the high culture's longevity, and, understandably,
he knew the nation could play a helpful role.

Today's literary mainstream gets much less help from the nation, and
much less popular attention, than did its counterpart during the boom years
of the 1950s, '60s, and '70s. The CBC had a major role in promoting literature
at that time, even to the point of helping to catalyze and sustain celebrity
for poets such as Layton and Cohen. Since the 1980s the CBC's budget and
presence has seemed constantly to shrink in an era of neoliberal governments
and the growing mass media of the private sector here and abroad. In 1981,
David Macfarlane argued that "[t]he Can Lit boom years of the '60s and
'70s—a period when names like Atwood, Richler and Laurence came to the
public's awakening attention—have given way to rampant commercialism
and fierce economic strictures. Our literary culture, so pessimists say, has
celebrated itself to death in the short span of 20 years" (14). He and the "pessimists" that he refers to were responding in part to Weaver's decision to cease
publication of the *Tamarack Review* in 1981. Macfarlane states that "many
saw the decision as symptomatic of the ultimate failure of Canadian literary

culture. The boom years of Can Lit were over. Many publishers had swung to rampant commercialism in an effort to stay out of the red" (15). Weaver's view was quite different: that *Tamarack* was no longer needed because the literary culture was now more firmly established (Everard 64). One reason that this view was possible is that medium-sized publishers (e.g., Anansi and Coach House) had grown and were pressuring their smaller competitors—a good thing if you valued stability, perhaps, but not good for new access to markets. Wearing his *Tamarack* and CBC hats simultaneously, Weaver might have understood the role of the government in supporting little magazines to be less crucial given that at least a few publishers seemed unlikely thereafter to fail. We have seen, however, that association with big government and big publishers didn't help a little magazine to become medium-sized.

Weaver's decisions related to the end of *Tamarack* and then *Anthology* were not and are not reducible to a nationalistic (e.g., governmental) agenda. But, as a product of the governmental establishment, the CBC's *Anthology*, starting in the 1950s, was earlier in publicizing nationalism than were printed anthologies that were products of a still maturing industry. Lecker's *Keepers of the Code* attempts to survey all published anthologies claiming national relevance from 1837 to the present. Notably, the number of such anthologies per decade gradually increased between the 1920s and the 1950s from six to around ten, then doubled in the 1960s to twenty, and almost tripled in the 1970s to fifty-seven. The difference in the 1970s was that alternatives, such as the aptly named *39 Below: The Anthology of Greater Edmonton Poetry* (1973) and Montreal's *Black Chat: An Anthology of Black Poets* (1973), were adding to the coast-to-coast nationalistic baseline. This is when, in print, the nation became many nations, or anthologists reacted to excessive nationalism by not mentioning the nation and by signifying other communities and social formations instead.

One such formation is the public, which as a concept is as encompassing as the nation but often without the national connotations. Within the public are publics or niches, and, from his perspective at the CBC, Weaver had remarked on their emergence in the mass media many years before literary anthologies opened up to publics. At the 1955 Canadian Writers' Conference he said, "The words 'mass media' suggest a search for a mass audience. Yet the same mass media are apparently beginning to create their own specialized publics, and this has been happening quite noticeably in the past ten years or so" ("Broadcasting" 106). As with nations within a nation, publics within a public might resist the bigger social formation and thereby test its willingness to be inclusive. So, counterintuitively perhaps, by virtue of being a part of the mass media as most printed anthologies were not, the CBC and *Anthology* might have been enabling a postnationalistic discourse before the print tradition caught up to them. But the CBC and Canada have been adept at seeming inclusive, or at least tolerant, as a strategy of co-opting postnationalistic discourse.

Weaver's remarks about mass media and publics predate by almost half a century Michael Warner's *Publics and Counterpublics* (2002). Warner's book dismisses the illusion of a single public, *the* public, and argues instead for a conception of the public that includes complementary niches or, more important for him, counterpublics and subcultures. Long before Warner, Weaver understood twentieth century media to "create their own specialized publics," partly because a radio and television station can broadcast a program at a regular time of day that tends to be convenient for specific demographics, which become publics. Weaver also noted that, nevertheless, "the moment we mention the words 'mass media' we seem to be implying the existence of a single mass public" ("Broadcasting" 104). According to Warner, this single public is dangerous because it helps to impose "norms" and "deep and unwritten rules" (25). The star poets that Weaver broadcast, such as Layton but also MacEwen, would have agreed with Warner. Both Layton and MacEwen demonized the public, and Weaver understood why, even if he was not so concerned: the public of electronic mass media was big, with 50 percent to 85 percent of households in Toronto, Montreal, and Vancouver using radio or television every night—already in 1955. Weaver explains that these statistics "make it easy to understand why so many writers and social observers have decided that, if our society is going to the bad, the mass media have something to do with the corruption. For the mass media are pervasive, and for better or worse, they are helping to form the society in which we live" (105). And yet Weaver was not really worried; he seemed to think that the publics of the various programs he mentions, including *Anthology*, were not so big and were not likely to produce a homogeneous set of "norms" or "rules." They were "minority publics" (Weaver, "Broadcasting" 112). Weaver guessed that *Anthology* might have been attracting "twenty-five to fifty thousand listeners" in its first year—"a small public by mass media standards; and yet a large public of its kind for this country; and also, I believe, a public for which serious writers need feel no contempt" ("Broadcasting" 112). One might add: and no fear.

Weaver's relativistic comment about writers in "this country" speaks volumes, as they say (an expression that seems apt to this essay about radio's voice for books). He was interested in volume not as a measure of loudness but as a measure of book sales, and he recognized that Canada was a small market, as it is today. The word *interest* too speaks volumes in his remarks. "If there is an international public," Weaver said at the conference, "then simple arithmetic suggests that Canadian writers ought to have a particular interest in that public" ("Broadcasting" 109). But he implied that there was a lack of interest: "Why wouldn't a certain kind of Canadian writer want to find a public abroad? The more serious, experimental, and individual the writer, the more need he is likely to have for an international public" ("Broadcasting" 111).[3] He might have meant that writers with these qualities sold few books and needed to look to bigger markets, possibly because Canada was usually inhospitable to such writers. Weaver said that the writers he approved of

> aren't obviously Canadian; they don't fit our recent nationalistic picture of ourselves. But there are other writers whose talents interest me much less, but who do receive substantial reviews and reasonable sales in this country; and I suspect that their popularity has at least something to do with the fact that, in the foreground, their books are so obviously Canadian. They feed our nationalistic pride, even if their literary abilities are rather ordinary. ("Broadcasting" 111)

Weaver's "interest" has a certain financial connotation: "sales." He realized that overtly nationalistic books could sell well in Canada, but that nationalism reduced the sales potential in bigger markets: "There are still a very limited number of Canadian writers who are likely to interest the international reading public" ("Broadcasting" 110). He implied that being less obviously Canadian helped Richler and Ernest Buckler to publish novels in the United States, and he predicted that their ambition to look abroad would help their books to "reach a new and larger public in their own country" (111). So, for Weaver, this "public" was in effect a book-buying readership that had no special interest in nationalism but that would be encouraged by international buy-in.

This view of the Canadian reading public is in contrast with the view Bennett proposes in one of her readings of *The Anthology Anthology*. She does recognize that Weaver's selections, "and the anthology as a whole, [point] to what Weaver evidently finds compelling—the locating, through encounters with the other, of Canada in an international context" (124). She also advances, however, a nationalistic interpretation of Weaver's project that takes into account (financial connotation intended) a range of nationalistic feeling. Reflecting humorously on the compulsion to buy copies of *The Anthology Anthology* nationalistically and nostalgically, she writes: "Right now, while we can still hear the voice of the land on publicly funded radio, let us purchase *The Anthology Anthology* as a talisman and hope that there is a way of keeping our oral tradition alive, of maintaining the literary arts in such a widely available form, so that we can continue to listen to our literature" (121). In this interpretation, *Anthology* and its printed companion address a public that is idiosyncratically regional (as "oral tradition[s]" tend to be), not global, yet national. The public here is in fact the nation, and, like any public or nation known as "the" and described as "our[s]," it is a potentially homogenizing entity that tries to assimilate the regions and voices that might not want to be involved so approvingly in such "tradition." It also needs our financial support. Bennett then self-consciously repositions her view, not to glorify the nation or literature but to explain how a national literature can reconcile high and low cultures:

> To speak the words that define ourselves is virtually a ritualistic act in Canada, and it is an act that calls for expression that is both literate (because it is a rhetorically important act and must not be debased) and comprehensible (because it is a public rite). The material contained in *The Anthology Anthology*, like that of its parent program, has been chosen not because it is literature but because it is a literate expression of Canadian culture. (124–25)

This revision is to me a sophisticated and nuanced statement about the literature that Weaver appreciated, but even this would probably have been too nationalistic a statement for Weaver to accept; he seemed to want the nationalist ideologies of his writers and the CBC to be less noticeable, just as realism can disguise ideology as seemingly natural.

Bennett is comparatively upfront; she leaves her revision in print as a record of the paradoxical desire to "[keep] our oral tradition alive," and this desire is part of a cultural anxiety (maybe "ours") about the longevity of ephemeral expressions such as the spoken word or a radio broadcast. As Bennett knows as co-editor of *An Anthology of Canadian Literature in English* (1982), longevity, or the impression of it, is one of the major results of anthologization and one reason why anthologies are instruments of canonization. Like a saint, a writer in the canon is remembered and even venerated for years to come, partly because anthologies usually recirculate previously published texts and can be reissued, thereby reasserting the importance of the included authors. The prefix "re" returns again and again. In *Keepers of the Code* and his earlier work, Lecker explains that the establishment of the canon in Canadian literature during the boom years was the result of increasingly corporate publishers that had additional help from new professorships and university courses that defined a field of study and created new readerships with each cohort of students (249–53). Compared to printed anthologies, *Anthology* was ephemeral on air, but it had the similar advantage of corporate, albeit national, backing plus frequent—in fact, weekly—opportunities to engage and renew the interest of listeners and readers. It was inevitable that Weaver would look back on his flagship program near the end of its run and produce *The Anthology Anthology*, a perfect example of the logic of canons. But *Anthology*'s ends were already conservative. It was not initially in print, and most of the radio program's content was never published as an anthology, but it compensated for the lacking durability of radio by helping to create a much larger public than most anthologies get, one whose critical mass was theoretically self-sustaining. Radio's publics have the advantage of scope, and perhaps if you can tell the same story to enough people then the story becomes mythic and hardly needs to be written.

Radio is thereby arguably more effective than print in conveying ideology. The propaganda of Nazi Germany would not have been so insidious if it had been restricted to brochures and newspapers. Radio's effect is partly the result of the sonic and emotional registers of the human voice, which can transmit feeling that overrides reason. A skilled orator can also be so casual that the listener might forget the fact of the performance and the fact that radio is a form of public address. Often seeming private and personal, radio broadcasts reach nations simultaneously. Such possibilities are a major interest of Jason Loviglio in *Radio's Intimate Public* (2005). Referring as Bennett did to the "ritualistic" aspects of radio, Loviglio claims that between the World Wars in the United States "radio seemed to conjure a ritual of national identity" (xv). He argues that, "[m]ore than any other mass medium, network radio in the 1930s and 1940s, by addressing a national public in an immediate and intimate manner, was perfectly situated to capitalize on the era's ambivalent romance with populism" (xxiii). Much the same ambivalence characterized the 1950s, 1960s, and to a lesser extent the 1970s in Canadian literature, when even Canadian poetry was briefly a *cause célèbre*. As I demonstrate in *The Metaphor of Celebrity*, Layton, Cohen, MacEwen, and Michael Ondaatje had a combined total of just over three hundred appearances on CBC Radio alone between 1955 and 1980 inclusive, and creative writers and literary critics debated the benefits and costs of reconciling high and low cultures. Since the heyday of modernism, privacy has been supposedly valued in the high culture, publicity in the low. For these four poets, one of the major themes of their work after the 1950s was the fusion of privacy and publicity that celebrity catalyzes. Close-ups in film and a closely mic'ed voice on radio are some of the techniques that enable this fusion. According to Loviglio, "[t]he tension between intimacy (interpersonal communication) and publicity (mass communication) was the defining feature of early network radio, its central problem and its greatest appeal. The 'intimate public' of this study's title refers to a new cultural space created by radio broadcasting in the 1930s that was marked by tensions between national and local, inclusion and exclusion, publicity and privacy" (xvi). He goes on to write that these latter two terms "have come to be understood as permanently 'in crisis'" (xvi). In my view, the crisis is that they become indistinguishable.

The fusion of privacy and publicity enabled by celebrity and radio might be reason to think that modernist ideology, with its pretense of separation between high and low cultures, was not the operative value system after the mid-1950s and through the 1960s in Canada. The 1950s and '60s are a little late for high modernism, yet Weaver's work at the CBC sometimes conformed to high modernist promotion of self and other. In *Modernism and the Culture of Celebrity* (2005), Aaron Jaffe shows how in the American context various authors promoted their own celebrity while endorsing the arts and personas of others. Although Weaver stayed behind the scenes on air, he had a habit of doing business at what Jeannine Locke calls "the *milieu* of Canada's mini-celebrities" (116): a trendy hotel bar across from the CBC headquarters in Toronto where popular writers, broadcasters, actors, and other public figures were often present. Given that his two major literary projects, *Anthology* and the *Tamarack Review*, both ended around the time of his retirement from the CBC in 1985, these projects seem not altogether different from star vehicles. Of course, Weaver was first and foremost promoting writers such as Munro and MacEwen, but he was also to some extent delimiting their access to national radio according to the limits of his own career. Jaffe argues that modernist writers attempted to devalue popular systems of promotion and disguise their own ways of promoting themselves with the goal of having distinction granted upon them (10). Weaver's dismissal of overtly nationalistic writers in a nationalistic era might have been one such attempt, because nationalism was one of the popular systems of promotion. Jaffe also explains that modernist celebrities had a "facility with promotional apparatus, its institutional agendas, and accompanying discourses," and that they created a "restrictive promotional system of introducing, editing, and anthologizing" (165), thereby enabling themselves to be gatekeepers of the exclusive cultures of both celebrity and literature. If Weaver had been in a different time and place, Jaffe could be describing him here—and even Weaver's self-professed *modus operandi* has modernist connotations of impersonality: "'I still have a certain innocence about this world,' he says, tamping the tobacco off his pipe and clearing his constantly unclear throat. 'I'm not really a member of the literary establishment. I maintain a certain degree of detachment'" (qtd. in Macfarlane 15).

This attempt at distancing himself from "literary" culture also involves a hint of smugness, as if he were almost anti-literary and yet elitist, and it anticipates and perhaps creates a precedent for the contradictions in later descriptions of him. It's funny to consider the high and low cultural inflections in Nave's summary of other views: "Once described by Al Purdy as the most important literary figure in Canada, Bob Weaver has been called 'a cultural pioneer,' by Mark Abley, 'a one-man national literary network,' by Robert Fulford, and 'radio's literary czar,' by David Staines. The most modest of men, he rejects these accolades, allowing only that he was a 'cultural bureaucrat,' simply doing his job" (17). Here, Weaver is "literary" but a "pioneer." One man but a "network." "Bob" but a "czar." He is either royalty or salt of the earth. These contradictions reveal that his friends and admirers did not know quite where to place him in a class system. He could move through the strata because his work was on the "'middle' writing" that Bennett identifies, and he had convinced others with more power to give him a sort of national authority—which no doubt invigorated his charisma in literary circles—to use the mass media for the promotion of literary, national, and ultimately personal ends.

Weaver worked in radio and print, combining their influence on culture. Involved in both publishing and broadcasting, he directed national funds toward writers he believed had the quality of strong silent nationalism. This preference guided his anthological practice so that he could reconcile two cultures, high and low, that were coming into alignment partly because of him and partly because of major changes in the mass media and its industries during the boom years in Canadian literature. Recognizing the financial situation of writers and the access to markets afforded by the media, he tried to develop writers and thereby developed some of the culturally literate publics that the CBC was promoting. It will always be too early to know if this literacy is permanent, but by expanding his publics through radio in the 1950s he had a major role—and celebrated career—in preparing the way for the diversity of nations that emerged through anthologies in the 1970s and later.

How does our concept of the anthology change when an anthology originates on the radio? In this case, perhaps not as much as we would expect. A *concept* is "[a] widely held idea of what something is or should be ... while a *conception* is a concept that is held by a person or small group and that is often colored by imagination and feeling" (*New Oxford*). As with *the public* compared to *publics*, the difference is of degree, just as radio affords the anthology a public of larger scope. We might expect this change to affect the character of the thing too, as many poets did in imagining the public, but Weaver's conception of the anthology reflected and affected a great many of the anthologies produced when he was active: it had national character, a concept, and its effect and perhaps intention was to integrate not only texts but also cultures—high, low, oral, literary—to maximize its public. If I may attribute intention rather liberally: a nation wants every public to be nationalized. This requires money and time. As a representative of the CBC, and perhaps not altogether comfortably or admittedly of the nation, Weaver used *Anthology* and *The Anthology Anthology* to multiply implicit, ideological, materialistic, national signs. If he produced widespread changes of concept, he did so through national public radio, which left its impression on both the texts it broadcast and the medium it was adapting.

NOTES

1   Consider, as a more recent example, the difficulty and even reluctance that the publishers at the small Gaspereau Press experienced in meeting the sales potential of Johanna Skibsrud's Giller Prize–winning 2009 novel, *The Sentimentalists*.
2   I leave it to others to determine whether *Anthology* should be considered an example of "middlebrow" culture.
3   In the *Literary History of Canada*, Hugo McPherson paraphrases Weaver somewhat differently: "As Robert Weaver has suggested, the artist who genuinely wants to write short fiction is now forced to compete in the international market" because the advent of television drew professional writers away from the form of the short story and, as a result, literary magazines "have become blind alleys for writers who wish to reach a mass audience" (721).

WORKS CITED

Bennett, Donna. Rev. of *The Anthology Anthology*, Ed. Robert Weaver. *Essays on Canadian Writing* 34 (1987): 119–26. Print.

"Canadian Broadcasting Corporation: The Advent of Television." *The Canadian Encyclopedia*. Historica-Dominion, 4 May 2009. Web. 2 Apr. 2012.

Deshaye, Joel. *The Metaphor of Celebrity: Canadian Poetry and the Public, 1955–1980*. Toronto: U of Toronto P, 2013. Print.

Everard, Mark. "Robert Weaver's Contribution to Canadian Literature." MA thesis. U of Toronto, 1984. Print.

"idea." *New Oxford American Dictionary*. 2nd ed. Oxford: Oxford UP, 2005. Print.

Jaffe, Aaron. *Modernism and the Culture of Celebrity*. Cambridge: Cambridge UP, 2005. Print.

Lecker, Robert. *Keepers of the Code*. Toronto: U of Toronto P, 2013. Print.

———. *Open Country: Canadian Literature in English*. Toronto: Nelson, 2008. Print.

Loviglio, Jason. *Radio's Intimate Public: Network Broadcasting and Mass-Mediated Democracy*. Minneapolis: U of Minnesota P, 2005. Print.

Macfarlane, David. "Leave It to Weaver." *Today Magazine* 24 Oct. 1981, 16–17. Print.

McKay, R. Bruce. "The CBC and the Public: Management Decision Making in the English Television Service of the Canadian Broadcasting Corporation, 1970–1974." Diss. Stanford University, 1976. Print.

McLean, Stuart. *The Vinyl Cafe Notebooks*. Toronto: Viking, 2010. Print.

McPherson, Hugo. "Fiction, 1940–1960." *Literary History of Canada: Canadian Literature in English*. Ed. Carl F. Klinck. Toronto: U of Toronto P, 1973. 694–722. Print.

Naves, Elaine Kalman. *Robert Weaver: Godfather of Canadian Literature*. Montreal: Véhicule, 2007. Print.

Warner, Michael. *Publics and Counterpublics*. Brooklyn: Zone, 2002. Print.

Weaver, Robert. "Broadcasting." *Writing in Canada: Proceedings of the Canadian Writers' Conference, Queen's University, 28–31 July 1955.* Ed. George Whalley. Toronto: Macmillan, 1956. 103–14. Print.

———. Introduction. *Canadian Short Stories.* Toronto: Oxford UP, 1969. ix–xiii. Print.

———. Preface. *The Anthology Anthology.* Toronto: Macmillan, 1984. xi–xii. Print.

Williams, Linda. "Melodrama Revised." *Refiguring American Film Genres.* Ed. Nick Browne. Berkeley: U of California P, 1998. 42–88. Print.

Canadian Literary Anthologies through the Lens of Publishing History

A Preliminary Exploration of Historical Trends to 1997

Janet B. Friskney

Scrutiny of Canadian literary anthologies has typically occurred through the lens of literary criticism, often with emphasis placed on specific titles and their contents alongside an assessment of the critical vision that animated the individuals who edited these works. Canadian literary critics have pursued aspects of the subject in article-length studies, but the only book-length work on the topic to date is Robert Lecker's *Keepers of the Code: English-Canadian Literary Anthologies and the Representation of Nation* (2013), whose discussion touches on over two hundred anthologies produced over the stretch of two centuries but whose "central focus is on those collections that define themselves as pan-Canadian in their perspective—books that are not restricted to a particular region, movement, age group, or period" (3).

This chapter approaches the topic of Canadian literary anthologies in English at a macro level and from the perspective of publishing history. Basic bibliographical detail serves as my primary point of entry: that is, the names of editors/authors/compilers, titles, places and years of publication, names of publishers, editions, and series. I focus on the period up to 1997 for a very practical reason: in 1997, Robert Lecker and his two associate editors, Colin Hill and Péter Lipert, published *English-Canadian Literary Anthologies: An Enumerative Bibliography*, a volume that records 2,093 anthologies issued up to the year of the bibliography's publication. This book therefore offers a handy corpus to exploit in my effort to gain an understanding of broad historical trends associated with the publication of Canadian literary anthologies in English nearly to the close of the twentieth century. Methodologically my impulse is to explore the ways in which basic bibliographical detail can be manipulated in support of an historical narrative about publishing trends in a specific topical area. Also I wish to test the limits of basic bibliographical data as a source of insight into historical trends up to the point at which it becomes necessary, for the sake of clarity or deeper understanding, to seek out other resources in the publishing historian's toolkit, such as the primary sources represented by books themselves, descriptors associated with titles when listed in library catalogues, secondary literature, or archival materials.

When analyzed at a macro level, the corpus provided in Lecker et al. reveals the publishing history of Canadian literary anthologies in English to 1997 to have been overwhelmingly a domestic affair. Of the 2,093 entries in the bibliography, 1,976 (94.41 percent) are Canadian imprints. Moreover, the 117 (5.59 percent) foreign imprints that are present can be more accurately expressed as 105 unique titles since some titles appeared multiple times over a stretch of years.[1] A total of only ten foreign countries issued these Canadian literary anthologies in English, with the United States and the United Kingdom vanquishing all other foreign countries, together claiming 99 (84.62 percent) of the 117.[2] A remarkable seventy publishers in these two countries issued these 99 titles over the stretch of thirteen decades (1870s to 1990s). Foreign-based publishers that engaged in publishing Canadian literary anthologies in English are therefore most notable for the typically one-off nature of their investments. The major exception is Penguin UK,[3] which published 10 anthologies involving English-Canadian literature between the 1940s and the 1980s. Even so, these were predominantly new editions of Ralph Gustafson's *The Penguin Book of Canadian Verse*, the first iteration of which—the Pelican *Anthology of Canadian Poetry (English)* (1942)—resulted from a request from the Canadian military to Penguin for a pocket-sized anthology for Canadian services personnel stationed overseas (Gustafson 74).

Domestically, the publishing history of Canadian literary anthologies in English to 1997 emerges from the corpus of Lecker et al. as a far richer, more complex, and messier story than what occurred abroad. That domestic story provides the focus for this essay. In general, domestic publication of Canadian literary anthologies in English experienced a sustained and ever-expanding commitment on the part of Canadian-based publishers. A fledgling activity in the mid-nineteenth century, it took firmer hold in the 1880s and '90s, and then demonstrated steady if modest growth during the first half of the twentieth century, buttressed by Canada's increasing population and the consolidation of provincial education systems whose curricular needs it addressed. By 1960, many of the anthologies produced in Canada bore the imprint of either Canadian-owned publishers or foreign-owned branch plants—after 1900, the latter increasingly set up shop in Canada (mostly in Toronto) to gain a piece of the country's market for primary- and secondary-school textbooks. These professional publishers also issued some anthologies with an adult reader in view. If they were lucky, these volumes found traction in both the general trade and postsecondary markets, the latter representing a growth area from the mid-twentieth century onward as Canadian literature made inroads into university curricula.

Yet, right up to 1997, domestic production of Canadian literary anthologies in English was by no means the purview of professional publishers alone. They shared the territory with a range of other Canadian-based agents, including enthusiastic editors and authors' collectives that published their own anthologies, writers' groups and cultural organizations that ran their own publishing programs, and religious groups and social agencies, some of which brought distinctly extra-literary aims to the publication of anthologies. Moreover, prior to 1970, anthologies that focused on specific geographical areas of Canada were predominantly the productions of such alternative agents, particularly writers' organizations. That situation changed rapidly in the last two decades of the twentieth century with the proliferation of smaller publishing firms based outside of Toronto, many of which viewed a regional focus as central to their mandates. Aided by a significant infusion of government funding into the Canadian book publishing industry after 1970, this expansion occurred at a time of social change and when the boundaries and preoccupations of Canadian literature experienced revision. These shifts influenced the visions of editors, scholars, publishers, and readers, bringing forth anthologies that, on the one hand, targeted such issues as ethnicity, gender, and sexuality, while, on the other, broadened the concept of Canadian literature to embrace more popular forms of writing, particularly science fiction, fantasy, and mysteries.

CORPUS AND METHOD

While some pertinent titles certainly will have eluded Lecker, Hill, and Lipert in their compilation of *English-Canadian Literary Anthologies* (an inevitability of such a bibliographical undertaking), my assumption is that the 1976 Canadian imprints they did identify provide a sufficiently large corpus from which to interrogate broad historical trends in the domestic publication of Canadian literary anthologies in English. Since my approach makes me entirely reliant on their corpus, let me reiterate here the criteria for inclusion used by Lecker and his associate editors for their bibliography. According to Lecker, who authored the introduction,

> we tried to be as inclusive as possible. We defined an anthology as a book that included the works of two or more Canadian writers; collaborative works (volumes that include only co-written pieces) were excluded. We have cited

anthologies that include both Canadians and writers of other nationalities since these anthologies provide a means of understanding how Canadian literature is represented in "cosmopolitan" as opposed to strictly national anthologies. For these cosmopolitan anthologies, the inclusion of one Canadian was sufficient for listing in the bibliography.... We have also cited anthologies that include French-Canadian poetry or fiction that is translated into English....

Our definition of "literature" includes hymns; inspirational verse; poetry; fiction; stage, radio, and screen-play drama; children's literature; and literature for and by children, juveniles, and young adults. We did not include [volumes exclusively focused on] folklore or legends [...]. We also excluded [dedicated] anthologies of Canadian essays, even though these are clearly literary anthologies, since our primary aim was to focus on anthology formation as it related to poetry and fiction. (Lecker et al. viii–ix)

Collections entirely devoted to works of Canadian journalism appear to have been excluded following the same rationale applied to volumes of essays. Therefore, titles such as *A Century of Reporting: The National Press Club Anthology* (1967) or *Flaunting It!: A Decade of Gay Journalism from the Body Politic: An Anthology* (1982) fall outside the corpus considered here.

The entries in the first section ("Anthologies") of *English-Canadian Literary Anthologies* include details of titles, editors, and authors, as well as the imprints of their publishers: that is, information around places and years of publication, the names of the publishers who issued the titles, and indication of inclusion in particular series. In order to acquire a better understanding of historical publishing trends associated with the domestic publication of the Canadian literary anthology in English, I have used the information associated with the publishers' imprints in conjunction with the topical insight provided by the individual titles. Moreover, *English-Canadian Literary Anthologies* codes entries based on the broad literary categories of "poetry," "prose," and "drama"; when the basic category is not evident in the title of a work, entries are annotated with a "[Po]," "[Pr]," or "[Dr]," or some combination of the three. As part of my preparation for analysis, I further coded entries with topical descriptors of various kinds (e.g., region, ethnicity, sexuality) derived directly from titles, or by consulting descriptions in library catalogues, or by examining the contents of the works themselves. For those entries lacking information about places or years of publication, I checked library catalogues in case new information had become available since 1997; when I found such information, I added it to the original entry. In the case of some titles, I also dipped into the paratextual elements (Genette) so often part and parcel of anthologies, particularly prefaces and introductions. Finally, I made occasional recourse to secondary literature. A combination of quantitative and qualitative research therefore informs this preliminary study of historical trends in the domestic publication of Canadian literary anthologies in English.

EXPLORING THE CANADIAN IMPRINTS

A basic historical narrative of domestic publication of Canadian literary anthologies in English can be derived by filtering, in various ways, the bibliographical data associated with the Canadian imprints listed in *English-Canadian Literary Anthologies*. When examined in terms of the number of unique titles (i.e., same title and same editor/compiler—though one editor might be added/subtracted, and the publisher might change), the 1,976 Canadian imprints captured in the bibliography falls to 1,868. In offering this figure, cautions apply: the reduced number does not account for the possibilities of new editions issued with stable titles but modified content, or of anthologies issued with modified titles but containing stable content. For some works, the bibliographical data for the entry does indicate that the title has been revised. In other cases, however, comparison of copies of the books issued under the same title would be necessary to clarify whether the volume with the later date is a new edition, or simply a new printing sporting a later publication date. In addition, certain titles exist within the reduced figure of 1,868 that, if investigated, would reveal themselves as new editions of earlier volumes with slightly altered titles. Subtle changes of language in a title combined with a consistent editor can hint broadly in this direction. For instance, Gary Geddes and Phyllis Bruce's *15 Canadian Poets Plus Five* (1978) represents a revised edition of the original *15 Canadian Poets* (1970), and further manipulation of the title occurred with subsequent editions (Lecker, *Keepers* 285).

Among the 100-odd entries that do share identical titles and consistent editors, remarkably few represent a work that appeared more than twice in the complete list of Canadian imprints. The most notable exceptions include: Desmond Pacey's *A Book of Canadian Stories*, recorded nine times, beginning in 1947; and J. E. Wetherell's *Poems of the Love of Country* (1905) and Clyde Rose's Newfoundland anthology *Baffles of Wind and Tide* (1974), both of which claimed five Canadian entries. Janice Cavell's revelation that Pacey's anthology represented a "staple" on the favoured list of books distributed internationally by External Affairs offers one explanation for that work's exceptional status (84); it also found a place on reading lists for courses in Canadian literature. While multiple entries for a single title are obviously suggestive of more successful works, it nonetheless remains impossible to determine definitively from bibliographical details alone which works sold the most copies, stayed longest in print, or had the greatest curricular and/or cultural impact. For such revelations, one must consult copyright pages for evidence of multiple printings, seek out historical data in publishers' archival records, and consult backlist catalogues, provincial textbook lists, memoirs, and secondary sources.

Filter the total 1,976 domestic imprints through the lens of time period and location, and further details of the narrative reveal themselves. More than 98 percent of the Canadian imprints appeared in 1900 or later. Almost 68 percent of the 28 titles that did appear in the nineteenth century emerged in the 1880s and '90s. The volume of publication continued on an upward trajectory in the first decade of the twentieth century (15 entries), with modest but steady incremental increases in the succeeding four decades: 25 for the 1910s; 37 for the 1920s; 57 for the 1930s; and 69 for the 1940s. After dropping down to 66 in the 1950s, the figure almost doubled (126) in the 1960s, and then, from 1970 forward, advanced at a breathless pace: 464 for the 1970s; 491 for the 1980s; and 598 for the years between 1990 and 1997 (see table 1). Almost 85 percent of the Canadian imprints listed in the Lecker et al. bibliography appeared after 1960; over 78 percent appeared after 1970.

Throughout the two centuries, Ontario dominated as the primary producer of Canadian literary anthologies in English, claiming almost 60 percent of the total Canadian imprints. Given that Toronto had emerged as the centre of Canada's English-language book publishing industry by the late

Table 1   Canadian Imprints Divided by Time

PERIOD	# OF IMPRINTS	PERCENTAGE (/1976)
pre-1900	28	1.42%
1900–09	15	0.76%
1910–19	25	1.27%
1920–29	37	1.87%
1930–39	57	2.88%
1940–49	69	3.49%
1950–59	66	3.34%
1960–69	126	6.38%
1970–79	464	23.48%
1980–89	491	24.85%
1990–97	598	30.26%
Total	1976	100.00%

nineteenth century, the position comes as no real surprise (Parker "Evolution" 28–31). Still, prior to 1900, Quebec represents a notable competitor—the source of just over one-third (35.71 percent) of the anthologies produced during that period. However, during the first half of the twentieth century, Quebec largely retreated from the field, and it demonstrated a significant resurgence in the production of Canadian literary anthologies in English only after 1970, although never again remotely close to the scale of Ontario. From the 1930s through the 1950s, the most significant production outside of Ontario came from Saskatchewan and Alberta, which respectively issued a total of 35 and 34 during these decades. In the 1960s, British Columbia joined these two provinces as a player, but it would be the 1970s before production of English-Canadian literary anthologies became more pronounced in Manitoba and the Atlantic provinces. (See table 2.)

Steady emergence after the turn of the century of a more sophisticated book publishing industry offers one significant reason for the dominance of the twentieth century in the history of domestic publication of Canadian literary anthologies in English. The regional diversity of the industry also increased significantly in the late decades of the century, an important contextual factor for understanding the increase in the publication of anthologies outside of Ontario after 1970. While vital political and geographical factors shaped the sector's development in profound ways both before and after 1900, expansion of the Canadian population during the twentieth century inherently supported these trajectories in Canada's book publishing industry: in 1901, the census recorded approximately 5.3 million Canadians (excluding Newfoundland, which did not join Confederation until 1949); by 1971, the population had risen to about 21.5 million. Even taking into account the significant number of Canadians who claimed French as their first language, a country with a population of 21 million in 1971 provided a much more substantial market on which to build an English-language book publishing industry than one of 5 million had in 1901. The general upward trend in the domestic rate of publication of English-Canadian literary anthologies during the first seven decades of the century occurred in tandem with this expansion in population. Moreover, the twentieth century was the first to experience the full impact of a public education system, one whose textbook needs encompassed literary anthologies. The remarkable acceleration in production of anthologies after 1960 and even more spectacularly after 1970 dovetails with two additional contextual phenomena: significantly expanded curricular interest in Canadian literature, particularly at the secondary and postsecondary levels, and the onset of government intervention in the book publishing sector. Whereas targeted "project" grants had characterized the

Table 2 Canadian Imprints Divided by Time and Province/Territory

PERIOD	TOTAL FOR YR	BC	AB	SK	MB	ON	QC	NS	NB	PEI	NF	YK	CAN
pre-1900	28	0	0	0	0	18	10	0	0	0	0	0	0
1900–09	15	0	0	0	1	10	1	1	0	0	2	0	0
1910–19	25	0	0	0	0	22	0	0	0	0	2	0	1
1920–29	37	2	0	1	0	30	2	1	0	0	1	0	0
1930–39	57	1	13	6	2	32	2	1	0	0	0	0	0
1940–49	69	2	9	19	0	31	3	2	3	0	0	0	0
1950–59	66	2	12	10	0	41	0	0	0	0	1	0	0
1960–69	126	11	12	7	1	84.5	4.5	1	4	0	1	0	0
1970–79	464	53	37	19	8	286	26	10	10	4	11	0	0
1980–89	491	44	57	33	21	280	24	10	3	4	15	0	0
1990–97	598	72	41.33	30.33	22.33	340.5	31.5	23	9	5	22	1	0
Total	1976	187	181.33	125.33	55.33	1175	104	49	29	13	55	1	1

government funding of the 1960s, the 1970s witnessed a shift to "block grant" subsidies designed to aid programs of original book publishing. That change in the funding model likely played into the dramatic jump in the issue of anthologies after 1970. Federal and provincial government support for book publishers during these decades also encouraged the founding of many new book publishing firms throughout the country. This greater density of publishers in the market enhanced overall volume of book publication, and some of that volume included the by then staple genre of English-Canadian literary anthologies.

Concomitantly, in the twentieth century the position of would-be editors of Canadian literary anthologies improved as the nature of financial arrangements between Canadian authors and Canadian book publishers shifted, with remuneration on a royalty basis emerging around the 1920s as the industry norm. While royalty arrangements were not absent in Canadian book publishing prior to 1900, the more typical contracts between Canadian authors and Canadian book publishers featured subscriptions (partial or total),[4] commissions,[5] or the authors' absorption of all costs and responsibilities related to editing, manufacturing, and marketing. The most well-known anthology of Canada's mid-nineteenth century, E. H. Dewart's *Selections from Canadian Poets* (1864), involved a subscription arrangement between Dewart and his Montreal publisher John Lovell. As part of the standard process of bringing a book into print on a subscription basis, Dewart issued a prospectus in 1863 to advertise the book and acquire subscribers. In this document, he stated: "the Editor anxiously hopes that the patriotic sympathy and favor of the public will warrant him in soon placing this volume before the people of Canada." (qtd. in "Rev. E. H. Dewart's"). An article in the Toronto *Christian Guardian* that highlighted the planned book and its prospectus further illuminated the arrangement: "As soon as a sufficient number of subscribers is obtained, to warrant the expense of publication, the volume will at once go to press" ("Rev. E. H. Dewart's"). The low volume of domestic production of Canadian literary anthologies prior to 1900 likely owed something—and possibly much—to an inability on the part of would-be editors to finance anthologies either by subscription or through their own financial resources. After 1900, these myriad forms of financial arrangements between editors and publishers endured for some time. For example, Toronto publisher William Briggs, book steward of the Methodist Book and Publishing House (MBPH) of Toronto, issued under his own imprint and on a royalty basis both Theodore Harding Rand's *A Treasury of Canadian Verse* (1900) and Mrs. C. M. Whyte-Edgar's *A Wreath of Canadian Song* (1910), but in 1911 published J. D. Logan's *Songs of the Makers of Canada and Other Homeland Lyrics* on a commission basis (Ledger). For its time, Rand's anthology did remarkably well: it appeared in

1900 in UK and US editions as well, and sold 2,000 copies in Canada by 1904 (Peterman and Friskney).

The Canadian imprints in the bibliography of Lecker et al. reveal quite dramatically that domestic issue of English-Canadian literary anthologies has been by no means the exclusive purview of professional book publishers. Indeed, roughly one quarter of the Canadian imprints they capture can readily be credited, fully or partially, to other types of entities that were motivated and able to fund anthologies of their own imagining. That is a vital factor to keep in mind when exploring the volume and topical preoccupations exhibited by the corpus of Canadian imprints. For instance, consider the social impetus behind the second earliest Canadian imprint recorded: *The Canadian Temperance Minstrel: Being a Collection of Hymns, Songs and Poetry, Selected and Original* (1842). Published by the Committee of the Montreal Temperance Society, its pages included the song "The Drunkard's Child" and the poem "The Rum Maniac."

Most prominent among the alternative players in the production of Canadian literary anthologies are writers' groups and educational institutions (e.g., schools, boards of education, colleges, universities, or units within them), but the organizations involved also encompass arts, heritage, ethnocultural, and religious groups, as well as periodical publishers, libraries, bookstores, book clubs, broadcasters, museums, galleries, and festivals. Social service organizations, groups variously focused on youth, women, seniors, prisoners, and military pilots have also issued Canadian literary anthologies, as have private businesses, foundations, special commissions and committees, and local governments. Publication of literary anthologies by writers' groups, educational institutions, periodical publishers, libraries, and bookstores engenders little surprise since these organizations represent, one might say, "allied trades" of the book publishing industry. From the 1880s, periodical publishers intermittently repackaged selections of texts from their magazines or literary journals and reissued them in book form, sometimes joining forces with an established book publisher to do so. Similarly, broadcasters relied on written content that could later be transformed into book publications, as the CBC did when it produced anthologies like *Poems for Voices* under its own imprint in 1970 or *The Anthology Anthology: A Selection from Thirty Years of CBC-Radio's "Anthology,"* published in 1984 in collaboration with Macmillan of Canada. In some cases, museums and galleries operated publishing programs as auxiliary functions.

Still, the anthological impulse behind some of the other entities identified above suggests a need for further investigation into the extra-literary social and cultural functions that anthologies have played in Canada historically. For instance, what inspired *Double Vision: Creative Vignettes by Manitoba*

Social Workers (1993), collaboratively published by the Manitoba Association of Social Workers and the Manitoba Institute of Registered Social Workers? What is it about the literary anthology as a genre that led such Canadian organizations to embrace it as a tool for communication and/or advocacy? Meaningful investigation would involve close examination of the anthologies in question and archival research into the origins and development of these works. The preface to one issue of *Words from Inside*, an annual anthology issued through the 1970s that garnered two entries in *English-Canadian Literary Anthologies*, suggests the broad social missions assigned to certain anthologies. This annual represented a component of "Prison Arts," an initiative sponsored by the St. Leonard's Society that aimed "to encourage creative activity, to recognize talent and to develop potential ability" (*Words* n. pag.).

The bibliographical details attached to anthologies associated specifically with educational institutions and writers' groups equally suggest that the organizations themselves funded the bulk of them. Anthologies capturing the literary efforts of primary, secondary, and postsecondary students all find a place, but with publications issued by educational institutions an examination of the contents is often required in order to determine whether they are composed of the writing of students (past or present), instructors, or others. In relation to writers' groups, branches of the Canadian Authors Association (CAA, est. 1921) must be recognized for producing a great many of these anthologies. The CAA's Edmonton branch deserves particular note; it annually published under its own imprint the *Alberta Poetry Year Book* from 1930 to 1989 (59 volumes). Equally striking for steadiness of production under its own imprint is the Saskatchewan Poetry Society (est. 1935) for issuing 43 volumes of *The Saskatchewan Poetry Book* from 1936 to 1997, initially on an annual basis and then from 1960 every second year. Indeed, these two regular publishing initiatives by writers' groups explain why Alberta and Saskatchewan stand out statistically for anthology production from the 1930s to the 1950s.

While writers' groups typically defined themselves on the basis of locale (community or province), in other cases concerns such as ethnicity, genre, and politics provided the delineating factor, with a clear impact on the topical focus of the anthologies they produced: for example, from the Canadian Hungarian Authors' Association came *Living Free: Selections/Szabadon: Valogatas* (1981) and from the Canadian chapter of Poets, Essayists and Novelists (PEN) *Writing Away: The PEN Canada Travel Anthology* (1994). The first title appeared under the imprint of its group. However, in the case of the PEN anthology, the name of the writers' group formed part of the title of the volume while the work emerged under the imprint of McClelland & Stewart. In this case, the introduction reveals that the publisher rather than PEN Canada initiated the volume: at a point when the group was "running dangerously low on funds ... McClelland & Stewart, in the redoubtable person of [the firm's owner] Avie Bennett, came to the rescue with the suggestion that M&S publish a book whose proceeds would go to PEN" (Rooke vii).

Exploration of the Canadian imprints also reveals self-publishing as a consistent and notable factor in the history of Canadian literary anthologies in English, one certainly not confined to the period before 1920. Just how many cases of self-publication exist in the corpus is difficult to pin down. While the bibliographical details associated with the imprints form a vital starting point, to determine the level of this activity more precisely would require consultation of additional resources—as well as some firm determinations about what constitutes self-publication. On the one hand, some self-published titles are easy to pick out because they appear under the imprints of their editors/authors. The absence of the name of any publisher can also be suggestive, if not definitive, in revealing a self-published title. On the other hand, rigorously identifying self-published titles in the corpus is complicated by the fact that, in the absence of a conventional book publisher, commercial printers and newspaper offices that undertook the physical production of self-published anthologies as printing jobs sometimes chose to include their own firms' names as part of the standard bibliographical entry rather than the author's. While the names of some printers and newspaper publishers clearly reveal their status, sometimes it is not so readily picked out based on name alone. In addition, some writers formed formal, named collectives, and when they produced anthologies featuring work by the collective they would sometimes self-publish together under that name. For instance, Squid Inc., comprising eight writers, published two anthologies found in the corpus under the imprint "Squid Inc." Such formal writers' collectives, self-publishing under the names of their groups, inhabit a middle ground; they are located between writers who spontaneously and informally come together to self-publish collaboratively a single anthology featuring only their own work, and entities like the Writers' Cooperative. This cooperative, whose 1973 anthology *Current Assets: Fiction and Poetry* offers a sampling of work by a limited number of members, operated with an "Editorial Committee," and self-identified as a small press resolutely set up as an alternative to conventional "commercial publishing houses" (Robbins n. pag.). The editorial selectivity with which the Writers' Cooperative clearly functioned in relation to its anthology situates the organization more closely to the professional publishers than to self-publishing authors.

Notwithstanding the aforementioned challenge of identifying—and separating out—the imprints of printers, newspaper publishers, and formal writers' collectives, all of which facilitated self-publication of anthologies by their editors/authors, examination of the Canadian imprints suggests that around 400 professional, Canadian-based book publishers involved themselves in the production of Canadian literary anthologies to 1997. My use of the term "Canadian-based" is very deliberate, since Canadian branch plants of foreign-owned publishing houses became an integral part of Canada's domestic book publishing landscape in the twentieth century. Such branch plants played a major role in the publication of Canadian literary anthologies in English to 1997. A first wave of British-owned branch plants came after the turn of the twentieth century; American publishers moved more strongly into the market after the Second World War (Parker, "Distributors, Agents, and Publishers" 50–54; Clark 227). The major attraction for these foreign firms was the Canadian educational market of primary and secondary schools for which textbooks, including literary anthologies, had to be produced in volume. However, the provincial educational authorities that wielded the power of authorizing textbooks also had the right, in their contracts with publishers, to impose domestic—or even provincial—manufacture as a condition. In Ontario, the largest of Canada's textbook markets, the province's "standard form of contract" with publishers through the middle decades of the century "provided for the work of printing and publishing to be done in Ontario at union rate of wages" (Parvin Day 324). Insistence on local manufacture would have provided a significant motivation for foreign publishers to establish branch plants in Canada.

Of the 400-odd publishing firms identified from among the Canadian imprints, fewer than half registered more than one entry. About 75 claimed 5 or more, and only 26 had their imprints associated with 10 or more entries in the list (see table 3). These 26 firms encompassed a mix of Canadian- and foreign-owned book publishers, with the Canadian-owned proportion representing 70 percent or more. (Gage is a problem in this accounting, since it was Canadian-owned, then foreign-owned, and then Canadian-owned again.) More than half of these 26 were Canadian-owned firms founded after 1960. However, with the notable exceptions of Coach House Press and Oberon Press, the 8 top-producing firms—each of which claimed more than 20 entries—were all active in the industry prior to the Second World War. In fact, the roots of the publishers Gage and Ryerson Press extended back into the nineteenth century. "William Briggs" and "Ryerson" are combined in table 3 because, in 1919, the latter name succeeded "William Briggs" as the trade book imprint of the Methodist Book and Publishing House in the wake of Briggs's retirement.[6] In the case of the Briggs imprints specifically, it is important to keep in mind that commission arrangements would have prevailed for some of these anthologies since such financial arrangements were common during the years of Briggs's management (Friskney 172–73).

From the early decades of the twentieth century, Ryerson, Gage, Macmillan of Canada, and the Canadian branch of the Oxford University Press all represented major players in Canada's educational market, and their involvement in the publication of Canadian literary anthologies in English formed part and parcel of that commitment. The high volume of entries

Table 3   Canadian-based Publishers Claiming Ten or More Entries

PUBLISHER	NUMBER OF ENTRIES	CITY OF PUBLISHER
Macmillan	74	Toronto
McClelland & Stewart	73	Toronto
Oxford UP	65	Toronto
Oberon	57	Ottawa
Ryerson / William Briggs	53	Toronto
Coach House	24	Toronto
Gage / Gage Educational	23	Toronto / Scarborough / Agincourt / Vancouver
Nelson	22	Toronto / Scarborough
NeWest	19.33	Edmonton
Breakwater	19	St. John's / Portugal Cove
Mosaic	17.5	Oakville, ON
Coteau	16.33	Moose Jaw / Regina
Quarry	16	Kingston, ON
Dent	15	Toronto
Simon & Pierre	14	Toronto
Holt	13	Toronto
Hurtig	13	Edmonton
Borealis	12	Ottawa
McGraw / McGraw-Hill	15	Toronto
Prentice	12	Scarborough, ON
Copp	11	Toronto / Mississauga
Playwrights Canada Press	11	Toronto
Women's	11	Toronto
Black Moss	10	Windsor, ON
Jesperson	10	St. John's
Véhicule	10	Montreal

linked with these four firms owes much to their repeated publication of the same titles over multiple years—frequently in new editions, but not exclusively so. Between the 1940s and the 1970s, for example, Gage published multiple editions of two highly popular anthologies used in Canadian post-secondary classrooms: the Canadian edition of A. J. M. Smith's *The Book of Canadian Poetry* (1943; 1957) originated by the University of Chicago Press, and Carl Klinck and R. E. Watters's *Canadian Anthology* (1955; 1966; 1974). Macmillan's 74 entries stand out in particular for the issue of the same titles multiple times over a stretch of years, although how many represented new editions versus later printings with new years of publication would require investigation. One Macmillan title in this category is J. E. Wetherell's *Poems of the Love of Country* (1912; 1915; 1917). Issued as part of the firm's Macmillan's Literature Series, this anthology first appeared under the imprint of Morang (1905; 1909), another Canadian publisher known for its investment in educational publishing and whose backlist Macmillan acquired in 1912.

Also among these repeated Macmillan anthologies are C. T. Fyfe and Lorne Pierce's *Our Heritage* (1948; 1956) and C. L. Bennet, J. F. Swayze, and Pierce's *Golden Caravan* (1948; 1962 with Pierce's name dropped). The firm co-published these two anthologies with Ryerson as part of the two firms' shared and extremely successful textbook series, The Canada Books of Prose and Verse, aimed at students in grades 7 to 12. In fact, Pierce served as editor of Ryerson Press from 1920 to 1960. According to Sandra Campbell, Pierce pursued textbook publishing for far more than financial reasons, "convinced that textbooks designed to inculcate patriotic feeling were essential to building Canadian national feeling" (95). At Ryerson alone, under Pierce's watch, another historically prominent anthology—*Our Canadian Literature: Representative Prose and Verse*—also made multiple appearances. It claimed three entries in 1922 and 1923, with Pierce co-editing the volume with A. D. Watson; in the mid-1930s, Ryerson issued another work with the same main title, but the modified subtitle "Representative Verse, English and French." This latter work appeared under the co-editorship of Pierce and prominent poet Bliss Carman. Even though the poet had died in 1929, Pierce claimed that Carman had participated in the compilation of the anthology during several years preceding his death (Lecker, *Keepers* 139–40). Carman's stature as a well-known Canadian poet lent authority to the 1930s edition of *Our Canadian Literature*, thereby playing a strategic role in marketing the book for Ryerson. Carman's name would have enhanced the anthology's appeal in both the general trade and educational markets.

Oxford distinguishes itself most acutely for embracing such a marketing strategy in relation to its Canadian literary anthologies. The firm recruited CBC broadcaster Robert Weaver, known for radio programming that highlighted

Canadian literature. Among Oxford's titles, Weaver's *Canadian Short Stories* (1952; 1960; 1966; 2nd ed. 1968; 1971) appears most repeatedly. The 1952 issue of the title included Helen James as a co-editor, but her name subsequently disappeared. Oxford also exploited the Weaver–*Canadian Short Stories* brand by issuing works in 1968, 1978, 1985, and 1991 with the same editor and main title, but with the subtitles "Second Series," "Third Series," "Fourth Series," and "Fifth Series." In addition, Weaver collaborated with Oxford editor William Toye to publish two editions of *The Oxford Anthology of Canadian Literature* (1973; 2nd ed. 1981). After mid-century, Oxford issued additional anthologies that benefited from the name recognition of such prominent figures as A. J. M. Smith and Margaret Atwood. Indeed, as the insertion of the "new" in the title signals, Atwood's *The New Oxford Book of Canadian Verse in English* (1982) clearly succeeded Smith's two earlier anthologies for the publisher, *The Oxford Book of Canadian Verse in English and French* (1960) and *The Oxford Book of Canadian Verse* (1968). Oxford also had Atwood join forces with the stalwart Weaver first to produce *The Oxford Book of Canadian Short Stories in English* (1986) and then *The New Oxford Book of Canadian Short Stories in English* (1995; 1997).

The entries associated with McClelland & Stewart (M&S) similarly suggest a firm producing anthologies for both markets, but with the boundaries more clearly drawn between them than in Oxford's case—particularly in relation to M&S titles issued after the mid-twentieth century. To be sure, an anthology like Donald G. French's *Famous Canadian Stories: Re-Told for Boys and Girls* (rev. ed. 1931) held the potential for cross-market appeal. However, E. S. Caswell's *Canadian Singers and Their Songs* (1919; 1925), which reproduced poets' photographs alongside a single autograph poem, was decidedly a trade book, and specifically a gift book. The five regional/ provincial anthologies M&S produced during the middle decades of the century also suggest trade books. Of particular note are W. G. Hardy's *Alberta Golden Jubilee Anthology 1905–1955* (1955), Carlyle King's *Saskatchewan Harvest: A Golden Jubilee Selection of Song and Story* (1955), and R. E. Watters's *British Columbia: A Centennial Anthology* (1958) since their association with provincial anniversaries raises the question of whether these volumes represented collaborative undertakings between the publisher and the three provincial governments. Paratextual elements in these anthologies hint that such was indeed the case. Toward the end of *British Columbia*, for example, Watters acknowledges "on behalf of the publishers and myself[,] the support of the British Columbia Centennial Committee," adding that: "Without such assistance this work could not have appeared in its present form" (576). Archival investigation would be required to clarify the extent to which the provincial governments associated with these three anniversary volumes contributed toward editorial and physical production costs.

Titles published by M&S after 1960 demonstrate its production of many more anthologies for use by students, including works like Eva Taube's *An Anthology of Prose for Secondary Schools* (1970), and six period-specific poetry anthologies produced as part of the New Canadian Library (NCL, est. 1958), the firm's Canadian literary reprint series aimed primarily, but not exclusively, at the postsecondary and secondary markets. Still, the years after 1960 also witnessed many anthologies from M&S whose titles suggest they were conceptualized for a trade audience, such as Irving Layton's *Love Where the Nights Are Long: An Anthology of Canadian Love Poems* (1962). On the basis of title alone, more ambiguous are anthologies like Al Purdy's *Storm Warning: The New Canadian Poets* or Muriel Whitaker's *Great Canadian Animal Stories: Sixteen Stories by Sixteen Masters* (1997). Also worth noting among M&S's anthologies is that, from 1989 through the mid-1990s, the firm issued the annual *Journey Prize Anthology*, whose subtitle proclaimed: "The Best Short Fiction from Canada's Literary Journals."

M&S was not alone among the top eight publishers when it came to annual series. In *Keepers of the Code*, Lecker argues that, to take advantage of increased library budgets in the 1970s and to stabilize their revenue streams, certain Canadian-based publishers adopted a marketing strategy of creating "anthologies in a variety of series that appeared annually" (219). The rationale: "once invested in serial anthologies," libraries "treated them as subscriptions rather than individual titles"; as a result, "publishers could count on libraries buying annual editions automatically, as soon as they appeared" (219). Evidence of this strategy certainly emerges from the entries associated with Coach House and Oberon, another two firms among the top 8 to claim more than 20 anthologies. For Coach House, it was The Story So Far series. While not rigorously annual in their appearance, between 1971 and 1979 six volumes in the series emerged, under various editors. In 1972, Oberon launched its New Canadian Stories series with *72: New Canadian Stories*. Four more volumes in the series appeared over the next four years, each bearing the truncated year as the main title followed by "New Canadian Stories"; then, in 1977, Oberon shifted the name to "Best Canadian Stories," with the first appearing as *1977: Best Canadian Stories*. Subsequent volumes appeared annually over the next eighteen years, two editors typically taking on the job for several years before handing it off to the next two. In 1980, Oberon commenced a second series, beginning with *First Impressions* and ending in 1982 with *Third Impressions*. In 1983, it launched a third series, *Coming Attractions*, which featured several writers in each volume. Further volumes appeared in this series annually over the next twelve years. Together the volumes in these three series account for 35 of the 57 entries associated with Oberon.

Examining all 1,976 Canadian imprints through the lens of topicality reveals notable trends, particularly when topic is intersected with time period and publisher. One or more of the three basic categories of "poetry," "prose," and "drama" applies to all of the Canadian imprints. "Poetry," applicable to more than 1,300 of the imprints, outdistances the other two categories by a wide margin; "prose" follows with about 1,000, while drama hovers around 200. In relation to pan-Canadian anthologies specifically, Lecker has noted that these works contained poetry exclusively until the 1920s, when Watson and Pierce innovated by including prose selections in *Our Canadian Literature* (Lecker, *Keepers* 74). That statement largely holds true for the whole gamut of Canadian literary anthologies in English published prior to 1920, with some notable exceptions: songs and hymns featured in a handful of anthologies; there emerged several late-nineteenth-century short-story anthologies directed at children; and prose did appear in a few works, such as D. G. French's *Standard Canadian Reciter* (M&S, 1918) and J. E. Wetherell's *Great War in Verse and Prose* (Wilgress, 1919). In 1926, French also edited for M&S *More Famous Canadian Stories: Re-Told for Boys and Girls*, but dedicated collections of prose aimed at adults began to appear only after that, the earliest being *A Short Anthology of French Canadian Prose Literature* (Longmans, 1927). Exclusive collections of prose appeared steadily from that point on. In the case of "drama," it made a debut as early as 1882 as one of the categories of literature found in *The Advanced Reader*. However, the first dedicated volume of Canadian drama appeared only in 1926. Entitled *One-Act Plays by Canadian Authors: 19 Short Canadian Plays,* it appeared under the imprint of the Montreal branch of the CAA. Four years later, Copp Clark became the first professional publishing firm to issue a dedicated anthology of drama, *Six Canadian Plays*, edited by Herman Voaden. During the next three decades, dedicated anthologies of drama made an occasional appearance, but it was only from the 1960s onward that they were published regularly.

As recounted in detail in Lecker's *Keepers of the Code*, pan-Canadian anthologies of Canadian literature in English have appeared steadily since the mid-nineteenth century. Study of the Canadian imprints listed in *English-Canadian Literary Anthologies* reveals that most were issued by professional publishers based in Canada, and occasionally by those operating abroad. Prior to 1997, professional publishers also dominated in the publication of anthologies whose contents included, but were not limited to, Canadian literary materials. In the case of the Canadian-based publishers that produced such anthologies, they frequently issued their books expressly for the educational market within Canada. Nonetheless, some trade books certainly appear in this category, such as Mordecai Richler's *The Best of Modern Humour*, published not only in Canada, in 1983, but also in the United States and United Kingdom.

Unlike the pan-Canadian and transnational works noted above, anthologies focused on particular Canadian geographies emerge from the Canadian imprints as a distinctive aspect of domestic publication, one that commenced in the early twentieth century with several contributions compiled and published in St. John's by James Murphy, including *Old Songs of Newfoundland* (1912). While the occasional anthology in this category focused on broad geographical phenomena, such as the sea or rural environments, the titles of most aligned themselves explicitly with particular regions (large or small), provinces, cities, or communities within Canada. Regional anthologies steadily appeared from the 1910s onward; however, to the end of the 1960s the majority were either self-published by their editors, issued under the imprints of writers' groups, or occasionally sponsored by businesses or government. For instance, J. D. Logan's *Pictou Poets: A Treasury of Verse in Gaelic and English* (1923), printed on the press of the *Pictou Advocate*, was likely self-published by Logan, while *Saskatchewan: Her Infinite Variety* (1925) appeared under the imprint of the Saskatchewan branch of the CAA. In the 1930s and '40s, the Edmonton branch of the CAA and the Saskatchewan Poetry Society dominated domestic production in the field with the issue of their aforementioned annuals, but branches of the CAA in Manitoba, Nova Scotia, and Montreal also engaged in singular productions. During these two decades M&S represented the only professional publisher to issue a regional anthology: Eliza Ritchie's *Songs of the Maritimes* (1931). The situation did not change much through the middle decades of the century. As already noted, most of the publishing of regional anthologies in which M&S engaged in the 1950s was most likely aided by provincial funds available due to milestone anniversaries. In turn, on occasion commercial enterprises also supported regional anthologies: for example, L. W. James's *The Treasury of Newfoundland Stories* appeared in 1961 thanks to the patronage of Maple Leaf Mills.

The situation changed dramatically in the early 1970s when both long-established publishers based in Toronto as well as small publishers scattered throughout the country began to take up publication of regional and provincial anthologies in earnest. Fiddlehead Books of New Brunswick signalled the first serious move of professional publishers other than M&S into the field, producing *Five New Brunswick Poets* as early as 1962, and then *One Hundred Poems of Modern Quebec* in 1970. Toronto publishers Oxford and Macmillan also began to issue regional anthologies in the early 1970s. On the west coast, Victoria publisher Sono Nis produced Michael Yates's *Contemporary Poetry of British Columbia* in 1970, while on the east, in Portugal Cove, Newfoundland, Clyde Rose's *Baffles of Wind and Tide* made its first appearance in 1973 under the imprint of Breakwater Books.

As the remainder of the century unfolded, professional publishers of myriad stripes—small, trade, educational, and scholarly—invested in anthologies of even finer geographical specificity than regions or provinces. From the mid-1970s forward, while the publication of broad regional and provincial anthologies continued apace, volumes focused on particular cities or smaller regions also began to appear more frequently. Joan Parr's *Winnipeg Stories* (1974) and Frank M. Tierney's *Poets of the Capital* (Ottawa, 1974) represented two early contributions. In general, expanding educational markets for Canadian literature in the late decades of the twentieth century, including the emergence of specialized courses in regional writing within the field, encouraged professional publishers across the country to engage in the production of these anthologies of geographical specificity. Such anthologies also fitted the regional/provincial mandates of many publishers based outside of Toronto. In addition to the educational market, publishers of these anthologies would have looked for sales through the local trade book market, with potential buyers split between local residents and tourists visiting their regions. Notwithstanding the substantial involvement of professional publishers in the field after 1970, the final decades of the century continued to witness the publication of geographically specific anthologies by alternative entities, with writers' groups remaining the most prominent among them.

While not entirely unknown prior to 1970, in the late twentieth century it also became much more common to see anthologies published in Canada that demonstrated an intersection of a specific Canadian geographic territory with some other element of topicality. Logan's *Pictou Poets* of 1923 represented an early example of this phenomenon by featuring writing both in Gaelic and English. After 1970, such occurrences became much more frequent: for example, an intersection with children's literature is found in Wenda McArthur and Geoffrey Ursell's *Prairie Jungle: Songs, Poems and Stories for Children* (1985); an intersection with two forms of popular fiction informs John Bell and Lesley Choyce's *Visions from the Edge: An Anthology of Atlantic Canadian Science Fiction and Fantasy* (1981); an intersection with gender is the basis of Beverley Daurio and Luise von Flutow's *Ink and Strawberries: An Anthology of Quebec Women's Fiction* (1988); and an intersection with ethnicity happens in George Elliott Clarke's *Fire on the Water: An Anthology of Black Nova Scotian Writing* (1991). In general, this intersection of geography with another topical element after 1970 paralleled a phenomenon also occurring in relation to pan-Canadian anthologies issued in Canada. Works such as Jon Pearce's *Marked by the Wild: An Anthology of Canadian Literature Shaped by the Canadian Wilderness* (1973) and Gerri Sinclair and Morris Wolfe's *Spice Box: An Anthology of Jewish Canadian Writing* (1981) offer two examples.

Topical emphases on ethnicity, gender, and sexuality equally characterized domestically produced anthologies after 1970. In the case of some books, these subjects formed the exclusive concern of the title with no explicit reference made to country, region, province, or community (e.g., Fictive Collective's *Baker's Dozen: Stories by Women* [1984]). Indeed, the interiors of some of these anthologies would need to be examined to determine to what extent the writing within their pages was authored by Canadians. Certain anthologies in this grouping are also notable for combining two or more of these topical foci (e.g., Makeda Silvera's *Piece of My Heart: A Lesbian of Colour Anthology* [1991]). The topical emphases of these anthologies reflected, on the one hand, general macro-level social and academic preoccupations active in the western world in the late twentieth century; on the other, issues of ethnicity, gender, and sexuality had particular currency in Canada in light of the federal government's adoption of an official policy of multiculturalism in 1971, and the introduction of a Charter of Rights and Freedoms into the Constitution in 1982. Two late chapters in Lecker's *Keepers of the Code*, "Nation Making, Nation Breaking, 1967–1982" and "Solidifying the Canadian Canon, 1982–1992," provide a detailed look at the impact of these new social and critical priorities on pan-Canadian anthologies and the editors who shaped them. And, as the closing chapter of the second edition of Carl Berger's *The Writing of Canadian History* (1986) attests, other fields of Canadian scholarship were equally affected by these forces (see Berger, chap. 11, "Tradition and the 'New' History"). It is therefore vital to locate this particular trend in the history of Canadian literary anthologies in its broad historical context.

While the prominence of geography, ethnicity, gender, and sexuality in the conceptualization of Canadian literary anthologies published in the late decades of the twentieth century may surprise few, this period also witnessed a much more marked concern for publishing collections of specialized literary forms, particularly anthologies highlighting popular genres. Earlier in the twentieth century, the word "humour" featured in the title of only four anthologies. Volumes dedicated to the topic continued to make intermittent appearances after 1970, averaging about three a decade during the remainder of the century. In the closing decades of the century, humour anthologies were joined by those devoted to other forms of popular writing, including works featuring science fiction, fantasy, ghost stories, horror, crime, mystery, action, adventure, sports, and cowboys.

Collectively these anthologies (excluding humour) accounted for about 50 Canadian imprints between 1970 and 1997. The broad category of science fiction/fantasy/horror/ghost stories led the pack, followed in second place by crime/mystery. The predominance of anthologies in these categories makes sense when one considers that a sufficient number of writers in these specializations had emerged by 1990 to establish the writers' organizations SF Canada (est. 1989) and Crime Writers of Canada (est. 1982). Imprints in the former category rose from 4 in the 1970s to nearly 20 in the 1990s, the increase from 1985 forward buttressed by the regular appearance of volumes in the *Tesseracts* series, the first of which was edited by prominent SF author Judith Merril. Oxford also gave critical heft to the field when it published in 1990 *The Oxford Book of Canadian Ghost Stories* under Alberto Manguel's editorship. In the realm of crime/mystery, the 1970s were all about the Mounties (e.g., Dick Harrison's *Best Mounted Police Stories* [1978]), but that soon changed. Several more titles emerged in the crime/mystery category in the 1980s, and then things accelerated in the 1990s, thanks in part to the productive partnership David Skene-Melvin formed with Toronto publisher Simon & Pierre. Together they produced four anthologies between 1994 and 1997, including *Investigating Women: Female Detectives by Canadian Writers* (1995). Finally, after only single anthologies in the 1970s and '80s, sports provided some modest competition in the '90s with five volumes, among them John B. Lee's *That Sign of Perfection: From Bandy Legs to Beer Legs: Poems and Stories on the Game of Hockey* (1995). The bibliography by Lecker et al. records no anthologies focused on popular romance fiction, a surprising absence given that throughout the latter half of the twentieth century Canada served as home base for multinational romance publisher Harlequin and a critical mass of romance writers was at work in Canada by the closing decades of the twentieth century. Anthologies dedicated to erotica did appear, however: one in the 1980s and three in the 1990s.

When looked at collectively, what stands out about these 50-odd volumes is that they appeared under the imprints of numerous publishers of myriad stripes, although most were Canadian-owned rather than foreign branch plants. Mosaic, based in Oakville, Ontario, is the only one really to stand out in terms of volume—it published about 10 of these works, largely thanks to its commitment to two series: *Cold Blood* and *Northern Frights*. *Tesseracts* must also be noted since this company, at the time an anomaly in the Canadian book publishing industry for being a specialist in science fiction and fantasy, emerged out of the anthology series of the same name, with its earliest anthologies appearing under the imprints of Porcépic and then Beach Holme, both of Victoria, British Columbia.

CONCLUSION

Roughly 95 parts domestic issue to 5 parts foreign represents the simplest quantification of the nearly 2,100 entries in *English-Canadian Literary Anthologies*. The tiny proportion of anthologies to appear abroad indicates that the genre commanded a sparse international market to 1997. Indeed, from their bases outside of Canada, foreign publishers that did produce a literary anthology with Canadian content rarely did so more than once. The same did not hold true within Canada. The lure of steady volume in textbook sales combined with contractual obligations for their domestic manufacture encouraged certain British and American firms—primarily those with interests in educational publishing—to found branch plants in Canada after 1900. The Canadian literary anthologies these subsidiaries produced therefore emerged as Canadian imprints, a circumstance that simultaneously complicates and magnifies the role of foreign publishers in the publishing history of the genre. Once established in Canada, some of these subsidiaries, chief among them Oxford and Macmillan (see Panofsky on both firms), gained a reputation for a broad commitment to Canadian writing. This engagement with Canadiana even encouraged certain of them to produce anthologies for the riskier trade book market, alongside those they issued for the more stable educational one. In Oxford's case, it strategized by recruiting editors whose names would resonate more strongly with the public, and produced Canadian literary anthologies in English designed to attract sales in both the trade and educational markets.

In contrast to the foreign-owned branch plants, Canadian-owned publishers issued Canadian literary anthologies in English from well back into the nineteenth century. However, the financial risk of publishing such works for Canada's small domestic market severely inhibited the extent of production, and the pace of issue only began to increase in the final two decades of the century. The relative success Briggs experienced with Rand's *A Treasury of Canadian Verse* was cause for cautious optimism by 1900. Still, one has to wonder how involved Canadian-owned publishers would have been in the genre in the twentieth century had Canadian literary anthologies not come into greater curricular use. The financial potential of large textbook orders attracted Canadian-owned firms just as they did the foreign subsidiaries. Ryerson Press is a case in point: it made a particular name for itself as a textbook publisher after Pierce joined the firm in 1920 and identified the potential of the textbook market. Yet, as Campbell makes clear, cultural as well as financial imperatives factored into Pierce's determined pursuit of textbook publishing. What needs to be investigated more thoroughly is the extent to which his colleagues at other publishing houses might also have brought a cultural imperative to the work of textbook publishing, and how that made a particular impact on Canadian literary anthologies in English expressly produced as textbooks. Though textbook anthologies obviously would have had to satisfy the curricular concerns of provincial educational authorities, more investigation into the editorial vision that Canadian- and foreign-owned publishing firms brought to these anthologies seems merited.

Study of the bibliographical corpus provided by Lecker et al. also reveals the impressive extent to which domestic production of Canadian literary anthologies in English represented a shared field of endeavour. Professional publishers cohabitated this territory with, among others, self-publishing editors and authors' collectives, writers' organizations, educational institutions, cultural bodies, religious groups, and social agencies. More research needs to be done to determine why such an array of entities viewed the Canadian literary anthology as a genre that could be embraced for their own purposes, some of which no doubt were quite extra-literary in nature. In addition, writers' organizations in particular should be noted for having tilled the soil of regional and provincial Canadian literary anthologies in English. They only began to give significant ground in that area to professional publishers after 1970, with the rise of smaller English-language publishing houses located outside of Toronto whose ambitions toward regionally specific books were facilitated by federal and sometimes provincial funding. Small presses similarly played a vital role in the issue of Canadian literary anthologies in English that highlighted late-twentieth-century concerns around ethnicity, gender, and sexuality, or called attention to more popular forms of Canadian writing, such as science fiction, fantasy, and mysteries. The commitment that small presses collectively expressed to such anthologies was one they shared with larger Canadian-based houses.

From the perspective of publishing history, the bibliographical corpus provided by *English-Canadian Literary Anthologies* has tremendous utility. Viewing the data variously through the lenses of time period, place of publication, publisher, and topic offers significant quantitative revelations about publishing trends for the Canadian literary anthology in English over the course of almost two centuries. Such quantitative data not only serves Canadian publishing history; it also provides helpful contextual information to literary critics and other scholars engaged in more particularized studies of specific anthologies and their editors and publishers. Still, quantification has its limits while the descriptive bibliographical detail associated with individual entries often simply hints at, or sometimes keeps entirely hidden, the contents of an anthology or the motivation behind its publication. For that reason, more nuanced understanding of the publishing history of Canadian literary anthologies in English to 1997 would involve more comprehensive examination of anthologies themselves, while investigation of whatever printed and archival resources survive in relation to these books would be highly recommended.

NOTES

1 That reduced figure needs to be treated with caution for two reasons. First, reduction based on title alone may eliminate later issues of a title that were, in fact, new editions—that is, later issues reflecting modified content though the title remained stable. Second, publishers have been known to change titles without otherwise modifying the content of a book.

2 Of the 99, the United Kingdom claimed 33.5 (33.84 percent) and the United States 65.5 (66.16 percent), the half imprint associated with each accounted for by one dual UK-US imprint listed in the bibliography. The UK issued more anthologies prior to 1930, and then the situation reversed itself, with the US becoming the more dominant foreign producer. The only exception was the 1960s, a decade in which there was equal activity in both countries. The other foreign countries to issue Canadian literary anthologies in English are: Germany (7), China (2), Denmark (2), Italy (2), Japan (2), Greece (1), Netherlands (1), Spain (1). Two of these works, both issued in 1945 (one in the Netherlands, the other in Italy) had imprints associated with Canadian military forces stationed abroad during the Second World War.

3 Walter Scott and Dent each claimed 5; all of the other US and UK publishers only 1 or 2.

4 Subscription arrangements required the author/editor of a work to solicit subscriptions—that is, partial or full payments in advance of publication from would-be purchasers in order to offset production costs. If insufficient subscriptions were secured, the book would not be published. See Mary Lu MacDonald, "Subscription Publishing," for a more detailed account.

5 In a commission arrangement, all of the manufacturing costs of bringing the book into print are absorbed by the author/editor, but, for a commission on sales, the publisher markets and distributes the book on behalf of the author/editor.

6 After the merger of the Methodist, Presbyterian, and Congregational Churches into the United Church of Canada in June 1925, "The Ryerson Press" became the trade imprint of the United Church Publishing House.

WORKS CITED

Berger, Carl. *The Writing of Canadian History: Aspects of English-Canadian Historical Writing since 1900.* 2nd ed. Toronto: U of Toronto P, 1986. Print.

Campbell, Sandra. "From Romantic History to Communications Theory: Lorne Pierce as Publisher of C. W. Jefferys and Harold Innis." *Journal of Canadian Studies* 30.3 (Fall 1995): 91–116. Print.

Cavell, Janice. "Canadiana Abroad: The Department of External Affairs' Book Presentation Programmes, 1949–1963." *American Review of Canadian Studies* 39.2 (June 2009): 81–93. Print.

Clark, Penney. "The Rise and Fall of Textbook Publishing in English Canada." *History of the Book in Canada, Volume 3: 1918–1980.* Ed. Carole Gerson and Jacques Michon. Toronto: U of Toronto P, 2007. 226–32. Print.

Friskney, Janet B. "Beyond the Shadow of William Briggs, Part II: Canadian-authored Titles and the Commitment to Canadian Writing." *Papers of the Bibliographical Society of Canada* 35.2 (Fall 1997): 161–207. Print.

Genette, Gérard. *Paratexts: Thresholds of Interpretation.* Cambridge: Cambridge UP, 1997.

Gustafson, Ralph. "The Story of the Penguin." *Canadian Poetry: Studies, Documents, Reviews* 12 (1983): 71–76. Print.

Lecker, Robert. Introduction. *English-Canadian Literary Anthologies: An Enumerative Bibliography.* Teeswater, ON: Reference, 1997. vii–x. Print.

——. *Keepers of the Code: English-Canadian Literary Anthologies and the Representations of Nation.* Toronto: U of Toronto P, 2013. Print.

Lecker, Robert, et al., eds. *English-Canadian Literary Anthologies: An Enumerative Bibliography.* Teeswater, ON: Reference, 1997. Print.

Ledger: Costs of Publication and Sale of Selected Works, 1908–1913. Board of Publication Papers. United Church of Canada Archives, Toronto. Archival.

MacDonald, Mary Lu. "Subscription Publishing." *History of the Book in Canada, Volume One: Beginnings to 1840.* Ed. Patricia Fleming et al. Toronto: U of Toronto P, 2004. 78–80. Print.

Panofsky, Ruth. *The Literary Legacy of the Macmillan Company Canada: Making Books and Mapping Culture.* Toronto: U of Toronto P, 2012. Print.

——. "'A Press with Such Traditions': Oxford University Press of Canada." *Papers of the Bibliographical Society of Canada* 42.1 (Spring 2004): 7–29. Print.

Parker, George L. "Distributors, Agents, and Publishers: Creating a Separate Market for Books in Canada 1900–1920. Part I." *Papers of the Bibliographical Society of Canada* 43.2 (2005): 7–65. Print.

——. "The Evolution of Publishing in Canada." *History of the Book in Canada, Volume Two: 1840–1918.* Ed. Yvan Lamonde et al. Toronto: U of Toronto P, 2005. 17–32. Print.

Parvin Day, Viola E. "The Authorization of Textbooks for the Schools of Ontario from 1846 to the Present." *Ontario Royal Commission on Book Publishing: Background Papers.* Toronto: Queen's Printer, 1972. 311–30. Print.

Peterman, Michael A., and Janet B. Friskney. "'Booming the Canuck Book': Edward Caswell and the Promotion of Canadian Writing." *Journal of Canadian Studies* 30.3 (Fall 1995): 60–90. Print.

"Rev. E. H. Dewart's Volume of Poems." *Christian Guardian.* 16 Dec. 1863. 202. Print.

Robbins, Wayne. Preface. *Current Assets: Fiction and Poetry from the Writers' Cooperative.* Montreal: Writers' Cooperative, 1973. n. pag. Print.

Rooke, Constance. Introduction. *Writing Away: The PEN Canada Travel Anthology.* Ed. Constance Rooke. Toronto: McClelland & Stewart, 1994. vii–x. Print.

Watters, R. E. Acknowledgments. *British Columbia: A Centennial Anthology.* Ed. R. E. Watters. Toronto: McClelland & Stewart, 1958. 573–76. Print.

Words from Inside. Brantford: Prison Arts Foundation, 1971. Print.

Confessions of an Unrepentant Anthologist

Gary Geddes

Some years ago, while attempting to write an essay in response to questions often put to me about my role as an anthologist in the shaping of tastes—what is, I think, mistakenly referred to as canon-making—I came across a comment by the American poet and critic Randall Jarrell, in which the typical anthologist is described as "a Gallup Poll with connections" (155). I laughed at this; it seemed so far removed from the facts in my case, especially when I considered how unconnected I was as a young graduate student at the University of Toronto, struggling through a makeup year, trying to learn a small portion of what my clever classmates had acquired quite casually through their honours degrees. Mine had been a patchwork BA from UBC with a major in both English and Philosophy, consisting mainly of courses available during those days I was not working at a variety of part-time jobs, in particular stocking shelves on the food floor at Woodward's department store in downtown Vancouver, where the fumes from detergents and other soap products would make me sneeze. If there was ever an unconnected and unprepared anthologist-in-the-making, it was me.

And yet, it appears, that I did have a serendipitous connection after all. I was enthusiastic about poetry, and as I taught students in Engineering, Nursing, Business Administration, and Literature at Trent, Ryerson, York, and U of T, I noticed that there were no anthologies that served my needs as a teacher. *Modern Poetry*, published in the United States and edited by Maynard Mack, Leonard Dean, and William Frost, contained no Canadian poets and no British or American poets after Dylan Thomas and e. e. cummings. Having just spent a year in a graduate course reading work by Irving Layton, Margaret Avison, and Earle Birney, and being fully caught up in the Canadian literary renaissance of the 1960s, which brought Al Purdy, Gwendolyn MacEwen, Leonard Cohen, Margaret Atwood, and Michael Ondaatje into the public eye, I was appalled by the lack of a decent and representative teaching anthology. I remember complaining to one of my colleagues, Patricia Owen, in the faculty room at Ryerson and being completely taken aback by her response.

"Why don't you edit one?"

I don't recall my exact words, but the import was this: who would allow an unknown schmuck like me to edit an anthology of poetry? As if her vote of confidence in my abilities were not enough, Patricia added that her husband, Ivon Owen, was in charge of Oxford University Press in Canada and that she would tell him I was interested in submitting a proposal. I won't go into the rest of the story here, but that was the beginning of a long career as an editor and anthologist, moving from the international to the national and the regional in the three poetry anthologies I edited for Oxford, and then to six more anthologies for other companies based on issues, place, themes, and constituencies, including the city of Vancouver. All this time, I was learning on the go, flying by the seat of my pants, reading voraciously, trying to plug those huge gaps in my education.

I have to laugh when I recall a subsequent chat in January 1971 with Margaret Atwood in a flat she shared in London, England, with her first husband, James Polk. I was in the city doing research for my doctoral thesis on Joseph Conrad and had just finished the co-editing with Phyllis Bruce of *15 Canadian Poets*. Peggy asked me what my next anthology project would be.

"Never again," I said. "I've learned my lesson. It's hard work and doesn't pay well enough."

She gave me one of her piercing eagle-eye looks and said with a wicked grin, "Once an anthologist, always an anthologist." This remark proved prophetic for both of us, two packrats with the same recurring disease.

T. S. Eliot wrote an essay on what he called minor poetry, in which he discusses the role of anthologists, with their blind spots and enthusiasms. I certainly have my enthusiasms and blind spots, like everyone else, and Eliot's poetry is a case in point. As an undergraduate, I did not like the way Eliot strutted his learning in "The Waste Land," a poem that requires footnotes, an encyclopedia, and an I.Q. of 150. I could not bring myself to fight for the inclusion of this poem in *20th-Century Poetry & Poetics*, although I knew it was widely taught and admired. However, I could identify completely with the poetics at work in "The Love Song of J. Alfred Prufrock," with its vivid imagery, heightened speaking-voice, and narrative line. I also found myself more drawn to free-verse experiments, to poems availing themselves of an organ base, an intricate pattern of stress and recurring sound, which might be called prosodic depth.

Along the way, too, I fell in love with the long poem and poetic narrative, in their various manifestations, and fought for their inclusion at every turn, sometimes at the expense of a poet's best lyrics. It's not fashionable to include long poems in anthologies or in glossy magazines such as *The New Yorker*, where cute little vacuities that can fit between ads for scotch, luxury cars, and lingerie are preferred, or to try to teach them in classrooms where the fast-food mentality prevails in literary studies. Anthologies, for a variety of reasons—time limits, so-called "teachability"—favour the short lyric rather than the long poem, privileging song over story, all the laurels going to songbirds belting it out to God and the angels. However, if you know anything about songbirds, you will realize that their outpourings usually have a purpose, most often to attract a mate or to signal danger. In other words, even the simplest lyric often has an implied, or submerged, narrative, as is so obviously the case with William Carlos Williams's imagist poem "The Red Wheelbarrow." In the great tradition of epic that stretches back to Homer, story or narrative figures prominently as a way of exploring, explaining, and, yes, critiquing the world. I have made an elaborate defence of the long poem and poetic narrative elsewhere, critiquing Edgar Allan Poe's notion that the long poem is a "contradiction in terms" and B. S. Johnson's dismissal of narrative poets as literary flat-earthers, so I won't belabour the point here that the long poem is particularly suited to our age.[1] Even Northrop Frye expressed his hope in *The Bush Garden* that poets would "maintain an interest in narrative form. For the lyric, if cultivated too exclusively, tends to become too entangled with the printed page" (156). I make no apologies for admiring Robert Kroetsch's "Seed Catalogue," Atwood's *The Journals of Susanna Moodie*, Ondaatje's *Collected Works of Billy the Kid*, Robert Hass's "My Mother's Nipples," and Anne Carson's "The Glass Essay," each of which manages to foreground the two dominant impulses of story and song and to remind us of the riches available to the poet who writes with a full toolbox.

Looking back at my built-in resistance to poetry that is academic, or experimental for its own sake, it occurs to me that what I considered a radical stance many years ago may have had more to do with the ingrained conservatism of the poor, or the poorly educated. Hopefully, this bias has, at least, had the beneficial effect of making me concentrate on the poem itself, rather than on theory or literary criticism. I wanted to provide ammunition for the student who, like me, had to struggle against the undue authority and privileging of critics, and who preferred to spend his or her time engaging with the primary texts rather than quoting and synthesizing secondary materials. The ammunition I had in mind came from an unlikely encounter with a book called *The Creative Process*, edited by Brewster Ghiselin, which contained essays by playwrights, painters, scientists, mathematicians, poets, sculptors, musicians, and novelists. Reading this collection of jottings by creative individuals was illuminating and awe-inspiring, a visit to Aladdin's cave of wonders. Having access to these "poetics" was like being invited into the creator's living room for a chat, becoming a confidant. So the anthologizing project, from beginning to end, was, for me, an attempt to create an intimate encounter between editor, poet, and reader, and to celebrate poems that had come to mean a lot to me, and to many others. Wherever possible, I included comments by the poets, not interpretations of their poems but tentative forays, intimate thoughts about the creative process. I believed these brief insights, admissions, and asides would draw readers into the poems rather than scaring them off, though I was not oblivious to what we call the pathetic fallacy or to Plato's admonition that the poets are often the least likely to be saying something useful about the craft.

Since I'm in confessional mode here, another idiosyncrasy/limitation I possess as an editor has to do with class and ideology. Growing up poor and disadvantaged, I was well aware of abuses of power and the economic disparities at work in our world, so I've had a tendency to favour engaged writers whose work addresses issues of the marginalized and disenfranchised, or micro-history, that which often falls between the cracks. This position has met with criticism and resistance, especially from those who consider poetry and politics strange bedfellows and who like to quote W. H. Auden's comment in "In Memory of W. B. Yeats" that "poetry makes nothing happen" (939). Auden was speaking here of Yeats's vision, not his own; his personal view on the matter is best expressed in the essays from *A Dyer's Hand,* where he argues that "the mere making of a work of art is itself a political act" (335) because it reminds the management that we are humans, not just automatons. I agree with Auden and with American poet James Scully, who insists that the phrase "political poetry" is "not a contradiction in terms but an instructive redundancy" (54). In other words, I've come to believe that all good writing is engaged, with language and with life, and that its ideological slip is always showing, for those who care to look closely.

It must have seemed to friends that I was hoping for a miracle to be born from the marriage of my ignorance and arrogance. However, I made it my task to study the field, consider a wide range of critical opinions, and play those opinions off against my own subjective responses as a reader. Blind spots and personal limitations aside, I tried to be eclectic in my selections and to represent a fairly broad spectrum of tastes and poetics. I did not think of myself as a scholar or canon-maker, only as someone lucky enough to be allowed to create a good teaching anthology that celebrated a number of the best poems written in English during the twentieth century. I never expected *20th-Century Poetry & Poetics* and *15 Canadian Poets* to have such a long life; they were creatures formed at a particular point in time and space, with all the blinkers and limitations that implies. I thought they would have their moment and be gone, replaced by anthologies edited by different eyes and reflecting different tastes. However, because the anthologies became successful, both pedagogically and commercially, what started as a pioneering venture inspired by passion and hope was transformed into a series of refittings influenced by changing tastes, my own included, and by market considerations. In retrospect, popular demand and the exigencies of the publishing world (competition and the cost of printing and permissions) have given these two anthologies longer lives and more influence than they probably deserved.

As I was pondering these matters, a letter arrived from Canadian publisher, professor, and critic Robert Lecker asking if I would be willing to answer a few questions concerning my work as an anthologist for a piece of literary history on which he was working. His questions were mostly related to the anthology *15 Canadian Poets*, which was first published in 1970 to fill an obvious vacuum and in enthusiastic response to the success of the international anthology. I thought carefully about Robert's questions, particularly his notion that the first edition was centralist, focusing mainly on poets in Ontario and Quebec. I came to Canadian poetry first as a graduate student in Toronto, where Raymond Souster, Eli Mandel, John Newlove, Victor Coleman, Avison, MacEwen, Purdy, Atwood, and Ondaatje were emerging voices, so it's not surprising that I was more familiar with poets from Central Canada. However, of the seven mentioned above, Mandel, Newlove, and MacEwen were born in the prairies; Ondaatje originated in Sri Lanka, coming to Toronto via England and Quebec. Alden Nowlan was the solitary Maritimer; Birney and George Bowering were the two British Columbians. The anthology also included three Quebec writers: D. G. Jones, Layton, and Cohen. Region, gender, ethnicity, and sexual orientation were not on my mind at the time. I thought of the anthology only as a treasure trove, a sampling of exciting new and not-so-new talent that might stimulate interest in and whet appetites for Canadian poetry.

To my surprise, and Oxford's, *15 Canadian Poets* not only succeeded in its modest aims, but also came to be used widely in Canadian literature courses. This fact created a number of challenges. Many teachers, especially in a developing field, were already leaning toward a historical approach to Canadian poetry, as well as hoping for regional representation and gender balance. With the advice of editor-in-chief William Toye, my co-editor Phyllis Bruce, and the editors at Oxford, the decision was taken to expand the anthology in all three directions. *15 Canadian Poets Plus 5* appeared in 1978, adding three well-known and respected poets, Dorothy Livesay, P. K. Page, and Phyllis Webb, and two relatively new voices, Patrick Lane and Pat Lowther. All five hailed from British Columbia, though Livesay was born in Winnipeg and Page, born in Calgary, had cut her poetic teeth in Montreal. Four out of five of the additions were women, so the first revision altered the historical range as well as the regional and gender balance of the anthology, eliciting the inevitable criticism that I was now favouring West Coast poets.

Anthologies have a life of their own, which can be problematic when revisions take place, as they often do. Inclusions and exclusions can be self-perpetuating. As Canadian Studies programs expanded, demand for the anthology grew, so there was pressure to expand its range backwards. The inclusion of E. J. Pratt, A. M. Klein, F. R. Scott, Miriam Waddington, and Ralph Gustafson pushed back the historical boundaries of the anthology. I was glad to showcase Pratt's narrative gifts; and he was a Newfoundlander to boot, though he had spent his creative life in Toronto. In *15 Canadian Poets X 2*, I made the difficult decision to drop Victor Coleman's work. I considered Victor a friend and respected both his experimental writing and his considerable work on behalf of the literary community. My initial inclusion of his poetry had been a gesture toward the avant-garde. However, a few years later my tastes had shifted and my enthusiasm for his work had cooled. I felt it did not stand up in terms of craft and development alongside that of several other poets whose poems I wished to celebrate. Robert Kroetsch seemed a more interesting experimental poet, as well as a master of the long poem or poetic meditation; and Bronwen Wallace spoke powerfully of the spiritual, physical, and poetic work being done by women.

With each new revision the matter of selection became more complicated and more controversial. If the anthologies had not been so much in demand, they might have died a quiet, natural death. By the time of the fourth edition, *15 Canadian Poets X 3*, published in 2003, which I thought would be my editorial swan song, I was determined to celebrate new and neglected poets, beginning with five of my then-current favourites: Don McKay, Jan Zwicky, Anne Carson, Dionne Brand, and Louise Halfe; and three well-known poets whose work I had previously overlooked: Fred Wah, Daphne Marlatt, and bpNichol. Over the years, I had come to feel less confident of my choices and uncomfortable with the fact that anthologizing was becoming more and more an act of exclusion. In fact, I agreed with some of the criticisms made over the years by Frank Davey, Alan Knight, and Michael Barnholden, particularly the latter's essay, "New Canadian Poetry: Anthologizing the Nation and After," and the last word he gives to Susan Schultz (from a interview in *How2*): "Bound anthologies are fixed, stiffly covered, and resemble small literary nation-states; they claim authority like territories that are governed, paid fealty to, often eventually invaded." Nation-state or invisible city, I could no longer determine which. Therefore, eschewing both canons and cannons, I decided it was time to bow out, to let a new generation, with all its own biases, theories, and constituencies, decide what was important to it.

My theatrical exit or grand finale proved to be premature. Three years later I received a letter from Oxford asking if I was interested in doing a fifth edition. It struck me as a preposterous idea. First, anthology sales had plummeted drastically and permissions and printing costs had escalated. Instructors, thinking they were doing students a favour by making cheaper course packs of their own favourites, had largely destroyed the market. These "curse packs," as I came to call them, actually shortchanged the students, denying them exposure to a broader selection of good poetry and the potential for a life of browsing in a beloved tome. Second, the number of fine poets excluded from my previous editions and the astonishing array of impressive new talents made the task of selecting seem daunting, if not impossible, especially if I were limited to another fifteen. Besides, I had become embarrassed by the proposed title, which seemed to anticipate an inevitable joke: *15 Canadian Poets Squared*, both a sly comment on the conservatism of the anthologist and an oddly appropriate description, given the explosion of extremely fine work from the two generations of poets who had emerged since 1970.

I should have bowed out, but couldn't let go. Besides, it occurred to me that I might take on the task responsibly with the help of a younger generation of advisory editors. Along with that suggestion, I proposed to Oxford that we drop the "15" designation and aim for an anthology with a greater representation of new poets. This proposal was greeted with cautious enthusiasm, because the costs had become prohibitive and the size cumbersome, a long way from the $4.95 price on my first slim teaching anthology in 1969. Meanwhile, a new generation had grown up expecting things to be free: music, movies, and now books and information. Why pay for an anthology when you could find some of the material online or convince the professor to make copies of specific poems for free, or a portion of the cost? Copyright itself was under assault by Conservative politicians, who had no respect for the written arts in general and even less for poetry specifically. Also, competing interests in English departments had reduced class time for poetry, which now had to compete with feminist, queer, postmodernist, film, cultural, vampire, Pop Cult, deconstructionist, and other studies.

What Oxford proposed was an impossible compromise. The press wanted the anthology cut from 622 to 480 pages to make it slimmer, marketable, and affordable. If I could do that, they were happy with whatever combination of new and "used" poets I might choose to include, as long as professional evaluators in the field were mildly supportive of my selections. I knew this procedure would require major surgery, removing not only poems but possibly poets as well; it also meant reading a huge number of books by new poets, plus all the recent books by the existing group.

By now, pan-nationalism had receded as Canadians became—unjustifiably, I believe—more comfortable about their cultural and political survival and more focused on issues both local and international. A growing sense of the importance of place made it imperative that more attention be given to the regions, where poets were busy writing the land. Ethnicity was another factor for me to consider, though one that could never be adequately satisfied. Was my vision of Canadian poetry blinkered by my gender and my origins and education? How open was I not only to new voices from Africa, Asia, South America, and the Caribbean, but also to First Nations writing, much of which has its roots in the oral tradition? Although I had included Québécois novels in translation in my Canadian literature classes, I never considered adding translations of French-Canadian poetry in my anthologies, because I wanted to avoid tokenism and because I felt ill equipped to address issues involved in translation, accepting, then, Frost's dictum that the poetry is what gets lost in translation.

So I signed a contract and set to work on the fifth edition, fully aware that it would exclude numerous fine poets, win me no friends, and take up more than a year of my life. I asked Di Brandt, Carmine Starnino, and Anne Compton, each of whose poems and critical intelligence I admired, to serve as associate editors, giving me advice about poets in their regions. And I wrote to the living poets from the previous edition asking for advice about their favourite poets, new and old. I borrowed hundreds of poetry books from the library and purchased at least another two hundred, thinking more than once of Yeats's sexist, and possibly apocryphal, remark to the Scriblerus Club: "Gentlemen, there are too many of us."

The more I read the less confident and the more uncomfortable I became. Along with these inevitable editorial crises, there were some wonderful discoveries and moments of sheer ecstasy over quality work, a good deal of it from relatively young poets, more than a few of them moving back toward more traditional forms. When my table of contents went out to academic readers, my surgical proceedings came under some harsh scrutiny. Why had I cut three of this person's favourite poems by P. K. Page? How could I have ignored the poetry of X, who has emerged as one of our most gifted? What made me think that more poets represented by fewer poems each was an improvement on what had originally been an inspired and tight little anthology of which any teacher could make good use? Of course, there was praise, too. I took all the comments to heart, restored a poem here and there, added the work of X after I'd absorbed it entirely and realized how good it was, and made sure the notes and selections were useful and accurate, if less inclusive than previously. My excuse in this regard was that the Internet now includes much of the bibliographical information I had originally felt obliged to pack into the notes.

By the end of eighteen, not twelve, months, I submitted to Oxford the final anthology, tentatively called *70 Canadian Poets*, in which A. J. M. Smith, Milton Acorn, Dennis Lee, and John Thompson are significant inclusions from the past, and in which Karen Solie, Ken Babstock, and Suzanne Buffam figure among the youngest of the twenty-six additional poets. The heaviest paragraph in the introduction is one containing the names of many of the poets I regretted not being able to include, and even that was too short by half. In spite of all my blind spots, editorial scars, and uncertainties, and considering the changes that might yet occur as a result of high permissions costs, I am convinced this is a work that should make us all proud as poetry lovers and as Canadians. I feel honoured to have been given the task and the responsibility of bringing this remarkable group of gifted poets together. And, of course, I am preparing myself, like Saint Sebastian, for the next volley of arrows.

NOTE

1 See Gary Geddes, *Out of the Ordinary: Politics, Poetry & Narrative* (Vernon, BC: Kalamalka Press, 2009). Print.

WORKS CITED

Auden, W. H. "In Memory of W. B. Yeats." *Norton Anthology of Poetry.* 5th ed. New York: Norton, 2005. 939–41. Print.

——. "The Poet & the City." *The Dyer's Hand.* New York: Vintage, 1962. 335–36. Print.

Barnholden, Michael. "New Canadian Poetry: Anthologizing the Nation and After." *The Poetic Front* 2.1 (2009): n. pag. Web. 3 June 2013.

Frye, Northrop. "Narrative Tradition in English-Canadian Poetry." *The Bush Garden: Essays on the Canadian Imagination.* Toronto: Anansi, 1971. 147–64. Print.

Jarrell, Randall. *Poetry and the Age.* New York: Vintage, 1953. Print.

Scully, James. *Line Break: Poetry as Social Practice.* Seattle: Bay, 1988. Print.

The Poet-Editor and the Small Press
Michael Ondaatje and *The Long Poem Anthology*

Karis Shearer

"Why edit at all?" Roy Miki asked at "Interventing the Text," a 1991 conference which "call[ed] for a more self-reflective consideration of the why in the doing" (*Broken* 34). One answer is that the editing of little magazines has allowed for the introduction and circulation of experimental work by new, young, avant-garde, and/or marginalized writers, while the editing and publication of poetry anthologies has played a major role in the establishment and disruption of academic canons, as Frank Davey has noted: "An intervention to re-publish one text rather than another ... can affect which texts can be placed on curricula, which are perceived as important for academics to write about, what story is told about literary history, what economic myths are acted upon, and ultimately how newly written texts are perceived" (*CLP* 107). If the editing of little magazines has helped to put the work of poets into print, the editing of anthologies has, through its organizing, evaluative, and recovery functions, helped to keep certain works in or return them to print. Moreover, as Miki observes, the force of this editorial work is even more profoundly felt in a country such as Canada,

> with its geographical spread, its small population of readers, its long history of anti-intellectualism, its colonial protestant ("puritan") ethic.... In the post-war years especially, the products of their "tastes," not only the literary journals but also the plethora of anthologies, have been instrumental in the canonization of writers and critics, and in governing what comes to be judged of *national* relevance. (*Broken* 35; italics in original)

The editing of anthologies does all that Miki and Davey indicate. Furthermore, as I will show, it serves to alter the work itself, in that it changes the optic through which the reader can approach the work, in this case, the Canadian long poem of the 1970s.

In 1979, Coach House Press published *The Long Poem Anthology* (henceforth *LPA*), an anthology that was remarkable for a number of reasons. First, it introduced into the national academic book market the work of nine small-press-affiliated writers who wrote from various localities, usually outside the commercial centres of Toronto and Montreal, effectively bypassing the normal hierarchy whereby small-press poetry was selected and fed into the academic market via commercial presses such as McClelland and Stewart, Ryerson Press, and Oxford University Press Canada. Secondly, and perhaps most significantly, it gathered writers who worked from a postmodern aesthetic and explored the self-reflexive construction of subjectivity through language in longer forms. In doing so, the anthology effectively introduced a postmodern poetry to Canadian classrooms, an event that did not go unnoticed: a French reviewer from the Centre d'Études Afro-Américaines et des Nouvelles Littératures Anglophones, at the Sorbonne, after listing each of the volume's authors, commented: "[i]l importe de les citer tous parce qu'ils représentent, chacun à sa façon, des directions nouvelles, des avancées de la poésie canadienne vers le post-modernisme" (Fabre 45).[1]

If, as Lynette Hunter suggests, "canons become a primary device for educating the populace into the ideology of the nation state" (18), then the canon presented by Coach House's *The Long Poem Anthology* disrupts the dominant ideology: it draws attention to the construction of identities, rather than reinforcing them as natural, unified subjects. Unlike that of *15 Canadian Poets* (1970), the title of *The Long Poem Anthology* clearly seeks to foreground form and downplay the Canadianness of its authors. *The Long Poem Anthology* belongs to a strange subset of Canadian anthologies that "could be an agency of critique as well as an embodiment of canonical value. Clearly, however, the positions advocated by any group of critics can readily turn into a new canon, over time inviting still further critique and further articulation of what is meant by the term 'representative'" (J. R. Struthers 33).

I begin this essay by situating *The Long Poem Anthology* within the context of the volume's own expressions of its value, as they are articulated in its paratextual material. The back-cover copy, for example, makes three assertions about the anthology's value: first, that "more than half of these poems are presently out of print," thus rendering the collection a valuable new source for these particular poems (we are never told exactly which poems they are); second, that "[i]n all but one case (Nichol's *The Martyrology*) the complete texts appear," thereby making the collection important in its comprehensiveness; and third, that "[t]his collection of book-length poems, for the first time, makes possible the serious study of this form and these poems in university and college classrooms." I test these articulations of value in order to explore their larger significance in the canon-making process, and then examine the strategic marketing of the volume to an academic audience. I argue that *The Long Poem Anthology* draws together texts that, in their original publications, were aesthetically and materially resistant both to the valorization of the individual author and to commodification in the literary marketplace. In their reproduction, those dissenting texts are integrated into the culturally legitimating form of the anthology and the capitalist structure of the academic book market, losing some (though not all) of their oppositional force in the field of Canadian literature. The anthology reasserts the valorization of the individual author by rhetorically and structurally decontextualizing the authors from their social communities and eliminating many traces of the collaborative nature of the original productions; simultaneously, however, it presents a newly collaborative text by involving—or at least consulting—its contributors in its design, layout, and marketing.

The production of the *LPA* is read against the background of Canadian publishing economics in order to situate it in relation to the changing conditions of literary production, and against its reception by reviewers. Overall, a picture of the poet-editor in the small-press environment, and his subjection to market beliefs and pressures, as well as to his own tastes and objectives, emerges, providing new insight into the process of poets' direct involvement with the process of canonization. The essay also demonstrates how the paratextual context of work matters to its meaning in the social sphere(s) in which it is read.

THE LONG POEM ANTHOLOGY

1. "More than half of these poems are presently out of print"

Almost thirty years after the appearance of *The Long Poem Anthology*, poet-critic Rob Winger, in his call for papers on the long poem for the spring 2008 conference of the Association of Canadian College and University Teachers of English (ACCUTE) session on the long poem, asked why, "given the generally laudatory reception of the book-length poems of the period [1970s], ... some of the best examples of the genre have long been both out of print and unavailable?" This apparent contradiction between reception and availability was already embodied in *The Long Poem Anthology* itself: the back-cover copy announced in 1979 that "more than half of these poems are presently out of print," while Ondaatje's introduction emphasized the form's ubiquity and importance in Canada through the following extended mixed metaphor, anthropomorphized: "long poems crawl out of cupboards, archives, gardens, long bus journeys, out of every segment of Canadian writing" (11). Its being "politely ignored by anthologists, schools, and the general reading public" would not be so egregious, Ondaatje continues, "if not much was happening with the form, but it seems to me that the most interesting writing being done by poets today can be found within the structure of the long poem" (11), a claim that echoes Dorothy Livesay's statement ten years earlier, in 1969, that "our most significant body of poetry exists in the long poem" ("Documentary" 268). Livesay admitted, however, that analysis of the form would be difficult "because so much of the material that would be of interest has not been made available throught [*sic*] republication" (268). Ondaatje both takes up her assertions of significance and makes material available through republication.

If there was really so much "happening" with this "interesting" and "significant" form in the 1970s, why then were more than half of these poems out of print? Ondaatje's introduction necessarily prompts the question: are the poems out of print because they have been ignored, or have they been ignored because they are out of print? What appears to be a contradiction is actually quite revealing, as it suggests two different sets of values. On the one hand, the long poem form is certainly of interest and value to Ondaatje (who won a Governor General's Award for his long poem *The Collected Works of Billy the Kid* in 1970), and presumably to other poets writing long poems, but its value is not recognized for some reason by educational institutions or the general reading public, so it is left to go out of print. On the other hand, the question itself presupposes a desire for an unproblematized link between literary value and availability, or circulation. Does the answer lie in publishing economics?

George Bowering provides a somewhat pointed answer in his author statement in *The New Long Poem Anthology*: "Book-length poems are often not kept in print because they were published by literary presses rather than oil company diversifications" ("Statement" 351), suggesting, it seems, the capitalist tendencies of the latter and the perhaps Marxist leanings of the former. Ondaatje too refers to poets' affiliation with small presses in his introduction: poets "emerged with these works and published them—mostly with small presses across the country" (12). This incantation is repeated again in Betsy Struthers's review of the *LPA*: "The nine poems collected here have previously appeared only in small press chapbooks and are, for the most part, not available to the general reader" (139), and is implied in Diana Brydon's comment that the *LPA* "makes work which was previously difficult to obtain or inaccessible available to a much wider audience, extending the range of what might be taught in courses on Canadian literature" ("Making" 99). Some of the poems Rob Winger could have been referring to (perhaps Roy Kiyooka's *The Fontainebleau Dream Machine*, or Don McKay's *Long Sault*) were originally produced by such small presses as Coach House, Applegarth Follies, and

Talonbooks, in what Pierre Bourdieu calls the "restricted field of production" (*Field* 36), as an aesthetic object with a relatively limited audience (often one that included primarily fellow artists). Even so, in general, the commentary on the anthology supports, or perhaps merely repeats, a causal connection between restricted availability and the poems' connections to small presses.

There is no disputing that this is a logical connection. The conditions of publishing economics in Canada are such that small presses depend heavily on support from the Canada Council Block Grants program, which for a long time subsidized only the first printing of a book; thus it has often been financially unfeasible for a press to keep a book in print after the first run. Consequently, it was difficult for small-press books to become part of an academic canon, since reprinting, until the onset of print on demand, was an ongoing problem. However, because literary presses relied almost without exception on state funding for support, they had to produce a minimum 300 copies,[2] a regulation that has been part of the Block Grant program since its founding in 1972.

Given the emphasis on their limited availability, it is interesting to note that the majority of the book-length poems included in the *LPA* were printed in editions of 1,000 copies—more than three times the minimum required number. Of the poems included, Robin Blaser's *The Moth Poem* had the smallest print run—a limited first edition of 300 copies (it was published in San Francisco, outside the Canada Council's jurisdiction). In contrast, Stuart MacKinnon's *The Intervals* also lists its print run as a "limited edition," but of 1,000 copies, raising the question of what exactly constitutes a "limited" edition. In addition to MacKinnon's *The Intervals*, Robert Kroetsch's *Seed Catalogue* also had an initial print run of 1,000 copies, as did Kiyooka's *The Fontainebleau Dream Machine*, and Bowering's *Allophanes*. According to the volume's colophon, Books 3 & 4 of bpNichol's *The Martyrology* were printed in an edition of 1,500 copies. In short, the sense that these volumes were scarce "chapbooks" seems more a myth constructed by the *LPA*'s back-cover copy (and then perpetuated without question by reviewers) than a description of the actual number of books still in existence. If anything, the problem of availability lay elsewhere.

The fact remains that, contrary to the press's claim that "over half of these poems are presently out of print," *Canadian Books in Print* (*CBiP*) shows that in the year of the *LPA*'s publication—1979—more than half of the poems (*Seed Catalogue, The Intervals, Allophanes, The Fontainebleau Dream Machine,* and *The Martyrology Book 4*) *were* in print—a fact supported by the Coach House Press year-end inventory in 1979 ("INVENT 79"). Indeed, all five would remain listed as in print in the *CBiP* for several more years, and nearly *all* of the poems were listed as being in print just the year before; only the volume's earliest poem, Blaser's *The Moth Poem* (1964), along with Don McKay's *The Long Sault* (which had gone out of print for the first time in 1978), were unavailable. For whatever reason, over half of the poems remained at least listed as being "in print" in *Canadian Books in Print* for years following the *LPA*'s publication,[3] suggesting that the anthology was marketed by Coach House Press as a solution to a problem that may not have existed in the first place.

However, there was good reason to try to sell readers on the anthology as a solution to a scarcity problem, all in one neat package. Coach House Press, as Frank Davey recalls in his memoir, was looking for a new audience, not only for the *LPA* but for other works they published, such as *The Contemporary Canadian Poem Anthology* (1983): "An added promotional advantage of such anthologies," he states, "was that their potential for high school and first-year university adoption could lead to the sale of our single-author collections to universities for graduate and senior undergraduate courses. In the 1980s the sale of titles by [Daphne] Marlatt, [Fred] Wah, Bowering, ... Nichol, [and] Ondaatje ... through graduate and senior undergraduate course adoptions became a substantial source of revenue" (49). This strategy may have worked for *other* volumes by those authors, but it was unlikely to have been useful for the particular books included in the *LPA*. By making the nine long poems available under one cover for $7.95, the press would probably have cannibalized their own market for the individual books. Consider, for example, that in 1979 it would have cost over $39.55 to purchase all nine volumes separately,[4] giving the anthology's purchaser a theoretical discount of over 80 percent. If readers could obtain nine long poems for the price of approximately two individual book-length poems, reassured by the *LPA*'s back-cover copy that they were getting "the complete texts," there would be no reason to seek out the supposedly rare individual editions—a quest only book collectors and devoted readers would be inclined to pursue. This conclusion may seem to contradict my observation that many of the titles included in the *LPA* stayed in print for years after the anthology's publication; however, their being in print does not necessarily mean that their sales were strong, only that there was stock available.

Rhetorically, *The Long Poem Anthology* positions itself as a bridge between what Pierre Bourdieu calls the restricted field and the large-scale field of production. As such, the back-cover copy and the editor's introduction construct a major shift in the publics addressed by the texts contained within it.[5] As I have already noted, the volume claims its value as a facilitator of increased circulation for long poems that were originally produced in Bourdieu's restricted field of production, perhaps exaggerating the limited availability of those poems in order to enhance its own importance in the large-scale field of production. Though the volume did mark a strategic shift in readership (Davey, for instance, notes that "the national aspirations of [Coach House Press] were marked by their frequent publishing of nationally framed titles [such as] ... *The Long Poem Anthology*" [*CLP* 85]), the division between the original condition of production and its subsequent reproduction is rhetorically configured in the introduction to the volume as an amplified division between "private" and "public" address. To this effect, Ondaatje describes two general types of poets writing in the 1970s:

> [s]ome writers became public personalities, ... at the same time some poets—
> from the generation of Souster's *New Wave Canada*—turned inward, away
> from the individual occasional poem, to explore, to take a longer look at
> themselves and their landscape, to hold onto something frail—whether the
> memory or discovery of a place, of a way of speaking. They emerged with
> these works and published them—mostly with small presses across the
> country. These private explorations are among the most significant poetry
> of recent years, and this book represents some of those "unofficial" voices of
> the 1970s. (12)

Again, later in the introduction, we are told that these "poems have more to do with open fields and quiet rooms than *public stages*," that "[i]n the 70s <some poets talked out loud and some listened. These poets listened to everything" (13; emphasis added), and also that "[w]e are not dealing with poetry whose themes are hardened into stone, into a *public cultural voice*. Between readings the tents are folded and the company moves on. In the daylight sometimes one can hardly see them at all" (12; emphasis added). When Ondaatje defines his poets against such "public" voices[6] he may have in mind poets such as Irving Layton, Al Purdy, or even Leonard Cohen, who toured nationally[7] with McClelland and Stewart in the 1960s: "The[se] poems are not parading down main street. Some jeer anonymously from the stands, some are written in such frail faint pencil that one can barely hold them, they shift like mercury off the hand" (11–12). In Ondaatje's configuration, there are the poets who are public personalities, who occupy public stages and whose poems parade down the main street, and then there are the "unofficial" poets who turn inward, residing in quiet rooms and producing private explorations that are frail and faint—ephemeral. Of the works included in the anthology, Stuart MacKinnon's poem, *The Intervals*, most explicitly echoes such a construction:

Eating lunch in cautious isolation
not wanting to be seen
trying to be a private man
in a public park
trying to look unapproachable
for whatever reason
afraid and defensive
wishing to be left alone
with my endless dreary speculations (49)

However, the degree to which the other poems collected in the *LPA* were really "private explorations" is debatable. Daphne Marlatt's *Steveston*, for example, is perhaps less a "private" poem, than an attempt to engage *personally* with the past and present of a local community, which is a type of public. Her own description of the poem, included in the anthology, consistently evokes the notion of community: *Steveston* is a "network, the ways in which all of the poems & the poem's parts, as all of us & where we live, are interconnected" (317). Likewise, Marlatt explains, "I wrote for Steveston to be, here now & myself now in it. The world I was writing was & is a world I in the company of everyone could continue to live in" (316). Marlatt's explorations also include, she tells us, "other people's speech, other voices my own moves with & against" (317). Rather than "turning inward" or engaging in "private explorations," Marlatt turns instead to collaborate with the photographer Robert Minden, and describes their collaboration as working "separately together," a process that constantly involves separation and return: "we often drove down together to Steveston, then separated to encounter the place and its people on our own terms.... Sometimes we met people together & sometimes one of us would bring the other to meet someone we had encountered previously. We exchanged our experience at every point ..." (317). This is not so much "inward" or "private" as it is a personal engagement with and commitment to a community.[8]

The public-private binary that Ondaatje establishes in his introduction places the reader—this new reader potentially located in a classroom or a university—as a kind of eavesdropping figure[9] whom the anthology permits to overhear "unofficial voices" that are involved in almost fetishized "private explorations." Possibly reacting to the literary nationalism of the post-centennial era, Ondaatje seems to invoke the "public" as *the* public, or the social totality of the nation-state, rendering those collected in the *LPA* on the other extreme, as solitary Romantic artists who turn away from community and public address to "private explorations" and "quiet rooms"—a vision of artistic production that echoes, perhaps unsurprisingly, his own "wish to come to each poem and let it breed in its own vacuum and have its own laws and order" (qtd. in Geddes and Bruce 288). It is also a construction that, as I will detail later, is reinforced by the material production of the anthology. It overlooks the possibility that in addressing a public, one must not necessarily address a national public; instead, one can address *a* public—a group of self-organizing readers or listeners—and indeed, I would suggest the poets collected in the *LPA* did just that. To name just a few examples, the involvement of poets like Bowering, Davey, and Marlatt in *Tish* magazine's community and at conferences such as the Vancouver Poetry Conference (1963) and "Writing in Our Time" conference (1979) attests to their commitment to a public address, as does bpNichol's involvement in the collaborative sound poetry group the Four Horsemen, and Roy Kiyooka's participation in different avant-garde arts movements—not to mention the prolific number of public readings these poets participated in during that decade. Ondaatje's binary construct of the public and private of the 1960s and '70s may gesture toward what Pauline Butling has described as those decades having witnessed a "reorganization of Canadian literary publishing into a rhizomatic, countrywide network of regional presses and grassroots magazines that linked literary production to local narratives of resistance and emergence. This replaced the former, centralized publishing system that revolved around nationalist agendas and was concentrated in central Canada" (*Writing* 29). In the former publishing system, she notes, "[i]n the 1950s, for instance, Ryerson, Macmillan, and McClelland and Stewart did virtually all of the literary publishing. Even the small presses were centralized" (46n6). Produced instead by regional artisan-run small presses—Coach House Press (Toronto), Talonbooks (Vancouver), Applegarth Follies (London, ON), Turnstone Press (Winnipeg), and Open Space (San Francisco)—the poems collected in the anthology represent the turn to the local that began in the 1960s.

To what extent, then, is the *LPA* a construction reflective of the cultural work of its poet-editor, Michael Ondaatje? I want to take a moment to explore the question of how Ondaatje is positioned and how he positions himself in relation to his own cultural work and the community he constructs. In the title of his review, "Ondaatje's Long Poem Anthology," Leon Surette refers to the volume as the possessive object of its editor (85); Diana Brydon suggests "[t]he most interesting aspect of this anthology is the way it has been shaped by its editor, himself a major Canadian poet of the 1970s who has written his own long poems" ("Making" 99). While Brydon's identification of Ondaatje as a "major poet" and writer of long poems confirms him as an authentic member of the community he represents in the volume, her comment also suggests that a reading of the anthology as an expression of its editor has as much value as the actual poems collected within it. Though she does not quite say that the volume is shaped to reflect Ondaatje's aesthetic practice, she comes very close: "When Ondaatje argues that 'the most interesting writing being done today can be found within the structure of the long poem' and that it is time to re-examine what we mean when we speak of the 'documentary poem in Canada,' he is really *advocating his own preference* for what Jack Spicer (invoked often in this volume) called the serial poem" (99; emphasis added). She might have said instead: "advocating his own *practice*." Certainly, in spite of being remarkably collaborative, the anthology also can be read as reflective of Ondaatje's own creative practice, since he is an interested editor by virtue of being a long-poem poet and since he has a reasonable degree of agency in conducting his work. As Donna Bennett asserts: "Most [canonical manifestos] are statements made by writer-critics.... It is in the interest of such critics that their school of writing ... fits into a pre-existing literary milieu" ("Encroaching" 41). Yet the absence of Ondaatje's own *Collected Works of Billy the Kid* is called "unfortunate" by Leon Surette in his review of the *LPA*, "because it is, in [Surette's] view, the finest long work of poetry produced by a contemporary Canadian poet" (85). Note, as Surette continues, his reassertion of the authority of the author as the definitive interpreter of his own work: "It was, perhaps, too long to be include [*sic*], or, it might be, *judged by the editor (who ought to know)* not to be a long poem at all, but something else" (Surette "Long Poem" 85; emphasis added).

Ondaatje, too, draws attention to himself as a subjective shaper of this canon; he chooses to be "governed by curiosity" and so the volume becomes his "explor[ation] [of] the poets who surprise [him] with their *step*, their process" (11; italics in original), at the same time as it becomes our discovery of *his* process—of "learning about something [he's] not sure of, [doesn't] fully understand" (11).[10] The similarities between his construction of himself as editor/canon-maker and as poet are remarkable, and echoed elsewhere: "My only emotion about my own work is curiosity," Ondaatje said of his poetry in a 1978 interview ("Moving" 134). The emphasis on the importance of "process" and "discovery" is repeated in his description of his own creative writing:

> I think any poem has got a sense of that <u>process</u> of investigating something—an emotion, a problem, a feeling, a celebration. In *Billy* [*the Kid*] and in [*Coming Through*] *Slaughter* I think it's the same thing but on a larger scale—it's a <u>discovery</u> of someone.... It's that sense of <u>finding</u> something out in the <u>process</u> of the poem or a novel. When I was writing these two books, I was in the state of trying to <u>find out</u> something about somebody else. It's the <u>process of unfolding</u>. If you already *know* the last line of the poem, how can you write the poem? You can't. But you can take the last line and make it the *first* line and go on from there. Anything else is boring, you know. If you know where it is going to end. ("Moving" 140–41; italics in original; underline added)

Again, the governing metaphors Ondaatje chooses to describe his own creativity are "curiosity," "process," "journey," and "finding," just as they were for his editing, indicating a coherent purposive relationship between his two roles.

2. "In all but one case (Nichol's *The Martyrology*) the complete texts appear"

During a discussion period at the 1984 Long-liners Conference on the Canadian Long Poem, bpNichol praised Smaro Kamboureli for having read "the book":

> what is terrific about it is that she's dealing with the book as a unit—all its component parts ... the thing that I dislike is that often you cannot read poets in the way they were published, in the books that they shape—what you're always reading is someone's edited version. So that's terrific. You read it, you read the significance of the preface and snuck in the photos ... that's terrific. I wish there were more people talking about "the books." ... [Applause] ("Discussion" 295)

George Bowering has noted that the "long poem does not fare well in a normal textbook" ("Statement" 351). How well does any poem fare in its reproduction? In any anthology, the tension between a text's original condition/mode of production and its subsequent reproduction in a collection alongside other poems—stripped of the original paratextual material and of its neighbouring poems in the original book—can significantly alter the way readers receive the poem. This is particularly true for *The Long Poem Anthology* which alleges to reproduce not just excerpts from original publications but the entire "text" of poems that were in some way considered subversive in their first edition. However, as several reviewers of the volume note, the "complete texts" are not really complete: they are missing some of the radical elements (particularly photographs and illustrations) of their original production. Among reviewers, Roy Geiger laments the "missing ... map that was part of the original *Long Sault*" (B3). While Michel Fabre reviews the book and finds that it is "d'une presentation impeccable jusque dans la reproduction des gravures de maîtres qui illustrent 'The Fontainebleau Dream Machine' de Roy Kiyooka" (45),[11] Eva Marie Kröller comments unfavourably on the reproduction of the images in the *LPA* (52). Similar observations could be made of virtually all the poems. The small-press origin of the poems has been consistently linked to their limited availability (Ondaatje, "What" 12; Bowering, "Statement" 351; Betsy Struthers, 139), with the *LPA* championed as a welcome solution to this "problem"; however, less frequently in the critical response have those small presses been acknowledged as producers of highly designed radical texts that combine visual images with the poems in a material object resistant to commodification by the normative book industry. In fact, all the poems included in the *LPA*, as they were originally produced, were non-standard sized texts that integrated graphics or photographs with poetry; some were produced collaboratively and/or had paratextual material that troubled the traditional notion of a single author. The absence of most of these visual features in the *LPA* effectively meant its readers may have missed what I will suggest are important interpretive connections both inside and outside of the texts. I will now survey several examples of these compromises and lost connections.

Out of necessity, issues of space and production cost ultimately governed the contents of an anthology with a projected list price of $7.95 a copy. There is also substantial evidence in the Coach House correspondence archive concerning what was affectionately known as the "longer anthol," suggesting that Ondaatje was involved in the production and design process and offered the authors opportunities to become involved in layout and marketing discussions. Moreover, the correspondence reveals that Ondaatje sought to include at least some of the artwork from the original editions, and given his own propensity toward the documentary collage—*The Collected Works of Billy the Kid* features graphics and images—perhaps it was the highly aesthetic aspects of the texts that drew him to include them in the first place. Correspondence between the editor and press's assistant indicates effort was made to reproduce the original editions' images in the anthology—something that is confirmed by other archived correspondence with the poets. Nevertheless, material constraints—namely production costs—inevitably limit what is achievable in any editorial project; the reproduction of those texts and their artwork in a volume destined for the academic market meant substantial changes in form would be necessary.

In the volume's introduction, Ondaatje's emphasis on landscape becomes somewhat ironic given the excision of the cover or title-page landscape images for the work by McKay, Marlatt, and even MacKinnon. Indeed, the title of the introduction, "What is in the pot," through its appositional placement, becomes a metaphor not for cooking but for mapping:

> The need to chart what is around us, to say what is in the pot, creates at first strange bedfellows with the contemporary poetic voice. However, one should remember that Nichol, who has spent years landscaping *The Martyrology*, used to be a cross-country runner. Or that George Bowering was an aerial photographer for the air force. Kroetsch dutifully planted bulbs and waited patiently for spring. McKay on the other hand saw his landscape erased, not created. The physical world, its habit, what is "given," is the map or backdrop

to these poems. If you forget that, you may assume that these poets are just pissing on the Porsche of Canadian literature. (16)

Of course, one reason we might "forget" that the physical world is the backdrop to the poems is because the maps that accompanied the original publications are missing. Their absence further decontextualizes the poems, removing them from the intertextual community created that linked Marlatt, McKay, and Kroetsch to the Black Mountain poetics of Charles Olson, Robert Creeley, and Robert Duncan. Olson's *The Maximus Poems* (1960), for example, featured a map on its cover that was then visually echoed in later publications not only by the three aforementioned poets, but also in George Bowering's *George, Vancouver* (1970); Robert Kroetsch's *The Ledger* (1975); and in two issues of *Tish* (see figures 2 and 3). Those poems link themselves through both their poetics and their visual images to Olson's *Maximus Poems*, a move that works to canonize the poems through the intertextual connection to an already canonized writer.[12]

In the world of commercial presses, to which such houses as McClelland & Stewart and Oxford University Press belong, the author is often far

Figure 1   Cover of Daphne Marlatt's *Steveston.*

removed from the production of his or her volume of poetry, not normally consulted on issues of design. According to David McKnight, "In the realm of design and material production, what distinguishes small presses from commercial presses is the consultative relationship that often exists between publisher and author in determining layout and appearance" (311). As Clint Burnham explains in his chapbook *Allegories of Publishing: The Toronto Small Press Scene*:

> Texts are produced by highly divided and alienated labour processes: a myriad of workers—including typesetters, secretaries, and publicists—participates in the creation, manufacture, and delivery of the modern book. This material division of labour is then replicated at the ideological level by the intricate structure of reviewing, promotion, criticism, and other forms of professional writing and reading in newspapers, magazines, trade and academic journals, conferences, and classrooms.
>
> It is this high level of the division of labour, the abstraction of tasks, and the structuration of ideological labour that demonstrates the similarity of book publishing to other industries, cultural or otherwise, and that also results in the alienation in all areas of production and consumption. (7)

In contrast to texts produced by these alienated labour processes, the highly aesthetic artworks produced by small presses were often the result of close cooperation between the poet and a visual artist, and/or designer, reducing the degree of alienation that occurs in commercial presses where the poet is far removed from the book's design process. While none of the volumes in question seems to have been produced under conditions in which the poet occupied all the roles to which Burnham refers (i.e., the most extreme form of anti-capitalist publishing, the vanity press production), the word "collaboration" is very frequently invoked: the colophon of *King of Swords* (1972), for example, indicates that the "book was designed in collaboration with Frank Davey / by David Robinson with Elizabeth Komisar" (n. pag).

King of Swords, as it was originally produced by Talonbooks, resists easy consumption or cataloguing: the volume measures 4.5 by 6.5 inches (smaller than the standard book size of 6 by 9 inches), and its two-tone dust jacket is designed to look less like a tarot card than a card from a secular playing deck in order to give the reader the impression of flipping through the card deck, rather than a book. The volume's title is suppressed, appearing for the first time in tiny letters on its spine and French flap, and again on the half-title page, rather than in the standard position on the front cover. In fact, the complete absence of typeface on the front or back of the volume prevents any sense of orientation; instead, the title is evoked through the image of the king of swords (see figure 4), appearing on one side of the volume as an

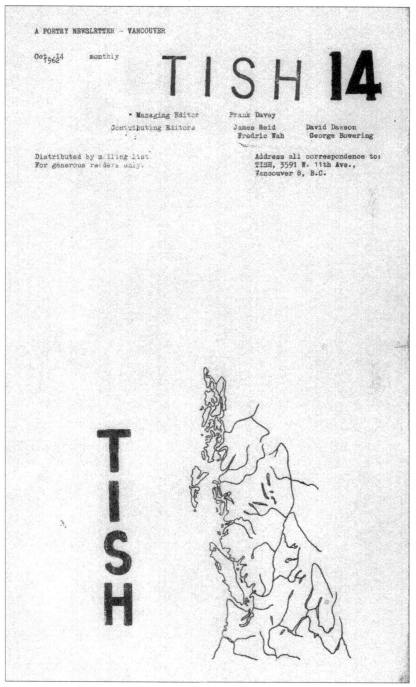

Figure 2   Cover of *Tish* 14 (14 Oct. 1962).

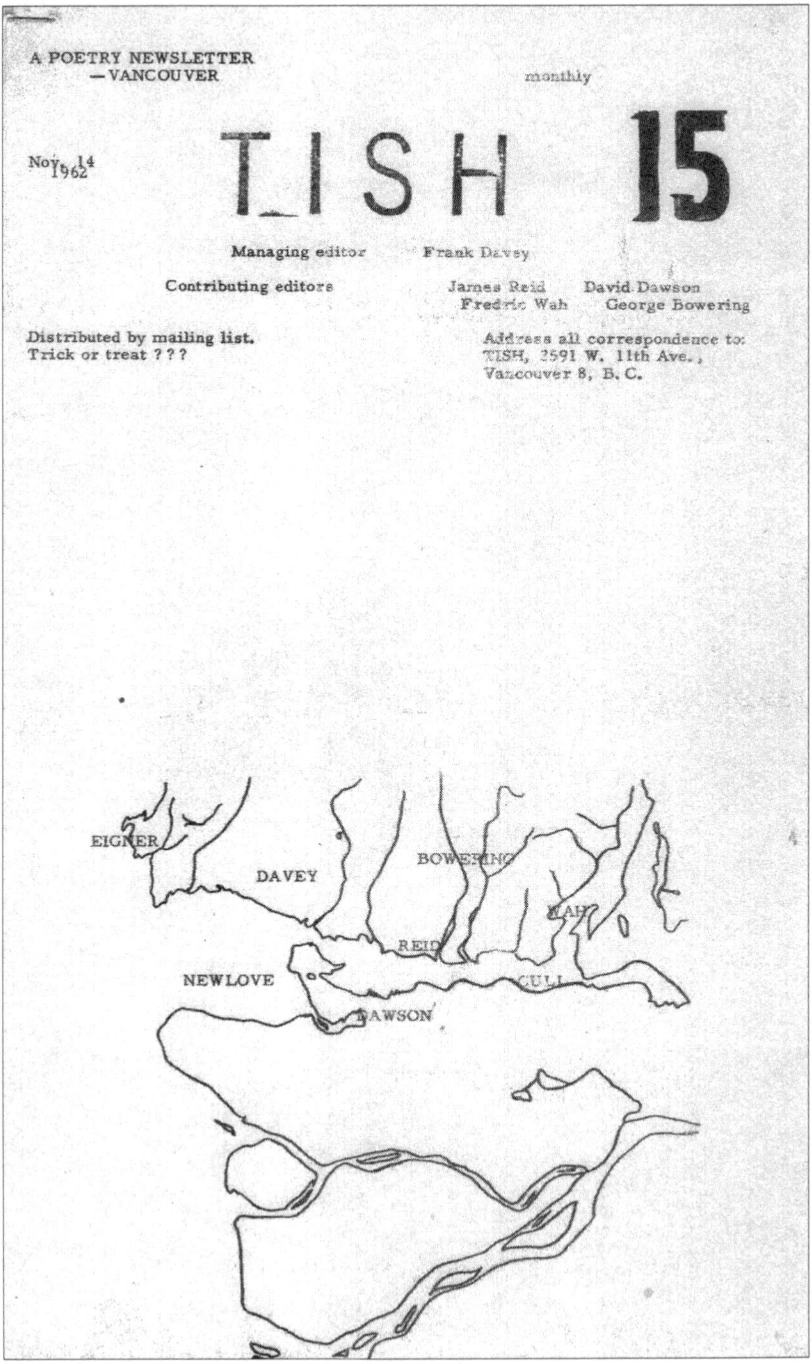

A POETRY NEWSLETTER
— VANCOUVER   monthly

Nov. 14
1962

TISH 15

Managing editor   Frank Davey

Contributing editors   James Reid   David Dawson
                             Fredric Wah   George Bowering

Distributed by mailing list.   Address all correspondence to:
Trick or treat ? ? ?   TISH, 2591 W. 11th Ave.,
                                             Vancouver 8, B. C.

EIGNER

DAVEY   BOWERING

                                                    WAH

                            REID

NEWLOVE   GULL

        DAWSON

Figure 3   Cover of *Tish* 15 (14 Nov. 1962).

angled mirror-image, which the reader can rotate 180 degrees to find herself looking at the exact same image. The other side of the dust jacket features the top design of a card, making it again unclear whether this is the front or back of the book, until the reader opens it. The inside front flap explains: "On this book's cover is a corrupt card, its sign female rather than male, its element earth rather than water, its bearing courtly rather than martial. Such confusion is hardly unlikely in the card of this 'hero' of the Tarot, of Gwenevere's bedroom, of your life and mine." Because the poem's title, speaker, and potentially its author are all signified by the cover image of the "corrupt card," which, along with the above passage, is absent from the *LPA*, the reader of the anthology risks mistaking the text's anti-hero for hero and missing the deliberate ambiguity of such an important sign that signifies on multiple levels. The sign of the King of Swords, normally a patriarchal figure of judgment and law in the tarot, is rendered ambiguous by the paratextual material that deliberately obscures such a straightforward reading.

Davey's volume is not the only one whose paratextual material cues the reader to questions of authorship. George Bowering's *Allophanes*, originally

Figure 4 Front cover of
Frank Davey's *King of Swords*.

Figure 5 Cover of
George Bowering's *Allophanes*.

published by Coach House Press, is also an unusual size (4 x 7.5 inches). Its
blue, heavy cardstock cover (see figure 5) has a triangular cut-out that reveals
"a text comprising geometric shapes and symbols suggestive of pictographs
or hieroglyphs and all decidedly non-phonetic" (McCaffery 133) printed on
a dark blue background—the inverse colour scheme of the cover itself. Not
only does the cover signal the primacy of the alphabetic system (the poem
is itself divided into twenty-six cantos), it also appears to cue its reader to a
particular pronunciation of its title by inscribing the word (itself of Greek
origin, of course) in Greek letters: "Αλλοphαηες." Of course, there is some
playfulness here, which should not be surprising since one of the meanings of
"allophanes" is "appearing otherwise": the title-word *appears* to be in its original Greek, but the spelling is in fact a corruption of the Greek (αλλοφανής)
and, in order to be pronounced "Allo-phan-eez," it must be read phonetically
as though it were actually the Latinate alphabet. As it appears on the cover,
the "φ", or "phi" sound is instead formed by a combination of the Greek letter
"rho" (the equivalent to the Latinate "r") with the letter Latinate "h". For a
reader of the Latinate alphabet, the "rho," or "ρ," appears to be the Latinate

"p." The "η," moreover, is the Greek "eta," making the word virtually unpro-
nounceable (*allorhaees?*), and certainly meaningless to a Greek speaker. Once
again, of course, there is a characteristic Bowering pun on the title; if the title
is loosely pronounced according to its Latinate letters, "Allophanes" becomes
a playful address to his readers: "allo-fanz" or "'ello fans."[13] This address sets
the reader up for the self-conscious considerations of authorship that occur
within the text of the poem itself:

> There is no perspective
> when the eye is transparent.
> When the author dies
> I disappear.
>
> Companionship is true growing up,
> I reach for the companionship of art. ("Allophanes," *LPA* 207)

Paradoxically, the lyrical eye/I which appears to be transparent actually has
no perspective—because, of course, it is not transparent at all, but mediated
by the text. Bowering's critique focuses here on "the transparent, quasi-realist
rhetoric of the contemporary free verse lyric [which] can be seen not only as
a canonical aesthetic but as an ideology, designed to appear natural and to
conceal its own constructedness" (Golding 167). Also present in Bowering's
poem is the complaining "reader," who, accustomed to the free-verse lyric,
occasionally objects parenthetically to this self-reflexive commentary on language and authorship, requesting instead the comfort of the "transparent"
lyric "I" of official verse culture: "(Aw poet, just tell us how you felt about
something)" (Bowering 211).

The facing-page collage images of Roy Kiyooka's *Fontainebleau Dream
Machine* make its poem even more resistant than Davey's or Bowering's to
being reproduced in a collection. To divorce Kiyooka's collage images entirely
from the poems would have posed a more obvious problem, since each section of the poem so clearly refers to its accompanying graphic. Nevertheless,
the Kiyooka images underwent a compromise, very likely due to space constraints (the ambitious volume was already 344 pages) and the cost of producing both the extra pages and larger graphics; in the end, the collages appeared,
as Kröller observes, "reduced to stamp-sized images" on the same page as
their poem-commentaries (52). It is worth noting that the subordinate position of the images seems to run counter to the way Kiyooka describes *The
Fontainebleau Dream Machine* as "the text & its co-equal, the illustrations"
("Statement" 332). Significantly, Kiyooka was also responsible for the cover
art, which functions as an extension of the interior collages. Eva Marie Kröller
finds "the ambiguities of the balloon as image" which is repeated throughout

the interior collages, to be "well captured in the cover of Kiyooka's book," but feels herself compelled to "describe [it] in some detail because it has been omitted" from the anthology (52). This statement, along with her near page-length description of the images, clearly implies that Kröller envisions her own readers having ready access to or being more familiar with the *LPA* version of Kiyooka's text than with the first edition. She also notes that the image on the cover of a man in overalls may in fact be Kiyooka himself (53)—an autobiographical link that has been omitted elsewhere as well.

Although the dedication[14] remains (to, among others, fellow poets George Bowering and bpNichol), the original edition's final signature is missing:

Roy K. Kiyooka
Oct. '76/ March '77
Vancouver B.C. (n. pag.)

In addition to situating the writer temporally and geographically, this passage connects Kiyooka's signature as "author" to the framing device of the caption through the bold typeface common to both, creating what Philippe Lejeune has called "le pacte autobiographique," in which the persona of the text is linked to the signature of the author on the text's cover. Most of those captions claim to reveal or conceal aspects of the collages, self-reflexively drawing attention to the way in which they are constructed by "the Hand of the unseen Poet"; for example, "<bold>the 2nd Frame<end bold> shows / all the dreams breath abides to the Queen of Hearts," while "<bold>the 3rd Frame<end bold> (hides) / the Morning Star under the Cowl of Breath," "<bold>the 6th Frame<end bold> exposes," and "<bold>the 7th Frame <end bold> shows / the Hand of the unseen Poet turning into a Palimpsest" (*Fontainebleau* n. pag.). Kiyooka, then, is "present" throughout the poem as a framer who "hides" and "shows," controlling what the reader sees or doesn't see. If, as Kröller suggests, "*The Fontainebleau Dream Machine*, besides presenting a critique of western civilization, also outlines the poet's autobiography ... in which the borderlines between subject and object have been dissolved" (56), then the absence of this textual connection will be a significant oversight.

Steveston is, today, probably the best-known collaboration to have been included in the anthology. Owing to its appearance in the volume as the solo work of "Daphne Marlatt," the poet is compelled to use the "author's statement" to contextualize the original conditions of production, emphasizing the collaborative aspect of the work: "I've been talking about *Steveston* as writing because that was what I was engaged in. But *the context of the writing was that it was half of a collaboration*, the other half being Robert Minden's photographs" ("Long as in time" 317; emphasis added). More than any other writer included in the anthology, Marlatt's statement troubles the marketing of the volume as containing "the complete texts," by naming her work *half* of a text that was complemented by the work of Robert Minden. It seems any elements of the original text—particularly the acknowledge-ments and epigraph—that might link Marlatt to Minden and raise questions about what is missing from "the complete text" have been suppressed. What is at stake in this suppression? For one, the Japanese-Canadian residents of Steveston, "Unosuke Sakamoto, Spud Matsushita, [and] Buck Suzuki," cannot be thanked "[f]or their time, their stories, their interest and kind-ness" because it is "our thanks"—Marlatt's and Minden's—that go to them in the dedication, just as it is "we" who "are grateful to the evocative work of those early photographers of Steveston: Philip Timms and F. Dundas Todd" (n. pag.). It seems even *Steveston*'s epigraph by the writer James Agee, "seek-ing to perceive it as it stands ..." (n.p.) could not be included, for it calls forth one of the most famous writer-photographer duos, James Agee and Walker Evans, a pair in whose footsteps Marlatt and Minden clearly felt they were following. Marlatt goes on to describe their collaborative process:

> We worked *separately together*: that is, we often drove down together to Steveston, then separated to encounter the place & its people on our own terms, he with his camera & me with my notebook. Sometimes we met people together & sometimes one of us would bring the other to meet someone we had encountered previously. We exchanged our experience at every point, although I found it difficult to convey to him the fullness of what I was sensing other than in the written piece that finally completed a day, even days later. ("Long as in time" 317; emphasis added).

As a poet who often collaborates with visual artists, Marlatt is likely to be more sensitive to the separation of photographic and textual elements of a single work. Furthermore, *Steveston* is the only one of the nine texts to have its authorship attributed to two separate individuals, both on the cover of the text itself and in *Canadian Books in Print*.

Minden and Marlatt's concern about their work's reproduction surfaces in an undated letter to Michael Ondaatje, written during the *LPA*'s produc-tion, in which Marlatt refers to "the latest instalment of the ongoing discus-sion re Robert [Minden]'s photos." In that letter, she expresses their mutual disappointment that the press seems to have opted not to print the photos with the poem, and refers to the collaborative precedent set by Evans and Agee in *Let Us Now Praise Famous Men* (1941). What becomes clear from Marlatt's correspondence is that there had been some intent to include the photographs, but reproducing "good quality" images, in keeping with Coach

House Press's commitment to aesthetic quality, seems to have been out of the scope of their budget. Marlatt and Minden remain concerned about the collaborative aspect:

> [Minden] says ... the quality of the Walker Evans repros in the paperback edition of *Let Us Now Praise Famous Men* was bad but that a reader still got the content of the photos &, *more importantly, the feeling of the book having been a collaboration between photographer & writer*.... But he does (& I do too, obviously) understand that there are financial considerations & if you & Stan feel that even that would be too costly for your budget for the book ... then, ok, we'll let it rest. (n. pag.; emphasis added)

The *LPA*'s budget[15] clearly, though unsurprisingly, governed what could be included and what would be excised from the original editions of these texts. While this is true of any anthology, what is interesting here is the seemingly new negotiation between cost and aesthetic quality at Coach House Press. In keeping with the publisher's precedent for producing highly designed volumes, Ondaatje demonstrates repeated interest in producing an anthology of aesthetic quality throughout his correspondence with the authors and the Coach House staff, suggesting that the original texts were altered to a certain degree so that the *LPA* could itself be an aesthetically attractive production.

While the reproduction and rhetorical positioning of the original texts may have streamlined them so as to privilege a single marketable, Romantic author, the production of the *LPA* did remain very much a collaborative event involving authors and editor at the levels of layout, marketing, promotion, and design; as such, it does avoid some of the alienation of commercial publishing. To this end, the process reflected the general operating policies of Coach House Press, which Stephen Cain explains:

> [T]he responsibilities of the Coach House editors during this period did not end with mere selection. Unlike at other publishing houses where stages of production—from selection, to editing, to copy-editing, to typesetting, to design—are demarcated and divided among various staff with "specialized functions," at Coach House once an editor took a manuscript under his/her direction, s/he often became responsible for more than what "editing" would normally imply. Hence, although the colophons of many of the texts produced during the "transition" period (1975–1976) only bear the print run and date of publication, by 1977 most texts also carried the line "edited by," or more commonly, "seen through the press by" one of the Coach House editors. (280–81)

Beyond the selection of poets and poems, Ondaatje was involved in the layout[16] and design of the volume; while there is no evidence to suggest he personally was responsible for designing the cover, the Coach House archives contain a handwritten note from Ondaatje to Sarah Sheard, accompanied by a scrap of the cover of the *Bradford Morrow Bookseller, Catalogue Five: Walter Reuben Collection of Jack Kerouac* (1978), featuring a cream background and Kerouac titles printed in blue, orange, and green print, respectively. The final design of the *LPA* does bear a resemblance to the Kerouac cover, particularly in terms of layout, with its emphasis on the printed word and absence of photos or other images, but unlike the Kerouac cover, the anthology's first printing was done in American Denford Green with red-orange lettering (see figure 6). In the *LPA*'s subsequent printings, the cover, with its now pale grey background and blue and black lettering, bears an even stronger resemblance to the Bradford Morrow catalogue (see figure 7). Ultimately, the volume probably was as good looking as Ondaatje had hoped, printed on the press's house paper, Rolland's Zephyr Antique Laid,[17] and it prompted several of the book's reviewers to comment on the quality. The *Globe and Mail* reviewer, for instance, reported that it was a "good looking volume ... handsomely designed & printed by Coach House Press" (Colombo E13), while Diana Brydon remarked on the "attractively produced volume, with wide margins, good paper and clear print" ("Making" 99). In addition to being involved in the production himself, Ondaatje invites the contributors to send him contributions to the list of "Further Reading of Long, Book-Length or Serial Poems" that has been "Suggested by the Poets and Editor" (341), emphasizing the collaborative nature of the volume.

3. This collection of book-length poems, for the first time, makes possible the serious study of this form and these poems in university classrooms.

The collaborative shaping of the LPA canon did not stop with the layout and design process; the authors were also involved in strategically positioning the text within the academic market. "It is hoped," the initial publicity flyers and early proofs for the anthology began, "that this collection of book-length poems will, for the first time, make possible the serious study of this form ..." (Coach House fonds n.pag.). By the time the volume was actually published, however, there would be no need to "hope" it would accomplish this function; as Ondaatje reports in an undated post-production letter to the authors, approximately half of the print run was pre-sold to colleges. This suggests they could be confident it had successfully tapped into the academic market. How did they do it?

In an early letter to contributors, pre-publication, Ondaatje sets out the objectives for the anthology: "The purpose of the book is two-fold," he writes. "Essentially it is to bring into wider circulation what we think are some of

Figure 6   Cover of *The Long Poem Anthology*, ed. Michael Ondaatje (first printing).

Figure 7   Cover of *The Long Poem Anthology*, ed. Michael Ondaatje (fifth printing).

the most interesting 'long' or 'serial' poems written in recent years.... And to make them (some out of print) available to the reading public" (qtd. in Shearer 21). The collection, as I discussed earlier, is conceived to reach a larger "reading public" than the conditions of production of the original works permitted.

As almost an afterthought—though a significant one—Ondaatje adds that "we also think the book would be a useful one for the university and college classroom, and we hope poets who have been overlooked because of the form they have chosen will sneak dangerously into the classroom" (qtd. in Shearer 21). Two things are worth noting here: first, the word "also" rhetorically separates "the reading public" from the university classroom, rendering them mutually exclusive—something I will return to shortly. Second, the metaphor of poets "sneak[ing] dangerously into the classroom" becomes strategically transformed in Ondaatje's introduction where, in the continued slippage between text and author, stealthy long poems become independent agents: "Long poems crawl out of cupboards, archives, gardens, long bus journeys ..." (11). This animation of the form[18] deflects attention from the poets toward the poems; in each case, it is the "form" that has been "politely ignored" by the readers and schools—not, as Ondaatje's letter to his contributors suggests, the poets. While this rhetorical move probably reflects Ondaatje's impression that "[a]t universities and schools teachers are preoccupied with certain aspects of content, with themes, with messages ... that's only half of poetry.... The other half ... [is] style, technique, the method and movement of the poem" (Ondaatje, qtd. in "Moving" 134–35), it also deflects attention from the poets, and the fact that they are all linked to Coach House Press.

Despite the missing visual links noted above, reviewers often recognized the poets' connection to Black Mountain poetics[19] and to *Tish* (Surette, "Ondaatje's" [86]; Brydon, "Making" [100]; Levenson, [6]), but few noticed their connection to Coach House or suggested the obvious parallel between the *LPA* and a book like Margaret Atwood's *Survival* to which Davey points:

> Ondaatje's very successful *Long Poem Anthology* (1979) publicized the press in a different way—by placing many of its authors and editors—George Bowering, Roy Kiyooka, myself, Daphne Marlatt, Robert Kroetsch, Don McKay, bpNichol—into the culturally legitimating format of a textbook, and by placing Ondaatje himself in a canon-making role. Small literary presses had to this time only rarely attempted to influence the legitimation of their own authors by publishing anthologies or criticism: John Sutherland of First Statement Press with *Other Canadians* in 1943, Louis Dudek and Irving Layton of Contact Press with *Canadian Poems 1850–1952* in 1952, and Margaret Atwood for House of Anansi in *Survival* in 1972. Another legitimating effect

of these Sutherland, Dudek/Layton, and Atwood books came from their placing of their own press's authors side by side with previously legitimated ones.
("Beginnings" 47–48)

Indeed, virtually all the poets who had attracted Michael Ondaatje's curiosity were affiliated in some way with Coach House Press.[20] While only one
third of the poems were published by the press, the other authors had all
published a number of works with Coach House Press in the past.[21] The
strategy of collecting small-press authors in an academic anthology was not
only an unusual move for small literary presses at the time, it was also a shift
in direction for Coach House:

> The appearance of these anthologies [*LPA* and Bowering's *Contemporary
> Canadian Poetry Anthology*] at this point in Coach House's history marks a
> direction which the press had been moving towards through the 1974–1982
> period: a desire to be accepted by, and to provide texts for, an academic mar-
> ket. While prior to 1974, Coach House had mocked or shunned the academy,
> producing work that deliberately avoided institutional acceptance, by the
> end of the 1970s the press was attempting to achieve the legitimacy that the
> academy could provide. (Cain 303)

Initially, there seems to have been some ambivalence about the academic market for the anthology. The press and editor clearly recognized the
academy would be a target market, but perhaps hoped the "general reading
public" (by which they seem to mean individuals not currently attending a
postsecondary educational institution) would make up a substantial portion
of their customers, as they had for the press in the past. While granting the
contributors permission to write what they want, Ondaatje also asks them
to keep the academic context in mind while composing their commentaries.
His emphasis in this early letter on strategically aiming the anthology at the
academy is still somewhat tentative: "If you have any spare time to suggest
some names of people [at universities and colleges] you think might be interested please drop me a list" (qtd. in Shearer 22). At this point, the poets'
participation in publicizing the book to an academic audience is something
they "might" do if they can spare the time.

By the time the anthology was in post-production and review copies
were ready, the realization that academia would be the primary market for
the anthology was much clearer. With the press having fully understood the
importance of the academic market for the book, the collaborative publicizing of the anthology became that much more urgent: "We want to push
the book for next year's courses. It would really help therefore if you can
think of <u>any</u> names and addresses or 'angles' we could use in getting teachers

interested in this book"; "for now the main thing is to get the book known and around and considered for courses"; "please talk it up, show it around to friends, and persuade them to buy it and put it on courses" (qtd. in Shearer 22; original underline). Where earlier advertising the volume to academic friends was something the poets "might" do, now the rhetoric is centred on "pushing" the book, thinking of useful "angles" to get this market interested, "persuading" friends to put it on courses. The contributors readily responded. Marlatt and Kroetsch even forwarded lists of American academics to whom a "circular" or desk copy might be sent; Marlatt sent an extensive list that included L=A=N=G=U=A=G=E poets Charles Bernstein and Lyn Hejinian, while Kroetsch requested a review copy for his co-editor of the SUNY Bing-hamton–based *Boundary 2*, William Spanos.

In many ways, the *LPA*—both in terms of its mode of production, and its content—challenged a number of tenets of the academic discipline of "Canadian Literature" as it stood in 1979. First, it refused to present or define an historical "tradition" out of which the collection could be understood to have emerged. In his review of the anthology, Leon Surette gestures toward this issue when he writes: "It is also rather disappointing that the anthol-ogy is exclusively contemporary. It would have been much more useful as a classroom text had it included some of the long poems from the Nine-teenth Century and the first three quarters of this Century" (85). Ondaat-je's anthology did not attempt to appeal to the authority of a tradition, but rather emphasized the contemporary Canadian writing scene by including poems written in the 1970s, with the exception of Robin Blaser's *The Moth Poem*, and by being "governed by curiosity" rather than the "chronological or historical" (Ondaatje, "What" 11). By collecting contemporary writers to insert into an academic canon, and suppressing the "national" from its title, the *LPA* eschews an "imagined totality," formed "by retroactively construct-ing its individual texts as a *tradition*," that would provide "the impression of totality or cultural hegemony. A tradition is 'real,' of course, but only in the sense in which the imaginary is real. A tradition always retroactively unifies disparate cultural productions" (Guillory 33–34). Instead, the *LPA* brings together nine texts produced under similar conditions within thirteen years of each other, avoiding both the nationalist grand narrative that governed Margaret Atwood's *Survival* and the construction of an historical tradition, for Guillory notes, "the larger and more disparate body of works to be ret-roactively unified, the more urgent and totalizing the concept of a tradition is likely to be" (33–34).

The situatedness of the *LPA* renders it a type of publication D. M. R. Bentley has linked to

the maturation in the late 'sixties and early 'seventies of a generation of writers—today's postmodernists—whose "new reading of experience" emphasized the here and now of personal, textual experience at the expense of the
there and then of traditional literary history. Whereas the high Modernists had at least engaged and anthologized representative samples of earlier
Canadian poetry as a means of demonstrating their own superiority, most of
their successors have chosen simply to ignore pre-Modern material and to
concentrate instead on publishing magazines and anthologies by, about, and
for themselves and their associates. ("Bibliocritical" 642)

The postmodern poets' focus on the publication of "magazines and anthologies by, about, and for themselves and their associates" marked a change
on two fronts. First, by engaging in activities that obviously had beneficial
outcome for those poets involved, the focus ran counter to the Victorian
values of self-sacrifice and Arnoldian disinterestedness. Second, and perhaps
more importantly, the act of self-publishing appears to disrupt the notion of
a "naturally" evolving national canon by overtly collapsing the arm's-length
production of value.[22]

This issue of self-publication likewise became a concern at Coach House,
as the press itself sought to become more professionalized around the time of
the *LPA*'s production. During the period of 1975–82, "accurate book-keep-
ing begins," Stephen Cain notes, "and the articles about Coach House in
the 1980s repeatedly emphasize the professional aspects of the house ..."
(270). Frank Davey explains in his Coach House memoir: "A related issue was
whether or not Coach House editors *should* publish their own books through
Coach House. Some editors felt strongly that editors should support the press
aesthetically and financially by publishing much of their best work through it.
[Sarah] Sheard sometimes expressed concern about the appearance of vanity
publishing" ("Beginning" 74n3). Thus, where on one hand "vanity publishing"
collapses the alienation brought about by the division of labour in capitalist
markets, the same process runs counter to the "professional" values of the
academic market Coach House sought to enter.

The purpose of a materialist study of *The Long Poem Anthology* such as
this is not to criticize the editorial process and find it either "flawed" or "successful," but rather to uncover—to the extent possible—the forces at play in
the anthology's production and to the reproduction of its poems in relation
to their first editions. As Charles Bernstein has observed, "[p]oetry, insofar
as it is published, is a social form, and the intersection of the text with social
institutions is *part of* the work, not a corruption of it" (167). As we have seen,
while some of the collaborative and visual aspects may have been lost in
the poems' anthologization, the works became part of a newly collaborative

effort among poets, in the common interest of strategically intervening in the academic book market and classroom.

NOTES

Unpublished correspondence printed with the permission of Daphne Marlatt.

Some portions of this chapter appeared previously in "*Imago* & the Canadian Long Poem: The Cultural Work of George Bowering," published in *Open Letter*, whose permission to reprint is gratefully acknowledged.

1 "it is necessary to cite all of them because they represent, each in its own way, Canadian poetry's move toward postmodernism" (my translation).

2 Now 350 copies.

3 Kiyooka's *Fontainebleau Dream Machine* and MacKinnon's *The Intervals* finally went out of print in 1991.

4 To obtain this figure, I tallied the volumes' list prices in 1979, or, if the volume had gone out of print by that year, I added its list price from the last year it was in print to obtain a total of $39.55. This total takes all volumes into account save for Robin Blaser's *The Moth Poem*, for which I could find no list price.

5 It also marks a major shift for Coach House Press, which, until this publication, had never explicitly marketed its books to an academic audience.

6 Consider also how similar this elision of "public" with "national" is to George Bowering's use of "public" in his introduction to the *Contemporary Canadian Poetry Anthology*, published in 1984 and clearly linked to *The Long Poem Anthology* through its similarly designed cover:

> The public & political hoopla meant almost nothing to the invention of the poetry you will find represented in this book. Diverse as they are, there is one thing these twenty poets hold in common, that being the assumption or belief that the animator of poetry is language. Not politics, not nationalism, not theme, not personality, not humanism, not real life, not the message, not self-expression, not confession, not the nobility of work, not the spirit of the region, not the Canadian Tradition—but language. The centre & impetus, the world & the creator of poetry is language. (n. pag.)

7 As Lynette Hunter notes, "reading tours ... were new to the 60s and may well have grown out of a perception of the popularity of the Beat poets' performances in the US [*sic*]. Jack McClelland was one of the initiators of this kind of publicity, touring Layton, Purdy and Cohen early in the 60s" (274).

8 Smaro Kamboureli is careful to point out that

> this correspondence between gaze and locality does not imply that the poet, as an outsider to the community of Steveston, engages in some version of voyeurism. Voyeurism, "le désir de posséder par le moyen de l'oeil," as Starobinksi defines it ..., is not what constitutes Marlatt's act of writing. Voyeurism is defined by the distance between the subject viewing and the object viewed. Marlatt's gaze, instead of freezing in its hold the motion of the town and keeping the town at a distance, introduces a different erotics: desire that brings together the body (the poet's / the locals'), the town, and language. (121)

9 This construction of the reader as eavesdropping figure is picked up not in the reviews of Ondaatje's anthology, but in a review of Sharon Thesen's 1991 volume *The New Long Poem Anthology*: "To the pleasures of disorder and the pleasures of the book, we

must add the pleasure of curiosity about other souls. The long poem often gives us a 'bio text' (Fred Wah) or 'gynotext' (Tostevin) or poetic diary. We read long poems because we're nosy. Or perhaps, as Bowering says, because we're lonely. We write and read long poems because we can linger in the presence of another" (Sproxton 41). In the *LPA* the reader is actually a double eavesdropper, since "overhearing" becomes a trope that is also used in its introduction to characterize the work of the poet: "In the 70's some poets talked out loud and some listened. These poets [in the anthology] listen to everything. Kroetsch hangs around bars picking up stories like Polonius behind the curtain, others recall childhood language, or hold onto dreams after they have awakened, or speak the unsaid politics of the day. They tempt things out of the quiet of the corner" (13).

10 Stuart MacKinnon's is the poem that most closely articulates the sentiments of Ondaatje's introduction. Consider, for example, how closely the following two passages resemble each other: "These poets do not fully know what they are trying to hold until they near the end of the poem, and this uncertainty, this lack of professional intent, is what allows them to go deep" (Ondaatje, "What" 13). In a self-reflexive passage on composition, MacKinnon writes:

> Not by any conscious act of will
> can we inhabit tense
> but must follow the drift
> of interest or amusement
> or necessity in consciousness
> wandering
>   wholly in the present
> only by surprise
> stunned into awareness (65)

11 "an impeccable presentation, right down to the masterful etchings that illustrate it" (my translation).

12 My thanks to Joe Zezulka for alerting me to this visual connection among these poets. My thanks also to Frank Davey for suggesting the link to *Tish* and for providing me with images of the covers from his own collection.

13 My thanks to Sean Henry, who pointed to this reading of the title.

14 *Allophanes's* dedication, "to Robin Blaser," is missing in its anthologized form, effectively severing its link to Blaser, perhaps in an effort to create the impression of professionalism as it enters, transformed, into an academic market, though this is inconsistent with Kiyooka's dedication of his text to Bowering and Nichol. These dedications, like Marlatt and Minden's epigraph, which I discuss later in this chapter, both gesture toward a larger artistic community. In the case of Bowering and Kiyooka, their dedications work against the bourgeois notion of individual, solitary authors by making these intertextual connections that work to foreground their group context.

15 I was not able to find the exact figures in the Coach House archive material, but the correspondence itself, including the list price of $7.95, suggests certain constraints.

16 In the Coach House correspondence, Ondaatje shows himself to be carefully attuned to the volume's layout and attentive to the integrity of the poems' relationship with the page ("Dear Sarah; Aug 79").

17 Rolland's Zephyr Antique Laid paper is a heavy, high-quality paper used by only a few presses in Canada. Coach House Press, The Porcupine's Quill, and now Gaspereau Press use or have used this paper regularly, marking their commitment to the book as an aesthetic material object. Gaspereau, for instance, describes the paper as "a creamy, sensual book paper" that represents part of their larger philosophy of "making books

that reinstate the importance of the book as a physical object, reuniting publishing and the book arts" ("Gaspereau Press: Background").

18 This same amplification of the poem, mainly through personification, is also deployed on the back cover copy of Don McKay's *Long Sault*, which appeals to the reader by resurrecting the Long Sault: "Long Sault lives! ... You might run across him playing sax and chasing women in a Kapuskasing bar.... Sometimes he works with Don McKay. In fact he's in this book. It's his energy running these poems ..."

19 Levenson sees this connection to be a drawback for the anthology:

> However, as much of this list [of the anthology's authors] indicates, there is a poetic party line at work here, one that involves *Tish* and Black Mountain, "composition by field" and theories of "the breath." What irritates is not that these theories are necessarily wrong but that their advocates talk and act as if theirs were the only possible kind of poetry that can be written today, that anything that does not derive from the apostolic succession of Pound, Williams, Olson, Creeley and Duncan could not possibly be relevant or worthwhile. (6)

20 In fact, included in the early proofs of the *LPA* was a list of "Other Coach House Books" that was to appear after the "Recommended Reading"; it seems, however, that this list of Coach House Books was included as an "insert" rather than part of the book itself.

21 Works published prior to 1979 by Coach House include George Bowering's *Baseball* (1967), *Geneve* (1971), *Curious* (1973), *Allophanes* (1976), and *Three Vancouver Writers* (1979); Frank Davey's *Weeds* (1970) and *Arcana* (1973); Roy Kiyooka's *The Fontainebleau Dream Machine* (1977), *Nevertheless These Eyes* (1967), and *StoneD-Gloves* (1971); Robert Kroetsch's *The Sad Phoenician* (1979); Daphne Marlatt's *Vancouver Poems* (1972) and *Zocalo* (1977), and her *What Matters: Writing 1968–70* would appear in 1980; Don McKay's *Lightning Ball Bait* was published in 1980; bpNichol's *Journeying & The Returns* (1967), *Two Novels* (1969), *The Martyrology Book 1* (1972), *The Martyrology Book 2* (1972), *The Martyrology Books 3 & 4* (1976), and *Journal* (1978).

22 Lynette Hunter touches on vanity publishing in her chapter on "Alternative Publishing in Canada" in *Outsider Notes*: "Publishing was one of the earliest capitalist ventures and has survived through a thorough understanding and exploitation of underlying economic practices of capitalism; printers simply run factories; booksellers will only stock items they think will sell, and that factor depends on readers with a regular disposable income. The only way to break this central control over production is to publish writing yourself, or print it yourself, or sell it yourself. There are two provisos: first, you have to be sure of an audience, and second you need to be able to afford the cost of printing" (31–32).

WORKS CITED

Bennett, Donna. "Conflicted Vision: A Consideration of Canon and Genre in English-Canadian Literature." *Canadian Canons: Essays in Literary Value*. Ed. Robert Lecker. Toronto: U of Toronto P, 1991. 131–49. Print.

———. "Encroaching on the Canon." *Open Letter 9.5–6 (Kroetsch at Niederbronn)* (1996): 33–42. Print.

Bentley, D. M. R. "Bibliocritical Afterword." *Early Long Poems on Canada*. Ed. D. M. R. Bentley. London ON: Canadian Poetry Press, 1993. Print.

Bernstein, Charles. "McGann Agonist." *Attack of the Difficult Poems: Essays and Inventions*. Chicago: U of Chicago P, 2011. 161–70. Print.

Bowering, George. *Allophanes*. Toronto: Coach House, 1976. Print.

———. "Statement." Thesen, *New Long Poem Anthology*. 351–52. Print.

Brydon, Diana. "Making the Present Continuous." Rev. of *The Long Poem Anthology*, ed. Michael Ondaatje. *Canadian Literature* 86 (1980): 99–100. Print.

Burnham, Clint. *Allegories of Publishing: The Toronto Small Press Scene*. Toronto: Streetcar Editions, 1991. Print.

Butling, Pauline, and Susan Rudy. *Writing in Our Time: Canada's Radical Poetries in English (1957–2003)*. Waterloo: Wilfrid Laurier UP, 2005. Print.

Cain, Stephen. "Imprinting Identities: An Examination of the Emergence and Developing Identities of Coach House Press and House of Anansi Press (1967–1982)." Diss. York University, April 2002. Print.

Coach House Fonds. Library and Archives Canada, Ottawa. LMS-0129 "Coach House 1987-14, Longer Anthol." Box 6C. Print.

Colombo, John Robert. "Length and Destiny: *The Long Poem Anthology*." Rev. of *The Long Poem Anthology*, ed. Michael Ondaatje. *Globe and Mail*. 8 March 1980, E3. Print.

Davey, Frank. "The Beginnings of an End of Coach House Press." *Open Letter* 9.8 (1997): 40–77. Print.

———. *Canadian Literary Power*. Edmonton: NeWest, 1994. Print.

———. *King of Swords*. Vancouver: Talonbooks, 1972. Print.

Fabre, Michel. Rev. of *The Long Poem Anthology*, ed. Michael Ondaatje. *AFRAM Newsletter*. Paris, France: May 1981. 45. Print.

"Gaspereau Press: Background." Gaspereau. Web. 20 March 2008. http://www.gaspereau.com/background.shtml

Geddes, Gary, and Phyllis Bruce, eds. *15 Canadian Poets*. Toronto: Oxford UP, 1970. Print.

Geiger, Roy. "Anthology of Samples Whets Appetite for More Long Poems." Rev. of *The Long Poem Anthology*, ed. Michael Ondaatje. *London Free Press* 29 Mar. 1980, B3. Print.

Golding, Alan. *From Outlaw to Classic: Canons in American Poetry*. Madison: U of Wisconsin P, 1995. Print.

Guillory, John. *Cultural Capital: The Problem of Literary Canon Formation*. Chicago: U of Chicago P, 1993. Print.

Hunter, Lynette. *Outsider Notes: Feminist Approaches to Nation State Ideology, Writers/Readers and Publishing*. Vancouver: Talonbooks, 1996. Print.

"INVENT 79/TXT at year end." Library and Archives Canada, Ottawa. LMS-0129 "Coach House Fonds, 1987–14, Longer Anthol." Box 6C. Print.

Kamboureli, Smaro. *On the Edge of Genre: The Contemporary Canadian Long Poem*. Toronto: U of Toronto P, 1991. Print.

Kiyooka, Roy. *The Fontainebleau Dream Machine*. Toronto: Coach House, 1977. Print.

Kröller, Eva Marie. "Roy Kiyooka's 'The Fontainebleau Dream Machine': A Reading." *Canadian Literature* 113–14 (1987): 47–58. Print.

Levenson, Christopher. "Editorial: The Long Poem in Canada." *ARC* 7 (1982): 5–8. Print.

Livesay, Dorothy. "The Documentary Poem: A Canadian Genre," in Mandel, *Contexts*. 267–81. Print.

MacKinnon, Stuart. *Intervals*. Toronto: Coach House, 1974. Print.

Mandel, Eli. Introduction. *Contexts of Canadian Criticism: A Collection of Critical Essays*. Ed. Eli Mandel. Chicago: U of Chicago P 1971. 3–25. Print.

Marlatt, Daphne. Letter to Michael Ondaatje, n.d. Coach House Fonds. Library and Archives Canada, Ottawa. LMS-0129 "Coach House, 1987-14. Longer. Anthol." Box 6C. Print.

——, and Robert Minden. *Steveston*. Vancouver: Talonbooks, 1974. Print.

McCaffery, Steve. *North of Intention: Critical Writings 1973–1986*. New York: Roof Books, 1986. Print.

Miki, Roy. *Broken Entries: Race, Writing, and Subjectivity*. Toronto: Mercury, 1998. Print.

Nichol, bp. "Discussion." *Open Letter* 6.2–3 (1985): 278–98. Print.

Ondaatje, Michael. "Dear Roy." Letter to Roy Kiyooka, Robin Blaser, Robert Kroetsch, Don McKay, George Bowering, Frank Davey, Stuart MacKinnon, and bpNichol. n.d. Coach House Fonds. Library and Archives Canada, Ottawa. LMS-0129 "Coach House 1987-14, Longer Anthol." Box 6C. Print.

——. "Dear Sarah." Letter to Sarah Sheard. August 1979. Coach House Fonds. Library and Archives Canada, Ottawa. LMS-0129 "Coach House 1987-14, Longer Anthol." Box 37. Print.

——. "Hello." Letter to Roy Kiyooka, Robin Blaser, Robert Kroetsch, Don McKay, George Bowering, Frank Davey, Stuart MacKinnon, and bpNichol. n.d. Coach House Fonds. Library and Archives Canada, Ottawa. LMS-0129 "Coach House 1987-14, Longer Anthol." Box 6C. Print.

——. "Moving to the Clear: Michael Ondaatje." Interview with Jon Pearce. *12 Voices: Interview with Canadian Poets*. Jon Pearce, ed. Ottawa: Borealis, 1980. 130–44. Print.

——. "What Is in the Pot." Introduction to *The Long Poem Anthology*. 11–18. Print.

——, ed. *The Long Poem Anthology*. Toronto: Coach House, 1979. Print.

Shearer, Karis. "*Imago* & The Canadian Long Poem: The Cultural Work of George Bowering." *Open Letter* 12.4 (2010): 13–29. Print.

Sproxton, Birk. "Lingering Longer: The Pleasures of the Long Poem." Rev. of *The New Long Poem Anthology*, 1st ed., ed. Sharon Thesen. *Border Crossings* 11.3 (1992): 39–41. Print.

Struthers, Betsy. Rev. of *The Long Poem Anthology*, ed. Michael Ondaatje. *Canadian Book Review Annual* 1979. Ed. Dean Tudor. Toronto: PMA Books, 1980. 138–39. Print.

Struthers, J. R. (Tim). "Anthologies." *New Canadian Encyclopedia of Literature in Canada*. Ed. William H. New. U of Toronto P, 2002. 31–35. Print.

Surette, Leon. "Ondaatje's Long Poem Anthology." Rev. of *The Long Poem Anthology*, ed. Michael Ondaatje. *Canadian Poetry* 6 (1980): 85–88. Print.

Thesen, Sharon. "Introduction." *The New Long Poem Anthology*. Ed. Sharon Thesen. Toronto: Coach House, 1991. Print.

———, ed. *The New Long Poem Anthology*. Toronto: Coach House, 1991. Print.
Winger, Rob. "Call for Papers." ACCUTE, 2008. 10 October 2007. Print.

Why So Serious?

The Quirky Canadian Literary Anthology

Lorraine York

A nthologies are a serious business. At least this is what anthologists and critics have told us. In 1928, though, Laura Riding and Robert Graves feared that English-language anthologies were in danger of becoming unserious. They launched a broadside against thematically organized, topical trade anthologies: treasuries of love poems, poems celebrating trees, flowers, cats, dogs.... Actually, Riding and Graves were critical of *any* anthologizing of poetry—any act of removing poems from the context of a poet's individual collection or oeuvre—but the topical anthology seemed, from their perspective, to embody the worst-case scenario and most egregious instance of this decontextualization. And so Riding and Graves derisively imagined the topical anthologies that were likely to spring up in the future, if this worrisome trend were not corrected: "*Vitamin E Poems, Poems of Television, Death-Ray Poems*, and so forth" (167). The classist assumptions of their attack are palpable, and perhaps, in the historical context of Riding and Graves's modernism, unsurprising. But in more recent critical works devoted to anthologies, such topical collections are no longer even much worth deriding; they do not even seem to be visible. In recognized texts like Jeffrey R. Di Leo's collection *On Anthologies: Politics and Pedagogy*, the anthology is assumed to be synonymous with the academic anthology, and every contributor assumes that the relevant field of cultural production is the academy and the academy alone. In his extensive essay "On Anthologies," David Hopkins is unusual in that he does "see" the topical anthology, but he uses it as a brief, amusing hook that prefaces a long argument about academic anthologies. Citing Riding and Graves's *A Pamphlet Against Anthologies*, he notes that "There are various practical and commercial reasons why publishers are still willing to produce, and why readers, both 'general' and academic, are still keen to buy anthologies" (285). Notably, the academic reader is not contained in nervous scare quotes, whereas the general reader (who are these people?) is. Hopkins notes the continued demand in "the 'general reader'" (scare quoted once more) to obtain thematic collections "which fulfil some of the traditional functions of poetry: to console in times of bereavement, to fortify against stress or anxiety, to give expression to love and friendship, to celebrate special occasions, or simply to entertain and amuse" (285). Tellingly, these "traditional" functions, implicitly characterized as naive and unsophisticated, are all marked by affect rather than intellect. And in describing them, Hopkins slides from the term "poetry" to the down-market moniker "verse": "And ordinary readers still seem to like to collect volumes of verse on their favourite interests or preoccupations: religion, gardens, food, sport, music, art, animals, birds, travel, topography, war" (285). Having established this quaint persistence of a hobbyist interest, Hopkins turns, for the rest of his lengthy article, to the anthologies that he clearly takes more seriously: the academic anthologies of the Oxford and Cambridge variety.

I am interested in a particular subset of the thematic, topical anthology as it continues to manifest itself in Canadian literary life: the quirky literary anthology. By quirky, I refer not necessarily to the mode of the writing contained therein, though the poems and stories may indeed assume a comic tone. Or they may not. What is quirky in the anthologies that I examine is their principle of organization. That principle is not, primarily, to identify the Arnoldian "best which has been thought and said"—or even that which is most representative of a cultural moment or movement. Their principle of organization could be summed up, instead, as taxonomy itself: categorization for the sheer pleasure of categorization. Titles like Greg Gatenby's 1977 *Whale Sound: An Anthology of Poems about Whales and Dolphins*; the stereotypically 1960s collection edited by Doug Fetherling, *Thumbprints: An Anthology of Hitchhiking Poems* (1969); *100% Cracked Wheat: The Exciting New Saskatchewan Breakfast Cereal in Book Form* (1983)—so successful that it germinated a second volume, *200% Cracked Wheat*; *$10 Cash Value: An Anthology of Assets* (2000)—poems that mention money; *Boredom Fighters* (2008)—a visual/verbal experimental volume that seeks to fight the boredom created by more staidly traditional anthologies; *Panty Lines* (2000)—an anthology of poems that mention underwear;[1] and that triumph of the taxonomical, *Desperately Seeking Susans* (2012)—an anthology of poetry by Canadian poets named Susan.

In this chapter, I ask how quirky anthologies relate to seriousness as a culturally mandated approach to anthologization. What relation does their quirkiness bear to the nation-building canonical operations of "serious" anthologies and to the academy, the bastion of those operations? How does their market operate and what, for that matter, is their market? I maintain that a study of anthologies that does not pay attention to the quirky/niche/popular anthology risks not recognizing a significant part of the literary activity of this country. Not studying these anthologies is tantamount to auto/-biographical critics not studying popular or celebrity autobiographies, those life writings that account for a considerable portion of the market share of auto/biographical texts in this country and many others.

"You Were Silly Like Us": Our History of Quirky Anthologies

A 2012 article published in *Maclean's* on the occasion of the publication of *Desperately Seeking Susans* argues that the quirky anthology is a new trend, but research[2] suggests that it is anything but. The author of this essay, Joanne Latimer, suggests that the unusually themed collection is a novel marketing device, "a new trend where publishers rely on quirky anthology themes to lure readers" (n. pag.). Marty Gervais, the editor and publisher at Black Moss Press, the publisher of the volume, agrees that market considerations are at the heart of his press's production of these volumes: "You need an edge, something unique," he notes (Latimer n. pag.). Black Moss Press has indeed carved out something of a specialization in this genre; John B. Lee, for instance, has edited several niche anthologies for Black Moss: *That Sign of Perfection: From Bandy Legs to Beer Legs* (1995)—writings on hockey; *Losers First: Poems and Stories on Game and Sport* (1999); *Henry's Creature: Poems and Stories on the Automobile* (2000); and *Body Language: A Head-to-Toe Anthology* (2003). And Black Moss seems poised to continue the trend; in 2011 they published, in addition to other themed anthologies, *The White Collar Book: Poetry and Prose of Canadian Business Life*, with a foreword by Conrad Black. Now that is quirky, to say the least.

But against the claim of *Maclean's* that these niche publications represent a recent, market-driven trend, we have evidence of a long history of such volumes in our collective literary life. As Robert Lecker, interviewed for the *Maclean's* story, pointed out, "Previously, Canadian poetry anthologies were grouped primarily around region, nature, gender and sometimes hockey, but the Susan project is part of the tradition of weird and wonderful themes" (n. pag.). Lecker's bibliographical survey *English-Canadian Literary Anthologies* (1997) amply demonstrates that tradition, with entries such as: *Crustula Juris: Being a Collection of Leading Cases Done into Verse* (1913); *Rhymes of the Miner: An Anthology of Canadian Mining Verse* (1937); *Beastly Ballads* (1954); *Cap and Bells: An Anthology of Light Verse* (1936); and, of course, *The Blasted Pine: An Anthology of Satire, Invective and Disrespectful Verse Chiefly by Canadian Writers* (1957). Some of these volumes have managed to migrate into our mainstream literary history, particularly John Garvin and Lorne Pierce's *Cap and Bells* and F. R. Scott and A. J. M. Smith's *The Blasted Pine*.

Cap and Bells was originally to be edited by John Garvin, but when he unexpectedly died shortly before publication, Lorne Pierce took over the honing of the selections and saw the volume through the press in 1936. In his preface to the collection, which was largely dedicated to a eulogy for Garvin, Pierce reveals, by the way, a fascinating perspective on the "serious" anthology and its less-serious confreres:

> He [Garvin] felt that our literature and art were too solemn, that they did not move blithely enough. While the oft-mentioned epic of nation building might be offered as some excuse for gravity and earnestness, it also presented innumerable occasions for gaiety and even robust nonsense. The absence of this note in a more marked degree appeared to John Garvin as a serious fault, a lack of poise and detachment in our life, some fundamental neglect. (vii)

In this passage, Pierce takes apart the basic assumption upon which rests the distinction between serious anthologies that document our national literatures and quirky ones that do not. There is nothing inherently serious about the subject of nation-building, he argues; it may be approached in any number of modes. But we have continued, in the decades since *Cap and Bells*, to invest cultural capital in anthologies that foreground nation-building as a serious—if problematic and anxious—act.

For all of the potentially disruptive nature of Garvin's insight, Pierce nevertheless strives to legitimize Garvin's opinions about the desirability of "gaiety and even robust nonsense" by making it clear that he was a serious, qualified scholar of Canadian literature. Before telling us of Garvin's concern about Canadian literature's lack of amusement and tonal range, Pierce recounts his signal "serious" achievements, as editor of the first definitive edition of Isabella Valancy Crawford's poems and, especially, his editing of *Canadian Poets*, an anthology that "none has surpassed" (vi). So in the framing of Garvin's career, the serious was mobilized to compensate for his interest in lighter fare.

In terms of content, *Cap and Bells* plays with distinctions between the serious and the light, sometimes reaffirming and sometimes playfully smudging them. Poets who were, and would continue to be, heavily anthologized as serious poets were amply represented (Charles G. D. Roberts, E. J. Pratt, Isabella Valancy Crawford), but so were poets whose reputations would now be described by a traditionally canonical critic as "minor" and less "serious" (William Henry Drummond, Jean Blewett, Robert Service). Drawing poets who were at home in Garvin's "serious" anthology *Canadian Poets* into this celebration of "light verse" reinforced Garvin's point about the integral role of comic writing in the Canadian canon of the day. Clearly, for Garvin, the Canadian poetic community was not to be unexceptionally divided into serious and light poets. Today, though, poets have had to work hard to smudge that line again.

Another reason for the coziness that editors like Garvin could imagine between "light" poetry and serious literary nation-building was that humour could, on occasion, be folded into earnest moral purposes. Looking to the late nineteenth century, a book like Charles Carroll Everett's *Poetry, Comedy, and Duty* made such an argument explicit in its very title. As Everett expatiated, "Comedy is the corrector as truly as the helper of the earnest life. Without it the poetic may become sentimental, and the heroic the burlesque.... Thus comedy may be the helper of the higher life in which the love of beauty and the moral sense have the controlling place" (314–15). As Canadian literature slowly became institutionalized over the next few decades, pedagogical imperatives were one reason for the widening gulf between occasional anthologies and those that explicitly thematized the growth and development of a national literature. As Robert Lecker argues in *Keepers of the Code*:

> In earlier decades [i.e., before the 1970s], anthologists had imagined a popular audience for their collections, underlining their assumption that the appreciation of Canadian literature was something that could be gained by the reading public at large. But now an important change set in: anthologists understood that the main readers of their books would be students and that in order to reach those students, they had to appeal to the professors and teachers who had become canonical gatekeepers ... (267–68)

Although Lecker focuses on "pan-Canadian" anthologies in his study—those that take the measure of the literature of the nation—his observation also illuminates what I see as the growing gulf between the academic and the quirkily specialist anthology.

Even at mid-twentieth century, as this process of professionalization was taking shape, and as modernist poets, in particular, called for Canadian writing to be taken seriously on an international stage, those same poets were some of the most enthusiastic participants in the anthology publication of comic poetry. The obvious case in point is F. R. Scott and A. J. M. Smith's *The Blasted Pine: An Anthology of Satire, Invective and Disrespectful Verse Chiefly by Canadian Writers* (1957). In their case, they saw the comic, particularly in its satirical forms, as wholly compatible with cosmopolitan disdain for parochial verities. As Scott wrote in his introduction, the poets anthologized in *The Blasted Pine* are sharply critical, in one way or another, of some aspect of Canadian life that has more often been accepted uncritically. They have been chosen because they sound a sour note. Their tone is harsh, sometimes unrefined, sometimes, perhaps, distorted, but always unsentimental—the noise that common sense makes, or the whisper of intelligence. It is a note which has generally been drowned out in the diapason of praise with which Canadian poets have hymned the glories of the True North Strong and Free. (xiii)

In one sense, then, this was Charles Carroll Everett turned on his head. But the satirical poets of *The Blasted Pine* were earnest in their own way, training their invective upon the Maple Leaf school of national culture; like Everett, who warned that, without comedy, "the poetic may become sentimental," Scott, Smith, et al. scorned sentimentality at all costs.

Quirkily themed anthologies, then, have served at various times to uphold or challenge prevailing ideas about the relationship between the quirky or humorous and national culture. They could uphold earnestness, duty, and patriotism just as readily as they could pillory those same national projects. Whichever position on these questions they assumed, there is no doubt that they were—and continue to be—a crucial part of the ongoing debates over our literary cultures and values.

WHY SO SERIOUS?: SERIOUSNESS AND THE ANTHOLOGY

There are good reasons why, in our pedagogical and critical practices, anthologies became serious, and why their editors moved away from Garvin's conviction that "the oft-mentioned epic of nation building ... also presented innumerable occasions for gaiety and even robust nonsense" (vii). The indigenous genocide that lay at the heart of the epic of Canadian nation-building is the most pressing and obvious reason. Accordingly, as Linda Tuhiwai Smith observes, for writers of colour, the anthology can be of tactical use; as she reminds us, "In the New Zealand context the lack of a literature was used at the beginning of the twentieth century to deny the teaching of Maori language in the university" (522). In the Canadian context, our scholarship on literary anthologies has been mindful of what is at stake, both in terms of visibility and in terms of contesting the nature of what is already visible in our national culture; as Robert Lecker notes:

As cultural texts, national literature anthologies carry a special burden. They transmit a particular world vision, a deliberate textual construction of the country that the reader is invited to join. By promoting this construction, these anthologies become deeply conflicted books. Their editors have to wrestle with questions about how the nation is mirrored in its literature and about the extent to which its existing literary canons (when such canons exist) should be repudiated or reproduced. ("Nineteenth-Century" 92)

Lecker's diction consistently underscores this burden: "anxious process"; "conflicted process"; "compromised," "anxieties" ("Nineteenth-Century" 93–94).

There is no question that our literature anthologies should continue to lead this conflicted existence and to shoulder this burden. However, this may not be all that an anthology can be understood to do, and those anthologies that do not understand their terms of reference in this way should not be consigned to invisibility in our critical discourses. In the article "Creating Anthologies and Other Dangerous Practices," in which she affirms the political exigencies at stake in their production, Linda Tuhiwai Smith also opens the door a crack to admit other reasons for assembling an anthology:

> However that sense of creating tradition or framing a canon as an act of resistance is but one motivation for producing an anthology. The anthology to some symbolizes an act of decentering and deprivileging the authoritative academic tome. It is a pedagogical process that creates a space for different voices and different possibilities. (523)

Although the anthologies that I consider in this essay are not even vaguely akin to the ones that Tuhiwai Smith considers in her essay, it is possible that niche anthologies, even those of the more quirky variety, are trying to create those spaces apart from academic understandings of what an anthology looks like and seeks to accomplish.

Robert Lecker's conclusion to his essay "The Canonization of Canadian Literature: An Inquiry into Value" is similarly rich in its implications for an alternative way to understand and value trade anthologies:

> My conclusion: Canadian critics find it impossible and even treasonous to deal with the Canadian canon in terms other than those embodied in the canon itself. We may hear calls for criticism that will uninvent, demythologize, or decenter text and world; and we may find occasional celebrations of noncanonized writing. But the canonized criticism, like the enshrined poetry and fiction, remains conservative, moral, documentary, sociological, and realistic in approach. (670–71)

Lecker's insight into the way in which the nature of the canon inflects criticism applies equally to the form of criticism known as the making of anthologies; it, too, remains "conservative, moral, documentary, sociological, and realistic in approach"—in a word, serious.

How, then, do quirky anthologies in Canada deal with this canonical anthological seriousness? In various ways, but deal with it they all do. Some seek to legitimize their quirky focus by hitching it to a serious cultural objective. For example, *Tributes to the Scarlet Riders: An Anthology of Mountie Poems* (2003) balances its niche focus (to quote the publisher's website: "Collectively, they will entertain anyone who has ever been or known a Mountie") with claims of seriousness. The publisher, Heritage House, observes that the poems contained in the collection range "from humorous to poignant" and "reflect the moods and adventures of Arctic survivors, plains horsemen, vulnerable trainees and witty veterans," and their chosen blurb, from retired Commissioner J. P. R. (Phil) Murray, similarly assures us that comedy will be counterbalanced by serious content: "The long and storied history of Canada's national police force is full of folklore, mythology and good humour but also, all too often, sadness and tragedy. Ed Kuhn's anthology captures all those elements" (Heritage House website).

A similar need for assurances of seriousness runs through the few reviews that are devoted to quirky anthologies. For example, Robert J. Wiersema, reviewing *Going Top Shelf: An Anthology of Canadian Hockey Poetry* (as stereotypical a national mythological subject as the Mounties) assures readers of *Quill & Quire* that it is "a pretty fine collection, despite the subject matter" (n. pag.).

On the other hand, there are those anthologies that seize upon Linda Tuhiwai Smith's strategy: "decentering and depriviliging the authoritative academic tome" rather than playing at the seriousness sweepstakes. For example, the editors of *100% Cracked Wheat: The Exciting New Saskatchewan Breakfast Cereal in Book Form* set up their volume as the antidote to the pedagogically familiar selection of prairie literature; one of their imagined people-in-the-street reviewers comments: "I always thought you guys were into the heavy-sledding, stuff with deep social significance, the existential angst of prairie survival, that kind of deal. Isn't that what Canadian writers are all about, especially in Saskatchewan?" (iii). The editors sound the same note in concluding their introduction to the volume: "No longer are our writers a stolid, doleful lot given to composing dirges about dust and drought" (iv). The selections familiar to student readers of the mainstream anthologies—Sinclair Ross's "The Painted Door" or Anne Marriott's "The Wind Our Enemy"—are nowhere to be found.

Desperately Seeking Susans, edited by Sarah Yi-Mei Tsiang for Oolichan Press, takes this approach even further, poking fun at the project of serious anthology-making in general. Her call for submissions made it clear that this would be an anti-anthology of sorts: "Though many anthologies purport to establish a new canon, *Desperately Seeking Susans* simply luxuriates in the ridiculous surfeit of talent that exists not only within Canadian poetry, not only within Canadian female poetry, but within female Canadian poets named Susan" (Steinberg 10). Here, again, is the contrast between the intellectual project ("purport to establish") and affect ("luxuriates"). And in its jokey honing of the anthology's taxonomy, from "Canadian poetry" to "Canadian female poetry" to "female Canadian poets named Susan," Oolichan Press implicitly asks, why is this taxonomy ridiculous, whereas a survey of "Canadian poets" or "Canadian female poets" is not? Where is the dividing line between serious and quirky taxonomies in anthology production, anyway?

The media did decide, though, that *Desperately Seeking Susans* was on the far side of seriousness, and so the volume received a certain amount of amused coverage, in both print and radio media. Sarah Steinberg, writing in *Broken Pencil*, reproduced the collection's call for submissions and then produced a parodic riff on the concept: "Well, after we went into a second pressing of our *What About Bob? Anthology*—and who would've thought that we'd sell out all 50 copies in that first year? Believe you me when I tell you we certainly did not see *that* coming" (10). The irony is compounded when one considers that *Broken Pencil* prides itself on its indie credibility and yet here, while it humorously takes up the implicit invitation from *Desperately Seeking Susans* to respond to their project in a quirky, non-serious spirit, its satire also serves to police the boundaries of mainstream and outré ideas. Ironically, small-scale production becomes a target for their indie lampoonery.

When interviewed for the *Maclean's* article on the volume, several of the Susans made it clear that the volume did not so much pose a direct challenge to standards of academic seriousness; it was more the case that those standards did not apply and that they circulated in another cultural field (as Pierre Bourdieu would say) entirely:

> When asked if such a light-hearted project could damage their reputations in serious poetry circles, the Susans roared. "We don't really know who those people are," said [Susan] Musgrave. "I've already been written off by everyone anyway!" laughed Susan Holbrook. (Latimer n. pag.)

Interviewed on this very question, George Bowering agreed that anthologies like *Desperately Seeking Susans* operate in another sphere entirely: "Academics won't even read it. They don't go to poetry readings and they don't buy poetry magazines" (Latimer n. pag.). What is more interesting than the relative or questionable accuracy of Bowering's assertions is the belief that these spheres are separate: that the academic anthology and the quirkily themed anthology have parted cultural company.

This perception of difference—what Linda Tuhiwai Smith calls the "decentering and depriviling [of the] the authoritative academic tome"—is one that contributors and publishers alike are willing to emphasize in their marketing of quirky volumes. Noelle Allan, Wolsak and Wynn's publisher, argues that "[d]eliberately idiosyncratic anthologies, like the Susans, help people get over any bad high school experience they might've had with a poetry book.... Canadians have the wrong idea about Canadian poetry— that it's boring and old-fashioned" (Latimer n. pag.). So these volumes are being positioned as alternatives to the purveyors of seriousness: academic and especially educational publishers' offerings.

In spite of the protestations of resistance to the criterion of seriousness, a supplemental justification for the seriousness of these avowedly non-serious books is always lurking in the background. Editor Sarah Yi-Mei Tsiang's introduction initially characterizes the collection as a product of a moment of frivolous comedy; one day she "idly" asked her husband to guess which Canadian poet named Susan she was thinking of—and he guessed seven Susans without lighting on the correct one. In a corresponding spirit of fun and games, she insists that this is an "unapologetically whimsical anthology," but immediately proceeds to justify the quality of the work therein, pointing out that all the poets included were chosen for "the beauty of their work" and adding that they "have won just about every major literary award there is to win in Canada" (n. pag.). Suddenly, the rationale for the collection is looking less apologetically whimsical and is nudging closer to more traditional mainstream rationales for canonical inclusion.

A similar dividedness appears in poet (and contributor) Sue Goyette's rationale for the anthology: "It'll help us break down the tired old reputation of poetry being inaccessible. The spine of what's connecting us—our name— isn't heavy, but the work is serious" (Latimer n. pag.). So Goyette is saying, in effect, we're not serious. Except that we are.

Another trade anthology that more consistently mocks the aspirations of mainstream literary collections is *Panty Lines: A Poetic Anthology*, published by Blue Moon Press in Lanzville, British Columbia, in 2000. It was the result of a contest in which poets submitted poems that contain at least one mention of underwear. In its paratextual sections—dedication and back cover blurb—it roundly parodies the language of politer, serious national anthologies. The epigraph reads: "To the hundreds of participants in the world-wide search for The Great Canadian Panty Poem whose enthusiasm more than matched our own—this book's for you" (n. pag.). This is a nod to the much-debated 1978 Calgary Conference on the Novel that produced, most controversially, a list of the Ten Best Canadian Novels to date. And on the back cover of *Panty Lines* appears another swipe at nation-building anthologies and their rhetorics: "Whether we wear them or not, panties define us."

ANTHOLOGIES, LIKE PANTIES, DEFINE US: NATION-BUILDING AND THE QUIRKY ANTHOLOGY

Decades of canon-questioning have taught us that anthologies, among other pedagogical activities, define us as a nation; as Robert Lecker opens his essay on "Nineteenth-Century English-Canadian Anthologies and the Making of a National Literature," "The publication and dissemination of national literature anthologies involves imagining a country, imagining a community, imagining an identity" (92). Many anthologies have made this act of imagination explicit, in their titles or section titles; even a "light" collection such as Garvin and Pierce's *Cap and Bells* contains a section called "Nation and Country." Still, the emphasis of many of the more recent quirky anthologies on actively subverting the academic, nation-centred anthology would seem to set them apart from this act of national imagination. The editors of *100% Cracked Wheat*, for example, are determined to depart from the NFB-wind-blown-wheat-fields image of the prairies, and the poems collected therein do not seem, collectively, to be selected or arranged so as to form a national narrative. Still, however much these anthologists would prefer to jettison "the nation" in favour of alternate means of organization, the fact of the nation does continue to affect their composition and arrangement.

First of all, historically, the quirky anthologies that have formed a part of our literary history have often taken as their raison d'être a stereotypical symbol of our national imaginary: hockey, mining, forests. This continues to be the case; examples include: *An Anthology of Steam Railroad Poetry* (1986); *Losers First: Poems and Stories on Game and Sport* (1999); *Tributes to the Scarlet Riders: An Anthology of Mountie Poems* (2003); *Going Top Shelf: An Anthology of Canadian Hockey Poetry* (2005). Even an anthology like *100% Cracked Wheat* that sets itself against such clichés of place is still defined by that place—and its clichés: hockey, for instance, in Geoffrey Ursell's "Last Minute of Play" and Mounties and wheat in Barbara Sapergia's comic tale "Orest Kulak's Wonderful New Wheat."

National clichés, then, are more difficult to overthrow than it would seem, and one sign that at least some of these quirky anthologies are working in tandem with those clichés rather than challenging them is their record of library holdings. The holdings in public and university libraries for volumes such as *Tribute to the Scarlet Riders: An Anthology of Mountie Poems* and *Going Top Shelf: An Anthology of Canadian Hockey Poetry* are far more extensive than those of other, less nationally themed collections.[3] A further irony that arises from these data is that, although quirky texts are understood by their editors, publishers, and contributors to be trade texts that speak to a non-academic general reader, they are much more frequently to be found in university libraries than in public ones. This raises the question: what, really, is the market for the quirky anthology?

SELLING QUIRKY

On the surface, the quirky anthology is a trade text that is, at least theoretically, directed to a general reader; they are seen as mass-market texts that are expected to generate some degree of profit (often as gift books). Bob Currie, Gary Hyland, and Jim McLean, editors of *100% Cracked Wheat*, subject this very assumption about markets to a rather revealing comic treatment:

> We ... decided that penury of the most profound sort should be no hindrance to our publishing a mass market paperback. If we couldn't woo writers with the promise of untold riches, we'd offer them the compensatory fame of having their works on the supermarket shelves prominently displayed somewhere between browning bunches of bananas and a special on rubber gloves....We also had one eye (the glazed one) on the legitimate book-store market. (i–ii)

The mass market is comically rendered as a literary supermarket, one haunted by the "legitimate" book trade. Comically, it is true, its wares are relegated to the realm of bodily rather than intellectual food. For all of the editors' joking about the elusive dream of riches, the fact is that the volume did sell exceedingly well. As of 1995, a dozen years after publication, the collection had sold 10,000 copies, "almost 20 times the volume of an average poetry title" (Melnyk), and gone through several printings. It is held extensively in Canadian and American libraries, both university and public, particularly in prairie regions, as one would expect. It was not, however, reviewed by an academic journal—and that is true of most of the quirky anthologies under study. Taken together, these findings tell us that the market for these volumes, like the mass market generally, is by no means homogeneous; furthermore, it is a market that is riven by ironies. These are collections that often, as I have demonstrated, pride themselves on their departures from academic anthologizing, and yet they are more often held by university libraries than by public ones. They are not often (or, in many cases, not ever) reviewed by scholars. But if their theme falls under the general category of "Canadiana," then they are more likely to attract media coverage, and will tend to be bought by libraries here and abroad. Again, the force of national narratives, most frequently analyzed in relation to academic anthologies, reaches into the general market for quirky, niche volumes. The power of nation to sell books reaches far beyond the classroom and the research library.

So too the force of individual literary celebrities or canonized writers. Although these collections do not, at first glance, appear to capitalize upon the workings of literary celebrity to boost their circulation or, at least, to provide an immediately visible marketing hook, a closer look shows that potent force at work in more circuitous ways. For example, in her review of *Desperately Seeking Susans*, Shannon Webb-Campbell sees Susan Musgrave's "Susanly contribution[s] … anchoring the anthology" (n. pag.). Perhaps in an effort to short-circuit this stargazing, *100% Cracked Wheat*'s contents page identifies poems by title rather than author, though the back-cover blurb highlights specific, canonically recognized authors: Lorna Crozier, Anne Szumigalski, Patrick Lane, Andrew Suknaski. Some of these poems are ones that appear in these poets' volumes and collected works: poems like Lane's "Annie She" and Crozier's "The Women Who Survive." But here, they appear collected alongside works that would never qualify for canonization: naughty limericks, for instance, of which the collection boasts quite a number. In the poems that are clearly not candidates for CanLit university courses, though, it's revealing to see a resistance to academic consecration at work. To quote Cy Shaw's "Academic":

In Ivory Tower
they yak by the hour—
academic pitter-patter.

But on the street
such talk's effete—
the alma doesn't matter. (298)

We have something interesting going on here: poems that have already been canonized, by poets who have earned a share of literary celebrity, sit side by side with downgraded poetic forms like the limerick, in a self-conscious blurring of the "proper" categorizations of anthology construction.

In these quirky anthologies, there is a measure of self-consciousness about their refusal to play by the rules or, indeed, to respect the rules of canonized literary value. A sign of this, besides the insouciant juxtapositions of a volume like *100% Cracked Wheat*, is the prevalence of the self-conscious poem or story: a text that revels in the thumbing of the nose at literary politesse that these collections specialize in. Consider, for instance, Bill Smith's self-conscious contribution to *$10 Cash Value: An Anthology of Assets*—a volume that is, like *Panty Lines*, the result of a poetic contest, in this case, to write poems that mention money. In "If You've Got the Money Honey," Smith's persona reflects that, although he has never worshipped money per se,

... he couldn't miss a contest
with a Clink connected theme.
Writing verses about Lolly or Doubloons
for a spot in an anthology,
immortalised perhaps,
he'd come down to earth
and sing a Loonie tune. (Langs and Smith 61)

This is all fun and games (or fund and games, more appropriately, perhaps), but even so, the poem's self-consciousness discloses its own anxieties. Smith's self-consciousness allows him to proclaim that he, for one, is not taking this cultural production too seriously, and that he is aware of the volume's earthy parameters. Roundly sending up the traditional poetic bid for immortality, Smith associates the monetary theme of the collection with a distinct, boastful lack of seriousness in this self-described "Loonie tune."

Desperately Seeking Susans has its own self-conscious poem that meditates quite brilliantly on the anthology as regulation, linking it to the social regulation of women's behaviour: Susan Holbrook's "Oolichan Books Is Seeking Submissions for a New Anthology of Female Canadian Poets Named Susan." In this prose poem, Holbrook riffs on the reputation of "Susans" as socially compliant women of their (postwar) generation: "Aside from B. Anthony, we don't make waves" (Holbrook 118). As the poem proceeds, the speaker calls upon the Susans to rise up, to "try road rage. Let's call someone the asshole that they are" (Holbrook 118). She imagines what might happen "[i]f all the Susans turned off the nice" (Holbrook 118). And, in a final stroke of self-conscious irony, she closes her poem with a found sentence from the call for submissions for which her poem is named: "If your poems are accepted, we will require a proof of your name as Susan, or a reasonable variant, (e.g., photocopy of your driver's licence" (Tsiang 118). Holbrook shows us the persistence of social regulation, the continuing reach of the law, but in leaving that final, found sentence unstoppered by a final parenthesis or a period, she leaves open the possibility that the Susans might just rise up to rage against the machine after all.

In another self-consciously quirky play on anthology construction, Portia Priegert, a contributor to *Boredom Fighters*, a graphic, visual-verbal experimental collection, parodies a common paratextual element of the poetry collection: the dryly technical-, arty-sounding note on the volume's typeface:

Times New Boring is the name given to a contemporary non-proprietary class of demi-serif typefaces. The reverse italic style is designed to reflect a sense of recreational recline, with the slope on the font's long extenders calculated as the average tilt coefficient of reclining chairs purchased in Canada between 1952 and 1993. (Poletto and Kennedy n. pag.)

With this riposte, Priegert takes aim at artistic pretension, with a side-swipe at postwar Canadian poetics in particular, here read as the cultural equivalent of a boring, ugly recliner. *Boredom Fighters*, by contrast, promises to reverse the tilt of modernist poetics in Canada by featuring texts in which "graphic doesn't always trump poetry and thus the ultimate tug of war is—in the most captivating sense—a real yawnyarn between word and image" (Poletto and Kennedy n. pag.).

As I have shown here, the quirky anthology is more than a postwar phenomenon; it has been with us as long as there have been anthologies produced in Canada. And its relationship to cultural seriousness is not as unremittingly oppositional as one might think, though many of these volumes do seek to blur the lines between the serious anthology that tells Canadian readers who we are as national subjects and the occasional collection that we might buy as a jokey gift for a friend. For that matter, nation does not figure as important solely in the pedagogical, institutional anthologies with which most of us, as former students or as scholars, are familiar. Nation exerts its anxious influence, strange to say, even on the likes of *Panty Lines* and *100% Cracked Wheat*. Quirky anthologies also ask us to question our often unexamined assumptions about cultural seriousness: a form of intellectual capital that anthologies have tended to produce and, in turn, to draw upon as a rationale for their existence. These are some of the reasons why any consideration of anthology production in Canada needs to take into account the academic anthology's much-maligned loopy cousin. Because there's something funny going on here.

NOTES

1 The collection seems implicitly indebted to the mother of all underwear poems, Lawrence Ferlinghetti's "Underwear," which opens: "I didn't get much sleep last night / thinking about underwear."

2 I recognize here the immense contribution made by my research assistant, Katja Lee, McMaster University, who researched the quirky anthology with enthusiasm.

3 Compare, for instance, *Tributes to the Scarlet Riders*'s holdings in 49 libraries in Canada and 2 in the United States, or *Going Top Shelf*'s holdings in 21 Canadian libraries, 11 in the United States, and 5 internationally, to *Desperately Seeking Susans*'s 3 Canadian library holdings (Worldcat.org). My thanks to Katja Lee for these data.

WORKS CITED

Currie, Bob, Gary Hyland, and Jim McLean, eds. *100% Cracked Wheat: The Exciting New Saskatchewan Breakfast Cereal in Book Form.* Moose Jaw: Coteau, 1983. Print.

Di Leo, Jeffrey. *On Anthologies: Politics and Pedagogy.* Lincoln: U of Nebraska P, 2004. Print.

Everett, Charles Carroll. *Poetry, Comedy, and Duty.* Boston: Houghton Mifflin, 1888. Print.

Ferlinghetti, Lawrence. "Underwear." *These Are My Rivers: New and Selected Poems, 1955–1993.* New York: New Directions, 1993. 130–32. Print.

Garvin, John, ed. *Cap and Bells: An Anthology of Light Verse by Canadian Poets.* Toronto: Ryerson, 1936. Print.

Heritage House Publisher's Website. Heritage House. Web. 10 Jan. 2013.

Holbrook, Susan. "Oolichan Books Is Seeking Submissions for a New Anthology of Female Canadian Poets Named Susan." *Desperately Seeking Susans.* Ed. Sarah Yi-Mei Tsiang. Fernie, BC: Oolichan, 2012. Print.

Hopkins, David. "On Anthologies." *Cambridge Quarterly* 37:3 (2008): 285–304. Print.

Langs, Lenore, and Laurie Smith, eds. *$10 Cash Value: An Anthology of Assets.* Windsor: Cranberry Tree Press, 2000. Print.

Latimer, Joanne. "Desperately Seeking Susans." *Maclean's* 2 Mar. 2012. n. pag. Web. 10 Jan. 2012.

Lecker, Robert. "The Canonization of Canadian Literature: An Inquiry into Value." *Critical Inquiry* 16:3 (1990): 656–71. Print.

———. *English-Canadian Literary Anthologies: An Enumerative Bibliography.* Teeswater, ON: Reference P, 1997. Print.

———. *Keepers of the Code: English-Canadian Literary Anthologies and the Representation of Nation.* Toronto: U of Toronto P, 2013. Print.

———. "Nineteenth-Century English-Canadian Anthologies and the Making of a National Literature." *Journal of Canadian Studies* 44.1 (2010): 91–117. Print.

McVittie, Deborah, and Ursula Vaira, eds. *Panty Lines: A Poetic Anthology.* Lantzville, BC: Blue Moon, 2000. Print.

Melnyk, George. "Tome on the Range." *Quill & Quire* 61:8 (1995), n. pag. Web. 16 Jan. 2013.

Pierce, Lorne. Foreword. *Cap and Bells: An Anthology of Light Verse by Canadian Poets.* Ed. John Garvin. Toronto: Ryerson, 1936. v–viii. Print.

Poletto, Paola, and Jake Kennedy, eds. *Boredom Fighters.* Toronto: Tightrope, 2008. Print.

Riding, Laura, and Robert Graves. *A Survey of Modernist Poetry and A Pamphlet Against Anthologies.* Ed. Charles Mundye and Patrick McGuiness. Manchester: Carcanet, 2002. Print.

Scott, F. R., and A. J. M. Smith, eds. *The Blasted Pine: An Anthology of Satire, Invective, and Disrespectful Verse Chiefly by Canadian Writers.* Toronto: Macmillan, 1957. Print.

Smith, Linda Tuhiwai. "Creating Anthologies and Other Dangerous Practices." *Educational Theory* 50.4 (2000): 521–32. Print.

Steinberg, Susan. "Introducing Sarah Steinberg." *Broken Pencil* 15 (Spring 2012), 10. Print.

Tsiang, Sarah Yi-Mei, ed. *Desperately Seeking Susans*. Fernie, BC: Oolichan, 2012. Print.

Webb-Campbell, Shannon. "A Sundry of Susans." *Saint John Telegraph-Journal.* 15 Dec. 2012. Web. 15 Jan. 2013.

Wiersema, Robert. Rev. of *Tributes to the Scarlet Riders*. *Quill & Quire* (2006), n. pag. Web. 10 Jan. 2013.

Reading Anthologies

Frank Davey

Like many university English Department faculty, I own a lot of anthol-ogies, most of which I didn't buy. Most of these I also haven't opened unless they've seemed relevant to an article I was planning to write about anthologies. The first that I purchased was in the Vancouver Eaton's store in 1951: Francis Turner Palgrave's *The Golden Treasury*, in a blue leather-bound Collins edition for ninety-nine cents. It had been re-edited to include W. B. Yeats, John Masefield, and a few Georgians. The next that I purchased vol-untarily was Donald Allen's *The New American Poetry 1945–1960*, when I was twenty, followed by Raymond Souster's *New Wave Canada* when I was twenty-seven. These were all anthologies that I had wanted to own because of my curiosity about poetry and how it could be written. I didn't think of them as national anthologies, although clearly all three in some way strongly marked an intersecting of nation and poetry. I thought of them merely as poetry anthologies. I still have all three, although the signatures of the Allen have become unglued.

Since then I have made similar purchases of Emmett Williams's *An Anthology of Concrete Poetry*, Jerome Rothenberg and George Quasha's *America a Prophecy*, Rothenberg and Pierre Joris's *Poems for the Millen-nium*, Bruce Andrews and Charles Bernstein's *The L=A=N=G=U=A=G=E Book*, and Andrew Klobucar and Michael Barnholden's *Writing Class*. These purchases would often lead me toward informed purchases of single-author volumes—a leading that is an important function of anthologies.

All of my poetry anthology purchases have come from my interest in the genre—I wasn't especially curious about how the British, the new Americans, or the newly waving Canadians had been writing poetry. I have also not pur-chased out of curiosity about how First Nations writers, Italian Canadians, Asian Americans, Canadian lesbians, British Columbians, Alberta labourers, or Canadians of African ancestry might be writing poetry, although I have followed some of these through book reviews. However, I can understand why readers interested in those communities might buy relevant anthologies, and—usually because of reviews or articles—I have myself bought single-author volumes by writers who are in some of them. As a poet curious about the continuing potential of the genre, I understand that I may not be a representative reader/buyer. Of course for voluntary anthology purchases no one may be a representative reader/buyer.

Except for a copy of Raymond Knister's *Canadian Short Stories* that I found at a church bazaar, I don't believe I have ever voluntarily purchased a short fiction anthology, although I own many that have come to me as review copies or possible desk copies. But I have purchased numerous historical anthologies that I've used in research on the Canadian anthology as a publishing genre—*New Provinces*, Louis Dudek and Irving Layton's *Canadian Poems 1850–1952*, A. J. M. Smith's 1943 *The Book of Canadian Poetry*, Ralph Gustafson's 1942 *Anthology of Canadian Poetry*, Edward Hartley Dewart's *Selections from Canadian Poets*, Fred Cogswell's *One Hundred Poems of Modern Quebec*, a 1934 edition of Bliss Carman and Lorne Pierce's *Our Canadian Literature*.

My anthology history illustrates how anthologies can play a variety of roles in one person's life—how they can be mandatory texts in one's education, celebrations or legitimations of one's community, materials for one's continuing self-education, arrestingly polemic introductions to emerging writers, tools one uses as an education worker, materials one uses in scholarly research, the objects that one creates if one is an anthologist, and a personal validation if one is a writer whose work becomes anthologized. They have played all those roles for me.

The editor of this volume, Robert Lecker, in his recent book *Keepers of the Code* makes a strong case that the commercially produced national literary anthology, designed for college and university course adoptions, is presently the pre-eminent version or sub-genre of the anthology genre—the sub-genre in which canons are most powerfully maintained, the most profits made, the largest readerships reached, and in which it is most meaningful for a writer to have work included. As he describes its current incarnations, it is mostly factors that we usually understand as non-literary that inform this pre-eminence—the concentrations of capital achieved by multinational publishers, the economies of scale that substantial capital permits (284–85), and the standardization of contents and permissions fees that dominance within a market presently both requires and enables (293–96, 305, 336–37).

A further characteristic of this pre-eminence is the narrow range of those anthologies' readers—mostly students between nineteen and twenty-two years of age and postsecondary teachers reading the texts as a requirement of their employment (267–68). That is, it is a readership rich in numbers but of indeterminate quality otherwise. Quite possibly it is not the imagined audience of many of the writers, although in recent decades I have heard poets discussing how to write Canadian "anthology poems"—poems less than a page long, with identifiably Canadian referents, a single unusual incident, a poignant or otherwise resonant ending, teachable within ten to twenty minutes. Poems suited to current material conditions. The poets' discussions were simultaneously ironic and serious. Quite possibly prose writers have similar conversations about the short story. The imaginary audience implied by such anthology poems, however, is more likely the editors of anthologies, and publishers' accountants, than it is any of the books' readers.

Lecker links these national postsecondary anthologies to canonicity—for a writer to have work in them is to be in the canon (279). I am not sure how firm this link may be. The assumed cultural power of such national anthologies rests in large part on hamburger-outlet quantity—copies sold, students served. Pierre Bourdieu has identified other possible sources of cultural capital beyond large quantity and mass production—including the scarcity of the object and the intellectual status of its consumer. In literature there is a canon of relatively scarce texts whose authors are sometimes called "writers' writers," or "poets' poets"—the writers that other writers admire, study, write about, and steal from but who do not themselves get into classroom anthologies: Louis Dudek, Hilda Doolittle, B. S. Johnson, Madeline Gins, Daphne Marlatt, Steve McCaffery, Christian Bök. There's also a dimly remembered canon of award-winners—in Canada poets such as Miriam Mandel, Don Coles, Fred Wah, David Donnell, Don McKay, Robert Hilles, Anne Szumigalski, E. D. Blodgett, Paulette Giles—who also rarely get into classroom anthologies. One might think of these metaphorically as the winners who—unlike the emphatically canonical Al Purdy—neglected to build themselves an A-frame house, or A-frame equivalent. As well, there is that canon of what could be called discussable texts, the canon created by the scholarly articles published by literary critics and theorists that may only slightly overlap with the national anthology canon. The discussable text has different properties from the teachable text. It can be much longer. How it ends may well be irrelevant, since the critic can reconstruct any ending. A single unique incident is probably a disadvantage, because what most makes a discussable text discussable is usually ambiguity, complexity, and current social relevance. But there are relatively few anthologies for such canons—Ondaatje's *The Long*

Poem Anthology is probably a writer's anthology, also bpNichol's *The Cosmic Chef,* Ron Silliman's *In the American Tree,* and Williams's *An Anthology of Concrete Poetry.* Smaro Kamboureli's *Making a Difference* appears in part to parallel and support her ongoing theoretical and critical publications, and to establish additional discussable difference.

Although Lecker's study gives very little specific attention to what writers aim for when they become interveners in national canon formation (it tends to treat such writer-editors as Wilfred Campbell, A. J. M. Smith, Earle Birney, Louis Dudek, Eli Mandel, John Robert Colombo, Margaret Atwood, John Metcalf, George Bowering, Dennis Lee, and Jane Urquhart simply as editors), it does pervasively imply that writers have wanted to be included in the national canon, and that they currently view inclusion in the national postsecondary anthology as a welcome recognition (321–24, 337). Again, I am not so sure. A writer could very well value contribution to a narrow constituency, or personal aesthetic achievement, more highly. The poem of mine that has been most often included in such anthologies strikes me as an anomaly in my writing; the writing of other quite different poems has given me more satisfaction, and a greater sense of having contributed to an expansion of the genre's possibilities. Of course such contributions may not be what a national anthologist wants to present. In writing a biography of bpNichol I realized very quickly that Nichol cared much more about his work on his continuing poem *The Martyrology* than he did about his inclusion (or non-inclusion) in any anthology—including Williams's international concrete collection. Writers whose main goals are to win prizes and be nationally anthologized rather than to take literature itself to new possibilities to my mind resemble the real estate agent who wins prizes for making the most sales or the political partisan who manoeuvres for an appointment to the Order of Canada. Achievements are achievements only within the constituency that values them. The young woman postie who efficiently delivers my royalty cheques, author's copies, and other mail could care less, alas, that bpNichol was a radically innovative poet or that Professor Lecker has invited me to contribute here to his anthology.

A decade or so ago it was Access Copyright's practice to track the authors and titles of texts that were being licensed for inclusion in course packs—the national anthology's chief rival—and report the relevant findings to the individual writers. Almost every year my multiple-page poem "Riel"—a poem that has never been included in a national anthology—was listed as having had two or three inclusions. In recent years, however, Access Copyright has sold to many Canadian educational institutions, on behalf of its writer members, all-inclusive licences, and its members no longer receive this glimpse of yet another Canadian canon that is being revised each year by postsecondary instructors unhappy with commercially produced anthologies. As well, many universities that have recently opted out of Access Copyright have redefined "fair dealing" in such a way that they believe it is lawful to use poems like my "Riel" in course packs without payment. Whether the university be inside or outside of Access, it is thus much easier today than it was a decade ago for many course instructors to custom-make collections for themselves and their students, and much more difficult to find records of their selections. The course pack has become the invisible anthology, the one that leaves little or no textual residue. There are few records accumulating of the Canadian literature course packs that are being produced, few copies are preserved for the antiquarian book market, no ISBN numbers are being assigned, and few copies are being preserved in the National Library. Some course packs lack the page numbers that would assure the completeness of a copy. No one is likely to be able to write a study similar to Lecker's *Keepers of the Code* about the ideological commitments that have been on display over the decades in the CanLit course pack.

In content, however, the course pack is not necessarily obliged to be all that different from the commercially produced anthology. At universities licensed by Access Copyright, writers who do not belong to the copyright collective—in literature mostly the higher-profile contemporary writers whose work can command high royalties—are unlikely to be included in course packs, either because of cost or because of the time needed to separately negotiate their inclusion. Universities that have opted out of Access licensing have usually hired special staff to research copyright and to handle such negotiations should they consider royalty payment necessary. Some have mitigated the costs of these hirings by defining their royalty payment obligations more narrowly than Access believes they should be defined, and have thus become able—in theory at least—to include a wider range of writers than the Access-affiliated institutions. The University of British Columbia, for example, in its current online policy document, "Fair Dealing Requirements for UBC Faculty and Staff," interprets the "fair dealing" exemptions of the Canadian Copyright Act as permitting the free copying of "one chapter from a book" or "a single article from a periodical" (n. pag.) into any course pack, effectively putting out of business the commercial essay anthology. The interpretation would permit royalty-free inclusion, for example, of several Northrop Frye chapters or essays, as long as each was from a different book. It would also, I believe, permit the royalty-free replication through a course pack of any current commercial Canadian short-story anthology, none of which appears to have more than one story from any one of its contributors' books. The UBC document also interprets fair dealing as permitting the royalty-free copying into a course pack of "an entire single poem ... from a Work containing other poems" ("Fair Dealing" n. pag)—allowing an instructor to come close to replicating almost any current Canadian poetry anthology. The course pack could, for example, contain unlimited numbers of Atwood, Purdy, Layton, or Ondaatje poems, without paying a fee, as long as each poem was copied from a different one of the poets' numerous books.[1] The only constraint would be the inability to reprint two or more poems from the same book.

The course pack's special attributes are also identifiable. Whether "assembled" through Access or through the more permissive UBC system, the course pack's contents can be changed much more frequently—every year or every term—than those of a commercial anthology. They can include exactly the texts that the instructor plans to cover; the student does not have to purchase numerous pages that the course will not designate as required reading, as is the case with a commercial anthology. The economics of the course pack's production are in some ways more like those of nineteenth-century subscription publishing than of current commercial publishing. The buyers can be known and counted before the book is printed. There is no distributor to pay. The publisher—usually the university bookstore—sells directly to the student, who in a sense is buying the collection wholesale. There can be almost no transportation costs—an aspect that adds a dimension of eco-friendliness. In the case of the e-book course pack, even physical production costs are avoided—or passed on to the rare student who prefers printed pages. The course pack can also be constructed very quickly. Although some university bookstores require two to three months to produce one, others, such as UBC's, can now produce them in less than a week—not all that surprising, perhaps, considering that university's self-benefiting understanding of fair dealing.

The course pack, then, does not appear to suffer much at all by comparison to the industrially produced anthology. While at some universities the course pack may not be able to include all the texts of the writers most consecrated by the mass market, it can usually be more economical, more likely to fit into a backpack, and much easier to produce and revise quickly. While for Access-affiliated institutions it might not be as useful as the commercial anthology for the teaching of a celebrity-names course, it could be equally useful in teaching the styles and modes of a period. If one wishes to teach poetry as a genre rather than as the creation of major figures, or as a history of changing styles and ideologies, there is probably no reason to prefer one over the other except on the basis of convenience and cost. For teaching alternative, regional, postcolonial, or minority writing, the course pack probably has the advantage.

As attractive as I find the course pack anthology for its flexibility, low cost, and openness to original choices and teaching, I am still troubled that its main audience is the limited and relatively captive one of the college student. I recall how impressed I was six or seven years ago to find my poem "The Piano" online on someone's website; I gathered from their commentary that they had posted it there merely because it had engaged them. Recently I encountered on someone else's website a video of four young people dramatizing the same poem. Like my voluntary purchases of anthologies, the voluntary engagement with a poem is of a higher order, it seems to me, than the involuntary—because it requires greater personal agency, and risk. One imagines—and hopes—that these and similar postings of other poems on sleepy Facebook walls could be the beginnings of personal anthologies, reminiscent of the "uncollected anthology" invented by Northrop Frye in a 1956 essay.[2] Certainly technology now enables that—just as it enables the more visible online anthologies of popular songs, proverbs, biblical quotations, and the hundreds of bpNichol photos and images that John Currie is presently assembling on flickr. Yes, as with the piracy of popular music, and the arguable piracy of some of UBC's interpretations of fair dealing, there would be copyright problems, but it would be good news for poetry to have such problems.

NOTES

1 Access is currently challenging by lawsuit, on behalf of its members, similarly self-advantaging interpretations of fair dealing by York University (http://www.iposgoode .ca/2013/04/access-copyright-initiates-lawsuit-against-york-university/). It would seem to me that if the commercial literature anthology, such as Robert Lecker's own *Open Country: Canadian Literature in English* or Donna Bennett and Russell Brown's *An Anthology of Canadian Literature in English,* is to have a future in Canada, its publishers should be joining Access in this suit and any similar ones.

2 See Northrop Frye's "Preface to an Uncollected Anthology," in *Studia Varia, Royal Society of Canada Literary and Scientific Papers,* 1957, 21–36. The essay was presented to Section II of the Royal Society in June 1956 in a session on Canadian literature, and reprinted in Frye's collection *The Bush Garden* in 1971. The "uncollected anthology" appears to be Frye's invention, and was treated as such by R. T. Robertson in 1973 in his "Another Preface to an Uncollected Anthology: Canadian Criticism in a Commonwealth Context," *Ariel* 4:3 (1973): 70–81.

WORKS CITED

Bourdieu, Pierre. *The Field of Cultural Production*. New York: Columbia UP, 1993. Print.

"Fair Dealing Requirements for UBC Faculty and Staff." *Scholarly Communications and Copyright Office*. Version 2.0. U of British Columbia, 9 Nov. 2012. Web. 25 June 2013.

Geist, Michael. "Supreme Court of Canada Stands Up for Fair-Dealing in Stunning Sweep of Cases." *Michael Geist*. n.p. 12 July 2012. Web. 28 May 2013.

Lecker, Robert. *Keepers of the Code: English-Canadian Literary Anthologies and Representation of Nation*. Toronto: U of Toronto P, 2013. Print.

The Poet and Her Library

Anthologies Read, Anthologies Made

Anne Compton

> *"I'm unpacking my library. Yes, I am. The books are not yet on the shelves, nor yet touched by the mild boredom of order."*
> —Walter Benjamin

When you think about anthologies, you can't help but agree with Solomon: "Of making many books there is no end ..." (*NIV* Eccles. 12:12). Nonetheless, with libraries turning into computer lounges, it's good to have these portable libraries. The Bible is, of course, itself an anthology, but then so too is Ovid's *Metamorphoses*. A double volume of visions, histories, or metaphorical stories (depending upon your view), gathered anciently in a collective binding, the Bible is, perhaps, the most reprinted of anthologies. Defined as a "compendium of mythological verse narratives" (Westling et al. 674), *The Metamorphoses* reminds us that the job of the compiler is to gather and to weigh, which is what compendium means: (*com-*, together + *pendere*, to weigh). Lurking within that word is another: commodious. Anthologies are remarkable for their roominess, a generosity that must be, nonetheless, wed to judiciousness. How many descriptors are there for anthology? I'm partial to the term "reader," which co-identifies the book and the user, and often brags of its portability: *The Portable Elizabethan Reader*, all you need to carry around with you in terms of sixteenth-century prose, poetry, and drama. Apocryphal or not, the story is that Ralph Gustafson's 1942 modest-sized Penguin *An Anthology of Canadian Poetry (English)*, small enough to fit in a pocket, was intended for soldiers heading for the front. In the history of anthologies, the notion of portability is a persistent one. In 2012, Penguin published the seventh edition of *Poetry: A Pocket Anthology*, edited by R. S. Gwynn. On the other hand, F. T. Palgrave's *The Golden Treasury of the Best Songs & Lyrical Poems in the English Language* (1861) promised the amplitude of a treasure chest and offered a "storehouse of delight" (vii). Commodious as a cabinet or conveniently pocket-sized, how many shapes—not to mention names—might an anthology take? Broadly speaking, it's an assembly of discrete, received materials—written or oral in their original form—collectively bound. In an anthology—whatever its size, shape, transportability—some metamorphosis of the original literary work inevitably takes place. Relocation alone changes how a work is received. Sometimes, although this is less frequent, an anthology features material not previously published, material solicited by the editors. Rarer still, sometimes literary works appear anonymously on the pages of an anthology, as they did, for example, in *The Poet's Tongue* (1935), edited by W. H. Auden and John Garrett: "As regards arrangement we have, after some thought, adopted an alphabetical, anonymous order ... free from the bias of great names and literary influences ..." (x). In a somewhat similar gesture, Seamus Heaney and Ted Hughes, in *The Rattle Bag* (1982), arranged the poems alphabetically by title—the author's name appended—to preserve a sense of "unexpectedness," allowing "the contents to discover themselves as we ourselves gradually discovered them ..." (19). Is there anything as plentiful, as various, as the anthology? Let us advance in open-mindedness.

1

As a child, my first school readers were those dreadful *Dick and Jane* books, but my ten older brothers and sisters had the pleasure of richer, more ample readers—anthologies of stories and poems—and these were lying about the house. Coming across those books made me a reader. Even beyond my primers, no school book, in spite of its promise of exotic travel—*More Streets and Roads, Highroads to Reading, The Golden Caravan*—quite matched the delicious, fugitive reading of the books that belonged to my siblings.

My first college anthology was *The College Survey of English Literature*, edited by the Dickensian-named Alexander M. Witherspoon, first published in 1942. In the 1960s, we were assigned the Revised, Shorter Edition, the shortness of which ran to 1,338 pages of text with an additional 40 pages for various apparatuses, including a prominently displayed "Rulers of England" chart. It boasts the first-time appearance in a college anthology of prose by Joseph Conrad, E. M. Forster, Virginia Woolf, D. H. Lawrence, and Aldous Huxley. Its poetry inclusions stop at Dylan Thomas. Although published in New York, it reflects a thoroughly British notion of literature in English. Our classroom view of the nineteenth century did not include, for example, Emily Dickinson or Walt Whitman. Looking at that anthology now, opening its musty pages, makes me feel old. And sad. T. S. Eliot and W. H. Auden were alive when I was reading their poems, although if my marginalia are anything to go by, in that first-year college survey Miss Barbara Worth, our teacher, did not take us beyond the Victorians, which suited me, the aspiring history major, just fine. Still, it's a bit of a shock—a telescoping of a half-century—to read the editor's words: "It is too early to assess Auden's work as a poet or to venture suggestions with respect to his further achievements" (1326). In the Contemporary Poetry course of my final undergraduate year, where I discovered my passion for poetry, we worked in an anthology-free zone, reading and studying those miraculously slim volumes recently published by W. C. Williams, Allen Ginsberg, and the like. When F. R. Scott visited the campus to give a reading, I'm not sure I made any connection between his work and the contemporary American and British poets we were studying. A literary education, it would appear, proceeds nation by nation. By the time I had an MA and my first teaching job (1971–72), I was using *The Norton Anthology of Poetry*, first edition, Coordinating Editor Arthur M. Eastman, "American poets conflated with British." Not a Canadian in sight. I have a vague memory of mimeographing Earle Birney's "David" and something by F. R. Scott for my students. It's a well-known fact that Canadian was *the* "foreign" literature in those decades. It would take another degree, and a decade-long project on A. J. M. Smith's work, before Canadian anthologies became part of my purview. Life might be thought of—if you're bookish—as a progression through the ever-expanding world of anthologies.

In "Confessions of a Compulsive Anthologist," Smith describes a discovery that contributed, at least in part, to his becoming a modernist metaphysical poet and an anthologist with a "sense of cultural mission," as Margaret Atwood puts it (xxvii):

> In the Westmount Public Library I came upon *The New Poetry* edited by Harriet Monroe and Alice Corbin Henderson, published in 1917. And here I read with delight and fascination the new poetry of Ezra Pound, Wallace Stevens, T. S. Eliot, Yeats in his middle period, Conrad Aiken, and H. D. This, I think is a complete list of the poets whom I deliberately began to imitate in the earliest apprentice verse I printed three or four years later in the *Literary Supplement* to the *McGill Daily* and *McGill Fortnightly Review*. (Smith 106–7)

In the *McGill Fortnightly Review* the probationary modernist poet published essays on Yeats's symbolism (5 Dec. 1925) and Eliot's *The Waste Land* (3 Nov. 1926), and in "Contemporary Poetry" (15 Dec. 1926) he worked out his theory of the "two-stage development" of modernism.

To the first of the modernists he attributed the "overthrow [of] an effete and decadent diction," and to the second "an attempt to recapture and exploit in a new way the poetics of the Metaphysical poets," a "turning back to the Seventeenth Century" that was born of the modernists' disillusionment with the present (Compton 67). What Smith particularly admired in the modernist poets was the coexistence in their work of conciseness and ambiguity, and these were qualities that he saw as well in the best of Canadian poets, poets such as Isabella Valancy Crawford, where these qualities were motivated not by the "psychological and philosophical concerns" of the modernists, but arose, rather, from the "geographical and spatial circumstances" that preoccupied Canadian writers (Compton 67). Smith's enthusiasm for modernism and his curiosity concerning a Canadian tradition moved forward in tandem, or, more accurately, in an action-reaction motion. With F. R. Scott, he published "the first anthology of 'modern' poetry in Canada" ("Confessions" 107), but within three years of *New Provinces: Poems of Several Authors* (1936), he was applying for a Guggenheim Fellowship, research funding for a solo exploration of "the historical development of a genuine Canadian poetry" ("Confessions" 109). Canadian modernism turned his head; he had to look back, had to see where, or what, modernism had emerged from. A poet, any poet, while going forward, creating new work—especially work that self-consciously participates in the "new"—is always mindful of predecessors, the work he's reacting against. Perhaps a similar forward movement, chastised by a backward glance, characterizes the work of an anthologist: Smith championed modernism in *New Provinces*, but the apologia turned him toward the past.

Smith's sustained, decades-long study of the Canadian poetic tradition found its fruition in *The Book of Canadian Poetry: A Critical and Historical Anthology* (1943), *The Oxford Book of Canadian Verse: In English and French* (1960), and *Modern Canadian Verse: In English and French* (1967). If *The Book of Canadian Poetry* "de-standardized" all preceding anthologies, as A. M. Klein suggests in a letter to Smith (qtd. in Compton 27), it is also true that Smith set the standard for future anthologies of Canadian poetry. As Atwood acknowledges in the introduction to her update, *The New Oxford Book of Canadian Verse in English* (1982), Smith is the progenitor of successive Oxford anthologies, including the most recent Oxford offering: *70 Canadian Poets*, Fifth Edition (2014), edited by Gary Geddes. But the real story here—taking A. J. M. Smith as an example—is the way in which an encounter with an anthology can be a determinant in a writer's career. Writing his "Confessions" in 1976, Smith might have said of the 1917 Monroe-Henderson anthology, "'I came upon' my future."

2

The New York Times Book Review celebrated the fiftieth anniversary of *The Norton Anthology of English Literature* by publishing a dialogue between M. H. Abrams, the founding general editor, and Stephen Greenblatt, the current general editor ("Built to Last" 31). Abrams is gratified "to meet middle-aged people who say: 'I still have the Norton Anthology that I used 20 years ago, I have it at my bed's head and I read it at night, and I enjoy it'" (31). Referring to the renewable pleasure they've experienced, Abrams's speakers testify to the fact that a so-called textbook—such an ugly word—can have life beyond the classroom, can be, in fact, a lifelong attachment. But what particularly gratifies the pair of editors is the current "counter-trend back to the basics" (31). Among present-day students, Greenblatt reports, there's a feeling "that they really shouldn't go through their undergraduate years without reading the great imaginative works of the past" (31). This renewal follows upon a period when university humanities curricula seemed in trouble—as indicated by a "decline in majors" and the clamour among those who did major for "contemporary topics" (31). The editors' conversation, ostensibly about *Norton*, is really a shared joy in "how fresh and new and powerful are the kinds of writings that are hundreds of years old" (31), a pleasure that they share with university students wherever one or another of the *Norton* variants is in use. Their words echo Auden and Garrett's introductory words to *The Poet's Tongue*: an anthology should present its poetry as "a spontaneous living product" (x). In spite of Auden and Garrett's aversion to names and eras, there is much, however, to be said on behalf of chronology, especially if the anthology is also a textbook.

Reading the Norton editors' conversation, I remembered that it was in an anthology that I discovered, as an undergraduate, the poetry of John Donne and the Metaphysicals, and how—years later—in reading A. J. M. Smith's poetry, I experienced again the sense of possibility that there was a kind of poetry that could address emotion and intellect, flesh and spirit at once. The Abrams-Greenblatt conversation prompted me to search my house, go through the books, for the anthology that had started me on my scholarly life. Although the Norton editors' exchange reminds the reader of the great, good intentions of anthology-makers—"it's worthwhile because you're presenting literature to students, many of them for the first time" (31)—that intention is not always recognizable in the slews of anthologies, the examination copies, that publishers impose on professors.

If you're a teacher, you've lived your classroom life with Norton—in its many incarnations—and with Oxford, Broadview, and all the rest, many of which, in the 1980s and '90s, abandoned the useful chronological arrangement for a subject structure, as if there were something political about chronology, similar to the way everything else, in those benighted decades of literary theory, was perceived as political. The unhinging of literature and "real events," real time, is neatly illustrated by a character in Jeffrey Eugenides's *The Marriage Plot*: "I contend, with Barthes, that the act of writing is itself a fictionalization, even if you are treating real events" (25–26). If "writing is itself a fictionalization," then anthologizing the already-written is a further fiction: the "real events" informing Tennyson's "The Charge of the Light Brigade," let us say, are aswim in undifferentiated time.

The "structure" of *Literature: An Introduction to Reading and Writing* (1996), containing fiction, poetry, and drama, edited by Edgar V. Roberts and Henry E. Jacobs, guarantees classroom confusion. In the poetry section, poems are presented higgledy-piggledy under poetic aspects—"Prosody," "Form," "Symbolism and Allusion," and so forth—even though, in the case of prosody, for example, rhyme and rhythm were differently practised, differently valued, before the twentieth century as compared to during it. Lifted from its cultural embeddedness, there's no understanding prosodic practice. Offerings, under the above headings, are followed by a stand-alone section, "Two Poetic Careers: Emily Dickinson and Robert Frost," which, in turn, is followed by seventy-six pages of poems—alphabetized by poet—for "Additional Study." Happily, chronology has been restored in most recent anthologies.

There are anthologies, such as Donald Hall's *To Read a Poem* (1982, 1992), possessing a structure somewhat similar to that of Roberts and Jacobs', foregrounding the elements of poetry, providing poems for further reading. Hall's is more of a how-to anthology, however, instructions for learning how to read a poem. Purpose and genre are confined. Printed on onion-skin-thin paper—print bleeding through—the Roberts and Jacobs anthology is a baggy monster, similar to many of the anthologies produced in the 1980s and '90s. Much as I love the marriage of prose and poetry in the best of prose poetry, an anthology, not to mention a college course, that aims for coverage in three or four genres dilutes all of them.

In the world of book production, the anthology is a peculiar item. It is rigorously tested for classroom use, which is where most anthologies are headed. Endless versions of the literary eras, in anthology form, flood a professor's office mailbox, and the chronological ones are the best of them. Novels and volumes of poetry end up in classrooms too, of course, but a single publication does not determine a syllabus the way an anthology can. It is frightening to think someone, somewhere, is making choices for you—this poet, not that one—based on the criteria of what's "teachable" and what's "usable." The buy-back guy visits your office in spring, giving you a few dollars for each anthology you have rejected, an exchange that has a taint on it.

3

A person rarely says, in a cherishing voice, "I was shopping today and bought the most gorgeous anthology that I can't wait to start." Anthologies don't often provoke love. Mine are in a separate room of the house, away from the other books, stacked in columns on the floor, not even their own bookcases. Given the word's Latin and Greek origins in garland (*anthos*, flower + *legein*, to gather), you'd expect more by way of tender preservation. Parenthetically, let me point out that a house is itself an anthology of rooms, each room with a story of its own. The rooms where my sons grew up, from infancy to adulthood and leave-taking, have stories to tell that are very different from the stories to be told by the room in which I read and write. The metaphor works, as well, in the opposite direction: an anthology houses. Its "architecture" reflects the sensibility of the maker or makers. It has designs on your mind, your taste, and future reading.

No one aspires to make an anthology in the lifelong way the incipient novelist longs to tell a family or local or homeland story. Rather, the anthologist is led by already-published material or by a perceived market opportunity or by career pressures—the need to get a book, any book, published. But there's another kind of anthologist—the idiosyncratic: shouldn't there be an anthology of poems about sparrows, the aspiring anthologist wonders, or a collection of stories about the tractor? These are the good ones, so much more satisfying—whimsical, quirky—than the machine-like annuals or biennials produced for classrooms. *A Convergence of Birds: Original Fiction and Poetry Inspired by the Work of Joseph Cornell* (2001), edited by Jonathan Safran Foer, is that kind of treasure, as is *The Poetry of Birds* (2009), edited by Simon Armitage and Tim Dee. Foer's anthology, prompted by the magic of Cornell's dioramas, is unusual in its first-time-published poems and stories. Most specialist anthologies are, however, a gathering of already-published materials, but even these can satisfy a reader by virtue of their tidy singularity, their concentration of a literary or cultural moment: *Aesthetes and Decadents of the 1890's: An Anthology of British Poetry and Prose* (1966), edited by Karl Beckson, or *The Imagist Poem* (1963), edited by William Pratt. Similarly, the anthologies that concentrate on a form—prose poem, sonnet, or ghazal—are useful in creative writing courses. An anthologist's obsession turned to good use.

The question "How is an anthologist different from an author?" might be a barroom joke. "He who can't, lists." Thinking about experiences—both positive and negative—in an anthology-filled life, you can't help but wonder about the various motivations activating anthologists. If not obsession or pragmatism—career advancement or market opportunity—an anthologist might be, psychologically speaking, an author *manqué*, determined, in lieu of the great novel, the grand poem, to exert influence over what's represented, what will last.

Even if this is not so—even if the anthologist is not a thwarted author— the aesthetic evaluations that he or she makes in creating an anthology are implicitly canon-making. An anthologist has power or, at least, assumes it. Wars erupt. Smith's *The Book of Canadian Poetry* (1943) elicited John Sutherland's three-stage attack: his editorial in *First Statement* (April 1944); his rebuttal of Smith's selections in the introduction to his own anthology, *Other Canadians* (1947); and the essay "Critics on the Defensive" (1947) (Compton 32). The history of anthology-making is riddled with these wars. The most virulent exchange of late took place in the pages of *The New York Review of Books* (24 Nov. 2011 and 22 Dec. 2011). In her review essay of *The Penguin Anthology of Twentieth-Century American Poetry* (2011), edited and introduced by Rita Dove, Helen Vendler took issue with the "[m]ulticultural inclusiveness" that, she believed, reduced the anthology to a sample-book: "No century in the evolution of poetry in English ever had 175 poets worth reading ..." (19). Vendler believed, as well, there was a privileging of accessibility over complexity in Dove's choices, and attacked the "mix of potted history ... and peculiar judgements" in the introduction, to which Vendler gives inordinate attention, concluding that "[t]he simplest thing to say about Dove's introduction is that she is writing in a genre not her own; she is a poet, not an essayist, and uncomfortable in the essayist's role ..." (19). Needless to say, Dove responded at length, marshalling rejoinders to six of Vendler's points but, interestingly, she did not take up Vendler's claim that a poet is not likely capable of an essay. "Can a rhymer write?" might be a barroom joke.

If you're a poet, certain books are always within reach—*Smith's Bible Dictionary*, Robert Graves's two volumes of *The Greek Myths*, Roger Tory Peterson's *A Field Guide to the Birds,* and similar guides to trees and flowers. Among such books, I keep—to the left side of my writing chair—Wes Davis's *An Anthology of Modern Irish Poetry*, a mammoth-sized collection of Irish poetry, selected from material published after 1950, its excellence due to its contents, and maybe something else. There are anthologies, you suspect, that aren't market- or classroom-determined, but are created in love. This is one. An anthology created in admiration and love is like a rooming house where you can open various doors, find a comfortable space, stay a while. Or perhaps it's a library—libraries as they used to be, where you could spend an afternoon or evening roaming the stacks and making discoveries, stumbling upon books that could, potentially, change your life.

Lucky readers, like the ones Abrams talked to, own a cherished anthology; others, if they are fortunate, will come across a life-changing one. Nonetheless, a reader will experience deficits as well as dividends in any anthology. I'm one who reads a book of poetry from beginning to end, rather than dipping in here and there. I don't use the word "collection" for a book of poems because I don't want to believe the book in my hand is constituted of poems that have merely been collected—like dust—since the poet published his or her last volume. There's a structure in the whole just as the individual poems are structured, or so I tell myself. An anthology, presenting one, five, or a dozen poems by a poet, drawn from a lifetime, violates my sense that a book of poetry has narrative drive, or an arc of ideas, or a pattern of recurring metaphors. This is one of the drawbacks of an anthology: it loses the context of the poem, its affiliation to the poem that precedes or follows it in the original publication. A depreciation of relatedness occurs, what Walter Benjamin refers to as the "decay of the aura" in his essay "The Work of Art in the Age of Mechanical Reproduction," by which he means a work's "authenticity" (222, 221). On the other hand, something is gained: an anthology can be an introduction to an era—*20th-Century Poetry & Poetics* (1969)—or a place—*The New North: Contemporary Poetry from Northern Ireland* (2013)—or a crossover topic—*Surrealist Painters and Poets: An Anthology* (2001). In this way, an anthology is *also* a setting of sorts—the poem is situated in its time, place, or cultural milieu.

It's an obvious truth that reading and writing are interrelated, or intimately related. We write the books that we want to read, and then, our interest exhausted, can't bear to read them in the years after. Anthologies have the advantage of inexhaustibility. It's a book of beginnings. Over and over again, you're in the company of a new author. Reaching the end of what's been selected of one poet's work, you are setting forth in the presence of yet another mind. If there's a sense of being thwarted, there is also a sense of possibility. Unlike a book of poetry or a novel—most of them, at any rate—an anthology is discontinuous, a start-and-stop engagement, but this discontinuity also contributes momentum.

It's wrong to think that all literary anthologies fill the same purpose. Classic poetry anthologies, marching the reader through the eras—medieval lyric to *vers libre*—possess a self-sufficiency. The relationship, excerpt to excerpt, exists within the covers. The evolution of the represented genre is its purpose. By contrast, an anthology of contemporary verse—where history has not yet sifted the wheat from the chaff, or bestowed its objectivity, as Vendler puts it (19)—tends to lead outward. The contemporary verse anthology is a search engine—to shift the metaphor—enabling the reader to see a scrap of a poet's work, a suggestion for what exists farther afield, outside the bounds of the editors' subjective choices. Perhaps it's best to think of such anthologies as research tools rather than literary works. Like dictionaries, encyclopaedias, and Google, they have pragmatic value. And then there are the idiosyncratic ones, already spoken about, compact, concerned about the one thing—saluting an artist or a moment in time. And, like Virginia Woolf's novel *Orlando*, some anthologies are love letters. Wes Davis's volume *An Anthology of Modern Irish Poetry* seems just such a work.

4

The making of *Coastlines: The Poetry of Atlantic Canada* (2002) was a three-and-a-half-year project—four editors, three of them in geographic proximity in New Brunswick and one of them in Newfoundland doing her research there, making lists, and sending those lists to the rest of us.

The enterprise arose in a conversation I had with poet Laurence Hutchman when he visited the Saint John campus of the University of New Brunswick (UNB) to give a reading, in winter 1999. Both of us were teaching courses in Maritime poetry; neither of us could find a regional anthology that was up to date or one that met our needs in terms of coverage and the quality of its selections. Excellent though they were, *Ninety Poems: Modern Poems from the Maritimes* (1974), edited by Robert Cockburn and Robert Gibbs, and *The Atlantic Anthology* (1985), edited by Fred Cogswell, were out of date as well as out of print. *Poetic Voices of the Maritimes: A Selection of Contemporary Poetry* (1996), edited by Allison Mitcham and Theresia Quigley, describing itself as "possibly somewhat more subjective than the traditional anthology" (15), contained twenty-two poets, five of whom would never make it onto a syllabus of mine. From the remaining seventeen poets, admirable though they were, the poems chosen were not the poets' best. The editors had made their selections from previous anthologies, "individual collections," and "Maritime poetry magazines" (17). The third source reflects the anthology's lack of rigour in research: in the 1990s, and for decades before that, Maritime poets were publishing nationally and internationally in journals. Lacking a bibliography of the poets' works, the volume offered no notion of a poet's career, and although *Poetic Voices*, in its subtitle, laid claim to *Contemporary*, three of the major poets included had died by 1985.

Well-meaning though it was, *Poetic Voices*, in what it lacked, illustrated the need for rigour in research and in the selection process. Its ahistorical character highlighted the importance of a comprehensive bibliography, the necessity of biographies that reflected on the poets' participation in a literary-cultural milieu, and an introduction that established the historical parameters of the anthology's inclusions. Individually, both Hutchman and I had had similar recent conversations with poet Ross Leckie, editor of *The Fiddlehead*. All three of us were aware that the remarkable productivity of Maritime poets in the 1990s demanded a new anthology, one that would place the decade's surge of activity in the context of a half century. By the time Hutchman, Leckie, and I had our first meeting, June 1999, in the Ice House on the Fredericton campus of UNB, we had heard from many of our teacher-colleagues in the area who, having got wind of our undertaking, insisted upon the importance of including Newfoundland in the anthology. We invited Newfoundland poet Robin McGrath to join us and the three-and-a-half-year task that would become *Coastlines* had begun. Having heard informally from interested parties, we formalized the conversation by sending out a survey to university teachers in the area, an inquiry as to the likelihood that they would use the anthology in their classrooms.

For the three of us working together in New Brunswick, it worked like this: we divided up the reading, assigned authors and their books to each editor. The initial reading of a poet's work had to include everything published by the author and any manuscript in production, gaining access to which was the editor's responsibility. The editor made photocopies of the best poems—could be a dozen, could be twenty or more—circulated those to the other editors, and then we met to discuss and pare down those selections. We read to one another. This is the most important thing to know about *Coastlines*. The poetry was chosen for its sonic value as much as its semantic. We couldn't imagine doing it any other way. This meant, of course, that we worked in person, not by email, not by phone or fax. On the hottest summer days, on the coldest winter ones—for three years—we read to one another. As our introduction indicates, "We were interested first in choosing the best poetry, and we defined *the best* as poetry combining a degree of intellectual and emotional complexity with an exceptional control of figuration and metaphor, voice and style, syntax, line and line break, rhythm and sound pattern" (18). In making our decisions, hearing, as well as seeing, was necessary. That's how we made our choices. How convincing the human voice can be! It was a blissful nightmare.

A shared keenness for a project, ardency for the poetry of a region, doesn't mean that the people involved in a project possess similar work habits. I'm an order-obsessed kind of person, an inveterate list-maker, useful on this kind of project, but hell to work with. A dozen years on, I'm embarrassed to think how cranky I was on occasion, but the reading together was magical, as were the occasions—and they were frequent—when we immediately agreed on choices. Speaking of the principles that guided him in anthology-making, A. J. M. Smith points out that "the emotional sources of critical insights are sometimes as significant as those of poetry" ("Confessions" 120). *Coastlines* is an anthology created by four poets.

The advantage of anthology by committee—even in the case of a committee of four—is that an editor's private tastes are checked and qualified by debate. I'm someone who has, for longish periods of time, four or five favourite poets to whom I turn again and again. My instinct in making *Coastlines*, and I'll confess it still is my inclination in the revising for a new edition, was to have a similar, or close to, number of favourite poets in *Coastlines*. No more than that. But an anthology is not about one's own reading habits. This is the *value* question—poems of value to whom? An anthologist is not so much a private reader as a public servant, a librarian of sorts, ranging widely, choosing judiciously, although, inevitably, choices will be affected by the anthologist's position in time and place, and by sensibility and experience. The checkmating of choices by co-editors in regard to the latter pair, sensibility and experience, is sometimes salutary. Nonetheless, as Paul Chowder, protagonist of Nicholson Baker's novel *The Anthologist*, says, the choosing is painful: "you have to decide over and over whether you are personally willing to stand behind a poem or not. And yet it's not your poem. It's somebody else's poem ..." (45), and even when that agonizing is over, there's still the need for explanation, an introduction to the whole, the not-writing of which paralyzes Baker's character in *The Anthologist*.

Here's the paradox: sharing a gruelling task—research, onerous reading, the discussion of hundreds of poems—does not mean that everyone involved agrees on what has emerged from the labour, on what should be said in an introduction. We almost foundered on that rock. But we didn't. An introduction is a compromise of viewpoints. Accommodating the work of sixty poets, *Coastlines* is retrospective and prospective. It looks to the excellence of the work done by the poets of mid-century—Milton Acorn, Charles Bruce, Alden Nowlan—and it is forward-looking in its inclusion of poets whose work was just beginning to appear in book publication in the early days of the twenty-first century. Besides the always-important issue of quality, the criterion for the new poets was one book in publication or in press. A sufficient number of pieces by each poet—established or emerging— makes *Coastlines* a useful representation of a poet's work. Responding to a perceived need, created in admiration and curiosity—who's out there? who's writing?—*Coastlines* gained a readership beyond the classroom. The truth is, anthologists often set out on a project with frightfully small lists and many gaps—with questions—allowing, as Heaney and Hughes say, "the contents to discover themselves as we ourselves gradually discovered them ..." (19).

If *Coastlines* was a response to the sharp rise in poetry production on the East Coast in the 1990s, *Meetings with Maritime Poets: Interviews* (2006), a solo venture, was a way of dealing with the scarcity of scholarship on recent, and earlier, Maritime poetry, a lack that students, searching for such materials, complained about. An anthology of interviews consisting of extended conversations on poetics with sixteen poets, *Meetings* resembles a collection of two-handed essays—my questions, their responses—and in other ways it resembles an anthology of poetry. The ideas in one interview appear to respond to the ideas in another, similar to the way in which there appears to be interaction between neighbouring poems in an anthology. The energy is in the talkback—the apparent clash or coincidence of ideas interview to interview. Second, because the poets did not see the questions in advance, their responses were full of accident and surprise. They backtracked and self-corrected. In the midst of a response, they made discoveries. Their answers have the halts and hesitations, the insights and self-surprise, that occur in the creation of a poem. Third, I wanted the respondent in the interview situation to feel as though she were talking to herself. I wanted to "overhear" (13), similar to the overhearing that happens when we read a lyric poem: "feeling confessing itself to itself, in moments of solitude," as John Stuart Mill would have it (71). The interviewer needed to "disappear" so that the poet could reclaim the condition that gave rise to the poems. It wasn't my talk. I was just the enabler, the arranger of meetings, collector of ideas. Asking questions, I needed to be as near-to-absent, as noiseless, as possible.

Achieving a condition of ease in the interview took months of preparation; it required, above all, that the poet's work be uppermost, the object of focus, in the interview. In preparation for an interview, I read everything that a poet had written, prose as well as poetry, manuscript as well as published work, and everything published about the poet. I read the poet's poems into a recorder, listened to them as I did chores or drove. I needed to internalize the poems, be as agile in moving around in the work as the author would be. In preparation for an interview, I was part critic—seeing the career as a whole—and part anthologist—choosing the best poems as the point of entry into conversations that were day-long, and in some cases two or three days long. Over the course of seven years, in and around other obligations, I read, wondered my way into questions, and travelled.

Unlike *Coastlines*, *Meetings* does not take up the work of Newfoundland and Labrador poets. Their work, I had come to believe, differed from Maritime poetry in "voice, syntactical structures, idiom, and accent" (12). And although both poetries have deep roots in the Gaelic ballad and the old English ballad, Newfoundland poetry remains closer to those sources than Maritime poetry does. A narrative inclination, within the lyric, is stronger in

Newfoundland poetry. As well, the topographies differ. Landscape is a prominent feature of both poetries, but it is a different landscape. Between the making of the poetry anthology *Coastlines* and the anthology of interviews *Meetings*, I had arrived at a clarification, or, rather, because of the interview work, I had reached a conclusion that seemed, for the moment, the right one. An anthology is an occasion for exploration. It is not a definitive account of a genre, a literary period, or the literature of a region or a nation.

The Preface in *Meetings* is followed by the Introduction which, in hindsight, should have been called Afterword. It is based upon the patterns I was noticing as the interviews accumulated. I kept lists of who was saying what on this or that subject; I created an inventory of the poets' prosodic practices, speech habits, patterns of syntax. The Introduction is perhaps counter to the spirit of the book—get them talking, stay out of the way—but after seven years, I wanted to have my say. Invited to talk poetics, no poet refused. I was grateful, and, further, I was gratified by the thoughtfulness of their responses. Even though I was, obviously, a presence in those conversations, to this day, I learn something new every time I reread one of the interviews.

To repeat, invited to talk poetics, no poet refused. Probably there is a 100 percent acceptance rate—or close to—when the editor of a poetry anthology asks a poet permission to include his or her work in an anthology—living poet, contemporary anthology—although the invitation is not desperately anticipated the way Paul Chowder, in *The Anthologist*, imagines it to be: "And you think: Maybe this very poem I write today will somehow pry open a space in that future anthology and maybe it will drop into position and root itself there" (86). As a contributor to a dozen or so anthologies, it's not my experience that a poet writes for, let alone lives for, inclusion in an anthology. Contrary to Paul Chowder's agriculture metaphor and its high estimate of inclusion, it's a little life—a second growth, not a first growth— that an anthology bestows. By the time the invitation comes, the poet has moved on, is involved in new work. The request, though, awakens ghosts. It's a strange feeling, that business of going back to poems composed, perhaps, a decade earlier. Nonetheless, you want it properly presented: Will it have its own page or be jammed up against someone else's work? Will the lineation, punctuation, spacing be maintained? You hope for, at a minimum, safekeeping. You're happier when what's requested is journal-published work rather than what's in one of your books. Even when a poem in your book is not part of a sequence, the thinking that resulted in its being placed *just there* in the original is sequential. A poem lifted from its environment has lost contact with what sustains it—the narrative, metaphor, or idea being worked out in the whole. Still, that's the test, isn't it? History and her handmaidens, the scholar and the anthologist, sift through the published work for what stands out, irrespective of the supportive surrounding pieces, and by choosing this one and not that one find the poem that will stand up to scrutiny in the years to come. As varied as anthologies are, and mixed though the motives of the anthologist may be, an anthology links present to future, reader to writer.

Bringing author and reader together is also the job of a reading series, although there is a difference. In that encounter there is a living immediacy that is reminiscent of the earliest days of storytelling when stories were passed village to village, generation to generation, in oral form. A reading series shares with an anthology the effort to select, and in selecting confers duration, but differs in that every reading—subject to time, place, and audience—is an unrepeatable event. It will never happen in exactly the same way again.

As a result, not all anthologies are between covers. There are dispersed anthologies. The reading over, the crowd of "readers" goes home. They have heard the story. Maybe they have bought the book in order to extend the experience. Likely, they will return for another instalment—different author, different book—but they are aware that someone, the director of the series, has been making choices for them. The director is part anthologist, part architect. The kind of reading series I refer to is one that is built up over years. I do not refer to those awful, one-off readings with an audience of five uncomfortable people.

For thirteen years I was Director of the Lorenzo Reading Series at UNB Saint John, and each year, from April to August, I produced an annual catalogue of essays on the books that would appear in the fall-winter series. Each essay in the brochure featured a paragraph on the author's career—books and prizes—followed by an account of the author's most recent book, the one he or she would read from. Neither a review nor a synopsis, each mini-essay was my attempt to become absorbed in the author's work, immersing myself in it as completely as possible, while, at the same time, suspending judgment, foregoing analysis. As with *Meetings*, my aim was to get out of the way so that the brochure-readers who would, in the months to come, make up the audience could have an advance encounter with the book.

Like an anthologist I made choices each year about which books to include in the series, but once having made those decisions, I enabled the reader to meet the book in as unfiltered a way as possible in the brochure essay. For each book chosen, probably five were rejected. The decision-making was not that different from choosing a poem for a poetry anthology. From the many advance reading copies of forthcoming books, I tried to choose the best. Once included in the series and the brochure, the book had to seduce the brochure reader. The brochure invited not just reader interest, but offered the reader, as well, the opportunity for a real-time encounter with the author at the upcoming reading, the experience of hearing passages in the author's voice. When a storyteller tells his or her story in a quiet space to two hundred or more people, the effect is magical. Abrams and Greenblatt remark on the freshness and power of "writings that are hundreds of years old" (31), but the experience of being proximate to the creation process, hearing about the inception and development of a story, adds intimacy to power. A good reading series is a library alive.

Those annual brochures, scattered across the country among authors and agents, publishers and publicists, audience members and journalists, are now archival items. Dispersed and no longer important, they are, nonetheless, evidence that an encounter—fleeting and unrepeatable—occurred. Author and reader met; they crossed over the page. A reading series shares with an anthology the maker's need to name what's fine, what's durable.

WORKS CITED

Atwood, Margaret. Introduction. *The New Oxford Book of Canadian Verse in English.* Oxford: Oxford UP, 1982. xxvii. Print.

Auden, W. H., and John Garrett. Introduction. *The Poet's Tongue: An Anthology Chosen by W. H. Auden and John Garrett.* London: G. Bell & Sons, 1937. v–x. Print.

Baker, Nicholson. *The Anthologist.* New York: Simon & Schuster, 2009. Print.

Benjamin, Walter. "Unpacking My Library." *Illuminations: Essays and Reflections.* 1955. Ed. Hannah Arendt. New York: Schocken Books, 1968. 59. Print.

——. "The Work of Art in the Age of Mechanical Reproduction." *Illuminations: Essays and Reflections.* 217–51. Print.

"Built to Last: 'The Norton Anthology of English Literature' celebrates its 50th anniversary. Dialogue: M. H. Abrams and Stephen Greenblatt." *New York Times Book Review.* 26 August, 2012. 31. Web. 28 May 2013.

Compton, Anne. *A. J. M. Smith: Canadian Metaphysical.* Toronto: ECW Press, 1994. Print.

——, et al. Introduction. *Coastlines: the Poetry of Atlantic Canada.* Fredericton: Goose Lane Editions, 2002. 15–18. Print.

——. Preface. *Meetings with Maritime Poets: Interviews.* Markham: Fitzhenry and Whiteside, 2006. 11–14. Print.

Eugenides, Jeffrey. *The Marriage Plot.* Random House Digital, 2011. Print.

Heaney, Seamus, and Ted Hughes. Introduction. *The Rattle Bag: An Anthology of Poetry Selected by Seamus Heaney and Ted Hughes.* London: Faber and Faber, 1982. 19. Print.

Mill, John Stuart. "Thoughts on Poetry and Its Varieties." 1833. *Dissertations and Discussions: Political, Philosophical, and Historical.* Vol. 1. New York: Haskell House, 1973. 63–94. Print.

Mitcham, Allison, and Theresia Quigley. Introduction. *Poetic Voices of the Maritimes: A Selection of Contemporary Poetry.* Hantsport, NS: Lancelot Press, 1996. 15–17. Print.

Palgrave, Francis Turner, ed. "Dedication: To Alfred Tennyson, Poet Laureate." *The Golden Treasury of the Best Songs & Lyrical Poems in the English Language*. 1861. London: Oxford UP, 1964. Print

Roberts, Edgar V., and Henry E. Jacobs. *Literature: An Introduction to Reading and Writing*. Upper Saddle River, NJ: Prentice-Hall, 1998. Print.

Smith, A. J. M. "The Confessions of a Compulsive Anthologist." *On Poetry and Poets*. Peterborough: Trent U, 1976. 106–22. Print.

The Student Bible: New International Version. Grand Rapids: Zondervan, 1986. Print.

Vendler, Helen. "Are These the Poems to Remember?" Rev. of *The Penguin Anthology of Twentieth-Century American Poetry*, ed. Rita Dove. *New York Review of Books*. 22 December, 2011, 19–20, 22. Web. 27 May 2013.

Westling, Louise, et al. Introduction. "Ovid." *The World of Literature*. Upper Saddle River, NJ: Prentice-Hall, 1999. 674. Print.

Witherspoon, Alexander M., ed. *The College Survey of English Literature*. New York: Harcourt, Brace & World, 1951. Print.

ABOUT THE CONTRIBUTORS

D. M. R. BENTLEY is a Distinguished University Professor and the Carl F. Klinck Professor in Canadian Literature at Western University. He has published widely in the fields of Canadian literature and culture and Victorian literature and art, and on the importance of the arts and humanities in Canadian society. Among his books are *The Confederation Group of Canadian Poets, 1880–1897* (2004) and *By Necessity and Indirection: Essays on Modernism in Canadian Literature* (2015). He was recently awarded the 2015 Killam Prize in Humanities.

RICHARD CAVELL is Professor of English and Principal Founder of the Bachelor in Media Studies Program at the University of British Columbia. He is the author of *Remediating McLuhan* (Amsterdam University Press, 2016), the editor of *McLuhan Bound: Essays in Understanding Media* (Gingko Press, 2015), and the curator of spectresofmcluhan.arts.ubc.ca. His most recent book is the critical performance piece *Marinetti Dines with the High Command* (Guernica Press, 2014).

CHERYL CUNDELL teaches Communication Skills for Engineering Students at Carleton University and continues to enjoy the empirical perspective of exploration writing.

ANNE COMPTON is a retired academic and the author of *A. J. M. Smith: Canadian Metaphysical* (1994) and *Meetings with Maritime Poets: Interviews* (2006); the editor of *The Edge of Home: Milton Acorn from the Island* (2002); and the co-editor of *Coastlines: The Poetry of Atlantic Canada* (2002). Her books of poetry include *Opening the Island* (2002), *Processional* (2005), *asking questions indoors and out* (2009); and *Alongside* (2013). She is the recipient of a Governor General's Award for Poetry (2005), the Alden Nowlan Award for Excellence (2008), and the Lieutenant-Governor's Award for High Achievement (2014).

FRANK DAVEY, FRSC, is professor emeritus at Western University and author of ten books on Canadian Literature and twenty collections of poetry. He edited the poetry newsletter *Tish* 1961–63 and journal *Open Letter* 1965–2013. His "Frank Davey's Blog" (http://www.londonpoetryopenmic.com/frank-davey-blog) began in April 2013.

JOEL DESHAYE is an Assistant Professor at Memorial University. His interests are in Canadian literature, its relationship to American literature, genre, cultural studies, and theories of metaphor. His essays on these topics and others have appeared in national and international journals. He is the author of *The Metaphor of Celebrity: Canadian Poetry and the Public, 1955–1980* (University of Toronto Press, 2013). His recent research has been on the Western genre in Canadian literature.

MARGERY FEE is Professor of English at the University of British Columbia, where she holds the David and Brenda McLean Chair in Canadian Studies. Her book *Literary Land Claims: The "Indian Land Question" from Pontiac's War to Attawapiskat* appeared in 2015 from Wilfrid Laurier University Press in the Indigenous Studies Series. With Dory Nason she has co-edited a collection of E. Pauline Johnson's Indigenous-themed writings, which is forthcoming from Broadview Press.

JANET B. FRISKNEY is a specialist in Canadian publishing history and the author of *New Canadian Library: The Ross–McClelland Years, 1952–1978*, editor of *Thirty Years of Storytelling: Selected Short Fiction by Ethelwyn Wetherald*, and associate editor of Volume 3 of the *History of the Book in Canada*. Her article credits include historical studies of the Methodist Book and Publishing House of Toronto, Canadian bible and tract and societies, and publishing and library services for the blind in Canada.

GARY GEDDES has written and edited forty-five books of poetry, fiction, drama, non-fiction, criticism, translation, and anthologies and won a dozen national and international literary awards, including the National Poetry Prize, National Magazine Gold Award, the Commonwealth Poetry Prize (Americas Region), the Lieutenant-Governor's Award for Literary Excellence, and the Gabriela Mistral Prize, awarded simultaneously to Octavio Paz, Vaclav Havel, Ernesto Cardenal, Rafael Alberti, and Mario Benedetti. His work has been widely praised, by Billy Collins, Philip Levine, and others.

BONNIE HUGHES is a graduate of the University of Ottawa, where she completed her doctoral dissertation, "'The Subtle but Powerful Cement of a Patriotic Literature': English-Canadian Literary Anthologies, National Identity, and the Canon." Her dissertation traced the careers of early Canadian authors in general anthologies published between 1922 and the present in order to clarify the relationship between anthologies, literary criticism, and the historical development of the English-Canadian canon. Her research interests include anthologization, canon formation, and censorship.

PEGGY LYNN KELLY has a Ph.D. in Canadian Literature (University of Alberta, 1999). She taught literature and communication at Canadian universities and colleges. Besides her publications on women in the Canadian literary field, especially Dorothy Livesay and Madge Macbeth, Dr. Kelly was a general editor for Tecumseh Press's Early Canadian Women Writers Series. She has retired to Lanark, Ontario, where she continues to write on Canadian literary history.

ROBERT LECKER is Greenshields Professor of English at McGill University, where he specializes in Canadian literature. Lecker was the co-editor of the critical journal *Essays on Canadian Writing* from 1975 to 2004, and the co-publisher at ECW Press from 1977 to 2003. He is the editor of several anthologies, most recently *Open Country: Canadian Literature in English* (2007). Lecker is the author of numerous books and articles, including *On the Line* (1982), *Robert Kroetsch* (1986), *Another I* (1988), *Making It Real* (1995), *Dr. Delicious* (2006), *The Cadence of* Civil Elegies (2006), and *Keepers of the Code* (2013).

KARIS SHEARER is an Assistant Professor in the Faculty of Creative and Critical Studies at UBC (Okanagan campus). She held the 2010 Canada–U.S. Fulbright Visiting Research Chair at Vanderbilt University and is the editor of *All These Roads: The Poetry of Louis Dudek* (2008). She has published critical work on Tomson Highway, George Bowering, Jane Urquhart, and has co-authored a chapter on the work of Sina Queyras.

LORRAINE YORK is professor and Senator William McMaster Chair in Canadian Literature and Culture at McMaster University. Her books *Literary Celebrity in Canada* (2007) and *Margaret Atwood and the Labour of Literary Celebrity* (2013) were finalists for the Raymond Klibansky and Gabrielle Roy Prizes, respectively. *Celebrity Cultures in Canada*, co-edited with Katja Lee, is forthcoming from Wilfrid Laurier University Press. Her new project examines the phenomenon of the reluctant celebrity.

INDEX